QUEEN OF THE CON

TRUE CRIME HISTORY

QUEEN

OF THE CON

From a Spiritualist to the Carnegie Imposter

THOMAS CROWL

The Kent State University Press KENT, OHIO

CONTENTS

ACKNOWLEDGMENTS

The author would like to acknowledge the following individuals and organizations without whose invaluable assistance this book could not have been completed: Kent State University Press, especially Susan Wadsworth-Booth, Mary Young, Christine Brooks, and Kat Saunders; Brian Meggitt, photo collection librarian, and the Cleveland Public Library; Mazie Adams and the Cleveland Police Historical Society; Ann Sindelar and the Cleveland History Center of the Western Reserve Historical Society Library and Archives; Valerie Ahwee, copy editor; Anne Salsich and the Oberlin College Libraries; the Oxford (Ontario, Canada) Historical Society; the Ohio History Connection Library and Archives; the Library of Congress; the Scott County (Kentucky) Public Library; and the New Castle (Pennsylvania) Public Library.

Introduction

In New York City in the spring of 1904, Mrs. Cassie Chadwick, a wealthy resident of Cleveland's fashionable Euclid Avenue, met a prominent Cleveland attorney—a florid-faced, prosperous man with a professional air and a propensity to gossip—in the lobby of the exclusive Holland House Hotel. Unbeknown to the barrister, he was about to become an unwitting accomplice in one of the most audacious frauds in American history. It was a pleasant carriage ride up Fifth Avenue to the magnificent mansion of Andrew Carnegie, where Mrs. Chadwick had promised her companion an introduction to the famous industrialist. Arriving at the mansion, Cassie tactfully suggested that the attorney wait in the carriage while she asked if Mr. Carnegie was home to visitors. The woman strode unhesitatingly to the front door, was admitted, and, with a jaunty wave to her companion, disappeared inside.

Mrs. Chadwick informed the butler that she wished to speak with the housekeeper about a former employee of the Carnegie household. The employee was unknown to the housekeeper and as the two women talked, Cassie took notes and stalled for time. Twenty minutes later, she reemerged from the mansion chirping pleasantly and waving. Once again seated in the cab, Cassie apologized to her companion, but Mr. Carnegie was not receiving visitors. Then, as if on cue, a package fell from her handbag. After the attorney retrieved it, Mrs. Chadwick said she wished to confide in him. After extracting a pledge of secrecy, Cassie admitted she was Andrew Carnegie's illegitimate daughter. Her mother died, and, according to Cassie, Carnegie had discreetly placed her with foster parents in Canada. The ironmaster was very generous to her, she said, and the package contained US Steel bonds. To seal the deception, Cassie displayed two six-figure promissory notes to her benefit bearing the signature of Andrew Carnegie. As the carriage pulled away from the curb, the attorney could not resist a backward glance at the mansion and later swore he saw a short, gray-bearded man standing in an upstairs window. Such was the power of Cassie Chadwick's persuasion.[1]

This tale has become part of the Chadwick mythology, and there are various versions. The attorney was never identified, and no one stepped forward to collaborate even a portion of the story. Cassie appreciated the importance of perception and appearance and was more than shrewd enough to plan just such an encounter. She was an expert at manipulating men of power and money in an era when swindlers and forgers flourished. This is the true story of the life of a poor Canadian farm girl named Betsy Bigley, who, before her fiftieth birthday, became the clever, persuasive, high-living Cassie Chadwick, a wealthy doctor's wife with a home on Cleveland's millionaire's row. With the suggestion that Andrew Carnegie stood behind her financially, Cassie succeeded in borrowing at least $10 million—$250 million in the twenty-first century—from some of the shrewdest businessmen in America on the flimsiest of collateral. In the press, she became known variously as Cleveland's Duchess of Diamonds, the Queen of Finance, the Queen of Swindlers, the Heroine of High Finance, and the Carnegie Imposter. After her downfall, any suspicion of association with her could cause banks to fail and powerful men to divert their gaze. Cassie's victims, and there were many, were said to have been "Chadwicked," and her methods, "Frenzied Finance."[2]

In the early twentieth century an anonymous pundit observed, "Men can lie, do lie, lie even on a gigantic scale, but the supreme liar is always a woman. Take all the great frauds of history which depend upon sheer invention and the fantastic creation of nonexistent things, they have, in nearly every case been the creation of woman." The newspapers of the Victorian age were filled with the exploits of feminine swindlers, imposters, and forgers. New York's Fox sisters—Maggie, Kate, and Leah—practically invented spiritualism in America in the 1840s. Eventually exposed as frauds, the sisters nonetheless launched the careers of thousands of spiritualists, mediums, and fortune-tellers. Ellen Peck, "a smooth-tongued pleasant little lady," according to one victim, defrauded a wealthy New York soap manufacturer of thousands, numerous Jewish diamond merchants of their wares, and a young physician of his life savings all while occasionally assisting the police in apprehending other swindlers. In the early 1890s two New York con artists, Sophie Lyons and Carrie Morse, opened the New York Women's Banking and Investment Company with the sole aim of defrauding women of all classes. Before the bank failed, the duo had collected at least $50,000 from unsuspecting victims. "Big Bertha" Heyman, described as "fair, fat and forty," operated in both the United States and Canada. She once claimed a fortune of $20 million and later swindled the Jewish community in San Francisco while bedecked in diamonds. Iowa suffragette and nationally recognized honeybee expert, Ellen Tupper, had an unfortunate tendency to forge checks, including those of the governor. But none of these nor the hundreds of women guilty of forgery, fraud, impersonation, check kiting, or telling fortunes came close to the audacity of Cassie Chadwick. Her closest competitor was a contemporary, Parisian Therese Humbert, who perpetrated one of Europe's greatest frauds based on a fabricated 100 million–franc inheritance in a swindle that lasted two decades. A French prosecutor admiringly said that Therese "raised burglary to the height of a work of genius." The American penny press made Cassie more famous.[3]

Author Amy Reading postulated in *The Mark Inside: A Perfect Swindle* that fraud flourishes when society undergoes major changes in accepted norms. "As those norms are shifting," she wrote, "as they did massively in the 19th century, you have the perfect conditions for exploiting the gap between old and new." From the 1850s onward, industrialization brought monumental shifts to American society. Industrialists, robber barons, and stock manipulators were acquiring huge fortunes, and women were demanding freedom and rights previously forbidden them. Cassie Chadwick exploited, in the words of a Canadian magazine, "the Victorian ideal of women as fluffy creatures with no money sense and certainly no brains for criminal activities" to her advantage. Cassie used the unbridled greed of the era to take advantage of smart and experienced businessmen and bankers.[4]

Mrs. Chadwick traded on her well-constructed illusion of wealth that resulted from her assertion that she was Andrew Carnegie's illegitimate daughter. This myth was accepted by able financiers who should have known better, yet failed to invest in even a two-cent postage stamp to verify the claim. So successful was Mrs. Chadwick's deception that while there was never any real doubt that she was not Carnegie's daughter, many of those men duped by her never quite gave up on the belief that somehow, some way, Andrew Carnegie was behind her. Even her lead defense attorney felt that she knew the man. Carnegie's place in Cassie's deception, and the public's reaction to it, says much about how America viewed its wealthiest industrialists in 1900.

Cassie Chadwick did not live a transparent life. She spent a lifetime dissembling to cover her tracks. Ferreting out the truth about her is not easy. Unable to navigate through the web of deceit, many earlier chroniclers of her career have chosen not facts, but rumor, innuendo, and pure fiction to fill the gaps. Cassie has been portrayed variously as a seductress, a gun-toting thief, or an insane con artist. These caricatures do her an injustice, for she was much more complex than any fictional depiction. The woman created from thin air a fortune worth millions and borrowed millions more against it. In a day when a $500 loan was significant, she declined loans of $10,000. She spent on an equally grand scale, purchasing everything from silver place settings to pianos in multiples of ten. Her personal jewelry box was said to contain seven trays, each filled with precious stones. She once owned the largest diamond ever imported into Canada.[5]

The *Cleveland Press* suggested to its readers that the mere fact of a woman being able to borrow such vast sums of money is itself interesting and unusual. "When it is known that she borrowed the money on personal notes giving no security but her promise to pay," an editor wrote, "the case becomes extraordinary and unprecedented in the history of local finance." One of the paper's reporters, Cynthia Grey, after touring Cassie's Euclid Avenue home, wrote, "It takes a smart woman to get any man's money. How much smarter a woman must be who gets the money of many men." A federal prosecutor in 1905 labeled her "the most dangerous criminal in the world today." Upon her death on October 11, 1907, the *Cleveland Plain Dealer* suggested that had she been a corporation with proper management, her talents might have made many people rich. One of her defense attorneys believed that she "was born with a mental disease which developed into a form of insanity." Mrs. Chadwick's last attorney simply called her "the shrewdest person I ever met." Her success as a swindler and imposter places her eighth on *Time* magazine's list of top ten imposters of all time.[6]

Financial chicanery has not been eradicated in the last hundred years. The names have changed, and the money has gone from thousands to billions. Yet greed has remained the common denominator since the nineteenth century, when a former British sailor, George MacGregor, invented a mythical Central American nation to fleece investors in 1817. An astute reader will note that some of the swindles discussed in this book—forged personal promissory notes, for instance—are no longer possible. Yet the reader will also see that some, like security fraud and embezzlement, are alive and well. In 2012, Rita Crundwell, comptroller of the small city of Dixon, Illinois, was arrested for embezzling $53 million from the city over a twenty-year period. Crundwell used the money to become one of the nation's top quarter horse breeders, well above her pay grade. Crundwell also spent $340,000 on jewelry and named one of her horses "Packin Jewels." After Rita had fooled city officials and outside auditors for years, a coworker finally discovered the crime. Crundwell pled guilty to one count of wire fraud, and for perpetrating the largest municipal fraud in American history she was sentenced to twenty years in prison. In 2019, a German woman living in New York, Anna Sorokin, was found guilty of grand larceny and theft for what prosecutors called "multiple acts of glamorous grifting." Sorokin was accused of defrauding her victims of over $200,000 while claiming a $60 million inheritance. The judge, citing the defendant's lack of remorse, gave her a four- to twelve-year prison sentence. In 1875, a noted swindler, alias "Professor Allyne," told the *New York Herald* that "All the fools ain't dead yet, this is a great racket!" It still is.[7]

CHAPTER ONE

Miss Bigley, Heiress to $15,000

The year 1857 is known to history for the Panic of 1857, the first worldwide economic collapse. During that momentous year, on March 28, Elizabeth Bigley, called Betsy or Lizzie, was born in Appin, Ontario, as the third daughter in an unremarkable Canadian family of six girls and two boys born to Daniel Bigley and his no-nonsense wife, Mary Ann. Three years later, Daniel, a dollar-a-day railroad section hand on the Great Western Railway, moved the family to a hardscrabble farm near Eastwood, Ontario, 125 miles east of Detroit. The Bigleys were solid, unremarkable folk of English descent and humble aspirations. Betsy, however, was destined to leave her mark in the history of crime.[1]

Betsy attended the Eastwood school, where her imagination impressed her teachers. At age sixteen, she ran away from home on her father's rail pass and was apprehended by police after attempting to obtain a $250 promissory note from a local farmer. After a night in jail, Betsy was remanded to her father by the local justice of the peace, one Charles Chadwick. By her twenty-first birthday, Betsy had developed what one Cleveland newspaper later described as "the notion that she ought to shine as a queen among women and live in luxury." She became obsessed with the expensive finery she saw in the shops of her hometown. In November 1878, Betsy was detained by police in Brantford, Ontario, for attempting to borrow money on a stolen gold pocket watch. Betsy's distraught father reached a settlement with the victim that allowed Betsy to escape the consequences of her petty larceny yet again.[2]

In her early twenties, Betsy drifted around Ontario. Some acquaintances claimed she worked the railroad Pullman cars passing through London, Ontario, mixing prostitution and blackmail. She appeared in Toronto representing herself as Elizabeth Cunard, a niece in the wealthy Cunard family of ocean liner fame. Betsy embarked on a manic spending spree, accumulating $10,000 worth of whatever took her fancy. It was all financed with a bogus letter of introduction and a worthless bank draft. The scheme collapsed in a couple of days, and Betsy fled Toronto.[3]

In March 1879, Elizabeth Bigley was arrested in Woodstock, Ontario, for attempting to redeem forged personal promissory notes. It was alleged that she had presented a forged promissory note from a local man to purchase $250 in dry goods and an organ, the beginning of a lifelong obsession with keyboard instruments. To supplement the note, Betsy produced a finely engraved calling card that proclaimed "Miss Bigley, Heiress to $15,000." When the note came due, she covered the debt with a second promissory note signed by a wealthy local farmer. The second note was denounced as a fraud by the farmer, and Betsy was arrested. Other forged notes appeared, including one for $500 signed by a "Mr. Virtue." Betsy was indicted for passing forged promissory notes.[4]

It was common practice for private individuals and businessmen in the Victorian era to obtain credit by offering a promissory note as collateral. Rarely legally recorded, the majority were secured only by a man's honor and integrity. These personal notes were frequently traded during their term. Banks speculated in them. If traded before the due date and for an amount less than full value, they were said to be "discounted." The amount of the discount varied widely depending on the creditworthiness of the note's maker. If they were redeemed early by the maker, again at a reduced amount, it was said the note was "taken up." Personal notes were not secure. Blank forms could be purchased at any stationery store, be completed by anyone, and a well-to-do individual's signature forged. Even a poor forgery might take days or weeks to be disavowed by the signer as fake, and even then it might end up in court before dueling handwriting experts. Personal promissory notes quickly became popular with forgers and swindlers whose schemes were regularly reported in the newspapers. Attempting to negotiate a fraudulent note was illegal. There were two specific crimes: creating a fraudulent note—forgery—and trying to pass a known fraudulent note, known as uttering.

Betsy's appalled family attributed her deceitful behavior to a prolonged high fever she suffered as a child that left her subject to occasional trancelike episodes. Elizabeth's Woodstock lawyers elected to employ insanity as a defense. Seeking to evade the law by claiming insanity was not novel in 1879, but if a defendant wasn't insane, he or she needed to at least evoke sympathy.

At her trial on March 22, 1879, twenty-two-year-old Betsy debuted her considerable acting talent by sitting motionless and disengaged at the defense table while clothed in an adolescent girl's dress and bonnet. Her head resting on one hand, Betsy rarely stirred except to make a silly face at someone or to stick her tongue out at the jury. Despite Betsy's odd behavior, many of the men present agreed with the Crown's prosecutor, who described Betsy as "rather attractive." The presiding judge, however, saw an obviously deranged girl. He strongly suggested to the jurymen that a verdict of not guilty by reason of temporary insanity would be appropriate. Nevertheless, it took two hours of debate and persuasion to secure the necessary number of jurors for the insanity verdict. Acquitted, Betsy left the courtroom with the notion that the legal system was another entity she could manipulate.[5]

Betsy would never formally live in Canada again. She was banished by her family to Cleveland to live with her older sister, Alice York, the wife of an enterprising machinist. Borrowing money from her brother-in-law, Betsy opened a dressmaking school in the Argyle Building on Euclid Avenue. Those who came to her establishment met a "pretty and lady-like" young woman. Beneath the veneer, Miss Bigley was making very little money dressmaking, and her prolific spending habits easily outpaced her legitimate income. In 1881, using the alias Alice M. Bestido, Betsy mortgaged the Yorks' household furnishings while the family was out of town. This type of loan was common among cash-strapped Americans during the nineteenth century. Mortgaging another person's property or goods bought on credit, sometimes multiple times, was a very common crime in the 1880s, especially for women. The crime news was full of such trickery, and many cases were settled outside the law for pennies on the dollar. Alice York convinced her husband to pay off the loan and not to have Betsy arrested. Instead, York expelled her from his house. Unrepentant, Betsy shopped on her sister's credit until her brother-in-law notified local merchants that, in the future, he would not be financially responsible for his sister-in-law's debts.[6]

Relocating to a Cleveland boardinghouse, Betsy mortgaged her new landlady's furniture and settled the debt by persuading the creditor to accept fifty cents on the dollar. In 1882, Betsy was prosecuted for another multiple mortgage scheme but avoided trial when the victim dropped the charges. In these instances, Betsy benefited from a critical advantage that favored women and would serve her well for the rest of her life—that men who were cleverly swindled by a woman were more likely to be concerned for their reputations than be vindictive.[7]

Fortune smiled on twenty-five-year-old Betsy in 1882 when she met, in Cleveland, a forty-year-old widowed physician from San Francisco, Wallace

S. Springsteen. How she met Springsteen remains a mystery, but Betsy likely sought his medical advice. She regaled the doctor with tales of Canadian wealth and tragedy that aroused his sympathy and perhaps a bit of greed. The middle-aged physician fell for this charming patient with an endearing lisp. The couple decided to marry. Unfortunately for Betsy, her creditors would soon spoil the romance.

Betsy had borrowed $100 using the Alice M. Bestido alias from a money lender named Hobday. Some elegant furniture served as collateral. Betsy said she was the widow of a wealthy Columbus man, but her lack of receipts made the lender skeptical. Betsy suggested Hobday ask her next-door neighbor about her respectability. Next door, Hobday encountered a well-dressed woman who said of her neighbor, "she is a fine lady." Hobday loaned Betsy the money. When the loan came due and was unpaid, Hobday made inquiries and was chagrined to learn that the furniture in that house had been mortgaged to several fellow money lenders by a different person each time.[8]

Betsy's wedding to Springsteen was set for November 21, 1882, the same day Hobday discovered he had been swindled. With the ceremony set for 8:00 P.M. at the home of a prominent local businessman, Hobday knocked at the door at 7:00 P.M. Ushered into the parlor where Betsy was dressing, Hobday demanded his money. Betsy begged off, saying she would get the cash from her husband tomorrow. Hobday declined and instead offered to take Betsy's dresses, trousseau, engagement ring, and the groom's gift—a gold watch—as collateral for the $100 loan, a very good deal for the lender. A chattel mortgage was signed thirty minutes before the wedding ceremony.[9]

Hobday's concern for his new collateral grew overnight, and the next day he took a wagon to Springsteen's house, where he took possession of the goods packed in several trunks. Springsteen was aghast. Hobday later found in one trunk a list of twenty men from whom Betsy had acquired between $20 and $100 each for a total of $1,100. Within days, additional creditors knocked at Springsteen's door. The doctor finally learned the truth from his sister-in-law, Mrs. York, and hired private detectives to spy on his new wife. Nine days after the wedding, Springsteen expelled his bride from his home. Dr. Springsteen did not immediately file for divorce, so on October 5, 1883, Betsy filed on the grounds of lack of support and neglect. She demanded $6,000. Springsteen made no response. The doctor's detectives presented proof of infidelity to the court, and on December 4, Betsy's petition was denied. Springsteen later told reporters that his wayward wife was a polished woman who shrewdly seduced him.[10]

Two weeks later, Dr. Springsteen filed for divorce on the grounds of infidelity, which Betsy denied. In a deposition taken by the doctor's attorney, Betsy claimed to own property worth $25,000 and to receive a yearly annuity payment of $1,600. Statements by other witnesses located by the private detectives were damning for Betsy. One was William Cross of the Reed House in Erie, Pennsylvania, who claimed that in the spring of 1883, Betsy took a room at his hotel using the alias Mazy DeLaylis under the pretense of wealth but was temporarily without funds. Betsy later faked her own death to evade the hotel bill.[11]

The evidence of infidelity and fraud presented to the court by Springsteen's detectives was damning enough to persuade Betsy to drop her challenge to the doctor's petition. The divorce was finalized on December 4, 1883. A press report some months after her divorce claimed that Betsy had a chance encounter with William Cross on a Cleveland street. Cross sarcastically remarked, "Why, I thought you were dead." To which she replied with seemingly no remorse, "I have come to life again." Indeed, Betsy Bigley would reinvent herself many times in the coming years.[12]

By 1884, the clever and imaginative Betsy was rumored to have launched a career as a clairvoyant, Madame La Rose, on Cleveland's Prospect Street. In addition to fortune-telling, Madame La Rose's rooms on Superior Avenue were known as a "resort" by some in Cleveland's fast crowd—a period term frequently applied to brothels or their close cousins, houses of assignation. Years later as Betsy's fame as an adventuress grew, some newspapers, in tabloid fashion, printed the story as fact, but in reality, the tale of Betsy Bigley pretending to be the clairvoyant Madame La Rose lacked any solid proof.[13]

America in the last half of the nineteenth century proved to be fertile ground for many radical ideas, and spiritualism was one. Based on the belief that an unbroken chain of communication existed between the Infinite and all beings, a spiritual telegraph was said to run from the hereafter through living mediums to the living. During the spiritualistic mania that swept the Victorian era, even keen men of affairs were known to consult clairvoyants, a pretentious nineteenth-century name for fortune-tellers. One unidentified man who frequently consulted clairvoyants told the *New York Sun,* "Oh, they know everything. I would rather believe one than my creator." In return for providing a peek at the future, most clairvoyants acquired cash, gold, confidential business information, and family secrets. The profession was ready-made for swindlers and blackmailers.

Spiritualism—the belief that deceased spirits could communicate with the living—was at its peak in the last half of the nineteenth century. Spiritualism traced its roots to the Fox sisters—Maggie, Kate, and Leah—from New York state who, in the 1840s, became the first mediums. Spiritualism came to be dominated by women and girls whose traditional purity and passivity made them, according to Victorian thinking, ideal mediums. To their advantage, mediums had the benefit of relaying messages from the departed with little responsibility for the content of the message.[14]

Some women saw something more in spiritualism and suggested that "spiritualism and women's rights . . . were responses to the control, subjugation, and repression of women by church and state." That may have been true, but spiritualism was quickly co-opted by fortune-tellers, mediums, palmists, and clairvoyants, who saw it as fertile ground for fraud. Police across the country agreed. There is nothing to support the idea that Betsy Bigley, if she adopted the Madame La Rose persona, saw it as anything other than a moneymaking scheme.[15]

As spiritualism spread across the land, so, too, did mesmerism, which at the time was considered synonymous with hypnosis. Its introduction in America was initially as entertainment—a sideshow or parlor trick. On rare occasions, subjects would demonstrate unexplained supernatural powers of precognition and clairvoyancy. Practitioners of mesmerism developed a haughty presence that, it was said, could seize control of even the strongest personality. Hypnosis, feminist adherents argued, offered women previously unknown opportunities to exert personal power. For those men purportedly in the grasp of a woman's hypnotic power, it provided a perfect means to deny responsibility for their actions. True or not, there would be men who later said they were unable to divert their gaze from Betsy Bigley's penetrating eyes, which had more to do with the power of suggestion than any hypnotic powers.[16]

Betsy's travels took her from Cleveland to Ohio's Mahoning Valley, where she reportedly married an unsuspecting farmer, John R. Scott, in 1883. In 1887 she purportedly swindled him out of his farm using a cleverly worded prenuptial agreement. This story lacks proof. Still, Betsy demonstrated some in-depth knowledge of the Youngstown-Warren, Ohio, area a short time later. A similarly vague rumor about the same time suggested a liaison with a Dr. Scott of Cleveland. Dr. William J. Scott did reside on Prospect near Betsy's address in 1882, but the physician was sixty years old and married.[17]

It was without a doubt Betsy who, in 1886, took up residence in a Cleveland boardinghouse operated by a widow, Mrs. S. C. Hoover. The widow Hoover, according to period Cleveland city directories, had several addresses prior to settling into the business of subletting rooms from a Euclid Avenue address.

In 1886, fellow boarders at Mrs. Hoover's knew the handsome young woman with a baby as Lydia Scott, Betsy's new alias. The father of Betsy's baby boy was never identified publicly. A well-connected, but anonymous, Cleveland attorney later pointed the finger at a prominent lawyer and Democrat politician who dutifully supported the child financially. Yet again, Betsy's activities while at Hoover's boardinghouse remain secret.[18]

In 1887, Betsy borrowed the widow Hoover's last name and perhaps elements of her biography to become Lydia Hoover. Lydia was arrested in Cleveland for her old standby fraud of mortgaging the same goods multiple times. She evaded prosecution by using her powers of persuasion to convince her creditors to settle for fifty cents on the dollar, which was better than nothing—the likely result if Lydia was jailed. Lydia departed Cleveland and dropped from sight, although a Lydia Hoover briefly appeared in both Columbus and Cincinnati. From the latter place, she absconded with $300 in jewelry obtained on credit.[19]

While Lydia Hoover's trail went cold, a Madame Devere surfaced in Leavenworth, Kansas, in 1887. A clairvoyant calling herself Mollie Devere disappeared, leaving behind several unpaid promissory notes bearing the endorsements of several prominent local businessmen. One victim who committed forgery and embezzlement to meet his obligation as endorser at the encouragement of the Devere woman was apprehended and committed suicide.[20]

CHAPTER TWO

MADAME DEVERE, EUROPEAN CLAIRVOYANT

Toledo, Ohio, was a hundred miles west of Cleveland at the western end of Lake Erie. In the 1880s it boasted a population of eighty thousand and was noted for its glass-manufacturing industry, hence the nickname "the Glass City." For Canadians entering the United States through Detroit, Toledo was familiar. Betsy Bigley arrived in Toledo from Cleveland in mid-1887 and established herself as Madame Lydia Devere, a clairvoyant. Her calling cards announced that she was a "European clairvoyant endowed with prophetic vision and power to read the future in the stars." The very term *clairvoyant* was French and hinted at an exotic connotation that to most Americans contained a whiff of mystery and the supernatural. Initially holding court on Toledo's Washington Street, Madame Devere's business—colorfully described in the press as "lifting the veil of the future"—was robust. Madame usually employed a couple of servants and kept a young black boy around to deliver her messages. The general consensus among her clients was that Madame Devere was around thirty, possessed penetrating dark eyes, and was quite charming. She spoke with a slight English accent and endearing lisp that many men found attractive. Lydia Devere had significant hearing loss, and the pauses in conversation that resulted were said to add dignity to her native politeness. The only thing European about her was her clothing, which was always in the latest fashion and of the best quality.[1]

Madame Devere claimed to be a widow. Putting her outsized imagination to work, Lydia created a romantic past that bore no resemblance to the truth. She told her clients in hushed tones that while living in Ontario, she met a dashing young military officer with roots in English nobility. They married and, after a suitable Paris honeymoon, returned to the man's ancestral English estate, where his parents were not impressed with their new daughter-in-law.

An agreement was reached in which the officer's father gave his son an annuity paying $1,000 a year if the bride and groom left the country. Before they could depart, according to Lydia, the young man was killed in a riding accident. Her husband's family offered the young widow the annuity if she left England forever. Madame Devere accepted the annuity and relocated to America. In time, according to Madame, she married a Dr. Hoover, a Rochester, New York, abortionist who was arrested and sent to prison. She said that Hoover's departure left her in the company of spiritualists and clairvoyants in New York. She dabbled in those arts for amusement at first before turning to it for a living in Cleveland and now Toledo. It was a fantastic story full of holes but sufficient when related by an attractive and persuasive woman.[2]

Madame Devere drew the attention of the police within three months of her arrival in Toledo. According to a police report she filed, someone—she suggested the ghostlike Dr. Hoover, purportedly recently released from prison—had absconded with $700 she had hidden behind a bureau drawer along with a cache of diamonds. The investigating Toledo police detectives, including veteran lawman John Manley, could find no evidence of a robbery. The diamonds, which were likely bought on credit, were discovered in a pawnshop, where Madame had traded them for cash. The clairvoyant confessed the robbery was a ruse and said her motive was to merely gain sympathy, an explanation that lacked credibility. Despite the lie and false report—no secret in Toledo—Madame Devere was not arrested and continued to prosper. Local police took note of her trotting about town in the finest carriages pulled by the best bay horses. She wore the latest fashions that flattered her figure, including expensive sealskin—the genuine article with the coarse outer hair removed and the soft undercoat dyed a dark brown or black.[3]

Not surprisingly, in the nineteenth century, fortune-tellers, clairvoyants, and spiritualistic mediums drew most of their clients from the lower classes. Yet the better, more practiced ones attracted clients of means. Madame Devere quickly developed a small but loyal following comprised of middle-aged businessmen, who found it within the scope of their conscience to visit a clairvoyant, an acceptable diversion in Victorian America. Madame was expert at managing to convey the hint of a promise of something more than lifting the veil of the future without ever losing her well-practiced ladylike poise.[4]

Some men who knew the woman swore that her eyes were hypnotic and confessed to feeling uneasy when they gazed into them. But Madame Devere made no claim to hypnosis. She relied on visions, trances, or other spiritualistic means to provide predictions on such mundane uncertainties as grain futures

and stock investments, solve disputes, eliminate evil spirits, and advise on affairs of the heart. Advice from Madame wasn't cheap. One man paid $1,500
to be rid of evil spirits plaguing him. There is no record of how the clairvoyant achieved this. In another instance, a young police officer wished to secure
an engagement to a certain young lady and consulted Madame. She informed
him that she could arrive at a solution by sleeping on a bag containing $250 in
gold to enhance her dreams. The outcome of the love affair was not revealed,
but Madame kept the gold. Among those who weren't fans was the policeman,
Manley, who had seen his share of fortune-tellers. "I remember that there was
nothing particularly brilliant about her," Manley would later recall.[5]

Operating without censure after the false diamond robbery, Madame Devere became famous among Toledo's young men about town, who told ribald
stories of extravagant late-evening parties with "the Devere." These lavish en-
tertainments were regular events at Madame's house on Washington Street.
The tables groaned with flower arrangements costing $40, more than many
men made in a month. These parties were usually enhanced by a comely female associate or two, who arrived by train from Cleveland. One of Devere's
younger sisters, Emma, who was also endowed with a bit of larceny, was a regular. Although lamed in a train accident, the sister was pretty, engaging, and a
popular addition to the ribaldry. Police detectives regularly encountered these
female associates in the course of their duties. One was apprehended leaving
Toledo with $20,000 in bearer bonds—unregistered securities that could be
negotiated by whoever possessed them—belonging to a local man.[6]

G. E. Knisely was a successful attorney with an office on the fifth floor of the
Produce Exchange Building. Knisely represented Madame Devere, who was
using the alias Eliza Clingan, in negotiations for the return of some valuable
papers, including a will, which she had acquired by less than honorable means
from an Elyria, New York, man. The papers contained information the upstate
New Yorker desperately desired to remain secret. Madame was not above a bit
of blackmail. Knisely contacted the man, who subsequently returned to Toledo to settle the affair. When the transaction was completed, Madame Devere
reminded the New Yorker to remain silent. "To publish the facts [of how she
acquired the papers] would not injure me," she told him, "and it would ruin
you." It wasn't until after the fact that Knisely learned that Mrs. Clingan was
Madame Devere. Within days the clairvoyant had purchased two $250 pianos
and shipped one to her partner in crime, sister Emma, while also outfitting
herself with a new wardrobe and a flashy new carriage horse.[7]

Detective Manley was convinced she was a fraud or worse. "I learned who was going to the woman's house, and went to the chief of police and complained," Manley told newsmen in 1890. "She had hypnotic influence over many people. Of this there is little doubt. She also made some claim of being a spiritualistic medium, and many of her victims were attracted that way. I told my superiors that I believed it was time that a stop was put to the business." The chief of police never explained why he chose to ignore Manley's suggestion. In 1900, claiming to be a clairvoyant, fortune-teller, or palmist became a misdemeanor in Ohio punishable by a fine of up to $100 or up to ninety days in jail.[8]

By late summer of 1887, Madame Devere was a frequent visitor to a boardinghouse on Toledo's Superior Street. The reason remains a mystery. It was at that establishment that she first encountered fifty-two-year-old Joe Lamb, also a regular, who claimed he was visiting a fellow lodge member who resided there. A nodding acquaintance developed between Lamb and Devere. An agent and cashier for the United States Express Company Toledo branch for almost two decades, the English-born Lamb was widely known and respected. His reputation was above reproach. In the 1880s, the safest way to send cash was by utilizing one of the many railroad express companies. When high volumes of grain were shipped through the city and its port, Joe handled hundreds of thousands of dollars without a slip. In September, Joe met Lydia Devere by chance on the street. On impulse, he presented her with a dahlia. On October 3, 1887, Lydia Devere arrived at Joe's express office to send money to Cleveland.

By the time their transaction was complete, Madame had invited Lamb to call at her residence on Washington Street. She didn't give a reason, Lamb later recalled, and he didn't ask. Joe stopped by the Washington Street house three days later because "she wanted to see me and I wanted to see her." Madame Devere wasn't at home. In Victorian America, a gentleman had fulfilled his social obligation by merely paying a visit to the home. If the person was not home or just not home to callers, it didn't matter. Joe clearly wanted to see Lydia Devere and stopped a second time. The lady herself answered the door. Lamb found Madame Devere at her most charming—talkative, ladylike, and modest. She was, she told Lamb, twice a widow. While she worked under the trade name of Madame Devere, her real name, she said, was Lydia Hoover. She charmed him with her fictional biography. In passing, she mentioned the murder of Lamb's brother in Toledo two years ago. That Madame Devere, new to Toledo, knew about the murder startled Joe and left him convinced that the lady had special powers. This opening led to a discussion about clairvoyants and spiritualists and "their strange ability to discover hidden secrets." Lamb told Madame Devere that he didn't believe in fortune-telling but did believe in mesmerism—hypnosis—as he practiced it as a young man. Madame invited him to call again but to give the name "Adams" when he arrived. Assigning Joe an alias should have indicated that something was amiss, but Lamb didn't seem to notice. He did not tell his wife.[9]

Lamb called again at the Washington Street house on October 22. Madame Devere was busy with clients but told Joe that her sister in Cleveland, a Mrs. Richard Brown, was deathly ill. Madame told Joe that she needed to go to Cleveland but was short of ready cash for a ticket. She asked Lamb for $20. Joe was sympathetic but explained that he made only $1,000 a year and had a wife and five children, neglecting to mention all were adults. "I will pay it back to you when I return," she promised. Unable to turn down a lady in distress, Joe gave her his last $5.[10]

Madame Devere returned from Cleveland within a week and summoned Lamb. She told Lamb she feared her sister might die. She needed money for a return trip to Cleveland and Lamb gave her $10. "I had become very much interested in her," he said by way of explanation. The following week brought news that the sister had passed away, leaving two children. Madame told Lamb that she had promised her dying sister she would see to the children's care. She asked Joe for $50, and he claimed he had no money to lend. She offered her jewelry or furniture as collateral and said that when she worked, she easily made $250 a month. Joe was persuaded. "I let her have $20," Lamb later said, "all the money I could spare." He gallantly declined the collateral, which, unbeknown to him, was likely already mortgaged to some local money lender.[11]

Lamb next saw Madame Devere around December 1. One of the sister's children had died, and the clairvoyant needed money to care for the surviving child because her sister's husband was "close about money matters." She borrowed another $50 from Lamb with only a promise of repayment. In a few days, she was back from Cleveland with a youngster of three or four, named Emil, who she said was the only surviving child of her deceased sister, and a man named Richard Brown.[12]

The tragedy with Madame's sister was not the end of the woman's troubles. Lydia Devere fell ill and took to her bed. She told Lamb that a few years ago she had contracted typhoid fever during a pregnancy and had an abortion, which left her badly scarred. This injury was, she said, the cause of her current illness. Only a very delicate surgical operation could cure her, and that could only be performed by a Dr. Samuel Gross in Philadelphia, one of America's preeminent surgeons of the Gilded Age. Had he not been dead for four years, Dr. Gross could certainly have charged the $1,500 Madame said was his fee—this was at a time when a tonsillectomy and anesthesia cost less than $20. The lady asked Lamb to serve as her agent—she being bedridden—and raise the funds for her surgery. She offered Joe a 2 percent commission for his trouble.[13]

Most of the money Lamb acquired for the woman's surgery fund was his own. In a matter of weeks in February 1888, Lamb borrowed or floated notes totaling almost $1,800 to assist the clairvoyant. She was not bashful about taking Joe's money for which she gave him her personal promissory note for $1,000 payable in a year. The note was likely not negotiable as it was payable to J. A. Adams—Lamb's alias—and signed by Devere using the alias of S. B. Hoover of Cleveland. Lamb got the impression that the aliases were to keep friends in Cleveland from discovering she was working as a clairvoyant instead of teaching French dressmaking. True or not, Joe accepted the explanation. Why did an upright man such as Joe Lamb accept her fabrications unquestioningly? This was a question many would later ask. Joe took the Hoover $1,000 note and used it to collateralize the clairvoyant's bill at a lace merchant. When the merchant's bill went unpaid, a Cleveland detective agency was engaged to find S. B. Hoover but could not. Lamb gave Madame his own $275 note as well, and it appeared at Toledo's First National Bank after the woman used it to pay a furrier.[14]

Lamb's family learned something of Joe's unusual relationship with Madame Devere when a local merchant notified Lamb that his personal check for $200—used to pay for a lady's custom sealskin coat that wasn't for Mrs. Lamb—was declined by the bank for lack of funds. Lamb conceded he had no funds for the coat, and Madame Devere herself eventually paid the bill.[15]

In April 1888, Madame Devere engaged a local seamstress, Lizzie Belanger, to alter some dresses. About thirty, the strikingly attractive widow was of average height with a sharp nose and chin, abundant curly auburn hair piled on her head, and piercing blue eyes. One male observer recalled that Mrs. Belanger had "a figure that would cause Venus to turn green with envy." The seamstress had lost her husband and her daughter in recent years, but she had not lost her positive outlook. Lizzie could talk, and, if nervous, she was inclined to "allow her heart to run away with her head," according an acquaintance.[16]

As she measured her new client and chatted, Lizzie told Madame Devere that she had some amateur experience with clairvoyancy. This was enough for Madame to ask Lizzie to fill in for her when she was feeling poorly. In

Lizzie's words, "she offered me a good thing if I would stay and help her out. It was nice easy work, and I accepted the offer." Overnight the Toledo seamstress became Madame LaFraie, a French clairvoyant. The two women were as different as night and day in appearance and manner. Madame LaFraie was stunning and chatty, whereas Madame Devere was a handsome, full-figured woman with much better control of her tongue. The men who came through Madame Devere's doors were all introduced to Madame LaFraie as widowers, which was statistically extraordinary. Madame LaFraie was popular. Lizzie would forever claim that she maintained only a professional relationship with the widowers and worked only days, hinting that something less honorable might occupy the nights. Madame Devere told her new partner that she had a quarterly allowance from an unnamed source and a good income, but since she had become ill, even her furniture was mortgaged. One regular caller at the house was Mr. Adams, and it would be months before Lizzie learned his real name was Joe Lamb. As to the financial aspects of the clairvoyant business, Lizzie preferred to remain blissfully ignorant, or at least that was her story.[17]

Dr. Albert Claypoole was a respected Toledo physician and neighbor of Lydia Devere. She selected him as her personal physician. In May 1888, with her attraction to physicians still strong, Madame informed Lamb that she and the forty-one-year-old doctor were considering marriage. Unfortunately, she confided to Joe that her Philadelphia surgeon had warned her she must abstain from sex for two years after her needed surgery, and that dampened her marriage prospects. This did not prevent Claypoole from taking an excursion to Detroit with Madame and mortgaging his horse and buggy—vital to any nineteenth-century physician—to loan her some money.[18]

Lamb saw little of Madame Devere the summer of 1888 as Dr. Claypoole hovered about and insisted his frequently bedridden patient have no visitors. With Madame LaFraie as intermediary, Lamb procured $900 between May 1 and August 23, 1888, for Madame, receiving a diamond pin worth $250 as collateral. Shortly thereafter, Devere left for a six-week stay in Philadelphia for surgery. Although Joe had given her well over $2,000, she thought she might need more and airily suggested she would get it from the wealthy Richard Brown. LaFraie gave Joe some diamonds of Madame's that summer to mortgage, and he borrowed $250 from a money lender. The naive Lizzie believed the man she knew as Mr. Adams was a banker.[19]

Madame Devere returned on October 18 from Philadelphia and a successful surgery. Reenergized, she relocated to a modest brick house with two front parlors on Broadway in Toledo. As usual, Madame needed yet more cash and turned to Lamb. At the time, Joe held $300 as a stakeholder in an election bet. He gave it to her, even though it wasn't his money. "I have always felt guilty over this," Lamb later admitted, "for it was the first time that I had compromised myself." When the winners came for their prize money, Joe gave one bettor a promissory note for $200 and borrowed $100 from another acquaintance to satisfy the other bettor.[20]

In October 1888, Ellsworth M. Beard, an apprentice in his father's Toledo law office, watched as Lydia Scott signed a chattel mortgage for $740 that Beard's father was lending on the woman's household goods. Only later did Beard discover "Mrs. Scott" was Lydia Devere.[21]

Madame Devere was a regular client of a Toledo notary public and yacht club denizen, G. Wade Morse. In January 1889, she visited Morse and asked him to draft a transfer deed for a Cleveland property on Euclid Avenue. Morse had done, in his words, "considerable work" for the woman and everything was always, in his words, "fair and square." The property was conveyed by one Florida G. Blythe to a J. Lamb. Morse also drafted a mortgage for $25,000 in favor of Florida G. Blythe. Morse's work involved creating unsigned documents, nothing more, and he asked no questions.[22]

Lamb's loans on Devere's behalf were coming due, and he asked her if she would sign her $1,000 annual annuity payment over to him. No, she said, it was already pledged to Richard Brown for money he gave her for her surgery. The more Joe pressured her, the more indignant Devere became, telling Lamb she "was wealthy and had means and property in England." She offered to give Lamb a $1,000 promissory note, made out to her, due January 1890 and signed by a Cleveland man, Charles Fagin. Madame Devere insisted this note be negotiated secretly and not in Cleveland. Lamb took the note to Ketcham National Bank in Toledo and received $400 for it, which he inexplicably gave to Devere. She used those funds to retrieve her jewelry from a pawnshop. Unlike most men caught in similar traps, Joe Lamb, the express agent, was an experienced bookkeeper and kept a detailed ledger of his transactions with the clairvoyant. To date, according to Lamb's meticulous accounting, he had either loaned the clairvoyant or negotiated notes for her amounting to $5,700.[23]

Dr. Claypoole's buggy mortgage came due on January 13, 1889, and Madame needed $700 to give to the physician so he could pay it off. She summoned Lamb and gave him an unidentified Cleveland man's promissory note for $700 to negotiate for cash. The dutiful Lamb got an unknown amount for it at Merchant's National Bank on January 14 and saved Claypoole's horse and buggy from seizure.[24]

In mid-March 1889, an unfamiliar woman with the dress and mannerisms of wealth and refinement arrived at the office of Jay O'Dell and Son, a real estate title firm located across the street from the Argyle Building on Cleveland's Euclid Avenue. The woman requested that O'Dell obtain the deed to the Argyle property and render an opinion as to its validity. Her reasons seemed legitimate to O'Dell, who did as requested. The document revealed that Florida G. Blythe and her sister had sold the property to the Alva Bradley estate, managed by one George Stone, and gave the financial details. Just a few months later, O'Dell was unable to recall the woman's name or even to describe her. He did say he supposed she had come from the Argyle Building across the street.[25]

In the late winter of 1889, Madame Devere gave Lamb a $2,000 promissory note made out to him paying 8 percent interest and due in one year. The note bore the supposed signature of Richard Brown, the deceased sister's purported husband. Devere asked Lamb to negotiate it for cash. However, she was adamant that the note not be sent to Cleveland. Joe was suspicious of this Richard Brown he had never met but heard a great deal about from the clairvoyant. Lamb ignored Devere's admonition and sent the note to a fellow express agent in Cleveland, William G. Yates, in early March with a request to make discreet inquiries about Richard Brown and to determine if any bank in Cleveland would be willing to purchase it. Yates contacted two local banks, where it was suggested that the only known Richard Brown was a principal in Cleveland, Brown and Company, a local iron and steel company. The banks declined to purchase the note, in part because Richard Brown was not from Cleveland, but Youngstown. Yates was referred to Cleveland, Brown, where he showed the note to the bookkeeper, Frank Strong, and the firm's manager, Frank Wilson, who was well acquainted with Brown's signature. Wilson looked at the $2,000 note and unhesitatingly declared it to be "a bad one." Yates wrote a reply to Lamb, telling him that Wilson had declared the note a forgery, and Yates, with over thirty years' experience as an express agent, agreed. Yates returned the note to Toledo along with a letter to Lamb. "I tried to make it plain to him [Lamb] that I thought it was a forgery," Yates recalled of the incident. Within days, Yates received a letter from Richard Brown himself, formally disavowing the note. Yates forwarded Brown's letter to Lamb.[26]

Creating and negotiating fraudulent promissory notes was a common crime during the last half of the nineteenth century—a Victorian form of identity theft. Forgers and swindlers were always active, and almost anybody, man or woman, rich or merely comfortable, could become a victim. Wealthy men like

Richard Brown had to constantly be on their guard. In many ways, the sixty-six-year-old Brown was an ideal mark—wealthy but not so famous as to be widely known outside his hometown. Brown was a self-made man who had arrived in the Mahoning Valley in the 1840s and went to work in the iron mills, rising through the ranks. In 1855, Richard Brown and William Bonnell purchased a shuttered iron mill in Youngstown that, thanks to demand for iron during the Civil War, grew rapidly under the Brown, Bonnell and Company name. In 1879, the company was sold to Chicago investors, making Brown a wealthy man. The Youngstowner had no children to succeed him and reinvested some of his money in other enterprises, including iron and steel broker Cleveland, Brown and Company. Brown had a sterling reputation in Youngstown, where he was recognized as a civic leader and successful businessman.

Brown was a loyal Methodist, heavy donor to his church, and married to the same woman for forty years. The word *scandal* and the name Richard Brown were never uttered in the same sentence. He apparently had no vices; in fact, he said he "never played a game of cards in his life." That didn't mean he was risk averse. The iron and steel business in the last half of the nineteenth century was described by one ironmaster as being "no game for a minister's son." While Brown was a believer in Christian values as practiced in his day, he was also a tough, shrewd businessman who had spent his life among rough laborers. Richard Brown was not a man to be trifled with, nor would he allow his reputation to be sullied. Forging his name on a promissory note was to invite trouble.[27]

Lamb had not been discreet in asking Yates to negotiate the Brown promissory note in Cleveland. Shortly after Yates returned the fraudulent note to Toledo, Madame Devere summoned Joe and scolded him. "Sir, these notes have been to Cleveland, to two banks and to Cleveland, Brown and Company," she lectured. "You have done just what I told you not to do." Dumbfounded, Lamb at first thought it was Madame's clairvoyant powers at work, but she informed him, "Mr. Brown himself told me and upbraided me." A nasty scene ensued with Lamb accusing Devere of deceiving him. She responded by admitting to Lamb that she *was* Florida G. Blythe, the daughter of a prominent Cleveland architect, the ex-wife of another architect, Walter Blythe, and heir to a large Cleveland estate. Upon her father's death, she told Lamb, she had inherited a two-thirds share of the Argyle Building on Cleveland's Euclid Avenue—the onetime address of Betsy Bigley's dressmaking school. The property, Lamb was informed, was being sold to a group of investors headed by Cleveland millionaire George H. Stone for $85,000, and Florida's share was $57,000. She told Joe that she held a $57,000 mortgage from Stone for the sale and a $25,000 promissory note from him as well. Blythe said she intended to negotiate with Stone to convert the mortgage into cash. Additionally, she stated that Richard Brown agreed to pay her $45,000 to raise and educate the boy, Emil. While the lady told Brown she preferred cash or an annuity, he had offered promissory notes. Lastly, Madame proposed to draft a new will that would make Joe Lamb her only executor—accompanied by the post's fees—and pay him $10,000 for managing her affairs, plus a percentage for managing Emil's share. According to this will, which no one ever saw, a Mrs. Bigley, Lydia Devere's mother, was to receive $5,000 and young Emil the balance. If Mrs. Blythe did not pass away in the near term, Lamb would still be paid $10,000 for managing her affairs. Considering Devere's frequent illnesses and precarious health, Joe Lamb had reason for optimism.[28]

Shortly thereafter, Joe Lamb approached a millionaire member of the Toledo Produce Exchange, Will Carrington, about negotiating a George Stone promissory note. Joe asked for a loan of $3,000 and offered a $25,000 personal note signed by George Stone as collateral. Carrington told Lamb "he could have all the money he wished on a note of Mr. Stone's" *if* it was good. As it was, Carrington knew Stone personally and met with him in Cleveland a couple of days later. Stone said that any such note was a forgery and nonchalantly told Carrington that the $25,000 note was likely not the only forged note of his in circulation—one of the burdens of wealth. Carrington declined to help Lamb. This prompted Lamb to insist to Carrington that the note was valid, but Stone had probably been warned by unnamed persons to disavow the note for reasons Lamb would not divulge.[29]

CHAPTER THREE

FAMILY TROUBLES

Not long after the failed attempt to negotiate the Stone note, Madame Devere sent Lamb to the *Toledo Daily Blade* printing office to purchase blank promissory notes. Within a week, Madame gave the blank notes back to Lamb, each now bearing the signature "Richard Brown." She instructed Joe to fill in the amounts, dates, interest, maturity dates, etc., according to her instructions. Joe thought this highly irregular, and he said so. What if the signatures were forgeries? It was all good, Madame Devere assured him, because Brown trusted Lamb, despite the two never having met. Lamb swallowed his doubts, took up a pen, and did as instructed. Lamb would later claim that he believed he was acting in "good faith" by assisting a helpless woman, which was hardly a satisfactory explanation. Lamb could not help but know the signatures were forgeries.[1]

Joe created at least four notes—purportedly for Emil's care—all dated April 22, 1889: two for $5,000, one for $10,000, and one for $25,000. A third $5,000 note similar to the others appeared later. Its origin is less clear. The interest rate varied from 5 to 6 percent, and the longest term was two years. The three smaller ones were made payable to Florida G. Blythe and the $25,000 one to Joseph Lamb. Madame Devere endorsed the three notes as Florida G. Blythe in Lamb's presence, naming him as her agent. Lamb was told to negotiate the notes for cash, but as before, not in Cleveland because neither Devere nor Richard Brown wanted anyone in the city to know about the notes or their reason for being.[2]

Devere told Lamb that she owned another property on Euclid Avenue in Cleveland that was pledged as collateral for the money she borrowed from Richard Brown for her Philadelphia surgery. This debt to Brown was not a recorded mortgage, she told Lamb and, therefore, she didn't hesitate to tell Joe to use the phony deed prepared by G. Wade Morse transferring the property to Joe Lamb as collateral for a loan—yet another instance of illegally mortgaging a property twice.

Joe concocted a story for the bankers to explain the various legal documents and promissory notes relating to Florida G. Blythe in his possession. There was some slight variation, but in general Lamb claimed that he was acting on behalf of Florida G. Blythe, a wealthy niece from Cleveland who had asked him a year ago to become her agent, a not uncommon arrangement in the nineteenth century. Mrs. Blythe had recently sold real estate to Richard Brown and had accepted promissory notes as payment. Contrary to standard practice, Lamb said that the property was sold without a mortgage because Brown's reputation was solid. Additionally, Mrs. Blythe, according to Lamb, had inherited Cleveland real estate—the Argyle Building on Euclid Avenue—that had been sold a year ago to a group fronted by millionaire George Stone for which Mrs. Blythe had received $57,000 in the form of a mortgage backed by a $25,000 Stone promissory note. In Lamb's telling, Mrs. Blythe wisely wanted to keep the real estate in her name until it was paid for and therefore the Stone mortgage was not legally recorded in Cleveland. Mrs. Blythe needed cash, Joe said, because she had serious medical problems and required money for doctors' bills and immediate living expenses. Lamb said that he and Blythe planned to try to negotiate the $57,000 Stone mortgage from the Argyle property for more cash. Lastly, Joe said Mrs. Blythe's health was so precarious that she had revised her will, leaving all her property to him.[3]

His back story memorized, the obedient Joe made the rounds of the Toledo banks with the Richard Brown paper and the deed. In March 1889, he approached Union Savings Bank in Toledo for a loan of $500, offering as collateral the deed to the Cleveland property, which was the most desirable collateral he had. The deed's format, the bank's lawyer informed Lamb, prevented its transfer and was of no value as collateral. While Lamb was having the problem fixed, Union Savings made quiet inquiries in Cleveland regarding Mrs. Blythe. The response was favorable—the lady was good for the amount. Still, the bankers were suspicious and while believing Lamb was upstanding, declined to loan on the deed. However, Leander Burdick, the bank's cashier, agreed to personally loan Lamb the money for thirty days using the Cleveland property as collateral.[4]

Lamb showed the Brown notes to Toledo's First National Bank's president Mars Nearing. Joe wanted Nearing to discount and buy the Richard Brown notes outright. This was an impossible request of a stiff-backed banker like Nearing, who had never heard of Richard Brown. Lamb violated his secrecy promise to Devere and reluctantly approved Nearing making his own confidential inquiries in Cleveland. Brown passed the test. Still not convinced, the ever-cautious Nearing declined to purchase any of the notes outright but instead told Lamb he could utilize them as collateral for short-term—a month or two—personal loans. Taking the $10,000 note as collateral, Nearing loaned Lamb $7,000 on April 29, 1889. Lamb asked Nearing to keep the notes secret and not to contact Richard Brown. The bank president never verified what Lamb told him about Blythe or the real estate. According to Nearing, "I took no steps to investigate. . . . I had confidence in what he [Lamb] said." Nor did he contact Brown regarding the notes during the summer and fall of 1889.[5]

Although Lamb and Madame had just received $7,000 from First National Bank, low-end money lender T. B. Tucker loaned Lydia Devere $450 on May 1, 1889. For collateral, Tucker had a chattel mortgage on a sealskin jacket and a set of silver-plate tableware. Tucker was destined to lose half of his loan money.[6]

Lamb's personal $500 loan from Union Savings' cashier, Leander Burdick, was not paid when due. A more surprised than agitated Burdick contacted Lamb, who said he wanted to borrow an additional $250 for what Joe claimed were probate fees on a $5,000 inheritance from a Cleveland estate. Burdick was no fool and told Lamb that the transaction had a very "sawdust"—shady—look to it. Why not just deduct the $250 from the $5,000? Lamb lamely claimed not to have thought of that. A few days later, Lamb paid off the $500 loan using some of the $7,000 he got from First National and got the property deed collateral back. He immediately offered Burdick a $5,000 note signed by Richard Brown for discounting. Burdick's trust in Lamb was fading, and the suspicious banker refused to have anything to do with the Brown note.[7]

Madame Devere owed Lamb several thousand dollars, and Joe's various creditors were growing impatient. Joe pleaded with the woman to settle her debts with him. She said she would go to Cleveland to see Richard Brown for more funds. When she returned without any money, she persuaded Lamb to give her two of his own promissory notes, one for $500 and another for $700. She would negotiate these for cash for Lamb, she said, in Cleveland, an unlikely scenario since Lamb was neither rich nor a Clevelander. She returned from the city and told Lamb she had failed to sell his notes and destroyed them. However, one note soon appeared at a Toledo jewelry store, and the other was presented at a local bank for discounting by an unidentified individual. When Lamb discovered the deception, he confronted Madame Devere. She condescendingly called him the biggest fool in existence, one of her few truthful statements.[8]

A month later, May 17, Mars Nearing at First National agreed to lend Lamb $2,800 on a $5,000 note, which went straight to Devere to purportedly save her family farm in Ontario from foreclosure. Madame left immediately for Canada, Lamb literally giving her the money, a bank draft, on a streetcar bound for the train station.

Madame Devere's sister, Emma Bigley, arrived to help in Toledo in late June. Shortly thereafter, a distraught Miss Bigley summoned Lamb and said her sister was very ill. Lamb found Madame in bed. He propped her up and gave her wine to stimulate her. She bemoaned requiring yet another surgery, which could only be performed by a physician in England. This surgeon, according to Lydia, required a $10,000 deposit on a $15,000 fee before he would take her case. Devere gave Lamb one of the $5,000 Brown notes she had endorsed as Florida Blythe and told Lamb to get cash for it. One lender refused him, but on June 24, Northern National loaned $3,000 in the form of a bank draft drawn against a New York bank. Lamb gave Devere the draft and $300 in cash. Six months later, while serving as a federal auditor examining the books at the Northern National Bank, Leander Burdick, the Union Savings cashier and onetime Lamb creditor, who had refused to loan on the note, discovered it was being held as collateral by Northern for a small loan to Joe Lamb.[9]

Lamb returned to First National on August 5, 1889, where he received $3,500 by producing a third $5,000 Brown note maturing in 1890 for security. It was after this last loan that Lamb told Nearing that the notes were actually not payment for real estate but a settlement for "family troubles" in Brown's household involving Mrs. Blythe. Lamb then offered Nearing a new explanation for the Richard Brown promissory notes. Lamb said that his niece, Mrs. Blythe, had a sister who was a servant in Richard Brown's household. Brown and the sister had a relationship that resulted in two children, one of whom was deceased. After Blythe's sister died, Joe's niece, Mrs. Blythe, took custody of the remaining child. A Cleveland attorney, Edgar Sowers, negotiated a financial settlement with Richard Brown for the boy's care. According to Lamb, Brown had pledged $45,000 for the task, offering two $5,000 notes and one $10,000 note payable to Mrs. Blythe and a $25,000 note payable to Joseph Lamb as Blythe's agent. Devere now wanted to negotiate the notes for her personal needs.[10]

That summer and fall Joe Lamb kept rolling over his short-term notes at First National and holding all his creditors at bay with new excuses. Devere told Lamb that the money would arrive soon in Toledo to make Brown's notes good. She assured Lamb that there was another unrecorded mortgage on another Cleveland property that she would give him to secure his borrowing. From Lamb's creditors' perspective, if Brown could be induced to take up his notes, the banks stood to make a tidy profit. But if not, they could lose the entire amount. How long could Lamb stall while waiting for Richard Brown to appear in Toledo?[11]

In November 1889, a woman calling herself Florida G. Blythe entered the office of an Oak Harbor, Ohio, real estate agent, John G. Metzger, and an attorney, Charles York. Mrs. Blythe requested a power of attorney be prepared for a Joseph Lamb to handle her affairs along with two mortgages for $57,000 and $25,000, respectively. The mortgages were to be undated and unsigned, headed "Cleveland," and in favor of Florida G. Blythe. She wanted the power of attorney backdated one year. Mrs. Blythe explained this highly unusual request by claiming she wanted to salvage something from her deceased husband's failed Cleveland business. The backdating was certainly a legally questionable request, but York and Metzger were undeterred. York took Mrs. Blythe across the street to George Gosline, publisher of *Oak Harbor Press,* to have the power of attorney notarized. Gosline asked if Florida G. Blythe was her real name, and she said yes. In a bit of irony, Mrs. Blythe insisted the power of attorney prohibit Lamb from making any speculative investments.[12]

Mars Nearing's concern for his loans to Lamb continued to grow. He told Lamb he wanted to see his power of attorney for Florida Blythe. Lamb told Nearing he would go to Cleveland to get it, along with Stone's $57,000 mortgage and another Cleveland mortgage. Lamb went on a Sunday and the next day gave Nearing the power of attorney. Lamb left the $57,000 Stone mortgage with Nearing for safekeeping.

Lamb felt increasingly nervous about the Brown notes he had a hand in creating and was solely responsible for negotiating. It was inevitable that the paper would find its way to Brown's bankers in Youngstown. Brown had already disavowed one note Lamb had sent to Cleveland. Madame Devere convinced Lamb that Brown had been to see her recently and was satisfied with Lamb as Devere's agent. But why, Lamb later said he kept asking himself, didn't Brown want to meet him? Most business was transacted in person. Madame Devere suggested that Joe tell Mars Nearing that he, Lamb, had met with Brown at a Toledo hotel, and the Youngstowner offered to pick up the outstanding notes. His conscience bothering him, Joe nevertheless lied to Nearing about meeting Brown. He tried to soften the falsehood by assuring Nearing he would bring Brown to the bank. When Devere learned of this, she patiently explained to Lamb that Brown would not go to the bank because he wanted to keep his personal indiscretions secret.[13]

Meanwhile, the money men at Northern National Bank, holders of a single $5,000 note, were also growing increasingly more adamant in their demands on Lamb. At the end of his rope, Lamb asked Northern National to write Brown directly and ask him to take up his notes at a discount. When Devere learned of this, she was furious, obviously knowing that exposure might doom both her and Lamb. Her eyes snapping and her finger jabbing the air, she lectured Joe. Uncharacteristically in his dealings with the clairvoyant, Joe stiffened and retorted that he had raised $18,000 for her on his own credit and her promissory notes, never taking a penny for himself for which she was never grateful. Joe Lamb began to finally appreciate what a dupe he had been.[14]

CHAPTER FOUR

A Clear Forgery

Putting pen to paper, Northern National's cashier, W. A. Eggleston, wrote Brown a confidential letter asking if he would like to redeem the $5,000 note, payable to and endorsed by Florida G. Blythe, at a discount over a year before it was due. From Eggleston's viewpoint, the worst that could happen was Brown could decline. On January 6, 1890, Brown responded through his Youngstown bank, Mahoning National, by requesting that the Toledo bank send the note to Youngstown for inspection. Northern National declined, afraid that the note might disappear. Brown replied by testily asking, "Why do you think it was my note?" He enclosed an old canceled check for a sample of his signature and requested that the forgery be brought to the attention of the local prosecutor. At Northern National's request, a handwriting "expert" in Toledo studied the signatures and labeled the note's signature "a bungling imitation." According to the *New York Sun*, "The forging of a man's name to a check or other piece of financial paper is something which requires a high degree of skill." That was true; however, it was usually simpler to just do a tracing. The Brown forgery appeared to be traced.[1]

First National Bank also held the $25,000 Brown note, payable to Lamb, as collateral. President Nearing succumbed to his nagging concerns about the Brown notes and had sent it to Cleveland's Commercial National Bank on December 27 to see if could be discounted. On Saturday, January 11, Richard Brown learned of the $25,000 note, coming on the heels of Northern National's $5,000 note, and rushed to Commercial National, where he was shown the paper.

Cleveland, Ohio, April 22, 1889.

Sixteen months after date, I promise to pay the order of Joseph Lamb twenty-five thousand dollars at 5 percent interest from date. Value received.

(signed) Richard Brown

Brown and Commercial National quickly determined that the note was a "clear forgery" and the signature "a poor imitation." Brown said he didn't know a Joseph Lamb. The *Cleveland Leader and Herald* reported the incident and concluded that this attempted forgery had been unsuccessful, *unless* "the Toledo banks discounted the paper without taking the precaution to ascertain if it was all right."[2]

The upper Midwest was struck by a massive winter storm on January 13, 1890, while in Cleveland, the press discovered another type of storm brewing. Bogus promissory notes were not uncommon, but a $25,000 one was. Banks, who regularly speculated in such notes, were frequently the victims of swindles, and the general public took a perverse joy in seeing a bank cheated when a note was disavowed by the signer. In addition, crime was always good copy for newspapers, which had a monopoly on reporting the news in 1890. And if a woman was somehow involved—like the elusive Florida G. Blythe— that was even better.[3]

Before the widespread use of wire services, newspapers often partnered with papers in other cities when reporting out-of-town news. The *Toledo Daily Blade* picked up the story from the Cleveland papers. The *Daily Blade*'s city editor, H. W. Hayes, dispatched his crime reporters to chase the story. Their job was to tap their sources, interview the principals, and gather the facts. Hayes would write the stories. Trying to make sense of the complexities of a story secondhand was not an easy task, and the result in this case was a series of front-page news reports that were sensational as well as confusing, not atypical of the sort of journalism that ruled the day in 1890. A reader attempting to make sense of them was likely left scratching his head.

In Toledo, the Joe Lamb who was named as beneficiary on the $25,000 note was quickly identified. A reporter for the *Daily Blade* found Lamb in his express office that Monday morning, pale and nervous, a condition the young reporter did not attribute to guilt. Asked to give a public statement, Lamb declined. When asked about Florida Blythe's identity, he said that she was a relative, although he had never actually met her. Joe had no reason to doubt her existence. "There is something strange in this whole affair," Lamb remarked to the reporter with sincerity. "If there has been a forgery, neither Mrs. Blythe nor myself has had any hand in it." The *Daily Blade* speculated that Joe was the unwitting victim of "a carefully laid and most cleverly carried out scheme."[4]

Nearing summoned Lamb to First National that morning and questioned him further about Florida G. Blythe's identity. Lamb's previous claims that she was a relative and a woman of wealth were no longer sufficient. Nearing wanted details. The banker thought Lamb "somewhat excited" when informed that the large note was disavowed by Brown on January 11. Joe told Nearing he would telegraph Cleveland immediately and have Mrs. Blythe come to Toledo. Lamb had been lying to Nearing, and it was time for the truth. Still, he wasn't afraid to manipulate the truth a little to his benefit. A short time later that Monday, Joe was back in Nearing's office, professing to have just discovered that Madame Devere and Mrs. Blythe were the same person. Nearing's reaction was predictable. "My God!" Nearing exclaimed. "You don't mean to tell me that your dealings have been with this spiritualist woman?" Looking intently at the floor, and dripping remorse, Lamb admitted it was so. He would later be called a practiced and artistic liar.[5]

Over at Northern National Bank, cashier Eggleston told reporters that the bank had much less than the $5,000 note's face value at risk. The matter could be settled, Eggleston suggested, by Joe Lamb giving the bank a mortgage on his Eighteenth Street home. Lamb was summoned to the bank. A hastily called meeting of Northern National's directors began at noon while Lamb and a *Daily Blade* reporter waited alone in the cashier's office. The youthful and naive scribe suggested that "Mr. Lamb's sincerity is so evident that no one questions his honesty."[6]

As the directors' meeting was in progress, Toledo police detective James "James D." Brown arrived and gave a letter with a Youngstown postmark to cashier Eggleston. The letter contained Richard Brown's request to prosecute the perpetrators of the fraud. Detective Brown and the *Daily Blade* reporter were acquainted. Asked about the letter, the lawman, with a twinkle in his eye, denied it had anything to do with forgery, quickly adding, "By the way, what forgery do you mean?" The bank's directors immediately examined the letter and gave the policeman some instructions—basically their desire not to have anyone arrested if they could achieve a settlement with Lamb. Joe was sent home to convince his sixty-year-old wife Amy, whose name was on the property deed, to agree to a mortgage as collateral for the money the bank had loaned on the fraudulent Brown note. Lamb assured the bankers he would telegraph Florida Blythe to come to Toledo and resolve the matter.[7]

The Toledo press also descended on First National Bank. President Nearing, dissembling, told the press that the bank was in possession of the $25,000 note and that they had merely been trying to negotiate it for a third party, which cost the bank nothing. Nearing failed to mention the other Brown notes his bank held. He told reporters the bank intended to do nothing further at present. When a reporter asked Nearing about Lamb's assertion that the notes were good, the banker replied that he hoped Lamb was correct, but "I believe he is mistaken."[8]

On the streets of Toledo, rumors persisted, as reported by the *Daily Blade*, that Lamb had been the victim of the most consummate piece of villainy, perpetrated by a well-known local woman. That afternoon while trolling for information, a *Daily Blade* reporter received a tip from an unnamed Toledo attorney. "Go and see Madame Devere," the man suggested.[9]

Taking a streetcar to the brick house at 133 Broadway shortly after 6:00 P.M., *Daily Blade* reporter M. P. Murphy mulled over his line of questioning to best get Madame Devere to admit involvement in the affair. Upon arriving, Murphy chose not one of the two front entrances but the side door. The lady herself answered and told Murphy that she had a client in every room and was too busy for an interview. She knew that her name had been connected with the case and admitted knowing Lamb as an express agent. Had she seen Lamb recently? Yes, she replied, he just left as you arrived, which confirmed the young man's hunch about the man the reporter saw leaving through a front door. "I sent for him," she continued because she had heard her name was involved and wanted Joe to "place my name right before the public." Lamb complained, as Madame recalled, that "I have had an awful day. I have had to mortgage my house to secure one of those notes, and my wife is nearly broken hearted. The Richard Brown of Cleveland, Brown and Company is not the Richard Brown, there must be another Richard Brown." Perhaps Lamb was correct, she suggested.[10]

Madame Devere admitted that Lamb had been to see her several times. However, she continued with rising indignation punctuated with sharp gestures, "I have a great many gentlemen visitors every day. Why, there are two or three grain merchants who, during the wheat season come regularly to see me every day as to their luck. You saw that old gentleman waiting for me before? Yes. Well, he came here to see me about a lottery ticket. And so it is." She even claimed confidential discussions with bank officials investigating the recent embezzlement of $85,000 from Toledo National Bank by its cashier. "I know many things like this," she concluded. "When it comes to that I could tell many things about the affairs of Toledo people were I to break confidences." Devere told the newsman, "Just on account of my profession, people will talk wickedly of me."[11]

Asked if Lamb was a relative, Devere said he was a distant relative. She admitted that she occasionally phoned Lamb's express office because there was a woman there who was a client. The calls were to confirm appointments.[12]

Did Madame have a relative in Cleveland named Blythe, Murphy inquired? She did, an aunt, Mrs. Florida G. Blythe. The reporter asked what she knew of her aunt. "I know that she is a lady of means and well connected and will pay any debt she owes." The interview concluded with the clairvoyant denying any knowledge of Lamb's business with Florida Blythe or if Brown and Blythe were in any way connected.[13]

Newsmen in Cleveland were combing the city for the illusive Florida G. Blythe to no avail. They discovered there had been a Mrs. Florida G. Blythe in Cleveland until last spring, when she relocated to Painesville, where her sister resided. The lady was the daughter of C. W. Hurd, a prominent architect, now deceased. Mrs. Blythe was described in the papers as "a most estimable woman, a lady of large means and social acquaintances," and any suggestion that she was involved in a forgery was "outlandish." She had married, divorced, and remarried Walter Blythe, also an architect but now likewise deceased. The fifty-one-year-old Mrs. Blythe had a confidential agent, James Walter Simpson of Cleveland, a real estate dealer and "manager of estates." G. M. D. Hurd, Blythe's brother, told reporters that Mrs. Blythe had only one child, a daughter Jennie, and mother and daughter were wintering in Connecticut. Mrs. Blythe's only recent business transaction was the sale of the Argyle Building in Cleveland in which she had inherited a share. Blythe owned two-thirds, her sister one-third, according to Hurd. The Argyle Building was purchased for $85,000 by the Bradley estate, controlled by the Cleveland millionaire George H. "Captain" Stone. The purchase, according to Hurd, included a $28,000 mortgage and $57,000 in checks and specie. Hurd was certain that neither of his sisters was involved with a Richard Brown. Hurd concluded, "I feel confident that she had no transactions with Mr. Lamb and does not know him." Simpson didn't believe any of the Florida G. Blythe signatures endorsing the notes were genuine. Hurd said he had documents with Blythe's signature available for Brown's inspection. Through intermediaries, Richard Brown declined the offer. He had his own detectives at work and was understandably suspicious of the middle-aged Mrs. Blythe, regardless of her pedigree.[14]

Not all swindlers looked the part, and Brown knew it. New York's infamous Mrs. Ellen Peck was near forty when she began her career and lived in a "handsomely furnished house" in Brooklyn, attended the Episcopal church, and was married to a respected maritime machinist. At age fifty-one, the pleasant and grandmotherly Mrs. Peck marked her entry into middle age by swindling a soap manufacturer out of $19,000, followed by a diamond fraud, in which she falsely claimed to have loaned a $4,000 diamond cross pendant to the New York governor's wife to wear at a reception. The stone later turned up in a pawnshop.[15]

Investigators seeking "Captain" Stone for comment on the affair in January met a stone wall. It was, the press learned, "impossible to ascertain his whereabouts or the names of his bankers." With the aid of his cronies in Cleveland's financial world, Stone proved remarkably adept at keeping a low profile. He later surfaced in Georgia, conveniently unavailable for investigators.[16]

Downtown at the *Daily Blade*'s office, reporter Murphy was given a message that a Cleveland paper wanted Mrs. Blythe's Cleveland address. A messenger boy was dispatched to Broadway to ask Devere, and he returned with a note from her declining to answer at the request of unidentified "officials." However, she would reply in person. The reporter reluctantly took the last streetcar of the evening to Broadway. Who were the unnamed officials, he testily asked the clairvoyant once inside the door. An attorney, possibly from Cleveland, had arrived just after their interview concluded earlier that afternoon. Madame did not have the man's name or address or know how this attorney knew she was implicated. As for Mrs. Blythe, Madame said she lived somewhere on Prospect in Cleveland. The scribe challenged the lady. "It is singular, isn't it, that he should come to you and warn you not to say anything about this matter, when you don't know the first thing about it?" Ignoring the reporter's sarcasm, Madame Devere readily agreed.[17]

As Murphy was leaving, two men were admitted to the house. On a hunch, the young newsman waited outside until they departed and followed them to a hotel. Murphy presented his press credentials and the men cautiously agreed to answer some questions, anonymously. They were from Cleveland and Youngstown, an attorney and a detective, in Brown's employ. They said that Madame told them she did not know Mrs. Blythe or Richard Brown. The men bluntly told her not to leave Toledo. "I am going to stay right in the city," Madame Devere declared and offered to let one of Brown's men stay in the house overnight to make sure she didn't decamp. One of the men warned her, "Madame Devere, you will undoubtedly be called upon to face the accusations that you are Florida G. Blythe." She replied, "Then I shall have to clear myself."[18]

The private detective told Murphy that Madame Devere was known to use many aliases. Besides her given name, which the man said was Lizzie Bigley, and her business name, Madame Devere, she had operated as Lydia

Hoover, Eliza Clingan, Lydia Scott, and Madame La Rose. The detective gave a thumbnail sketch of the lady's past and suggested the reporter talk to a Toledo attorney named Knisely, specifically about the transaction he handled between Madame Devere and a New York man. The detective further claimed that Madame had an unidentified confederate in Cleveland. She supposedly had an extensive correspondence with "him," never employing the mail or telegraph but rather via a hired messenger boy whose wages and fares she paid. A newsman from the *Daily Blade* would pay Knisely a visit.[19]

The two Toledo banks were concerned both about losing money and face in this swindle. Identical forged notes bearing Richard Brown's signature had been used as collateral for loans to Joe Lamb at both Northern National and First National Banks.

Cleveland, Ohio, April 22, 1889.
One year after date, I promise to pay to the order of Florida G. Blythe,
Five Thousand Dollars at 6 percent interest, value received.
Richard Brown
Endorsed Florida G. Blythe

The preprinted blanks had been purchased from the *Daily Blade* printing office and included a "Toledo" dateline. On the notes held by First National, the dateline "Toledo" had been crossed out and "Cleveland" handwritten instead. Who filled out and signed the notes? Was it Richard Brown or a forger? Mars Nearing had a letter from Brown and had the signature carefully examined. The Youngstown man's handwriting, on the whole, was described as "poor" and "messy" by those familiar with it. Superficially, Brown's signature on the letter appeared similar to that on the notes. Under magnification, the signature was described as a bungling forgery that had been carefully, painstakingly traced and then filled in—a skill possessed by many schoolchildren. Nearing had handled four notes, all dated April 22, 1889. Three were made out to Florida G. Blythe, two for $5,000 and one for $10,000. The last was for $25,000 and payable to Joe Lamb. The Blythe notes were presented already endorsed. Lamb endorsed his note in the presence of Mars Nearing. Holding a fistful of phony paper and no solid collateral, First National Bank was backed into a corner.[20]

First National officials had spent January 13 huddled with police detectives, handwriting experts, and officials from the United States Express Company. The bankers had to take into consideration that Richard Brown might be lying—in fact, that scenario was their best way out of the mess. The next morning, January 14, the bank's directors met to determine a course of action. An ever-present newspaper reporter asked what First National's monetary risk was. A bank officer avoided a direct answer, preferring to spin the narrative to put the bank in the best possible light. "Well, we accepted a $5,000 collateral as did Northern National on a loan," he said. "The case is exactly similar to that of the Northern National, save in this exception, the Northern National has been secured, the First National has not." Mars Nearing had made a serious mistake by not contacting Brown before loaning on the note. Greed, and his trust in Lamb, had clouded his judgment. Contacting Brown might have pushed the Youngstowner to take up his notes, ruining a potentially lucrative transaction for the bank.[21]

That same forenoon as the bank directors met, a *Daily Blade* reporter arrived at attorney Knisely's office in the Produce Exchange Building. Following up on last evening's tip, the newsman wanted information about the incident between Madame Devere and the New York man. Knisely agreed to talk—but within the bounds of client privilege. The attorney said he had known Madame Devere as Eliza Clingan since 1887. He also admitted his role in the affair with the New York man, but he refused to give particulars. Knisely left the reporter with more questions than answers when he summarized the case: "I will say that the present forgery, in the matter of planning and plotting, pales into insignificance before the boldness and premeditated cold-bloodedness of the scheme in the case which I handled."[22]

Madame LaFraie's name came to the newspapers' attention thanks to a tip from a moneylender. President Nearing was asked if he believed this Madame LaFraie was the forger of the notes. "No, I do not," Nearing replied. Furthermore, Nearing had consulted with United States Express officials and concluded, "An expert tells me the writing in the body of the bogus notes was that of Joe Lamb." Nearing was asked if Madame Devere was involved in the case. "That I don't know," Nearing admitted. "In fact, we do not know who wrote the signatures. That's what we would like to find out." When asked directly by a *Daily Blade* reporter if the bank had lost money in the deal, an unnamed bank official was evasive. "Well," he remarked vaguely, "there are 100 stories afloat and none of them are true."[23]

The morning of January 14, the *Daily Blade*'s Murphy decided to gauge Joe Lamb's reaction to the suggestion that Madame was implicated in the forgeries. When the reporter showed Lamb his newspaper's latest edition with the report that Madame Devere was involved, Joe's hands shook visibly as he held the paper. Still, Lamb maintained he knew nothing and would not discuss the matter. The newsman felt that Lamb was "evidently sincere" in his denial but was obviously befuddled. The reporter uncharacteristically withdrew quietly.[24]

After leaving Lamb, Murphy made a third visit to 133 Broadway. Once inside, Murphy noted that the doorbell rang with annoying regularity. The reporter was shunted into an unoccupied room. More comings and goings resulted in a musical-chairs shuffling of the various rooms' occupants. When the rooms were full, the next visitor, Dr. Claypoole, was left standing in the hall. Through it all, a young messenger boy slept in a chair next to the warm stove in the kitchen.[25]

When he was finally alone with Devere, the newsman asked her if her real name was Florida G. Blythe. "Just say I don't deny it or confirm it," she said. Then to confuse matters even more, Madame claimed to have had a dispatch that morning from Mrs. Blythe, who was now in Philadelphia. The newsman pressed her for a full statement. After a moment's thought, she declined, lamenting that no less than ten detectives, reporters, and lawyers had hounded and annoyed her. Perhaps "one of these days" she would tell all. Just as the reporter was heading out into a cold drizzle, he mused that "the Madame's popularity has grown amazingly." The last caller seen by the scribe was later identified as a bill collector.[26]

Detective John Manley had known Joe Lamb since childhood. Manley was at Devere's Broadway house on January 14 to "see that she didn't get away, understanding that she was making preparations to leave." During a previously unrelated visit to Devere's home, Manley had seen moving boxes and barrels in the house and had spoken to a man who had been packing the lady's household goods since just after Christmas. The packer said that Devere's silver plate and flatware had already left the house for parts unknown. Manley discovered Lamb in the house and pulled him into an empty parlor. The detective told Lamb he had gotten into quite a scrape. Joe showed Manley the $5,000 note that Northern National Bank had released in return for a mortgage on Lamb's home. Despite this, Joe assured Manley that he would come out fine in the end.[27]

Madame Devere was a good customer of the local moneylenders. Billy Wilson was a collector for one, H. V. Ketcham. Wilson had been to the house on Broadway early the morning of January 14 to make certain that the diamonds and household goods on his inventory list that served as collateral for a loan of $1,500 hadn't left the premises. "I am watching her very closely," Wilson told reporters. Billy Wilson left the impression of a man experienced in dealing with less than sterling borrowers, and who made it his business to know his debtors' secrets. The name on Devere's chattel mortgage, according to Wilson, was Lydia Scott. Wilson also proved to be the source of the theory that it was Madame LaFraie, a partner in "the clairvoyant game," who was the perpetrator of the fraud, not Madame Devere. "It was Madame La Fraie who got her and Lamb into all this trouble," Wilson claimed convincingly. When eager reporters inquired about Madame LaFraie's whereabouts, Wilson replied that he had asked Madame Devere that same question. "She got out of the way, it seems," Wilson said, "before the cloud-burst come, and now they want her." Wilson was deliberately providing misleading information to the reporters. Was it to protect his investment in Devere or to make trouble for Madame LaFraie?[28]

Lizzie Belanger, alias Madame LaFraie, proved easy to locate. Her home was a cluttered second-floor apartment owned by a Toledo police detective. Clearly, the Toledo police knew where to find her. Lizzie was known about town, and reporters learned that she had "a reputation beyond question." A seamstress once again, the talkative former Madame LaFraie was more than willing to reveal the details of her time spent with Madame Devere to the press.[29]

After interviewing Mrs. Belanger, a *Daily Blade* reporter asked Detective Manley, the veteran detective in charge of the investigation, his thoughts on Mrs. Belanger. Manley indicated to the reporter that he was convinced that Lizzie wasn't Florida Blythe in reality or as an imposter. In fact, she was not a suspect in the Brown forgery case. "It is a pretty scheme to throw it off onto a third party, but it fails to operate readily," the detective told reporters while deflating Wilson's theory. Manley based this on Mrs. Belanger's and Madame Devere's claims not to have seen each other since last April—flimsy evidence. In truth, Toledo detectives were already convinced, based on their circumstantial evidence and what they read in the newspapers, that they had solved the case. "The first opinion, that Devere and Blythe are identical," Manley stated with confidence, "will prove to be correct." The banks were as yet unwilling to admit this fact in hopes of finding a miracle to save either their money, reputations, or both, opined Manley. In response to Richard Brown's demand for prosecution of the perpetrators, Toledo police chief O'Dwyer sent Brown a letter saying that Lamb was a respected citizen. However, if Brown would come to Toledo and "make information against Lamb, he would be arrested."[30]

The Toledo police were not pleased with the banks' indecision about filing criminal charges. One police official told the *Daily Blade,* "They [the banks] appear to be wanting to cover up something and it has been with the utmost difficulty that we have obtained a bit of information from them." For the po-lice, longtime Toledo resident Joe Lamb didn't pose a flight risk. But Madame Devere had nothing to keep her in town and a history of not staying in one place very long. Manley and Brown had warned Devere not to leave town, but she was not under surveillance.[31]

United States Express Company employees had been involved with the bo-gus Brown notes from the start, thanks to Joe Lamb. By Tuesday, Lamb's Toledo supervisor, Calvin Cone, had heard the rumors that Madame Devere was in-volved. Cone asked Lamb directly about Madame Devere's identity, and Joe ex-plained she was a relative and he was her agent. Cone thought the whole busi-ness "looked very hazy." Express companies and railroads made huge profits shipping all manner of freight, including gold and currency, across the country every day. United States Express could not afford to have its reputation sullied by scandal. Cone wanted to interview Devere himself, primarily to see if she and Lamb told the same story. From the perspective of the express company, if Joe Lamb was involved in something criminal, he would have to be fired.[32]

Although First National wasn't admitting it, the bank had just under $13,000 at risk in the affair. Northern National Bank was even more tight-lipped, but they had loaned Lamb $3,500 on a $5,000 note, which was now partially cov-ered by that mortgage on Lamb's home. The men at First National knew from the private detectives they had hired that Madame Devere's criminal past in-cluded passing forged notes. Police and bank officials agreed it was time to question Madame Devere. Lamb, First National's Nearing, Calvin Cone of the express company, police clerk Will Cook, and police detectives John Manley and James Brown formed a delegation and were on their way to Madame's home by mid-afternoon on Tuesday, January 14. Devere had boasted to report-ers that if all parties would come before her, "I will tell all I know." The answers she gave would determine her future. Cook had two blank arrest warrants in his pocket because the detectives were ready to act. All the police needed was for one of the banks to swear out a warrant.[33]

Nearing and Cone, however, were hoping to quietly salvage something that would avoid a public court action and its inevitable press coverage. Both men felt that Madame Devere might be more cooperative without an intim-idating police presence, so only Lamb, Nearing, and Cone rang the doorbell at 133 Broadway. Cook, Manley, and Brown reluctantly waited outside.[34]

Shown into one of the clairvoyant's overstuffed parlors, Lamb introduced Madame Devere as Mrs. Blythe to Nearing and Cone, who politely continued to address her as Mrs. Blythe during the interrogation. Nearing asked Devere what her relationship was to Lamb, and she attempted to defer to Joe because, in reality, she didn't know exactly what Lamb had told Nearing. The banker pressured Madame, and she said she was Lamb's niece. Joe readily agreed, and the woman's relief was evident. Lamb and Devere both assured Nearing that the Richard Brown notes were good and genuine. The clairvoyant said she "regretted very much that they had not been paid." She was reluctant to disclose any details. Cone tried to loosen her tongue by cleverly suggesting that "if it was all straight the facts could not injure them." Eventually, Devere began to relax. Questioned about Richard Brown's appearance, she said that the man was about sixty years old and had gray hair. She claimed that the promissory notes in question represented a settlement between herself and Brown. The deceased sister, who remained nameless, had been a servant in Brown's Youngstown household. The sister's husband died, and, according to Devere, her sister became Brown's mistress. As a pillar of his community, Brown was desirous of keeping the extramarital affair quiet. To that end, he had leased a home for his mistress in Cleveland and corresponded with her only by typewritten letters signed "Dick." Brown and his mistress had two children, according to Devere, one of whom died. Madame said she lived with her sister for a while, and when the sister passed away, Brown offered a settlement of $45,000, channeled through a Cleveland attorney, for the child's continuing care. Brown chose to employ promissory notes of varying due dates as the means of payment, believing them less public than an annuity or trust. Devere told Nearing and Cone that she had turned the notes over to Lamb to negotiate. The two men were left with the impression that Lamb "paid all the money over to her."[35]

To support the Brown promissory notes, Devere claimed to hold a $57,000 mortgage and a $25,000 promissory note from Cleveland millionaire George H. Stone from the sale of real estate. The Stone note had been given to Lamb, she claimed. Nearing knew of the Stone paper, having seen the note. Lamb had given him the mortgage, along with his power of attorney, for safekeeping with the explanation that Blythe was being sued and there were parties in Cleveland who wanted the mortgage and note. Nearing was likely convinced by the time he questioned Madame that the Stone note was also a forgery.[36]

Nearing, understandably, wanted to know what had happened to the money from the notes. Cone later remarked of her answer, "Nothing was said, that I recollect about what became of the money, except that she said she had none of it then." This, no doubt, deflated Nearing. To deflect criticism, Madame Devere hastened to explain that her medical bills over the past two years had been nearly $10,000. Not mentioned was a rumor around Toledo that Madame Devere had invested as much as $8,000 in questionable Kansas City real estate and inflated western mining stocks. She lost most of it.

Devere told Nearing that she had recently met Brown in Detroit and had been assured the money would soon arrive in Toledo to cover the outstanding notes. As two hours of questioning drew to a close, Madame Devere agreed to go to Cleveland the next day to straighten things out. According to Cone, "I wanted to identify Mr. Brown and Mrs. Blythe manifested a disposition to help us the next day." There would be no criminal charges filed on Tuesday. First National's directors would meet in the morning and decide on a course of action. In Toledo's bars and on the city's streets, Joe Lamb was said to be "either crazy or else the dupe of a designing woman."[37]

Calvin Cone planned to accompany Madame Devere and Joe Lamb to Cleveland the morning of January 15 as he attended to express company business in the city. Lamb arrived at the express office early on the 15th with the news that Madame Devere had been warned by "some more parties" from Youngstown not to go to Cleveland because Richard Brown was coming to Toledo tomorrow. Cone told Lamb he should stay in Toledo in that case and left for Cleveland alone.[38]

CHAPTER FIVE

AN UNPRINCIPLED
ADVENTURESS

The morning of January 15, 1890, the directors of the First National Bank met to hear the reports of their private detectives and consider their options. They were aware of Madame Devere's unsavory past. All the evidence indicated that Devere and Lamb knew the Brown notes were fraudulent. First National Bank had loaned Lamb just shy of $13,000 and had only the bogus Brown notes and the questionable $57,000 Stone mortgage as collateral. Lastly, Devere had contrived an excuse not to go to Cleveland that morning. The directors were out of options. That afternoon, First National Bank vice president Spencer D. Carr went to the central police station and filed a criminal complaint against Lydia Devere and Joseph Lamb for forging and passing a single fraudulent $5,000 promissory note. The remaining notes could be used as the basis for further criminal charges if needed.[1]

While the bank directors were meeting, a *Daily Blade* reporter went to Devere's residence in an attempt to get her to disclose more details about the financial settlement with the New York businessman that attorney Knisely had facilitated. The newsman found the Broadway home overflowing with clients, moneylenders, the ever-vigilant Dr. Claypoole, and lastly Joe Lamb. Madame was blunt with the reporter: "I don't care to talk with you, and I have nothing to say to you." The young scribe parried by telling her, "I have a great deal to say to you . . . facts that came all the way from New York this morning . . . but you are not obliged to listen to them." It was a bluff on the reporter's part, and Madame responded that an attorney had forbidden her to give any interviews. The *Daily Blade* called Madame's unwillingness to talk "a bitter disappointment."[2]

Lamb and Devere argued for two hours in the early afternoon over what course of action to take to avoid arrest. Joe wanted her to help him reach an understanding with his creditors. She refused, sarcastically suggesting that the problem with promissory notes was that people were always wanting their money. She told Lamb he should obtain a lawyer—any lawyer, as long as he was smart—and bring him to her, and the three of them would concoct a story to defeat justice. Lamb stiffened and refused, telling Madame as he left to await arrest that she was "one of the vilest, most dangerous women that modern history has known."[3]

Toledo's chief of police personally sent Detectives Manley and Brown to Broadway to arrest Madame Devere the afternoon of January 15. The lady was out, but a servant expected her soon. The two lawmen took up concealed positions in the neighborhood—Brown, a large man, hiding in the bushes—where they could observe the house. Late that afternoon, Lydia Devere returned, and moments later, she was peacefully arrested just inside her front door. Lamb surrendered quietly at his home a short time later and left voluntarily with Detective Manley.[4]

Lydia Devere and Joe Lamb were booked for forgery at 6:00 P.M. on Wednesday, January 15, 1890. The detectives lodged Lamb in the cramped, unappealing city jail proper and Devere in the jail matron's apartment, at least until a cell was available for her. Madame was accompanied by youngster Emil Hoover. Shortly after midnight, a judge was roused from bed and set bail at $800 apiece. Lamb's wife and son-in-law promptly provided Joe's bail. No one appeared to cover Madame Devere's bail, as all her "widowers" remained silent.[5]

On Thursday, January 16, Lamb and Devere were arraigned in police court. According to the *Youngstown Vindicator,* "The opinion still prevails [in Toledo] that the clairvoyant is an unprincipled adventuress and that Lamb is one of her many victims." A haggard and pale Madame Devere was escorted into court—normally the haunt of drunks, petty thieves, and prostitutes—and sank heavily into a chair. She was clad in the same white tea gown with green stripes that she wore when arrested. A likewise pale and dazed Joe Lamb stood behind her, resting his hand on her chair. One reporter with a literary bent wrote that Lydia Devere's face was "painful to look into, devoid of a line which could suggest the expression of happiness." The clairvoyant and her dupe, as many were now referring to Joe, came away from the proceedings with further charges for passing or uttering forged notes, one count for Lamb and two for Madame. Bail was increased to $2,000 for Madame Devere, who remained in custody. First National also filed a civil suit for $3,500 against her for the cash the bank had loaned Lamb on a $5,000 Brown note. Madame was supported by the jail matron as she left the courtroom. From behind bars, she issued a threat to make any number of bankers squirm if they didn't help her secure bail. But no Toledo banker was foolish enough to be associated with an accused swindler. The threat proved to be a hollow bluff, and Devere remained in jail. Rumors spread through the city that her victims "are numbered by the score" and included, among others, a banker, two physicians, and an aged real estate investor.[6]

From her jail cell on January 16, Madame told a *Daily Blade* reporter, "I have made no statement yet, but when I do it will be easily traced, line for line, and Lamb and I will be found innocent." The newsman concluded, "She said this with such an air of sincerity that it would be hard to doubt but that she meant just what she says." Despite her threats, Madame Devere kept her secrets to herself throughout. The police and prosecutors tried politeness, pleading, and finally threats to get her to talk, all to no avail. And in the face of mounting publicity and evidence, there were still those in Toledo who believed that both defendants would clear themselves. To further muddy the waters, Madame told the reporter, "There is another Madame Devere in Cleveland and perhaps she has been mixed up in what the papers say. She is a clairvoyant, and I called on her once."[7]

The sixty-year-old Mrs. Lamb was so prostrated by the blow of her husband's arrest and duplicity that her physician sent her to bed and banned visitors. Lamb's family and friends tried to explain Joe's seemingly illogical and atypical actions. He had been behaving strangely for some time, and some unexplained involvement with Madame Devere was known to his family. However, it wasn't until the forgery was made public that Lamb's family came to appreciate the depth of Joe's involvement. In nineteenth-century America, it was common to blame a man's aberrant behavior on a woman's irresistible persuasion. Some went so far as to suggest that because Joe had practiced mesmerizing as a young man, his mind was so constructed that it was unable to resist mesmeric—hypnotic—influences of the type a clairvoyant might employ. Nevertheless, Joe's supporters maintained that he did not intend to defraud anyone and was "more sinned against than sinning."[8]

Guilty or innocent, Joe Lamb had become a liability to the United States Express Company. A reporter calling at the company's Toledo office on January 16 found Lamb absent. When asked if Lamb had been fired, a coworker told the newsman he didn't know when Joe would return.[9]

Joe Lamb had come to the realization, with some persuasion from family, friends, and his lawyer, that he was on his own in this criminal proceeding. Madame Devere was not going to save him. And so on January 18, the *Daily Blade* headline read, "Lamb Says He Will Tell the Whole Story. He Will Leave

Madame Devere to Her Fate." He would have to present his own explanation for the events surrounding the forged notes. Lamb gave the prosecutors his detailed journal of his transactions with Devere. The handwritten journal began in January 1887. In the history of fraud, no victim of a swindle ever kept such accurate records with every transaction recorded in detail. The question for the prosecutors centered on the journal's authenticity. Was the journal genuine or had Lamb concocted it from thin air? If genuine, could it be used as evidence? The prosecutors were uncertain.[10]

A *Daily Blade* reporter interviewed Madame Devere in the confines of jail, where she appeared anxious but confident of a favorable outcome to her troubles. "Lamb and I will be found innocent," she said while dropping hints of her political influence. Another experienced newsman familiar with the ways of the upper classes suggested that Madame Devere "will make some very wealthy gentlemen hustle around and settle her little case rather than have themselves too intimately associated with her."[11]

The police matron, Miss Coates, told reporters that her new prisoner was bright, talkative, and a good conversationalist. Madame was well supplied with the city's newspapers, and her droll sense of humor was best displayed when discussing newspaper accounts of her troubles. Since her personal possessions had been seized by creditors, she was reduced to begging her jailers for a change of clothes and toys for Emil. Nevertheless, Madame and Emil dined well on catered meals prepared by a local hotel and charged to an anonymous benefactor.[12]

Mary Ann Bigley and her daughter Emma, who was to marry a Cleveland machinist in a week, were en route from Canada to take charge of six-year-old Emil. Initially believing the clairvoyant ill, Emma had discovered the truth in a newspaper. She also identified Joe Lamb by a description and woodcut of him published by the *Daily Blade* on January 20. "He is the man who went by the name of Adams when I was in in Toledo!" Emma exclaimed. "He told me he was a widower."[13]

Associated Press reports from the evening of January 19 confirmed that Toledo's First National Bank had lost $13,000 on three forged notes and that Devere received an estimated total of almost $20,000 from various forged instruments. Where was the money? One report claimed that Madame's valuable plate and silverware had already been shipped to Canada. Madame had promised that she would care for Emil no matter what, and some newspapers speculated that some of the cash "has been placed to the credit of some such fund somewhere." One of the bank drafts from First National Bank had been negotiated through the Imperial Bank of Canada.[14]

A preliminary hearing in Toledo's police court on the charges against Lamb and Devere began promptly at 9:00 A.M. on Tuesday, January 21. Proving that there were few things more interesting than a notorious woman, two hundred people had requested admission to the courtroom, which held no more than eighty. Six burly policemen regulated the flow of spectators. Friends of the presiding judge were permitted to watch from the door to his chambers while his wife sat with him on the bench. Onlookers even perched in windows across a courtyard opposite the courtroom's high windows. The spectators were a mixed lot comprised of businessmen, laborers, and, according to the *Daily Blade*, "the bummer element." There were women in attendance seated in the first row of chairs behind the bar. They were described by one newsman as "women who dress in silks and sealskins but have the misfortune to be afflicted with morbid curiosity."

After hastily disposing of two drunk and disorderly cases, Judge Humphrey gave the signal, and, with a dramatic flair, the doors at the rear of the room opened. Madame Devere's lead attorney, a dignified veteran barrister, Lew Richardson, led the parade, which included Madame Devere, still wearing the rumpled green-and-white tea dress and daintily dabbing a handkerchief to her tearful eyes. Mrs. Bigley, dressed solemnly in black, followed her daughter with Emil. More lawyers and bankers followed. All but unnoticed, Joe Lamb was already present in court, sitting jauntily with his chair leaned back against the bar.[15]

The spectacle and the crowd were all for naught. The star witness—the critical witness, Richard Brown—was ill and unable to travel to Toledo. A physician's note said the Youngstowner had influenza. Judge Humphrey granted the prosecutor a continuance until Friday, January 24. The issue of unequal bail was raised by the defense. Lamb's was set at $800, while Devere's had been raised to $2,000 after the additional charges were filed. The prosecution argued for the status quo because Lamb was a longtime resident of the city, whereas Lydia Devere was colorfully described as a "bird of passage" in Toledo and "may have friends to help her escape." Judge Humphrey's response to the bail question was not devoid of bias. "It is apparent that a crime has been committed, she [Devere] the principal actor and Mr. Lamb used as her cat's paw. . . . He has been known here many years and highly trusted, yet he was entrapped. I think she should be held in $1200 bond for this [second] charge of uttering and publishing the notes." Judge Humphrey left bail unchanged. Rumors flew around the courthouse that bail for Madame Devere was imminent, but they proved false.[16]

Mrs. Mary Ann Bigley remained in Toledo until January 22 before returning to Canada with young Emil. Mrs. Bigley told her errant daughter as she
prepared to leave, "If it was a case of sickness or death, Lizzie, you should
have my last cent, but as it is, you have brought yourself into trouble, and it is
your own fault." Some newspapers suggested that the old woman had taken
important papers needed by the prosecution, but the jail matron denied it.
Meanwhile, young Emil, who called Lydia Devere "Mother," had been convinced they were staying in a hospital, not a jail. The boy was destined for his
uncle Arthur Bigley's Ontario stock farm.[17]

Joe Lamb was seen in Cleveland on Wednesday, January 22, where he
talked to employees at Cleveland, Brown and Company. He also wanted to
speak to his former colleague, William G. Yates, about the $2,000 note. Lamb
believed if he could get Yates's correspondence, it would support his explanation that he was not trying to negotiate the note, only determine its validity,
which was not a crime. Yates was conveniently ill and "unavailable" to Joe
and reporters. Lamb admitted to the Cleveland press that he had been a dupe
of Madame Devere and "had lost all—reputation, property and situation"
through his dealings with her. He told Cleveland reporters that Devere had
realized nearly $20,000 from the notes. Joe said that before he left the city, he
intended to call on Madame's relatives in Cleveland.[18]

Would Richard Brown attend Friday's proceedings in police court? Detective James Brown of the Toledo police, acknowledged by the papers for "doing good work on the forgery case," was dispatched to Youngstown to talk to
Brown. Upon his return, Detective Brown told everyone that "Mr. Brown will
be here." Still, the detective said he would not blame the man if he didn't come
because "he is predisposed to lung troubles . . . but he purposes to come even
it should kill him."[19]

Richard Brown, not quite recovered from the influenza and plagued by a
sharp cough, was on a train Thursday night, January 23, from Cleveland to
Toledo. The *Daily Blade,* seeking a leg up on its competition, sent a reporter to
intercept Brown when the train made a scheduled stop at Fremont, Ohio, east
of Toledo. Through a combination of luck and guile, the young reporter located
Brown, "a tall, fine looking middle-aged gentleman," in the first passenger car
on the westbound Lake Shore train. Presenting his credentials to Brown, the
persuasive young newsman succeeded in gaining Brown's confidence.[20]

Richard Brown found the forgeries "a very singular case, and it puzzles me
to know how I ever came to be mixed up in it." He said he learned of Devere's
arrest from Pittsburgh newspapers. Brown did not recall ever meeting the

woman; however, the sketches of her in the papers *might* have resembled a woman who came to the parsonage of Brown's church several years ago seeking assistance. He gave her $2. The woman claimed she was going to Meadville, Pennsylvania, and promised to repay him. Brown and the woman had exchanged correspondence at a later date, which might have provided a sample signature. Brown had seen the forged notes in Cleveland and believed the signatures on the notes were "made evidently to imitate mine" but were "poor imitations." The forged ones were steady and polished to Brown's eye, unlike his unsteady, rambling hand.[21]

Of Joe Lamb, Brown said, "I do not know that I know him." Brown was aware of Lamb's recent inquiries and visits to Cleveland regarding the notes. "I do not really think Mr. Lamb is guilty," Brown said. He had read that Lamb's family "are very good people. I trust they may be able to save him." Brown said he intended to stay in Toledo only long enough to testify.[22]

The *Toledo Daily Blade* reporter persuaded the Youngstowner to detrain in East Toledo and take a carriage into the city to avoid the expected crowd awaiting him at the central station. Learning from Brown that he usually stayed at the Broody Hotel when in town, the reporter suggested another lodging, the Madison. The reporter had a coconspirator at the hotel write "R. Brown, Youngstown" in the Broody register. Rival newsmen and city authorities were left fuming and searching high and low for the critical witness. The enterprising reporter came away from his conversation with Brown believing that the man had "spoken only the absolute truth in regard to this matter." Furthermore, in the newsman's opinion, "There is no art or guile in the soft blue eyes, and not a single trace of duplicity or cunning in his bland and sunny smile."[23]

Public fascination with the forgery case on Friday exceeded that of the previous Tuesday. Two tables were reserved for the press. The police court hearing would determine if there was evidence of a felony and, if so, send the forgery case on for consideration by the county grand jury. Spectators were packed in like sardines, and the atmosphere was stifling and reeking from dozens of closely packed bodies. Madame Devere entered theatrically, supported by the jail matron, a fresh handkerchief held to her face, and curls piled atop her head. To confirm her poverty, she wore the tired green-and-white frock of her arrest. Seating herself at the defense table, Lydia Devere crossed her legs in a manner calculated to show entirely too much ankle for 1890. Her attorneys, J. D. Ford and Lew Richardson, reseated her between them at the defense table. Madame sat, feet planted on the floor, elbows on the table, and hands supporting her head. Although appearing dejected, the defendant's eyes betrayed her. She was intensely interested and remained so during the daylong proceeding.

Joe Lamb arrived fashionably late, his graying Vandyke beard and hair neatly trimmed and a fresh paper collar encircling his neck, just as the judge was inquiring of his whereabouts. Each defendant was entitled to a separate hearing, and Joe was scheduled to go first. Lamb dropped into a chair facing the spectators and assumed an air of nonchalance as he leaned his chair back against the railing. A *Daily Blade* reporter thought him pale and his hair possibly a bit whiter. Yet, Lamb's expression remained blank and his eyes fixed on the floor as he worked hard to ignore the testimony. Lamb's fate would be determined first.[24]

The center of attention that Friday morning would be Richard Brown. Everyone wanted to know if Brown was an upstanding citizen or a scoundrel trying to weasel out of a debt. When the silver-haired gentleman with the white Dutch beard in the solemn black suit entered, all eyes were on him. To its readers, the *Daily Blade* described Brown as a "mild and kindly faced, dignified old gentleman" who entered court "erect and calm."[25]

The honor of testifying first went to First National Bank, the primary victim of the swindle. President Mars Nearing took the stand clutching, as if attempting to squeeze money from them, three promissory notes. Under examination by the prosecution, Nearing gave a recap of what Lamb had told him over the preceding several months and a synopsis of what Madame Devere had said when Nearing and Cone had interviewed her earlier in the month. "Both represented the notes were given by Mr. Brown. The notes, they said, were given in settlement of a family difficulty," Nearing explained. He then admitted giving Lamb a $3,500 loan on a $5,000 note, the source of the charges the defendant faced. Did the bank communicate with Richard Brown? "I took no steps to investigate until the matter came out," Nearing admitted. "I had confidence in what he [Lamb] said."[26]

Richard Brown followed Nearing. He forcefully denied meeting Lamb in December or any other time and said the first time he saw Joe Lamb was that morning. Pointing to Madame Devere, the prosecutor asked, "Are you acquainted with this lady?" Brown responded, "I don't know that I ever saw her until this morning. I think I never had any transaction with her." He was asked if he ever had any transactions with Florida G. Blythe. "No, not personally, and I do not remember that the firm ever did," Brown said. Asked if there was any scandal associated with his household, Brown replied, "None!" Shown the $5,000 note in question, the prosecutor asked Brown if it was his signature at the bottom. "It is not," Brown replied. "Did you at any time execute a note of $5,000 to Florida G. Blythe?" inquired the prosecutor. "No, sir, I never did" was Brown's answer. Brown was shown the other notes bearing his purported signature and denied signing his name to them or authorizing anyone else to do so. When he was asked if the signatures were a fair imitation of his, Brown admitted they were, but he had no trouble picking his own genuine signature from a grouping. He was asked if he ever sent $10,000 to an English physician to treat Mrs. Blythe, and Brown denied he had. Brown's responses were given with such conviction that he was universally judged to be truthful by the time he rose to leave the witness box.[27]

The Oak Harbor attorney, Charles York, was called to the stand and testified that he had drawn up papers for a lady in which the names Joseph Lamb and Florida G. Blythe appeared—one was Lamb's power of attorney and two were mortgages for $57,000 and $25,000. Indicating Madame Devere, the prosecutor asked York if she was the lady who identified herself as Florida G. Blythe. "I believe that's the lady," York answered. "The power of attorney was acknowledged [notarized] across the street by Mr. Gosline."[28]

Around noon, a gong sounded in the hallway indicating lunch. The spectators had stood all morning in close quarters, yet, according to the *Daily Blade*, "they reluctantly left the room."[29]

Resuming at 2:00 P.M., the courtroom was again packed. When Mr. Chapin of the United States Express Company took the stand, he was asked to confirm that the handwriting in the body of each note was Joe Lamb's. However, Irving Belford, Lamb's attorney, said his client would admit to that fact. The prosecution rested its case. Lamb's defense presented no witnesses.[30]

Madame Devere was next. Brown repeated his testimony, establishing that forgery occurred. Mars Nearing connected Lamb to Florida G. Blythe and established that Madame Devere identified herself as Mrs. Blythe. Nearing also testified that Devere admitted she gave the notes to Lamb to negotiate. Nearing stated that when he questioned Madame Devere about the proceeds from the notes, she told him that "she had no money then." Calvin Cone was asked if Madame Devere had represented to Lamb that the notes were made by Richard Brown of Cleveland, Brown and Company. According to Cone, "she answered decidedly that she had" and that all the money Lamb raised from the notes he gave to her.[31]

All during the trying day, a young man wearing fine clothes and flashy jewelry and sporting a gold-headed cane sat with Madame Devere and became the source of some speculation. His name was A. L. Dent, an old Canadian neighbor of the Bigleys. Dent was called to briefly testify and said he had known the defendant for fifteen years. Dent said he believed Devere's husband was named Hoover and that he, Dent, had received several letters from Devere signed S. B. Hoover. This testimony established a connection between Madame and the alias S. B. Hoover.[32]

The prosecution wanted Lamb to take the stand. This was an unusual request, and Lamb had every right to refuse. After several minutes' consultation, Lamb's attorney, Belford, declined to let Lamb testify "because it is in most cases not wise to do so." Thus, with Lamb not inclined to testify, both the prosecution and defense rested.[33]

Judge Humphrey didn't hesitate to bind the duo over to the grand jury. "There has been a base forgery committed," Judge Humphrey said, "and I cannot do otherwise than allow the grand jury to figure it out." The judge acknowledged that Lamb was highly spoken of in the community. "The higher courts will have to find how deeply he [Lamb] has become involved." The question of unequal bail arose—Lamb's $800 versus Devere's $2,000. The prosecution argued that Lamb was "a mere tool of the woman and wielded by her power." As for Devere, the prosecution declared, "It was her act." Judge Humphrey left bail unchanged. It was 5:00 P.M., and as the judge made his docket entries by gaslight, Richard Brown shook hands all around.[34]

The day concluded as one last bit of excitement rippled through Toledo when it was rumored, yet again, that bail for Madame was in the city. At first, speculation swirled around her brother, Arthur Bigley, and the neighbor, A. L. Dent. Neither of them supplied bail. A second rumor was that Madame Devere had placed some of the proceeds from the forged notes with a well-known local man. According to the *Daily Blade,* "the gentleman's name is known, but there are reasons why it should not be published." The local professional man had advised Madame Devere on some investments and would supply bail. The prosecutor told the press that the story was being investigated. It was a moot point. Prosecutors planned to rearrest Madame on other charges should she ever post bail. Freedom for the shifty clairvoyant was not an option.[35]

Lydia Devere was transferred from city to county custody after the hearing and endured the indignity of a ride to the county jail in the police paddy wagon, pulled by ordinary horses and guarded by two officers. Some observers felt the woman deserved better, but no one offered a different means of transport. In the county jail, she complained about her cellmate and the food, which was served on worn tin plates. When she wasn't complaining about those things, she objected to her treatment by the press. Lastly, Madame Devere complained of illness, but, abandoned by her personal physicians, including Dr. Claypoole, she refused the services of the jailhouse doctor.[36]

A day or two later, H. V. Ketcham foreclosed on Madame Devere's chattel mortgage. Her goods were to be auctioned. The mortgage holder allowed her, accompanied by the sheriff, to visit her former Broadway residence to collect her clothes. Although Madame had a taste for the finer things, an appraisal estimated that her remaining chattels wouldn't bring fifty cents on the dollar owed. Of extraordinary interest and potential value was a mysterious photo album, which, the clairvoyant maintained, contained the pictures of more than sixty "widower" clients. The *Daily Blade* chortled, "Each man of these sixty men wants it. He wants it badly. He needs it." The album, if it ever truly existed, quietly disappeared.[37]

Women found the jailed clairvoyant fascinating and a source of endless gossip. Many of Toledo's ladies seemed to have an insatiable curiosity about women of ill repute. The more curious, who would never have crossed the threshold of the clairvoyant's residence, found that arriving on visitation days at the jail bearing fruit and other delicacies guaranteed them a brief interview with the notorious lady. The county jailers were hospitable and sympathetic to Madame Devere, granting her privileges usually not extended to most inmates.[38]

CHAPTER SIX

A Most Novel and Unique Defense

On February 18, 1890, the Lucas County grand jury indicted Joseph Lamb and Lydia Devere for negotiating forged promissory notes. Each defendant was indicted on two counts based on First National Bank's complaint. One count was for the $10,000 Brown note and one for the two $5,000 notes. To avoid the carnival-like atmosphere of her police court appearances, Madame Devere, wearing a fine black cashmere dress, was quietly arraigned in the county sheriff's private office during the recess in the trial of a horse thief. Despite her fashionable attire, Madame looked haggard and had trouble hearing Judge Lemmon's questions. She pled not guilty. The judge set Madame's trial for two weeks hence. Joe Lamb was arraigned in open court and also pled not guilty. Bail was set at an equal $2,000 for each defendant on the grand jury charges. Lamb made bail, but Devere remained confined in the county jail.[1]

There was little doubt that Lydia Devere had well-placed friends in Cleveland who remained in the shadows. These mysterious benefactors retained a prominent Cleveland attorney, Harrison Ewing, to assist Madame Devere's defense. When Cleveland newsmen asked if defending Madame was an uphill battle, attorney Ewing said no. Would evidence of her previous Canadian forgeries hurt? "Not at all. She was acquitted in Canada," Ewing replied. On what grounds was Madame acquitted, a reporter asked. "On the grounds of insanity," Ewing replied, smiling.[2]

The trial of Madame Devere began on Wednesday, March 19. The crowd was predominately women, who came to judge her for themselves instead of through the lens of the male press. Before court proceedings began, the women exchanged whispered critiques of Madame's stylish attire—all black, highlighted by a large turban hat with bright ribbons.[3]

Devere's defense lawyers were led to believe that Joe Lamb would be tried first, but a last-minute change was made. Madame Devere would be first. The Cleveland attorney, Ewing, was unable to be in Toledo on March 19. Madame's defense council asked for a delay, but the judge was unmoved and pushed ahead. Jury selection began, and it was immediately apparent that most potential jurors—all men in 1890—held no opinions about the Devere case. The *Toledo Daily Blade* sarcastically noted that when the attorneys questioned prospective jurors, they failed to discover "anything but a wild and barren waste of opinion and an ignorance of the Devere case so dense and profound as to excite admiration and awe." In truth, almost every man in the jury pool wanted to be on the Devere jury. To hear the details of the case first-hand would be a pleasant break from the monotony of daily life. By the end of the day, a jury was impaneled. Twelve men, mostly tradesmen, mechanics, and small businessmen, would decide the defendant's fate.[4]

Defense council J. D. Ford closed the first day of trial by telling the jury that Madame's defense was that she had no connection to the promissory notes in question. Ford pointed out that only Joe Lamb had ever seen her with the notes, and even then, never outside of her home. How could she be guilty of passing them? Ford reminded the jury that Lamb might lie to save himself. Devere's defense would claim, Ford said, that nervous First National Bank officials got Lamb's superiors at the express company to coerce him into blaming Madame Devere to cover the bank's failure to verify the signatures on the notes.[5]

The second day of the trial, Thursday, found Madame Devere in good humor, her mood buoyed by the presence of young Emil, returned from Canada and seated beside her. The appearance of a child in court with the defendant was a common tactic to evoke sympathy. The first witness for the prosecution was William Eggleston, cashier of the Northern National Bank, who identified a $5,000 Brown note as one Joe Lamb had presented to him in the spring of 1889, alleging it belonged to Richard Brown of Cleveland, Brown and Company. Eggleston's testimony demonstrated that Lamb and Devere knew who Richard Brown was. Eggleston was followed by three witnesses, each of whom had loaned Devere money on furniture, jewelry, clothing, or household goods for a total of almost $2,400, creating the picture of a woman who lived on credit.[6]

Richard Brown entered the witness box and proved to be as unwavering as ever in his claim that the notes were forgeries. In fact, nearly all of his answers began with "Never!" Attorney Ford tried to twist and squeeze Brown into admitting anything even remotely resembling scandalous behavior. When the defense accused Brown of losing $2,500 at cards in a Cleveland club, the straightlaced Brown retorted that he had "Never played in a game of cards in his life." Madame's defense failed to discredit Brown, and the fact that a forgery was committed was established.[7]

After Brown testified, Mars Nearing was summoned, repeated his police court performance on the stand, and offered no new revelations. Court adjourned for the day, and a bevy of ladies not bold enough to approach Devere, but willing to accept Lamb as a proxy, crowded around the express agent to shake his hand and look in the eye of the man who knew Madame Devere so intimately. Madame was limited to the attentions of two black ladies who were regular spectators in County Court.[8]

On day three of the trial, Ewing, the Cleveland defense attorney, heretofore an unknown quantity in Toledo, was seated at the defense table. A rotund man whose "entire physique was constructed on the spherical plan," according to a clever *Toledo Daily Blade* reporter, was dressed in a black broadcloth coat of the finest wool, complete with a black velvet collar that marked him as a successful barrister. Mr. Ewing sat beside Madame Devere, chatting and making "bright little comments." The press found him to be a wit, bordering at times on sarcasm. When Ewing directed his sarcasm at the press, the reporters got their collective back up, having come to see themselves responsible for solving the case. However, none of those reporters seemed to question why, and at whose expense, the Cleveland man was in Toledo.[9]

The testimony of Lizzie Belanger, alias Madame LaFraie, caused quite a stir. The comely widow entered court tall and erect, wearing a huge black hat with nodding plumes pressed down upon a mass of curly auburn hair. County prosecutor James Southard questioned her about Madame's family two years ago. Obviously nervous, Lizzie giggled to the point of annoyance after every answer and put her gloved fingers to her lips in a vain effort to suppress it. Lizzie recalled that one of Devere's sisters and a black messenger boy resided occasionally in the Washington Street house and that after relocating to Broadway, the child Emil lived in Devere's home. According to Lizzie, Madame Devere never discussed her marital history or Emil's parentage. Lizzie indicated that she worked for Devere until April 1889. Lizzie said that she "couldn't say a word against her [Madame Devere] and tell the truth." She diplomatically put Madame's only fault as being "too free with her money," buying whatever took her fancy. The onetime suspect's lack of guile and sweet face led one reporter to write that the seamstress "looked little like a lady who would forge a name to anything."[10]

The first defense witnesses on Monday morning, March 24, were two girls who worked briefly for Devere as domestics. They were questioned about a mysterious lady from Cleveland—hopefully the illusive Florida G. Blythe—who visited Madame Devere often. Their credibility evaporated when they admitted they had been coached by Devere's attorneys. Defense attorney Lew Richardson breezily dismissed this violation of protocol, saying, "Oh well, we'll admit that." After introducing handwriting samples purportedly from the real Florida G. Blythe into evidence—they were dissimilar to anything on the forged notes—the defense rested. The defendant didn't take the stand, disappointing everyone in Toledo.[11]

In rebuttal, the prosecution shocked the courtroom by calling Joe Lamb to testify. Joe froze and blanched at the sound of his name. His attorney, Irving Belford, objected, but he was overruled. Southard explained, "We ask that he be sworn. We don't object to his not answering our questions." Judge Lemmon cautioned Lamb against self-incrimination. Joe was shown a voucher for $3,000 from a New York bank—proceeds of a loan on a $5,000 note obtained at First National—that was payable to Florida G. Blythe and endorsed by Lamb. Southard asked Lamb what he did with this draft. Joe leaned forward, his voice raised and his hands shaking, and replied, "I delivered the draft into the hands of Mrs. Blythe, the lady sitting right there," indicating Devere. The scowling clairvoyant's dark eyes snapped at Lamb. Imperial Bank of Canada stamps on the paper indicated it was cashed while Devere was in Canada in August 1889.[12]

Lamb completed his testimony Tuesday morning with no revelations, and closing arguments began that afternoon. The defense was quick to point out that there was no solid evidence that Madame Devere was the forger. As for passing the forged notes, Joe Lamb had incriminated himself perhaps more than Devere. The prosecution chose to dwell on the abundant circumstantial evidence. The honor of the last argument went to venerable white-haired J. M. Richie, an attorney and former judge hired by the First National Bank to assist the prosecution. This was not an uncommon practice in the nineteenth century, when prosecutors were poorly compensated and the job tended to attract the young and inexperienced or the old and incompetent. Southard was the former. Richie lectured the jury for three long hours. His sharpest words were leveled at Madame Devere for conveying the impression that young Emil, who clearly seemed to be the woman's son, was the product of her sister and Richard Brown. Using her son as a prop in the fraud had the most pronounced effect on the all-male jury and predominantly female spectators. "A mother's love is the most unselfish thing that earth can yield or heaven can bestow," Richie told the jury. "And yet this woman would bastardize her own son and send him forth into the world with brand and story of illegitimacy to protect her ownself."[13]

On Wednesday afternoon, March 26, Judge Lemmon began his lengthy fourteen-point charge to the jury by reminding them that there were two indictments to be considered: one for forgery and one for passing paper known to be forged. A guilty verdict rested upon Madame Devere knowing the notes were forgeries *and* then passing them through Joseph Lamb. The judge concluded his instructions by telling the jury that a guilty verdict required such "a preponderance [of evidence] as enables you to support the finding beyond a reasonable doubt." The jurymen began deliberations late Thursday morning while the defendant awaited her fate in her jail cell.[14]

By 5:00 P.M., there was a verdict. Madame Devere was brought from jail, and her brown eyes darted from lawyer to jurors to judge. The prosecutor, Southard, nonchalantly chewed gum. Madame's lead attorney, Richardson, was visibly nervous.

The clerk read the verdict written on a piece of foolscap: "Not guilty." Madame understood and smiled. Once clear of the courthouse, Richardson threw his hat into the air and gave a shout of triumph. Ford chided reporters, "I told you so. I suppose that's the proper thing to say." The *Toledo Daily Blade* credited the presence of only circumstantial evidence and the judge's charge that emphasized reasonable doubt for the acquittal. The newspaper had little trouble unearthing the jury's actions during the four hours they spent behind closed doors. They dispensed with the first indictment with one unanimous ballot. Four ballots were required on the second count for the stronger wills to prevail.[15]

Although acquitted, Madame Devere would nonetheless remain in jail until the next judicial term to face trial on those other indictments. Lamb's trial was also set for next term. The general opinion around the courthouse, the *Daily Blade* reported, was that Lamb might reveal enough to convict the clairvoyant next time but that he would be convicted, in part, because he was not a woman.[16]

The trial of Joe Lamb began just two weeks later on Monday, April 15, with Judge Pugsley presiding. A twelve-man jury was impaneled by 10:30 A.M. Although Joe was facing multiple indictments also, this trial was for one count of forgery and uttering, stemming from First National Bank's complaint. Mrs. Amy Lamb was in attendance, a veil masking her emotions. The crowd had thinned considerably, and seating was not at a premium to see Joe Lamb in the dock.[17]

Searching for a forger other than his client, Lamb's defense attorney, Irving Belford, attempted to get handwriting samples from "certain men" by sending decoy letters that tricked the recipients—unidentified Clevelanders believed close to Madame—into writing "Brown" in their replies. Two men responded, and one was a close match to the Brown forgeries. But this information was not presented in court. Belford believed "that the introduction of this evidence would not help the case," perhaps because similar handwriting was not sufficient to accuse someone of forgery.[18]

Much of the testimony presented in Lamb's trial was a rehash of that given at Madame Devere's. The prosecution attempted to demonstrate that Lamb was aware the notes were frauds as early as February 1889, when he sent one of Brown's notes to Yates in Cleveland for verification and it failed the test. Domestic help employed by Lydia Devere testified that Lamb was introduced to them as "Mr. Adams." One, Bessie Talbot, said that young Emil was introduced to her as Lamb's nephew. The dazzling Lizzie Belanger, more relaxed, testified that she met Lamb on three or four occasions to get money from him for Devere. Wanting to avoid any hint of impropriety, Lizzie had insisted that the meetings be public, so some shade trees on Superior Street were the chosen site. Prosecutor Southard quipped, "The transaction was a little shady then wasn't it?" It was a bit of levity in a proceeding that had become tedious for all present. In need of an unspecified medical operation, Madame Devere would take Lamb's money, Lizzie said, and supposedly shake it in the faces of her doctors, who were apparently reluctant to do surgery on credit. Lizzie admitted that she argued with her employer over the ethics of taking the man's money and refused any cut for herself. Madame Devere justified it by saying she would pay it all back.[19]

The trial's only sensation was the testimony of the real Florida G. Blythe, whose appearance answered the question "Who is Florida G. Bylthe?" in Toledo. Blue-eyed with silver hair framing a kind face, the trappings of wealth were clearly visible in the form of her expensive fur wrap and a jet-black cross that hung from her necklace. Weary from her trip to Toledo from Connecticut, she nevertheless gave every appearance of being annoyed at being in court and forcefully denied knowing Brown, Lamb, or Devere. Her time on the stand was brief but crucial.[20]

Late Thursday afternoon, April 18, Joe Lamb took the stand in his own defense. The *Daily Blade* condensed Lamb's tale by suggesting it was "a strange, unaccountable story, a story of a man who ran every risk in the world to provide a strange woman, evidently an adventuress, with a fortune believing in the most improbable stories, which never a bit of tangible evidence supported." The papers had begun calling Madame Devere an adventuress, the highest compliment Victorian-era writers could pay a woman accused of scandalous behavior and financial chicanery. Lamb's highly detailed explanation of his actions, aided by his journal to jog his memory, were presented as those of a man assisting a poor, sick woman in her hour of need whose story he believed completely. No one in the courtroom totally believed Lamb, but it was a defense strategy that put him in the best light.[21]

The cross-examination of Joe Lamb was a frustrating exercise for the prosecution. Lamb had spent the better part of the two previous days relating his dealings with Madame Devere in excruciating detail. Now he repeated his lengthy, accountant-like answers in response to each of Southard's questions. Finally, an exasperated Southard, fearful of alienating the jury if he let Lamb continue in this vein, let him go. Court was adjourned until 2:00 P.M. on Monday.[22]

When Lamb's trial resumed on Monday afternoon, April 22, the defense presented eight men as character witnesses, then rested. The prosecutor exhibited an air of confidence in his closing arguments. And why not? Joe Lamb had all but confessed to his role in the swindle. The prosecutor reminded the jury that the defendant had admitted filling in the blank promissory notes over Richard Brown's signature, even after Lamb knew Brown had disavowed similar notes. Despite Lamb's reputation for honesty, most observers of the trial believed he would be convicted. As to a motive, experienced courtroom observers saw Joe as either naive in his blind belief that he was aiding a poor woman or greedy for the fees he stood to gain from Emil's guardianship, the $10,000 Devere had willed him, and the 2 percent commission on the loans he negotiated for her. The obvious third possibility was only mentioned in hushed tones: that sex and blackmail were involved.[23]

In the face of seemingly overwhelming evidence against his client, Lamb's attorney, Irving Belford, had a stroke of genius. Belford later said that it came to him while he was reading an article about the theories of hypnosis advanced by the famous pioneering French neurologist, Jean-Martin Charcot. The article argued that hypnotized subjects could be ordered to go so far as to physically attack others on command of their operators and later not recall why. Belford, needing a miracle to save his client from serious prison time, decided to gamble by proposing to the jury that Joe Lamb had been cleverly hypnotized by the clairvoyant. Once she controlled his will, according to Belford, Lamb would do anything for her no matter how absurd or out of character. Legal observers suggested that this was the first time the so-called hypnotism defense was used in an Ohio court. The *Toledo Daily Blade* called Belford's inspiration "a most novel and unique feature of Lamb's defense, and one, too, entirely new to criminal cases." Another paper labeled Belford's clever and articulate defense "the best ever heard in this county's court."[24]

The jury returned in short order with a verdict of not guilty, which left thinking men shaking their heads. Perhaps the jurymen believed the hypnotism argument Belford advanced, since in 1890 it was an acceptable criminal defense for a man to claim to be under the spell of a woman. Or perhaps they believed their poor, gullible townsman had suffered enough and Belford's hypnosis defense offered a way to extract Lamb from his predicament. Either way, Joe Lamb was free. The prosecution had more indictments waiting for him, and they huffed about trying him again. In the end, they never did, perhaps because while Joe Lamb had been an unwitting accomplice, he was also, banks aside, Devere's primary victim. Charcot's theories failed to stand the test of time. Medical historian Edward Shorter, in *A History of Psychiatry*, suggested that Charcot was "quite lacking in common sense and grandiosely sure of his own judgment."[25]

CHAPTER SEVEN

GUILTY AS CHARGED

County prosecutor James Southard had so far failed to gain a conviction in two attempts. His next chance came on April 29, 1890, with Madame Devere's second trial. Madame's attorneys had not revealed the source of their fees for the first trial. However, this time around, there appeared to be no Cleveland benefactor and J. D. Ford and Lew Richardson, her previous attorneys, had declined to act as public defenders for the paltry fee of $10 a day in court, $50 maximum per case. Ford told the judge, "I do not feel justified in continuing in the case for the limited compensation the state provides." Richardson followed suit. The judge ignored their protests and both were reappointed to defend Madame primarily because of their familiarity with the case.[1]

Public interest in swindle, and thus the second of Devere's trials, was waning in Toledo thanks to months of press coverage. The newspapers didn't intend to give this proceeding as much ink. Severe weather limited spectators. The jury was impaneled with ease. Madame's defense attorneys had quietly arranged for their fees to be covered a second time by an anonymous benefactor, and the Cleveland lawyer, Ewing, was present. Madame had remained in good spirits since her acquittal a month ago and appeared confident. The prosecution had no new revelations to offer in this trial and presented a straightforward case of passing a forged promissory note that was not much different than one for a note with a $100 value.[2]

The witnesses in this trial were the same as the first, except that Richard Brown was upstaged by Florida Blythe, who brought along her young granddaughter in case anyone on the all-male jury doubted her grandmotherly purity. Growing weary of having to defend herself in court, Mrs. Blythe barely concealed her anger. She sharply denied any acquaintance with the defendant, and her contemptuous tone indicated disgust at the very insinuation.

She denied ever endorsing any of the forged notes. Madame Devere, notable for her penetrating gazes, preferred not to meet Mrs. Blythe's eyes. No one in the courtroom doubted the dignified grandmother's testimony.[3]

Lizzie Belanger had seated herself near the press table and enjoyed the admiring glances of the newsmen, who were impressed by her attire. Her testimony was less impressive and offered nothing new.[4]

The Oak Harbor men, Metzger and York, clearly identified Madame Devere as representing herself as Florida G. Blythe. Madame Devere had stated that an attorney from Cleveland named Edgar Sowers had negotiated the child care arrangement between her and Brown. Sowers had been subpoenaed to testify under oath, and he declared that he never met Madame Devere or Richard Brown and had no knowledge of any child care settlement. He admitted he knew who the real Florida Blythe was but never performed any legal work for her. Asked who S. M. York was, Sowers said he was a client and Devere's brother-in-law. This was the unfortunate lawyer's only connection to Madame Devere.[5]

Joe Lamb was the next prosecution witness, and he gave an abbreviated version of his relationship with Devere. Lamb offered no new information and emphasized his belief that Madame was Florida G. Blythe. When it was the defense's turn, Ford took the gloves off. Under hard questioning, Lamb conceded that he never saw Devere outside of her house with the notes. Furthermore, Lamb admitted he lied when he said the person who gave him the Brown notes was in Cleveland. He admitted that he accepted the mortgage for the Argyle property without reservation, that he procured the blank promissory note forms for the defendant, and that he filled them in, all in the belief that they were perfectly legal, if a bit irregular. Lamb said he might have been reluctant to fill out the promissory notes if the amounts were $50,000 or $100,000, but the smaller amounts concerned him less. He denied signing the notes himself as well as knowing when or where the notes were signed or even if the signatures were Brown's. Lamb admitted he lied to Nearing when he said he had met Brown at the Oliver House hotel in Toledo. When the court adjourned shortly after noon on that Friday, Lamb was glad to escape Ford's probing questions.[6]

On Monday morning, all the actors in Madame Devere's trial appeared refreshed save for Joe Lamb, who resumed his place in the witness box. Lamb remained on the stand all day as the defense developed its strategy of proving him a liar and blaming him for the forgeries. Ford had Lamb write "Richard Brown" on a scrap of paper, which, when compared to the genuine signature of the Youngstown iron maker, was sufficiently similar to create a stir in the court and excite the defendant, yet it was dissimilar enough to be of no real value to the defense. The defense took a new tactic. "Did you ever meet a woman from Cleveland at [Devere's] house?" Lamb denied he had. Ford pressed ahead. "Did you never go to the house to meet a woman of medium height, with light hair and light eyes, in fact, such a looking woman as this one?" Ford asked, pointing to Mrs. Blythe. "Never. I never met any woman there except the Madame's sister, Miss Bigley." Lamb was adamant that he had never seen any woman resembling the real Mrs. Blythe at Devere's home. The fraudulent power of attorney for Florida Blythe that Madame Devere gave Joe Lamb was introduced. Rare smiles appeared across the courtroom when the clause forbidding Lamb from putting the money in anything shady was read, the irony of a forger preferring only rock-solid investments proved amusing. Joe had been forced to admit to lying to bankers, police, and prosecutors.[7]

The *Daily Blade*, analyzing the trial thus far, suggested that Devere's defense lawyers needed to do more than show that Lamb lied to save their client. They needed to reveal a real perpetrator to succeed, or perhaps have the defendant testify.[8]

The defense called as witnesses three of the clairvoyant's former domestic servants. Mary Williams admitted to being coached by the defense and was dismissed. Tressie Fanning and a mulatto girl, Nellie Franklin, took the stand. The servants knew Lamb when he visited Madame's home as "Mr. Adams." Tressie Fanning, who was currently working as the defendant's jailhouse maid, said she worked for Madame Devere from May to September 1889 and during that time, Lamb met four or five times with a mystery woman from Cleveland. The woman was in her mid-twenties with light-brown hair and light eyes and usually wore a black-and-white dress, black jacket, and gray hat. When this mystery lady came to the Superior Street house from the Toledo railroad depot, the messenger boy was dispatched to summon "Mr. Adams." These meetings occurred even when Madame Devere was out of town. Nellie Franklin confirmed that she saw Lamb at Devere's with a woman dressed in black with light hair and in her late twenties "a good many times." Lamb and the mystery woman remained alone in a room for an hour or two with Joe always leaving first, Franklin testified. With no positive identification of this woman available, this line of questioning was left dangling. The mystery woman was obviously younger than the real Mrs. Blythe and, while never accused in print, almost everyone suspected she was a prostitute. The defense council wanted to show that despite Lamb's denials, he and a lady vaguely resembling the real Blythe were seen regularly at the clairvoyant's house.[9]

Devere's defense rested on Tuesday afternoon, April 30. Madame did not take the stand in her own defense, leaving no one to dispute Lamb's damaging testimony against her.[10]

Closing arguments began Wednesday morning. Richardson, in defense, suggested that had Madame been guilty, she would have fled Toledo, but she hadn't. Richardson called Lamb "an accomplished and artistic liar, because it must have taken an artistic liar to get $10,000 out of Mars Nearing!" It was a bit of humor at the flinty bank president's expense that brought chuckles from the spectators. The defendant did her part by weeping all day while comforted by her sister, Mrs. Emma Pine. Little Emil was present for whatever pity he might evoke among the jurymen.[11]

In closing, attorney Ford rhetorically asked the jury, "Don't you feel satisfied that you are only skimming over the surface of the matter? Don't you feel that there is a further mystery concerning this scandal in high life in Cleveland and Youngstown which hasn't been explained?" The defense offered the lame contention that forgery had not been proved, largely because the scrawling signatures on the notes might or might not be forgeries. This implied that Brown had lied, which no one seemed to consider a real possibility. Ford concluded by attempting to cast all blame on Joe Lamb.[12]

Prosecutor Southard got the last word. Devere had represented herself as Florida Blythe to attorneys in Oak Harbor, Southard pointed out. Suggesting that Lamb's testimony amounted to a confession, the prosecutor declared both Lamb and Devere guilty, despite Lamb's reputation for honesty and recent acquittal. What hold did the clairvoyant have over the express agent? Southard chose his next words carefully. "He [Lamb] was a too frequent visitor at that house to account for it on the ground of business," Southard argued. "Your experience may tell you what was the cause," he told the jurymen. This carefully worded reference to the mystery woman brought titters and chuckles from the female spectators. Southard suggested to the jury, "Gentlemen, if you are blessed with what is called good horse sense this is the place to use it. We are here to find out who forged that note . . . and who published it, and we want the truth." He finished his argument by reminding the jury that Madame Devere, through Joe Lamb's efforts, had received more than $18,000—close to a half million today—and purportedly spent it all.[13]

Handicapping the trial's outcome was no easy task. The *Daily Blade* observed that "to one who has watched the progress of the trial and the faces of the jurors, what their verdict will be is a thing on which he would not care to gamble." The paper reported that the courthouse consensus on a verdict was no verdict at all but a hung jury.[14]

The jury got the case on Thursday, May 2. In his charge to the jury, Judge Pugsley instructed them that they must first agree that the promissory note was forged by Devere. Merely possessing a forged note was not a crime. Secondly, intent to defraud must be proven. The defendant could be guilty of passing a forged note if she knew it was a forgery and procured another person to pass it. Legally, Judge Pugsley informed the jurymen, circumstantial evidence was acceptable in the absence of any other if it was beyond a reasonable doubt. With those guiding words, the jury was sent off to do their civic duty.[15]

The jury returned at 4:30 P.M. with a unanimous verdict. "Guilty as charged in the indictment" were the words the jury foreman had written on a scrap of paper. Madame and her sister burst into tears. The defendant was immediately removed by a deputy. In the court of public opinion, on the streets of Toledo, most agreed that Madame was guilty of passing the forged note, but who actually forged Richard Brown's signature would forever remain a mystery. The jurors had similar doubts. One juror interviewed by the *Daily Blade* explained the thinking in the jury room. "It was a question as to whether the woman was guilty on the first count that bothered us. The first vote was unanimous for conviction on the second count."[16]

Judge Pugsley sentenced the defendant to five years in prison on *each* count—a stiff penalty. The judge seemed to agree with his colleague, Judge Richie, who assisted the prosecution and grandly said of the case, "The proof shows a wide-spread, profligate, daring conspiracy to bleed the public." Madame Devere remained confined in the Lucas County jail as her lawyers appealed. Not until January 20, 1891, was a ruling by the Appeals Court rendered. It sustained the lower court in all areas, except the Appellate Court found that the sentencing on both counts was excessive since they were linked, not separate, charges. "It appears that the double sentence must be reversed," the Appeals Court said. "It appears that she [Devere] has been properly convicted of the crime of forgery."[17]

The Common Pleas Court in Toledo corrected the error by sentencing Lydia Devere to nine-and-one-half years in prison for both counts on January 21, 1891, a reduction of six months. She was transferred to the penitentiary in Columbus on January 23. Like all prisoners, upon arrival she was interviewed and examined. She exchanged her fine stylish clothes for coarse prison garb. On the prison entry record, Madame Devere acknowledged Emil was her son but lied about her age and birthplace, claiming twenty-eight and England, respectively. Prison officials put her to work cutting cloth and sewing shirts and dresses for fellow convicts. Further appeals to the Ohio Supreme Court failed to free her from incarceration.[18]

Behind bars, the once high-living and scheming Madame Devere proved to be a model prisoner. One matron recalled, "She was one of the best prisoners that ever fell under my observation. I do not think the woman was possessed by hypnotic powers, but her remarkable persuasive powers held spellbound all persons who came in contact with her." She reportedly demonstrated her clairvoyant powers for the warden, Charles James. She told him he would lose several thousand dollars in a Cincinnati business deal and that he would die of cancer. Both prophecies eventually came to pass. Mrs. James, the warden's widow, later recalled that Devere was "always kind and attentive to her fellow female prisoners." However, "they considered her a 'hoodoo,' attributing many distressing experiences to her." The former clairvoyant's unidentified Cleveland friends were generous and powerful, and they provided generous "tips" to her jailers to insure an easier life in prison. Madame Devere never had any visitors.[19]

Her attorneys applied for parole on January 27, 1892, after one year of incarceration, and because of her sterling prison record, she was recommended for parole on March 1, 1892. It was claimed that she was in declining health due to prison life—tuberculosis was mentioned—and might die. Letters supporting her parole were introduced from three Toledo attorneys, the Lucas County sheriff, former prosecutor and now congressman James Southard, the director of the county workhouse, and a former congressman. Her sister, Alice M. York of Cleveland, agreed to employ her as a dressmaker for $1 a day. Nevertheless, there must have been those who doubted her character. Lydia Devere was not paroled until December 9, 1893, and then only with the intervention of Gov. William McKinley, who was told she was ill.[20]

The *Daily Blade* sent a reporter to witness Devere's release. "The Madame was a strikingly handsome woman, but prison confinement has told upon her appearance," he wrote of the effect that three years behind bars had had on the woman. "Her eyes are sunken, her once black hair is quite gray, and the 'prison pallor' has obliterated almost all trace of her former brilliant complexion. Her once gentle features now offered an unflattering sternness. Her sense of hearing has also become impaired, and her once voluptuous and graceful form is now sadly emaciated." Devere was just thirty-six years of age; the newspaper described her as looking fifty.[21]

Lydia Devere walked out of prison and into the Panic of 1893, where a falling dollar and collapsing railroad companies left one in five American workers unemployed, and three-quarters of the country's wealth was in the hands of the top 10 percent. In mid-December 1893, even Andrew Carnegie—obviously one of the 10 percent—was forced to admit, "Never such stagnation in business here, as now." Thousands of Americans were homeless and hungry. Poor Joe Lamb was reduced to selling brooms. What was an ex-convict with a taste for the finer things in life to do? Many women in Devere's situation would have fallen into a life of petty crime, alcoholism, or prostitution. Lydia Devere, however, emerged from prison unrepentant and determined to pursue her grand dream "to shine as a queen among women and live in luxury."[22]

CHAPTER EIGHT

A Sort of a Business Arrangement

Madame Devere was a model parolee. Her monthly parole reports, beginning in January 1894, were mailed in by her sister, Mrs. Alice York, who was purportedly employing her for $1 a day as a seamstress. There were few, if any, visits with a parole officer. During this time, postal clerks in Cleveland recalled that she was a frequent visitor to the post office—as often as five times a day—who badgered them about her mail delivery. According to postal clerk Winfield Parr, she wore a "gorgeous" dress of a different color on each daily visit. "The gowns were magnificent and on some women would have been stunning," Parr recalled with some delicacy, "but I don't think that she was the woman." The new parolee was using three names: Mrs. Bigley, Madame Devere, and Mrs. Hoover. The postal clerks warned her that she couldn't receive mail under multiple names and finally, to make their point, sent her mail to the dead-letter office. Forced to choose a name, Betsy selected Mrs. Cassie L. Hoover. Changing one's name in the 1890s, when many people lacked even birth certificates, was as simple as that.[1]

Parr, the postal clerk, was still a teenager when he met Cassie as she lingered in the post office lobby for an hour at a time. She had a $350 watch attached with a brooch pin to her dress over her breast. She bragged that no man would ever get it away from her. According to Parr, "I got it once in fooling with her . . . she said I was the only man that ever got ahead of her." Eight months after her release in August 1894, Cassie took young Parr to her home and showed him the gowns she had stored there. Parr estimated there were fifty, most mounted on forms and filling several rooms. Parr—a teenager with no real point of reference—estimated their value at $20,000. Cassie told the lad that she was the American representative of a Parisian dressmaker. She also told Parr that she owned a row of houses on Cleveland's Tracy Street.

On August 31, 1894, Cassie requested the penitentiary send more blank employment forms to Mrs. Emma Pine, her younger sister.[2]

Cassie Hoover and Emil resided on Cleveland's Franklin Avenue near Emma Pine—the same easily misled Emma from Cassie's Toledo days. Reunited with her son, Cassie vowed that they would never be separated again. When Madame Devere was officially released from parole on January 28, 1897, she was almost forty years old and officially had a flawless parole record, although it appears that no one in authority was paying much attention. Three years out of prison, Cassie was wearing dresses in the latest styles and owned property. The old insatiable lust for a life of wealth was undiminished. In the eyes of the law, however, the former convict appeared to be successfully rehabilitated and intent on making Madame Devere disappear.[3]

A dollar-a-day seamstress could not afford what Cassie possessed. Her mysterious, wealthy, and influential Cleveland benefactors were obviously still in the picture. Emil's father was said to be an unscrupulous city politician, possibly a lawyer. The man or his cronies likely paid for Madame Devere's Toledo defense attorneys and some support for her and Emil after her release from prison. Emil's father was rumored to have died in the mid-1890s. There were few career options for an unmarried woman and an ex-con to boot in the 1890s, especially one with Mrs. Hoover's ambition and expensive tastes, so she returned to what she knew.

Her own family believed that during the mid-1890s Cassie Hoover was the madam of an exclusive brothel in Cleveland. There is no proof, and likely this was an exaggeration. In Toledo, Madame Devere was known for her wild parties and out-of-town hostesses. In Victorian America, establishments where such morally questionable activities took place were called "houses of assignation." In the 1890s the term referred to any place, short of a brothel or tavern, where morally questionable activities were sanctioned. Some were boardinghouses that rented rooms by the hour; others sold wine and hosted parties without benefit of licenses. One example in Akron, Ohio, offered phony evening prayer meetings followed by drinking and "shameful orgies." While they avoided the obvious trappings of a brothel, houses of assignation were nevertheless unwelcome in any respectable neighborhood. Semiprivate assignation houses were "greater pests in a city than the avowed houses of ill fame," lamented Canton, Ohio's, *Stark County Democrat* in 1888. "Assignation houses are established in the most respectable residence neighborhoods" and there was no simple remedy for their removal. According to the *Democrat*, the house's proprietor "generally has 'influence' somewhere that compels the policeman to give the house a wide berth." Public exposure of the house's visitors and bribing the proprietor to move were the only recourses for upright neighbors.[4]

Arranging rendezvous, leasing rooms, and hosting parties could be financially lucrative, but there was more. For a good listener and clever conversationalist like Cassie Hoover, the bankers, lawyers, businessmen, and politicians who had clandestine rendezvous in such establishments were eager to boast of their financial maneuverings and share their investment knowledge. The political connections and insider information gained could be invaluable to a shrewd woman who sought to understand, and profit from, the world of finance.[5]

Nevertheless, old habits die hard. Cleveland attorney John Smith, who would cross paths with Cassie frequently over the next decade, admitted that in late 1894/early 1895, he assisted her in arranging a couple of financial settlements with men that were obviously blackmail. Why wouldn't Cassie Hoover engage in blackmail? It was easy money, and the old Madame Devere had been good at it. The victims usually threatened legal action, but eventually they paid the hush money as had that unfortunate New Yorker back in Toledo almost a decade ago.[6]

Despite her desire to put Madame Devere in the past, Cassie had been too notorious to be easily forgotten, especially by those involved with her case in Toledo. Irving Belford, Joe Lamb's able defender, chanced upon her doing business in a toney Cleveland jewelry store. Belford had risen to clerk of the Federal Court in Cleveland and was a man of some power. He quietly alerted the manager of the store to Cassie's criminal past, prompting the proprietor to sternly question the woman. Cassie produced a sterling and easily verified bank letter of credit indicating her ability to pay. "Oh, that was mean of you," she told Belford. "I have had enough trouble already to live down my past life." Belford was unmoved.[7]

John Manley, the police detective who arrested Madame Devere, was now a private detective in Toledo. Manley saw Cassie on a Cleveland street, her fine carriage and horse catching his eye. Cassie saw Manley, stopped her horse, and called him over. "We shook hands," Manley later recalled, "and she thanked me for the way I had treated her during the trouble in Toledo." Cassie left Manley with the impression she was doing very well.[8]

Sometime in the last half of 1896, Cassie encountered, by chance or design, her sister Emma's family physician, the widowed Dr. Leroy Shippen Chadwick. The doctor was making a call at a house with a notorious reputation when he encountered Cassie Hoover. Mrs. Hoover presented herself as a wealthy, well-bred widow. Chadwick accepted this but pointed out that she was lodging in a boardinghouse of questionable repute. Cassie feigned surprise, then embarrassment, and finally indignation, followed by a fainting spell. Roused, she demanded the doctor immediately assist in her removal to a respectable establishment, which he gallantly did, the old lady-in-distress ploy proving effective. Although a physician, Dr. Leroy Chadwick was neither rich nor successful, but he was modestly handsome and, more importantly, owned a home on Euclid Avenue, Cleveland's most prestigious address.

Medicine in the 1880s and 1890s was becoming a more scientific and increasingly prosperous profession. Physicians had status in society, and the public believed they generally had money. As Dr. Springsteen and Dr. Claypoole discovered, they were no less immune to swindlers than any wealthy industrialist. New York's notorious con-woman, Ellen Peck, slowly and methodically swindled a much younger physician of $10,000 while posing as a wealthy Danish admiral's wife. Dr. Chadwick was exactly the sort of man to attract the attention of Cassie Hoover.[9]

Leroy Chadwick was four years older than Cassie with a full head of hair and a full mustache typical for the Victorian era. Unlike most of his contemporaries, he neither smoked nor drank. Dr. Chadwick graduated in 1877 from the Medical College of Wooster in Cleveland, which later became Western Reserve Medical College. Affiliated with Charity Hospital, the college stressed anatomy, physiology, and clinical medicine. As a physician, the doctor was average on his best day, and his only public recognition came when he occasionally testified in court as an expert witness in, of all things, psychological matters. His real passion was music, and he possessed some talent on the organ. Although Betsy was partially deaf for most of her life, the piano and organ were lifelong obsessions that made Chadwick that much more desirable. The doctor's first wife, who died in March 1894, was the slim, attractive Martha Heward Chadwick, the daughter of one of Leroy's father's domestic servants. Martha and Leroy had a daughter, Mary, born in 1885, whom Leroy adored and who greatly resembled her mother. Martha had been accepted, if not embraced, by the Euclid Avenue social scene, despite her plebian roots. Had the widowed Leroy made the effort, he could have easily found a new wife among Cleveland's upper-class widows and divorcées.[10]

Leroy's father, Elihu Chadwick, had been one of the beneficiaries of America's first oil boom. Elihu had been a successful farmer, surveyor, and land agent in Venango County, Pennsylvania, where crude oil—called rock oil at the time—seeped from the ground. Chemists eventually discovered how to refine the black goo that was rock oil into useful distillates, like kerosene. In the late 1850s, Edwin Drake successfully drilled for oil along Venango County's aptly named Oil Creek, and an industry was born.

Elihu Chadwick controlled a critical five-mile stretch of land along Oil Creek down which crude moving to Pittsburgh had to pass. The first undercapitalized oil prospectors leased the land they drilled on. One forward-thinking and aggressive Pittsburgh businessman, William Coleman, had the money to buy the land outright. Coleman and his partners purchased land in the epicenter of the oil boom. In 1861, Coleman formed the Columbia Oil Company and invited his young Pittsburgh neighbor, Andrew Carnegie, a Pennsylvania Railroad superintendent and budding capitalist, to buy in. The young Scotsman was impressed by the entrepreneurial spirit he saw in the oil field and purchased some shares. Chadwick sold his land holdings to the oil interests, as Carnegie eventually did his share of Columbia Oil, for a substantial profit.[11]

The elder Chadwick, his oil riches in his pocket, moved west from the Pennsylvania hills to Cleveland. Euclid Avenue was relatively undeveloped open land, and Chadwick bought real estate there. He built a country-style residence, reminiscent of his old Venango County farm, on a wooded lot at the corner of Euclid Avenue and Genesee. Eventually, Euclid Avenue would become home to industrialists like oil magnate John D. Rockefeller and political kingmakers like Ohio senator Marcus Hanna. By the 1880s, Euclid Avenue would be one of America's most prestigious addresses and was nicknamed "millionaire's row."[12]

Dr. Chadwick was one of Elihu and Isabel Chadwick's younger children, born in 1853. The doctor was even more unsuccessful as a businessman than he was a physician. His father had willed him considerable real estate in Cleveland, but under the son's ineptitude, it was crumbling. One former patient and family friend observed that by the mid-1890s, the widowed Dr. Chadwick was "struggling" and almost ruined by tangled finances. The doctor's new friend, Mrs. Hoover, had more of an eye for business than Leroy, and it took little convincing for him to turn the management of the declining properties over to her. One source claimed he transferred title of some properties to Mrs. Hoover so, as she disposed of them, the Chadwick name would not be attached to the public record, protecting the reputation one of Cleveland's old families.[13]

The doctor and Mary had recently moved back into the old mansion on Euclid to care for Chadwick's gravely ill sister and his mother, who had broken a hip. Little time lapsed before the widow Hoover became a fixture in the Euclid Avenue home. Cassie assumed control over the Chadwick household, including Leroy's financial affairs, and raised cash by liquidating the real estate inheritance and investing the proceeds.[14]

Mrs. Hoover's business methods were hardly ethical. Around the time Cassie met Dr. Chadwick, in early 1896, she was living across Franklin Avenue from her sister, Alice York. Mrs. York went to a local but unidentified attorney and told him that her sister, "Mrs. Dr. Hoover," was ill and wished to see an attorney. Seated at Cassie's bedside, the lawyer was told that she was the paramour of a very wealthy railroad man in Cleveland who was seriously ill. According to Cassie, the man wished to settle a "considerable amount" on her, but this matter had to be done secretly so as to not alert the man's nieces and nephews. The attorney inquired about the railroad man's assets. Cassie told him they amounted to stocks, bonds, and "a beautiful home on Lake Avenue."[15]

If some of the property was converted to cash and turned over to Cassie, the attorney assured her, it could not be traced. After a two-hour consultation, the attorney was convinced she was telling the truth. Every few days thereafter, Cassie stopped by the lawyer's office to discuss the case. Finally, the president of a Cleveland railroad trunk line and a millionaire bachelor died. Cassie claimed he had willed her the Lake Avenue home.[16]

Cassie took the attorney out to the house and convinced him she owned the place. Cassie did not want the attorney to contact the estate executor as this might make the affair public and she wanted discretion. Having bought into Cassie's story—a generous commission would often overcome a man's doubts—the attorney cosigned a $10,000 loan from the Superior Street Savings Bank, which had accepted the house as collateral.[17]

In a more rational moment, the attorney had second thoughts about the arrangement and checked the court records. He discovered that Cassie had purchased the house from the bank trustee for $5,000 down and a first mortgage on the balance. The attorney summoned Cassie in early 1897. She arrived accompanied by Dr. Chadwick. The attorney called her a liar and pointed out that mortgaging the home twice in that fashion was illegal. Cassie freely admitted it, saying she had done it just to get a loan. Dr. Chadwick objected to the accusation that Cassie was a liar, but she told Leroy "to be still and not to be a fool."[18]

It was Wednesday, and the attorney gave her until Saturday to produce the $10,000. Cassie met the deadline. The property eventually went into foreclosure, and the bank gained control of the house. The attorney had brokered other loans against the house for Cassie, and she secured others herself. The fate of those other creditors was never publicly revealed. It was apparent from this episode that Cassie had a network of sources, never publicly identified, who fed her the information she required to plan her schemes. The attorney, who no doubt wished to cast himself in a favorable light, would claim that this was her first transaction and was an example of the "cunning and effrontery" Cassie employed. At the end of the day, this anonymous attorney was only one of many men fooled and defrauded by Mrs. Hoover.[19]

Dr. Chadwick likely received a logical explanation for the affair from Cassie, who could be nothing if not convincing. So much so in fact that Leroy Chadwick and Cassie Hoover were married in Pittsburgh on February 5, 1897, just days after Cassie's release from parole. The Steel City was Mrs. Hoover's choice and far enough removed from Cleveland to keep the marriage from the public eye. The ceremony was low key, bordering on secret. Dr. Chadwick had gone alone to the Allegheny County clerk's office and succeeded in purchasing a marriage license without the presence of the bride-to-be. The clerk interpreted the doctor's signature—Leroy S. Chadwick—as "Leroy Schadwick," age forty-three. The bride's name was given as Cassie L. Hoover. At the doctor's request, the clerk wrote "Don't Publish" across the front of the license, insuring it would stay out of the papers. The ceremony was performed by Rev. Dr. A. H. Jolly, a solid local clergyman who was Dr. Chadwick's cousin. Dr. Jolly knew his cousin by the nickname "Ship," after his middle name Shippen. The Schadwick misunderstanding Jolly later chalked up to the clerk's "hasty writing," which was transcribed incorrectly. Jolly had "quite a talk" with Cassie the day of the wedding. She told him her mother was French and she lived in Cleveland before she met the doctor. If there were any other revelations, Jolly kept them to himself.[20]

This clerical error in Pittsburgh, Cassie eventually realized, had the potential to void the marriage. To correct the problem, six months later, on August 26, 1897, and at Cassie's insistence, the couple was married again in a Methodist church in Windsor, Ontario, near Detroit, once again miles from Cleveland. The Windsor marriage certificate gave their names as Leroy Chadwick and Elizabeth Hoover, aged forty-four and thirty-two—shaving almost a decade off the bride's age. Mrs. Hoover claimed to be a widow and born in New York. Her parents were listed as Osborne Riddleman and Katherine Turner. Later it was suggested that Cassie's American citizenship was in doubt, hence the Canadian ceremony. Whatever the case, on the surface, these two out-of-town weddings suggested someone had something to hide and would forever raise questions about what Dr. Chadwick really knew about his wife's past, her financial dealings, and when he knew it. In Cleveland, on Euclid Avenue, it seemed not to matter since the new Mrs. Chadwick was never really accepted into Cleveland society. Most of her wealthy neighbors knew her as the lady in the high-seated carriage with a yellow wicker body pulled by a bay horse— Cassie associated gray and black horses with hearses—regularly seen cruising the Avenue. Later, the carriage was replaced by a French Panhard motor car. Some Cleveland society matrons knew her as the overdressed and bejeweled Mrs. Chadwick, who occasionally appeared at social events.[21]

Whether the Chadwicks' marriage was based on romance or business was a matter of debate even among close friends of the Chadwick family. One family friend went so far as to call the marriage "a sort of business arrangement." By the late 1890s, Cassie was in her forties and had lost much of her youthful beauty. Her hair was gray, she was almost deaf, and she rarely smiled due to ill-fitting dentures. Some years later, when a newspaper mistakenly printed a photograph of a Gibson girl with an hourglass figure in place of Cassie's, Dr. Chadwick, seemingly in all seriousness, said, "That's not her picture. She is much better looking." Nevertheless, Leroy Chadwick appears to have been more interested in his wife for her engaging conversation, business acumen, and wealth than as a lover.[22]

Dr. Chadwick had maintained a business relationship with Wade Park Banking Company on Euclid Avenue near Cleveland's Wade Park for many years. When Mrs. Chadwick assumed control of the family's finances, she kept the doctor's bank and banker. Wade Park was a small bank with just two suburban branches. Nevertheless, it was considered one of the city's strongest consumer banks with over $1.7 million in assets. The president was Frank Rockefeller, the brother of Standard Oil's John D. Rockefeller and a respected Civil War veteran. The secretary-treasurer was Iri Reynolds, a conservative, stiff-collared, sad-eyed banker who was Dr. Chadwick's boyhood friend. Reynolds had been a banker for twelve years and was discreet, loyal to the bank, and honest. He met Cassie shortly after the couple was married in 1897. Cassie continued to do business with Wade Park, eventually owning thirty-odd shares of Wade Park stock.[23]

Mrs. Chadwick saw in Reynolds an exacting banker who unquestioningly trusted his old friend's new wife and could keep a secret. There was also a subservient streak in the man that rendered him malleable. What she told Reynolds shortly after their introduction astonished him, even if his expression remained impassive. During a private moment, Cassie told the banker that she was the illegitimate daughter of Andrew Carnegie and that the ironmaster was financially behind everything she did. According to the new Mrs.

Chadwick, she was born out of wedlock in Pittsburgh to the young Carnegie, who was then the chief assistant to the superintendent of the western division of the Pennsylvania Railroad, and an unknown mother. As a baby, Cassie had been entrusted to the care of the family of a railroad section hand in Canada. Although Carnegie supported her, she had not met her biological father until she was well into adulthood. Her biological mother had disappeared. She swore Reynolds to "eternal" secrecy, and he accepted Cassie's claim at face value. The story was fantastic, but if nothing else, the woman could be persuasive and convincing. In the Victorian era, it was not uncommon for men of wealth and status to have such quiet arrangements. It would be a few years before Reynolds and Mrs. Chadwick would engage in serious financial business and until then, Iri and Cassie's relationship would be strictly social and proper. It would take even longer for Reynolds to break his vow of confidentiality to Mrs. Chadwick and even then, it would be under great duress. There was not even a hint of a sexual relationship.[24]

The best merchants in Cleveland quickly became familiar with the new Mrs. Leroy Chadwick. One dry goods salesman was impressed when he saw her in two different formfitting $4,000 sealskin suits on successive days. She was an exacting customer but a very good one who bought lavishly on credit. She usually paid, but she was often tardy. Merchants recalled that her methods of settling her debts could be unorthodox. To one butcher's son she gave several suits of the latest style in lieu of cash to settle her bill. A lawyer, who performed some minor work for her, billed for $300. She returned the bill without payment, telling the attorney that she regarded him like her physician, as a friend and therefore above a sordid commercial transaction for money. However, as a friend, a present would be sent instead of payment. A short time later, the lawyer received delivery of a piano worth three times the amount due. The lucky barrister laughed when he postscripted his tale by noting that the piano dealer later sued Mrs. Chadwick for the cost of the instrument. Cassie had perfected the trick of paying off small debts with goods she acquired on credit.[25]

Mrs. Chadwick could be generous. She gave an expensive sealskin coat to her cook. She would randomly pluck an unknown urchin from the street and shower the bewildered child with lavish roses or orchids for no obvious reason. At a dinner party for some of Leroy's family, Cassie emptied a small leather pouch of uncut diamonds into her hand. She allowed the only little girl present, niece Lauretta Chadwick, to select one of the gemstones to keep. One Christmas, Mrs. Chadwick anonymously sent $800 in toys to orphanages, hospitals, and the like. The gifts were, she was emphatic, to be anonymous.

When her stepdaughter, Mary, had her society coming out, Cassie took her and twelve of her teenage friends to Europe to celebrate. Each young lady received a porcelain miniature by a Parisian artist framed in fourteen-carat gold as a remembrance. Closer to home, on Christmas Eve 1897, Mrs. Chadwick presented her husband with a $6,000—at least $120,000 today—complete makeover of the old Chadwick mansion between the appetizer and dessert while the couple was dining out. Leroy's now deceased mother's tastes were replaced by those of the new Mrs. Chadwick, cementing Cassie's position as mistress of the house. Cassie ended the evening by giving her husband a $1,200 fur-lined overcoat.[26]

The last half of the nineteenth century, the Gilded Age, was given over to unbridled capitalism. Tycoons like Andrew Carnegie, Jim Fisk, J. P. Morgan, and John D. Rockefeller, to name a few, led a period of unprecedented economic growth and opportunity in America. But it came at a price. The free markets they espoused were rigged, manipulated, exploited, and rife with fraud. And it was a man's game. Only one woman left her mark in the world of finance in the Gilded Age: the eccentric and miserly Hetty Green, who acquired a $100 million fortune by following a strict contrarian investment strategy. According to a contemporary journalist, a successful investor during the Gilded Age required "a clear, cool head, a large amount of brains and unfaltering nerve to thread one's way through the intricacies of the business of finance."[27]

Almost no man believed that women were up to the task. Throughout the nineteenth century, women were generally viewed as having no aptitude for business or finance. Women were believed to be "constitutionally lacking in the sense to handle money." One wag called women "agreeable blunderers." This attitude was changing by the 1890s as women became more publicly visible and assertive in their demands for suffrage and equal rights. Bankers who were once amused by their female customers' ignorance—"Why, my money is gone and my check book is not half used up!"—began to take them seriously. Hetty Green, the foremost businesswoman of the day, wrote in 1900, "A certain amount of business training would be an excellent thing for women." Beginning with New York's Chemical Bank—Mrs. Green's favorite haunt— bankers began to see women as potential profit centers. Larger banks began to install separate well-lit and cheerful teller cages for women, writing desks, parlor-like areas, and separate toilet facilities. Women began to move from being customers to managers. The *New York Sun* wrote, "with far less technical training than a man requires, a woman becomes the keenest and most accurate of managers." By 1895, women owned a quarter of national bank stock in the United States. According to the Wilmington *Evening Journal,* "In banking, especially, their [women's] influence is remarkable, and is constantly on the increase." More progressive bankers began to think like this New Yorker, who said, "About all the faults that can be found with women depositors apply equally to men. . . . Women are quite as prudent as men . . . I mean that they are quite as honest as men, if not more so."[28]

Mrs. Leroy Chadwick became known in Cleveland's financial and legal community for her exceptional financial acumen, considered extraordinary for a woman of her time. She did not rely on her husband or an agent to handle the family finances as did even the wealthiest of American women. Cassie, with a mediocre formal education at best, learned the jargon and the basic principles of the financial system. She borrowed heavily to finance her lifestyle, but why not? A good many wealthy American women borrowed against future income. She discovered that the ability to talk to bankers in their own tongue, combined with her well-practiced persuasiveness, were keys to successful borrowing. Cassie Chadwick saw opportunity in this new relationship between women and their bankers and was employing it to her advantage.[29]

The woman was no stranger to mortgages and mortgage schemes. By September 1900, she had mortgaged the Chadwick home at the corner of Euclid Avenue and South Genesee Avenue for $25,000 to the Savings Deposit Bank and Trust of Elyria. An additional mortgage for $13,000 from the same institution was made in April 1901. Cassie was paranoid about keeping her financial activities secret, and mortgaging her home outside of Cleveland was a means to this end since in 1900 there was no centralized bureau tracking an individual's credit history. A tax appraisal in 1904 listed the Chadwick home's value at $19,400—about a half million a century later. In addition, Dr. Chadwick owned an adjoining lot valued at $1,380. The couple's personal property was estimated at $3,100, a vast underestimate.[30]

Rumors of her Madame Devere past continued to follow Cassie. In the late 1890s, a Cleveland bank loaned her $8,000 on good collateral. In 1900, bank officials became suspicious of Mrs. Chadwick and nervous about the loan, although it was not delinquent. An investigation uncovered Madame Devere. The bank retained a lawyer, John Smith, the same attorney who claimed to have negotiated blackmail claims against Cassie Hoover, to force an immediate settlement of the loan. Smith summoned Cassie to his office and demanded immediate payment. She refused. Smith laid a prison picture of Madame Devere before her and recited her criminal history. Cassie Chadwick was astounded but deftly shifted her reaction to one of indignation. She repaid the loan in sixty days when it was due, while Smith took undeserved credit for his cleverness. Attorney Smith and the bank kept Cassie's past to themselves. Still, it was too good a story to remain buried, and the woman's role in the Toledo swindle was shared among bankers in their boardrooms and private clubs. A few Cleveland banks began to refuse her loans. Cassie, a liberal user of credit, was going to have to search farther afield for cash.[31]

In June 1900, less than seven years out of prison, Cassie Chadwick had come far. She was married to a physician; had an address on Euclid Avenue; had all the trappings of wealth; and employed a housekeeper, Irish cook and servant, and an English coachman. Her son attended the best schools. This was an extraordinary rise for a woman who had left prison six years ago, supposedly penniless, to work as a dollar-a-day seamstress. How had Cassie done it?[32]

While Mrs. Chadwick was living the good life on Euclid Avenue in 1900, Joe Lamb, forgotten and broken, died in January 1900 of heart failure in a Toledo housewife's kitchen as he demonstrated a broom. One of Lamb's former coworkers remembered him as "one of the best and most trusted men. His integrity was never questioned." The *Toledo Blade* reminded readers that Joe Lamb was "fully exonerated" of his "unfortunate difficulty." Cassie Chadwick probably never knew the fate of Joe Lamb.[33]

CHAPTER NINE

The Greatest Bull
Market in History

Cassie Chadwick was an avid consumer of newspapers. She would not have missed the financial news that broke on March 3, 1901: the formation of the world's first billion-dollar corporation, United States Steel. The new corporation marked the sale of Andrew Carnegie's steel interests to J. Pierpont Morgan, which, when combined with Morgan's steel investments, put two-thirds of American steel production in the hands of one entity. The two tycoons were long acquainted but hardly friends. Carnegie had come to dislike men like Morgan, who became wealthy speculating in stocks and bonds instead of making something tangible like steel. Furthermore, Carnegie was said to be appalled by Morgan's morals, especially his habit of keeping mistresses. "Carnegie was always faithful," explained Charles Schwab, Carnegie's business associate and friend, of the ironmaster's personal life. "Carnegie frowned on anything savoring of flesh and the devil. He was very narrow in some respects, and he had no forgiveness for human weaknesses—because he couldn't understand them."[1]

Morgan, however, saw Carnegie as a dangerous capitalist adventurer, an old-fashioned businessman who enjoyed hard-nosed competition, rather than the more orderly monopolization of American business that met with Morgan's approval. Nevertheless, Carnegie was ready to retire and Morgan had the money to buy. "If Andy wants to sell," Morgan is quoted as telling a subordinate, "I'll buy." Carnegie's price was $480 million. Morgan agreed.[2]

While the minority partners in Carnegie's steel companies received payment in common and preferred stock in the new US Steel as was the custom, Andrew Carnegie wanted what amounted to a first mortgage—5 percent gold corporate bonds issued by the new corporation. The bonds represented a debt secured by the company's hard assets, unlike stocks. US Steel was capitalized at $1.4 billion on paper. Carnegie and Morgan knew US Steel wasn't worth that lofty amount, but its assets were worth more than the $300 million Carnegie and his family would receive in gold bonds. Even in the unlikely event that US Steel failed, the gold bonds were redeemable at par ahead of all other creditors. United States Steel bonds were indeed "golden." Carnegie himself would receive $226 million—something around $6 billion in today's inflated dollars.[3]

Late in the winter of 1901, Mrs. Chadwick visited her husband's relatives in Franklin, Pennsylvania. She told them that an uncle of hers had died, leaving a vast fortune to Andrew Carnegie to hold in trust for the uncle's special-needs son. Should the son die, the money was to go to Cassie. She also told her in-laws that Pittsburgh industrialist and Carnegie contemporary, Charles Schwab—a "master hustler" in Thomas Edison's words—was her investment adviser. Cassie took a variation of this tale to the First National Bank in Franklin in pursuit of a loan of $30,000. Mrs. Chadwick told the bank that an uncle had died in New York City and left her $7 million in stocks and bonds, but the estate attorneys demanded $30,000 before they would assist her in securing the fortune. The bank offered $10,000, the most they could lend one person based on federal banking regulations. Cassie refused, telling the bank she would take nothing less than $30,000.[4]

Traveling south to Pittsburgh, Cassie and Leroy made the rounds of local banks and attorneys where Cassie presented herself as a woman of great wealth—aided by an ample display of diamond jewelry with an expensive gown as a backdrop—who was temporarily hard-pressed financially. She wanted a loan and offered lenders the couple's personal notes as collateral. There were old-timers in western Pennsylvania who still recalled Leroy's father and the fortune he made during the oil boom forty years ago. Reverend Jolly, Leroy's cousin who had officiated at the Chadwicks' wedding, served as an additional reference. Nonetheless, Pittsburghers willing to lend to the Clevelanders proved elusive.[5]

After also failing to secure a loan from the banks in Ashtabula, Ohio, Cassie looked west to Oberlin, Ohio, a small village in Lorain County twenty miles southwest of Cleveland. Founded in 1832 by Presbyterian clergy, Oberlin was home to Oberlin College, a very liberal and nationally prominent educational institution known for its support of abolition and women's rights. Village residents and the college community didn't always see eye to eye on the issues of the day, from women's suffrage to temperance, but the college was good for business. The village had three banks of which the larger two were the Oberlin Banking Company and Citizen's National Bank. When it came to borrowing,

Cassie never thought small. She wanted to borrow $25,000 and knew her best chance was with a local attorney as intermediary. Cassie selected prominent attorney A. E. Tillotson, and she asked him if he possessed sufficient influence with Oberlin Banking to secure a loan of $25,000 for her. "I am a poor man and have not enough influence to swing such a loan," Tillotson told her as he begged off, "and in addition, it seems to me that $10,000 is about as much as you could expect to raise in a town this size." Cassie stood and let her coat fall open to reveal a fine dress that served as a backdrop for a stunning diamond necklace holding a sizable gemstone. "Oh, well," Cassie sighed with an air of impatience, "I am not a pauper. I am not asking for a gift, but simply an accommodation for which I will amply pay." Cassie asked Tillotson what she owed him for the financial advice. "A dollar is all I could charge," he said. Mrs. Chadwick replied with a flourish, "Well, here is ten dollars."[6]

Cassie was nothing if not persistent and sought out another Oberlin attorney, W. B. Bedortha, a director at Citizen's National Bank. With Bedortha, Mrs. Chadwick adopted a pleading tone when she asked him to assist her in obtaining a $25,000 loan in return for a $5,000 fee. Bedortha declined because the fabulous offer of a $5,000 fee made him instantly suspicious. He later shared his concerns about this Cleveland doctor's wife with his fellow directors at Citizen's National.[7]

At the beginning of April 1901, the Chadwicks owed about $53,000. Mrs. Chadwick had liquidated much of her husband's deteriorating real estate and had invested, or spent, any loose cash. The six months following Republican president William McKinley's reelection in November 1900—the same man who as Ohio governor had paroled Madame Devere in 1893—experienced what the *New York Tribune* described at the time as "the greatest bull market boom in the history of the United States." The *New York Sun* saw it more darkly as "wild speculation." Winter and early spring of 1901 was one of those periods when small investors charged into the market. Wall Street clerks pooled their funds to buy stocks. Waiters quit their jobs to become full-time investors. Private secretaries and typewriter operators sold tips gleaned from the correspondence of businessmen and brokers. Brokerage house traders and clerks worked long hours and slept three to a room in downtown hotels to process the trading volume. April 30, 1901, was a record day for prices and volume, exceeding a then astounding three million shares.[8]

The bull market juggernaut was fueled with credit. Buying stocks on credit—on margin—was easy, too easy, with some brokerages requiring only 1 to 3 percent down to make a purchase. The brokerage would happily loan a good client the rest. At the ridiculous rate of 1 percent down, $10 would put $1,000 worth of stocks in your portfolio. It was easy to make money, substantial money, in a rising market with that kind of leverage, especially when banks offered just 4 percent annual interest on savings.

The problem with credit was that the loans had to be eventually repaid. If an investor took his profits and exited a rising market, all was good. However, if there was a falling—bear—market and a margin investor's stocks fell in value, the cash value of the account would be wiped out. As stocks fell, losses would mount until the stock, purchased with borrowed money, was sold and the investor was liable for these losses. During the trading day, seconds mattered, but in 1901, financial news might take hours or days to reach the account holder. Many investors, small and large, might be bankrupted in such a scenario. If enough clients at a brokerage were wiped out, the brokerage itself could collapse.

What made this bull unique was the presence of women in the market in large numbers for the first time. Women had always had a small presence in the stock market—fur-clad wives of businessmen, spinster schoolteachers, and bare-shouldered madams were occasionally seen entering brokerages. Many Victorian men believed "that women were constitutionally lacking in the sense to handle money," according to one journalist. Women, even if relatively well-off and educated, usually needed a husband, agent, or other species of male guardian to manage their money. Frequently, whatever money a wealthy woman had was tied up in trust and borrowed money would be repaid in what one New York banker called "driblet installments." When a woman found a lender willing let her have some money, he would want to pass judgment on the intended use. "The slightest suspicion that a woman had stock speculation in mind," one banker opined, "would probably lead to polite rejection of the loan, even on the best collateral."[9]

Another deterrent to women who wanted to participate in the bull market was that Wall Street did not have a good reputation in much of the country. Many Americans saw Wall Street as morally corrupt. One husband was quoted as saying, "only women who were ill-bred and vulgar even went down into Wall Street to speculate." An English banker working on Wall Street told a reporter that "Wall Street is not the place for a lady to find either fortune or character." Nevertheless, with women's rights a growing issue in America in 1901, a good many women chaffed under the restrictions placed on them by the male-dominated financial and investment community. They were determined to participate in this bull market by buying stocks on the sure tips they received from male friends or, often as not, just unsubstantiated rumors.[10]

A few brokerages saw catering to women as a profitable niche. A reporter for the *New York Sun* found one such brokerage on May 1, 1901. The newsman observed a trading room where fifty to seventy-five women "without enough space to prevent the bumping of elbows"—a clear breach of social etiquette—huddled in clusters around four or five stock tickers placing orders to buy as prices rose. A broker told the reporter, "There are women who started with a shoestring shortly after the first of January and they've made anywhere from $10,000 to $20,000." Three thousand dollars was a good average—about $75,000 today. "It's not difficult, generally speaking," the broker continued matter-of-factly, "for the small trader to make money on a bull market if he or she gets started right and the rising tide holds on long enough." That was a big "if." The broker suggested that "in a week or two, if this market holds there will be more Hetty Greens [purportedly the wealthiest woman in America] around this town than you can shake a dozen sticks at." Reportedly, a New York chorus girl, Marie Wilson, retired from the stage after making $250,000 in the market in April. On May 3, the *Stark County Democrat* told its readers, "Even women are struck with the gambling craze and as they have so far refused to sell stock in Wall Street deals where all have made money." It was true. The consensus on Wall Street was that women rarely sold stocks; most just kept buying. To make money on Wall Street, you not only had to buy low, but you had to *sell high*. Experienced hands and gray heads on the Street warned that the bull market could not last. Nevertheless, "a woman never believes the time to sell is coming," one broker ominously observed of the femininity crowding his trading room.[11]

Mrs. Chadwick readily admitted investing in the bull market. It was also rumored that she was a regular at Cleveland's premier, albeit illegal, bucket shop, something she never admitted. Bucket shops, an unscrupulous form of stock brokerage, flourished in the United States between 1870 and 1920. They were essentially stock brokerages that allowed individuals to "invest" based on the direction a stock's price might move in time frames as short as an hour. These unregulated establishments took securities orders from retail customers but never actually placed the order on a stock exchange, instead holding it in house. It was said the order went "in the bucket." This form of investment was further aggravated by the employment of margins levels as low as 1 percent. If a stock rose on Wall Street and exceeded the bucket shop's listed share value, the customer stood to gain. A decline in value, even as little as 1 percent for just one hour, resulted in a total loss of the customer's investment. Since bucket shops never actually purchased securities for individuals on the stock exchange, the customer's loss was limited to the money he had put up. This was unlike regular stock brokerages, which expected an investor to cover his losses even if the loss exceeded the customer's actual cash investment.[12]

The downside of bucket shops was that unscrupulous operators, who were the majority, often sold large blocks of stocks on Wall Street to drive the price down artificially, even briefly, wiping out their customers' accounts and fattening the bucket shop's profit. Bucket shop–style trading appealed to small investors and gamblers, because it basically was a form of gambling, and to speculators like the perennially cash-strapped Cassie Chadwick, who could realize potentially huge gains with minimal cash up front. Inevitable abuses by bucket shop operators led most states to outlaw them by 1920.[13]

An anonymous Cleveland attorney with some knowledge of Mrs. Chadwick's finances would claim that she had funneled $800,000 through Cleveland's largest bucket shop during the bull market. Was she a winner or loser? Was the story even true? Cassie never admitted it, and those who might have proof chose to remain silent.[14]

On Thursday, May 9, 1901, the New York World ran the headline "Fortunes Are Lost in Stock Panic." The bull market had collapsed. The New York Tribune called what transpired "one of the most disastrous panics ever recorded" on Wall Street. May 9 became "Blue Thursday" to differentiate it from the disastrous "Black Friday" market collapse thirty-two years earlier. One Wall Street broker told the New York Sun, "The wonderful trading down here is to be accounted for not by the enormous transactions of the big fellows, but by the operations of thousands of men and women who were led to believe that it was easy to make quick fortunes in stock gambling." Andrew Carnegie despised the practice. "Gambling is not business," Carnegie wrote, "it is a parasite feeding on values and creating none."[15]

That was true, but the market's collapse was precipitated by wealthy stock manipulators with names like Harriman and Morgan, who battled for control of Northern Pacific Railroad stock. Northern Pacific opened the day at $155 a share, shot up to $1,000, and then fell to $325. This volatility dragged first railroad stocks and then the entire market into a massive sell-off. Inexperienced traders on the exchange floor became hysterical in their efforts to unload falling stocks and had to be physically restrained by cooler heads. By noon it was over and order was restored, but almost every stock was down. One lady, upon learning the price drop of US Steel preferred stock, buried her face in her handkerchief and wept as if afflicted by great grief. While being helped down the steps of the exchange, the woman was heard to say,

"I'm utterly and completely ruined. I haven't a dollar to my name." A younger matron, who had turned a borrowed $300 into $7,000 only to lose it all, admitted she still owed her broker the original $300. The aggregate loss for small investors was pegged at $30 million, over $750 million today. Many margin buyers' accounts were wiped out, and brokers demanded customers cover their losses.[16]

Over at the bucket shops, speculators who jumped in during the morning's initial explosion of prices found themselves wiped out minutes later. The bucket shops closed for the afternoon after their operators had made huge profits on the backs of their clients, who lost every penny in their accounts. One Wall Streeter speculated that the bucket shop operators would be wearing diamonds again after "Blue Thursday."[17]

Cassie Chadwick borrowed $400,000 during the market's run-up to underwrite unsecured railroad stocks and bonds—an astounding $10 million investment in today's dollars. These railroad securities were the riskiest of investments and most often manipulated in the late nineteenth century, yet they offered the possibility of a huge return, especially if bought on margin. Cassie likely borrowed for this railroad investment and admitted to not securing a legal opinion on the investment's safety, which likely meant the investment was not all aboveboard. Her railroad venture went off the rails with the general market collapse. Additionally, Dr. Chadwick, like many Americans with some money, was buying stocks. Considering the doctor's poor head for money matters, it was no surprise he lost money. Cassie later complained that her husband's losses were also charged to her.[18]

Cassie Chadwick had plenty of feminine company in the loser's circle that day. The New York Sun ran an article a day after the crash headlined "Women Plungers Hard Hit" with "plungers" being the derisive term Wall Street professionals were using to describe the small investors who had helped drive stocks up. The Wall Street moneymen were blaming the market panic on these small investors. Wall Street brokers saw the small investors as easy scapegoats when they looked for some place to assign the blame for the crash. This disdain extended to the unprecedented number of women who were in the market. Worse, from a broker's point of view, many of the women were slow to make good their losses to the brokers, which caused some brokerages to collapse. One failed broker said, "It shows to my mind, that they [women investors] can't be counted on and if one decides to do any of this kind of business with women he has got to start out by insisting on good sized margins."[19]

The *New York Sun* located a rare woman manager at a Wall Street broker-age who was quoted as saying that "women are better on the long [up] side of the market, because they lack the courage to hold out on the short [down] side." Nevertheless, the lady defended her sex against charges they didn't pay their debts by saying, "Women are pretty good losers." The *New York Tribune* lamented that "so many small fortunes have been wiped out and so many persons of small incomes have been ruined" because "they were led to believe that it was easy to make quick fortunes in stock gambling." The stock market panic was best summed up by that woman manager when she decried the ob-vious gambling that occurred on the Street: "I want to say that there is more harm done in gambling in Wall Street than in any gambling house." Mrs. Chadwick would spend the next few weeks furiously searching for money to cover her losses.[20]

Many an attorney or banker would later comment on Cassie Chadwick's financial acumen. There is no doubt she possessed a higher level of knowledge than the majority of Victorian women. This was remarkable because she was self-taught, unlike Hetty Green, who frequented Wall Street in 1901 and who had learned much from her father and grandfather. Mrs. Green—called the "Queen of Wall Street" by some and the "Witch of Wall Street" by others—was a contrarian investor who, according to one biographer, was "buying when everyone else was selling and selling when everyone else was buying." Hetty herself said of the stock market, "I never speculate. Such stocks as belong to me were purchased simply as an investment, never on margin." Furthermore, Mrs. Green was a noted miser who, in the words of one journalist, "never per-mitted any expensive drains on either principal or income." Mrs. Chadwick did neither. She lacked the discipline to go against the ticker tape and never saved a penny of her profits. The latter was neatly summarized by her former partner in the Toledo clairvoyant business, Lizzie Berlanger, who said Cassie was "too free with her money." Although Cassie Chadwick possessed a rare depth of investment knowledge for a Victorian woman and was not lacking in audacity, she never employed those traits to her advantage on Wall Street.[21]

Cassie started her search for loans to cover her market losses in Cleveland. She approached an unnamed Cleveland lawyer—in later years most men who dealt with her preferred anonymity. She told the barrister that she owned a half million dollars in real estate in Pittsburgh, Boston, New York, and Phil-adelphia. She said that she and Dr. Chadwick were about to go abroad on an extended European tour. Mrs. Chadwick asked the lawyer to take complete charge of the properties during her absence, including collecting all rents. As was Cassie's modus operandi, the attorney had connections with a large financial institution. A second meeting between the two took place there, and Cassie broached the subject of a loan. The attorney was interested in brokering a loan but said he needed to investigate Mrs. Chadwick's real estate holdings. Unable to get an immediate loan, Cassie became indignant and threatened to go elsewhere. The attorney was firm, and Cassie gave the address of just one of the properties she offered for collateral. At a later third meeting, Mrs. Chadwick demanded to know if the loan would be made. "Well, Mrs. Chadwick," the lawyer replied, "I have discovered that the property you have described to me is worth just $60,000 and there are mortgages upon it now amounting to $58,000. Unless you can produce something more than that, we will have to call the whole business off right now." Cassie left without the loan.[22]

There were other lenders on the landscape with more liberal standards and greedy enough to take a risk on this persuasive woman. By the end of July 1901, Mrs. Chadwick had located enough willing lenders and covered her stock market losses with $175,000 in borrowed cash and $400,000 in her own promissory notes and the notes of men she endorsed and guaranteed. Guaranteeing these promissory notes was risky, but Cassie had few alternatives.[23]

In New York, Andrew Carnegie broke ground for his Fifth Avenue mansion in July 1901. At the same time, Mrs. Chadwick, her husband, their children, his in-laws, and a private maid—twelve people in total—prepared to depart on an extended first-class tour of Europe. The tour party sailed from New York on a Cunard liner in mid-July without Cassie, who remained behind in Cleveland tidying up her finances. On July 23, 1901, Cassie paid a travel agent $1,189.40 up front before leaving for London on July 27, a down payment on a tour that cost $15,000, or about $375,000 today. Upon her arrival in Britain, the Chadwick family was so happy to see her that Cassie "forgot" to inform her husband of her financial losses. The Chadwicks' grand European tour, a common excursion for wealthy Victorians, was guided by a British Army captain and included a private railcar. The American tourists passed through northern Europe, Germany, and Austria, and they concluded in Venice, Italy, on August 13. From Italy, Cassie and the younger members of the party went on to Paris, while Dr. Chadwick chose to explore the Roman ruins before the party was to reunite in London. This first-class excursion cost over $20,000 and included a drawing room on every train and other "special accommodations." What better way to impress the in-laws?[24]

In the fall of 1901, as the grand tour was concluding, Dr. Chadwick, on his way to London, fell ill in Brussels with Roman fever, a particularly virulent form of malaria found in Italy, and was hospitalized for four months. Four days after the doctor fell ill, one of his nieces sickened in Paris. A short time later, Mary Chadwick was hospitalized in London. For six weeks, Cassie traveled across Europe to hospitals in various countries nursing the sick. In November, the niece was sufficiently recovered to return to America, and Mary went to Brussels to tend her father on December 12. Cassie received a telegram on December 16, informing her that Emil was gravely ill with typhoid at the University School in Cleveland and not expected to live. On December 17 Cassie and Mary sailed for the States, leaving the doctor, who was still too weak to travel, in Europe. Arriving in Cleveland on December 23, Cassie was relieved to find Emil—at this point in his life a quiet, shy boy of eighteen— making a rapid recovery. Two days later, on Christmas, however, Cassie collapsed with appendicitis, a dangerous disease in preantibiotic 1901.[25]

Before sailing for home, Cassie had cabled Iri Reynolds at Wade Park Banking for expense money. Reynolds, forever trusting when it came to his old friend's wife, advanced her $15,000 from his personal funds. After Christmas, Cassie, bedridden with appendicitis, summoned Reynolds. She told him that her doctor said she would die. As for the $15,000 loan, Cassie pointed across the room to a dresser drawer. "There is a letter there which if I die, you must take to Mr. Carnegie. He will settle every one of my debts." It was a skillful performance, and Reynolds accepted what the woman said, possibly on her deathbed, without question. When it came to Cassie Chadwick, Reynolds, the experienced banker, proved to be the most gullible of men.[26]

CHAPTER TEN

SPLENDID BUSINESS

The Everett-Moore investment syndicate had been founded by two Cleveland-ers, Henry Everett, a director of Cleveland's Garfield Savings Bank, and Edward Moore. The syndicate's portfolio included trolley lines, telephone companies, and short-line railroads in northern Ohio and Michigan. The syndicate was funded by small investors and dozens of banks across northern Ohio and Michigan. By 1902, Everett-Moore was capitalized at $125 million and con-trolled twelve hundred miles of trolley lines with more under construction. In January 1902, one of the syndicate's subsidiary construction companies went bankrupt when it failed to meet a $2 million debt payment. Unlike many syn-dicates of the era, Everett-Moore investors put their money in the subsidiary companies, not the syndicate as a whole. It was revealed that thirty banks in Cleveland were Everett-Moore creditors and several teetered on the brink of collapse should the syndicate fail. It was also discovered, not surprisingly, that the banks held the choicest security and small investors the worst. A trustee assumed control to liquidate parts of the syndicate. In the end, Everett-Moore survived, as did all but one bank. However, hundreds of small investors lost money. Cassie Chadwick had guaranteed—endorsed, in the vernacular—the personal promissory notes amounting to $200,000 of an unidentified Cleve-land banker who bought into the syndicate. The man was bankrupted when the Everett-Moore subsidiary collapsed and he couldn't cover his notes. Cassie Chadwick was obligated to find the $200,000 to make those notes good.[1]

While Everett-Moore fought for its life, Mrs. Chadwick celebrated her re-covery from appendicitis by adding to her jewelry collection. In the spring of 1902, she met with her favorite gemstone agent in Toronto. The man had sold her fifty-six rings, plus other pieces of jewelry since 1899. While in Europe, Cas-sie had seen a huge diamond solitaire ring in Turin, Italy, that had belonged to

a member of the royal family, and she had to have it. She sent the Toronto agent
to Europe to attempt to purchase it. After traveling across the continent, the
agent secured the ring, which contained, according to gem experts, the largest
diamond imported into Canada to date. The agent's expenses and commission
reached $15,000—all paid by Mrs. Chadwick. The value of the piece was never
revealed, nor was it clear if Cassie paid the 10 percent US Customs duty on it
when she brought it home. Unsurprisingly, the Toronto gem agent later praised
Mrs. Chadwick for her beauty and "particularly engaging manners."[2]

That same spring, Cassie Chadwick asked her brother-in-law, James Chadwick, a Franklin, Pennsylvania, attorney, for a loan to help her out of a "tight
spot." James, believing in the importance of family ties, and fresh off Cassie's
all-expenses-paid European tour, unquestioningly loaned her the $9,000 he
had set aside for his young son. Cassie failed to repay her brother-in-law on
time. James became alarmed and applied quiet but ineffective pressure on
Cassie to repay him. In lieu of payment, she instead gave James a very ornate
mechanical organ weighing three-quarters of a ton.[3]

The family was unaware of this loan until after James's death in June 1903.
James, apparently no more successful an attorney than Leroy was a doctor,
left an estate of only $16,000, including Cassie's past-due note. James Chad-
wick's estate was administered by a local Franklin bank, which demanded
immediate repayment on behalf of the son, James Albert Chadwick, then
age nineteen. When Cleveland banks failed to give assistance in collection,
the Franklin bank informed Leroy Chadwick of the debt. Leroy wrote to his
brother's widow, vowing to set things right. Despite Leroy's assurances, the
Chadwicks stalled and offered numerous ingenious excuses for not paying.
The frustrated bank finally threatened to declare the Chadwicks involuntary
bankrupts if payment wasn't immediately forthcoming. This was an extreme
option open to creditors that would force a public accounting of the debtors'
assets, which could be sold to meet the debt. A snowball effect could ensue
with other creditors jumping on the bandwagon, lest they risk being left out
of an accounting. A check for $2,000 from Cassie and Leroy was promptly
received. The bank continued to press for the full amount. In September 1904,
another $2,000 check arrived. The remaining $5,000 never materialized. According to one Chadwick family descendant, the massive organ remained in
the Chadwick family for decades, too big to sell, and jokingly referred to as
James Albert Chadwick's "college education."[4]

Mrs. Chadwick's never-ending quest for money led her in the spring of
1902 to W. L. Fay, in Elyria, ten miles northeast of Oberlin, Ohio. Winslow L.

Fay, fifty-six, was an attorney, businessman, and financier who had attended Oberlin College. In the 1880s Fay had invented and manufactured the oddly named Fairy Tricycle for use by women and Civil War amputees. Fay was instrumental in the formation of the Elyria Savings and Loan Company, where he was secretary and a director. According to a Lorain County history from 1894, "Whatever business he [Fay] has undertaken, he has made a success."[5]

Mrs. Chadwick wanted a loan of $50,000, but this was more than Fay was willing to risk, so he approached Henry Wurst, an Elyria businessman of means. Wurst had a reputation for being shrewd, tough, and secretive. Wurst once said of a $10,000 check, "I don't know a thing about it and I don't remember a thing about it." Wurst was interested in lending to Mrs. Chadwick but would have none of her paper collateral. Cassie, with a pressing need for funds, reluctantly offered jewelry instead. She gave Wurst an eighteen-inch diamond-and-pearl necklace and a pearl ring said to have belonged to European royalty. Wurst's son, a New York advertising executive, later described the pieces for the *New York Times*. "I thought at first they were only toys," Charles Wurst said, "as I never had seen pearls so large. The necklace was eighteen inches long, of graduated pearls, the center one as large as a big marble. At either end of the necklace, were two steel blue diamonds, the extreme one on each end being fully three karats in weight. The three pearls in the ring were so large that they covered three fingers of the hand on which the ring was placed." According to Wurst, his father had the pieces examined in Cleveland by an expert, who "appraised the necklace at $80,000 and the ring at $5000." That was $85,000 for the two pieces to collateralize a $50,000 loan. Fay, acting as broker, received a commission. Henry Wurst continued to make loans to Mrs. Chadwick. By 1904, Wurst was complaining that he held two of Cassie's personal notes for $20,000 and $18,500 that he was unable to collect.[6]

Fay had his fingers in a number of enterprises, and he offered Cassie Chadwick stock in one of his manufacturing concerns. Desirous of keeping Fay's favor and his lender contacts, Cassie gave him her personal note for $4,000 for some stock. Before Mrs. Chadwick received the stock certificates, the factory burned. Although the investment was a total loss, Fay, nevertheless, pressed for payment of the note when it came due.[7]

Charles Beckwith, president of Citizen's National Bank in Oberlin since 1896, had learned that the Elyria businessmen, Wurst and Fay, had loaned to Mrs. Chadwick. When a description of this Cleveland doctor's wife, and especially her jewelry, reached Beckwith, who was once a jeweler's apprentice, his interest was piqued. Beckwith might have gone so far as to stop by Wurst's office to have a look for himself. He knew Wurst and Fay were shrewd moneymen, and Beckwith was always on the lookout for a good investment either for Citizen's National or himself personally. "I began to inquire," Beckwith explained, "for as a businessman, I wanted to accept every opportunity to turn an honest dollar. . . . Mrs. Chadwick was greatly interested the moment she learned that inquiries for business had been made by me." Beckwith was living up to the observation made by Samuel Clemens, the nineteenth century's premier humorist: "The only people that a bank will loan money to is the very people who don't need it."[8]

Citizen's National Bank was founded in 1856 as the third bank in Ohio to become a national bank. The national bank designation stood for soundness and integrity at a time when banks failed in every economic downdraft. The National Bank Act of 1863 was passed by Congress to add a measure of security to the American banking system, which was a hodgepodge of state regulations governing local banks, with varying degrees of security and success. National banks were required to have a capitalization of at least $25,000 and be audited regularly by federal examiners. State chartered banks often had less than $10,000 capitalization and audited each other. National banks did achieve a lower failure rate. From 1865 to 1896, 6.5 percent of all national banks failed, while over 17 percent of state chartered and private banks collapsed. Furthermore, depositors in failed national banks recovered three-quarters of their loss compared to less than half for state banks. Of the national banks that failed, almost 80 percent did so as a result of criminal acts or other chicanery on the part of their officers, directors, or employees. A crime against a federally chartered bank was a federal felony punishable by prison time.[9]

Citizen's National Bank was located in a merchants' block in the heart of Oberlin, where a wide, welcoming awning protected customers from the elements—a subtle sign of strength and security. Citizen's National was capitalized at a healthy $60,000 with a $20,000 surplus and had $440,000 in deposits. It had survived the Civil War and the financial panics of the 1870s and 1890s. Its eight directors were a who's who of Oberlin: the mayor, the postmaster, a college professor, an attorney, and local businessmen, one of whom owned $10,000 in bank stock. Stock dividends in the range of 4 percent were declared like clockwork. By the banking standards of the early twentieth century, Citizen's National was a very sound bank.[10]

If the bank was sound, president Charles T. Beckwith was rock solid. A wealthy man in his own right, Beckwith was born in Portage County, Ohio, in September 1839. Beckwith had received a public school education and had traveled extensively with his consumptive father whose diseased lungs required dry air. At eighteen, young Beckwith apprenticed in the jewelry business in New York State. Afterward he returned to Ohio and worked in the family hardware business. When the elder Beckwith passed away, Charles, an only child, inherited the business, which he promptly sold, beginning a life of leisure focused on trading securities and mortgages. Beckwith's wife of forty years was an intelligent and accomplished former Oberlin co-ed, Ellen Fletcher. The couple had one daughter and three sons.[11]

Befitting his status, Beckwith engaged in many charitable activities. He served as a member of the Oberlin school board for fifteen years, and his personal checks kept the local kindergarten afloat. He was a member of the Second Congregational Church for more than a quarter century and its treasurer. At age sixty-four, Beckwith was a thin man with an unhealthy pallor, thinning hair, and the soft hands of someone unfamiliar with manual labor.[12]

Beckwith's father had been a heavy investor in Citizen's National, and his son continued the relationship. The bank's directors elected Charles vice president in 1892, but in truth, he was the de facto president. The actual president, Albert Johnson, had numerous mining investments in the west that required his almost constant attention. Four years later in 1896, when Johnson died suddenly, Beckwith became president. He was a natural banker whose precision and caution won favor with his directors. It was universally agreed that the Citizen's National Bank of Oberlin prospered under Charles Beckwith's direction. One contemporary said of Beckwith, "He possessed to an eminent degree the power of converting a small sum of money into a large sum." Beckwith owned real estate in Oberlin, including the city block that contained the post office. His personal fortune was estimated at a respectable, but modest, $75,000, close to $2 million today.[13]

Despite his philanthropy, public service, and over fifty years as a resident of Oberlin, Charles Beckwith was not a popular figure in the village. The banker was respected as "a hardheaded businessman," but on a personal level, he was gruff and didn't make friends. In his business dealings, Beckwith was considered cold and grasping, working solely for his and the bank's interests. As a banker, Beckwith was very exacting, requiring gilt-edged collateral on all his loans. Personally successful, he prided himself on never having less than $200 in his pocket, when the average laborer made just $600 a year. Charles Beckwith, the stereotypical small-town Victorian banker, was not a man people felt comfortable approaching on the street.[14]

When it came to searching for a willing banker, Cassie Chadwick was like a bird dog, always sniffing the air for a lead. Having learned of some interest in her finances at Citizen's National, she hastened there in early 1902. The first bank officer she encountered was the cashier, Arthur B. Spear, number two in the bank's hierarchy. An Ohio native, Spear had left Oberlin College in 1891, where he studied bookkeeping, to join the bank. He was thirty-five, a shade over six feet, of medium build with sky-blue eyes and a strong chin. As cashier for the last six years, Spear was, in effect, the bank's chief executive officer. Although relatively young, Spear was pragmatic, clever, and cool under pressure. Although Mrs. Chadwick would change Spear's life forever, he never publicly revealed his first impression of her.[15]

This woman, bejeweled and attired in the latest finery, gave every impression of wealth and was seeking a loan. Spear introduced her to Charles Beckwith. The old banker recalled of meeting Mrs. Chadwick: "She was the most remarkable woman I had ever seen. She was a splendid conversationalist, and there was no subject that seemed foreign to her." When the conversation turned to business, Beckwith, with visions of Henry Wurst's glittering collateral in his mind's eye, asked what security for a loan Mrs. Chadwick could offer. She swore him to secrecy before telling Beckwith that her assets were in a trust and unavailable to her. As Cassie doled out the details, her already deliberate speech slowed for effect. The income from the trust was pledged, she said, to unspecified obligations. Beckwith came away from the interview convinced that Cassie's income was so tied up that she was "absolutely helpless" financially. All she could offer for collateral was her personal promissory note. Beckwith didn't refuse, but he wasn't a man to make snap judgments where money was concerned. He was impressed, but the banker in him wanted to know more. A second meeting was arranged.[16]

What Beckwith learned with a few telephone calls, he said, was that "Mrs. Chadwick had secured big loans from many other bankers. She had met those obligations." At the second meeting, Beckwith offered her a personal loan of $15,000 from his funds, not the bank's. Beckwith accepted Cassie's personal note as collateral. The loan was short term, and Beckwith likely received a hefty interest rate. Cassie repaid the loan promptly. More loans followed, and Beckwith recalled, "We secured considerable splendid business all transacted in a business-like way." Beckwith was pursuing a very conservative course.[17]

In the summer of 1902 and recovered from Roman fever, a reinvigorated Leroy Chadwick took his wife on a tour of western cities with a side trip to

Mexico. Mrs. Chadwick was drawn to a fellow traveler, a bank vice president from New Castle, Pennsylvania, Lewis Hoyt. Impressing Hoyt with her financial acumen, Cassie asked him how she could obtain some cash on two bank drafts—$58,000—she had brought along to purchase real estate. Hoyt, a direct, no-nonsense banker replied, "By being identified at any bank." Mrs. Chadwick asked Hoyt if he would vouch for her when the party reached San Francisco. Hoyt flatly refused to sign off on the drafts for this woman he barely knew. When the western tour concluded in the late summer of 1902, Leroy Chadwick hastened back to Europe, where he remained for the next eight months.[18]

As the "splendid business" with Mrs. Chadwick grew, Beckwith considered a bank loan. Cassie invited Beckwith and cashier Spear to her Euclid Avenue home. One visitor to the Chadwick house described the furnishings as "oriental luxury" yet lacking in a welcoming warmth that left a cold feel to the house. Upon arrival, Beckwith and Spear would have entered the old-fashioned hallway, where an imposing antique mahogany hall clock greeted them. The old clock was so finely carved that one visitor guessed that not even a pencil point could find an area untouched. An observant caller would be impressed by the number and uniqueness of the multiple timepieces that graced the formal rooms. The front parlor to the left of the hallway, where the two bankers would have been directed, was the most elegantly furnished of the rooms and tightly packed with costly European tables and chairs. One chair, an obvious conversation piece, was made entirely of solid cut glass. So crowded was the furniture that the parlor could barely accommodate visitors.[19]

The walls were covered by haphazardly hung artwork, some of which, to the untrained eye, were "undoubtedly" old masters. Beckwith, the former jeweler's apprentice, was given the chance to peruse Mrs. Chadwick's jewelry. He was shown three chests full of jewels so impressive he later called Cassie a gem expert. "She has a wonderful array of diamonds," Beckwith later said, "great big gems, the kind that make your eyes water. She had one necklace, a string of pearls, which was valued at $15,000. Her jewels alone must have been worth a half million dollars."[20]

Mrs. Chadwick's home tour stopped at the portrait of an elderly, white-bearded gentleman that hung in the upstairs hallway. She explained that the gentleman was her Uncle Fred—Frederick Mason—who kept her family supplied with money when she was younger. According to Mrs. Chadwick, Uncle Fred never appeared wealthy, and she did not know the source of his money or the reason for his largesse. It was a mystery. Alas, Uncle Fred was near death when he summoned Cassie to his bedside, swore her to secrecy, and told her that the family was related to Andrew Carnegie. The proof was in a safety deposit box in the vault of a New York bank, which Cassie declined to name.[21]

Mrs. Chadwick told the bankers that she was the beneficiary of a considerable trust. Control over the trust was in the hands of three New York trustees, Cassie explained to the bankers, chief among them was a William Baldwin. It was Baldwin who handled the proceeds of the trust and provided Cassie with what she alleged was a $750,000 yearly income. What the lady proposed, and the bankers readily embraced, was the suggestion that her trust be transferred to Citizen's National on July 1, 1903, when the current trust agreement expired. In return for overseeing this trust, Beckwith and Spear would each receive a yearly fee of $10,000, and the bank a $40,000 fee, after all outstanding loans were paid. This kind of business was unheard of for small-town bankers. Cassie was offering the Oberlin bankers a huge return for little risk. As the *Washington Post* would later point out, "To get something out of a shrewd banker, the banker must believe he is getting something big." The two men were left to ponder how they could accommodate Mrs. Chadwick's needs and make this golden harvest happen.[22]

The Chadwicks' fortunes further improved in July 1902, when Cassie found Pittsburgh attorney Thomas D. Chantler. The helpful Chantler introduced Dr. and Mrs. Chadwick to one of his clients, James W. Friend. The fifty-eight-year-old Friend was "the best and most shrewd financier in Pittsburgh," according to one local newspaper. Friend had grown his business empire in just two decades from a single steel company to include twenty-one financial and manufacturing firms. At the head of the list were the Pressed Steel Car Company and Pittsburgh's German National Bank of Allegheny. While not wealthy by Carnegie standards, Friend had both done business with the ironmaster and, for a time, was an "intimate" friend. The men even used the same New York law firm. However, Friend and Carnegie had experienced an unexplained falling-out, and the days of friendship and crony capitalism had morphed into intense jealousy on Friend's part. Friend and three other German National Bank officers—bank president Frank H. Hoffstott, director and brother T. W. Friend, and an unnamed fourth director—were principals in an investment syndicate, Friend, Hoffstott and Company. Hoffstott was also president of the Pressed Steel Car Company, which manufactured railroad rolling stock with a Pittsburgh workforce composed of immigrant labor. The company's factory was nicknamed "The Slaughterhouse" because, according to the county coroner, one worker died in the factory every workday.[23]

Cassie Chadwick learned of the Friend-Carnegie relationship and intimated to the Pittsburgh men that Andrew Carnegie was behind her financially. Just what she told them is unclear but was convincing. The opportunity
to loan to this woman who claimed a secret Carnegie connection was too
good for Friend to pass up. After making inquiries, the Pittsburgh men were
convinced that Mrs. Chadwick was "a woman of great wealth." The offer of
promissory notes from herself—one for $110,000—and her husband as collat-
eral was accepted. With Friend's assistance, loans from private lenders among
Pittsburgh's upper-class elite were arranged. Both the Pittsburghers and Mrs.
Chadwick were equally publicity shy, and later all anyone would admit was a
total of $225,000 in loans, $75,000 from Friend and $150,000 from his acquain-
tances. Later rumors estimated the loans to Mrs. Chadwick totaled between
$600,000 and $800,000—an astounding amount equivalent to $20 million
today. It was acknowledged in Cleveland banking circles that the woman had
deposited $100,000 in a Cleveland bank after one visit to Pittsburgh, a story
embellished by the suggestion that she brought the funds to Cleveland in a
market basket on the train. This event was even more memorable in Cleveland
banking circles because on the same day, so the story went, she deposited several New York bank checks drawn on the accounts of Pittsburghers, which in
aggregate was said to total into the "hundreds of thousands." These Pittsburgh
loans were initially secured only by Cassie's promissory notes, although the
shrewd Friend got solid collateral in the form of gems valued at $50,000 to
$75,000. As for the attorney, Chantler was sufficiently impressed to person-
ally loan his client $20,000, secured by a mortgage on the Chadwicks' already
mortgaged Cleveland real estate. Whether this was an actual loan or a disguised commission is unknown. Chantler later said his loan was repaid and
the mortgage document was indeed marked "cancelled." However, Chantler
never had the lien on the property officially canceled by the Cuyahoga County
Recorder's office. Was the loan really repaid or was Chantler unwilling to admit being swindled by a woman?[24]

Months later, on March 5, 1903, Mrs. Chadwick asked Iri Reynolds to stop
by her Euclid Avenue home. With Dr. Chadwick present, Cassie told Reynolds she wished to entrust him with some important papers on the advice of
an attorney in New York whose name she gave as Butler. Pittsburgh industrialists Carnegie and Friend were both clients of the prestigious New York law
firm Butler, Notman, Jollee and Mynderse.[25]

The next morning, the Chadwicks arrived at Wade Park and gave Reynolds an envelope that contained a $5 million promissory note. The actual note

was of the simple, unadorned stationery store–type preprinted "New York" and dated "May 20th, 1902." It read: "Fifteen months after date I promise to pay to the order of C. L. Chadwick five million dollars at No. 1824 Euclid Avenue, Cleveland, Ohio." The note was signed, "Andrew Carnegie." In addition, there was an $1,800 mortgage on Cassie's brother-in-law Daniel Pine's Cleveland home on Avondale Avenue.[26]

Lastly there was an envelope containing a trust agreement written in somewhat cramped longhand:

Know all men by these presents that I, Andrew Carnegie of New York City, do hereby acknowledge that I hold in trust for Mrs. Cassie L. Chadwick, wife of Dr. Leroy S. Chadwick, of 1824 Euclid Avenue, City of Cleveland, County of Cuyahoga, and State of Ohio, properly signed and delivered to me for said Cassie L. Chadwick by her uncle, Frederick R. Mason, in his lifetime, now deceased, which property is of the appraised value of $10,246,000, consisting of 2,500 shares of Great Western Railway stock of England and Wales, valued at $2,100,000; 1,800 Caledonian Railway stock of Scotland, valued at $1,146,000; and bonds of the United States Steel Corporation of New Jersey, bearing 5 percent interest of the par value of $7 million.

The income from the above described property I agree to pay over to said Cassie L. Chadwick semi-annually, between the first and fifteenth days of June and December of each year, during the life of the trust, without any deduction or charges for services or expenses of any kind, this trust to be in full force until August 28, 1902. In the case of the death of said Andrew Carnegie, said trust to terminate immediately, and said property, together with all income and proceeds thereof, to be transferred and turned over to the heirs-at-law or legitimate representatives of said Cassie L. Chadwick.

I further agree to faithfully carry out all of the above provisions and that all of the said stocks and bonds have been indorsed over in the name of Cassie L. Chadwick, so that no further or other act will be necessary on my part or on the part of my legal representatives to put said Cassie L. Chadwick or her heirs-in-law in full possession of same on the termination of this trust.

Witness my hand and seal this twenty seventh day of February 1901. Andrew Carnegie.[27]

The trust's securities, Mrs. Chadwick told Reynolds, were in New York currently administered by three trustees, chief among them was a mysterious Mr. Baldwin. The promissory note would be due in August 1903. She asked

Reynolds to sign a receipt for the documents, which he did without question. "To whom it may concern: I hereby certify that I have in my possession five million dollars ($5 million) in securities belonging to Cassie L. Chadwick, and that neither myself nor Wade Park Bank nor any other person has any claim upon same. Iri Reynolds." Reynolds, with some justification, apparently believed the Carnegie promissory note and $5 million in securities—approximately $125 million today—were interchangeable. The lack of claims clause was important. If either of the Chadwicks used them as collateral for a loan, Reynolds was to keep track of such transactions and duly record them. Should anyone inquire of the Chadwick securities, Reynolds could helpfully provide an accounting of any and all claims against the $5 million. Reynolds later admitted to hearing an unsubstantiated rumor that the securities were pledged as collateral for a $300,000 loan.[28]

Reynolds was so under Cassie's spell that he didn't question the Carnegie connection. "She gave me the impression that Andrew Carnegie was back of everything she undertook," Reynolds later explained. "She told me she was Carnegie's child and swore me to secrecy." Mrs. Chadwick took the original receipt, and Reynolds didn't keep a copy. For added security, Reynolds wrapped Cassie's envelopes with paper tape and had Mrs. Chadwick sign her name across it. She requested that Reynolds return the package to her on January 1, 1907, which was irrelevant since Cassie could have it back whenever she wanted it. However, this made sense if she never intended to collect from Andrew Carnegie but use his note as loan collateral.[29]

Even a stoic, poker-faced banker like Reynolds would have difficulty remaining expressionless as he read the trust agreement. It looked official and read, to a layperson, as if drafted by a skilled attorney. Reynolds was unfamiliar with Carnegie's signature, but he knew that United States Steel came into being just four days after the February 27, 1901, date on the trust document. The US Steel gold bonds were the most desirable corporate bonds in America. Their interest was payable in gold, biannually in June and December, which coincided with when Cassie was to receive her trust dividends. The bonds had a fifty-year life and were mostly in denominations of $100,000.[30]

The paper Reynolds had signed for Mrs. Chadwick raised questions. A receipt was one thing, but if what he had signed was considered in banking circles to be an "attest"—meaning Reynolds offered his personal guarantee as a banker that he had the actual securities—then the envelope's contents could be used as collateral for loans. Reynolds would forever deny that what he signed indicated that he had possession of the stocks and bonds. However, it was an assertion open to question. Many bankers would interpret it as an attest. Reynolds locked the envelope in his office safe and would strictly control any access. Not wanting the package to be opened by Wade Park officials should he unexpectedly pass away, Reynolds gave Dr. Chadwick a key to the safe and left a letter at the bank granting his old friend access.[31]

Was the uncle Frederick R. Mason mentioned in the trust agreement real or a product of Cassie's imagination? She gave him some credence by hanging a picture of a white-bearded gentleman she identified to visitors as Mason in the upstairs hall in her Euclid Avenue home. The source of Mason's money and his reason for giving it to Mrs. Chadwick's family was a topic Cassie was always reluctant to discuss. However, she was not reticent to relate that on his death-bed, Mason had told her, in confidence, that the family was related to Andrew Carnegie. According to Cassie, the definitive proof of this relationship was in a safe deposit box in a New York bank she declined to identify and was unavailable for public inspection. Upon Uncle Fred's demise, according to Cassie, she became a wealthy woman. If there was a real Frederick Mason, alive or dead, who served as Cassie's inspiration, he remains a mystery.[32]

It took the Oberlin banker, Charles Beckwith, a year of questioning and gentle pressure to get Mrs. Chadwick to admit, albeit with feigned reluctance, that Andrew Carnegie was behind her financially. Beckwith was shown in strict confidence an unsigned (skeleton) copy of the agreement for Cassie's trust sometime during the summer of 1903. It was, as Cassie had surmised, just what Beckwith wanted to see. After coming to believe that Mrs. Chadwick was connected to one of the two wealthiest men in America, more loans followed. Beckwith would later admit that thereafter, his financial dealings with the woman led into a "maze."[33]

Mrs. Chadwick appeared at Iri Reynolds's Wade Park office on May 23. Feigning mild embarrassment, she told the banker she had misplaced the handbag with the receipt for the securities and would like another receipt. This was Reynolds's chance to clarify what he possessed and held in his safe. However, having convinced himself that he was providing a simple receipt, Reynolds didn't hesitate to provide another identical one.[34]

Why had bankers with years of experience like Reynolds and Beckwith been deceived so easily by Cassie Chadwick? It was, in part, because she was a woman and, as conservative Victorian gentlemen, both men underestimated her. Reynolds and Beckwith were of a generation that held that upper-class women, which Mrs. Chadwick appeared to be, had no head for business, could not acquire money on their own, and were reliant on someone to stand behind them financially. And lastly, women of that class were honorable. Despite the increasing outcry for women's rights and suffrage in the early years of the twentieth century, most middle-aged men of the day remained skeptical that women could manage their own financial affairs. A clever observer of human nature like Cassie was able to exploit this conventional wisdom.

By the spring of 1903, Cassie Chadwick still had outstanding loans in Pittsburgh collateralized by her personal promissory notes and some jewelry. Rumors questioning the Chadwicks' authenticity had reached Pittsburgh, and they were behind on their loan payments. Mrs. Chadwick's efforts to get Friend and his associates to extend the loans were rebuffed. In June 1903, Cassie visited the New York law office of an unnamed attorney. The man's first impression of the "well-dressed, distinguished looking and business like" doctor's wife was favorable. She came right to the point, telling the barrister, "I am in great financial trouble."[35]

Mrs. Chadwick told the attorney that she had several million dollars in securities held in trust in a Cleveland bank in the custody of a Mr. Reynolds. Her annual income was, she said, $175,000. She further explained she had lost $200,000 in the Everett-Moore failure and had borrowed to cover the loss from Pittsburgh men, giving valuable jewelry and securities as collateral. The loan was due and the lenders were threatening to sell the jewelry. Telephone James Friend, Cassie told her new attorney, and persuade him to delay foreclosure briefly. To that end, she extracted a roll of cash from her handbag and gave the man $20. "Have a thorough talk with him," Cassie urged.[36]

To the attorney's amazement, he reached Friend by telephone immediately. "She knows how she can stop the sale," the voice on the line said. "Let her send in the rest of her jewelry." Cassie readily agreed and planned to use the extension to raise other funds to pay off the Pittsburghers. The attorney asked her why, if she had a $175,000 semiannual income, she didn't just pay the debt. Or go to her husband for assistance as most wealthy Victorian women would have done. Mrs. Chadwick replied that "that would never do." Her husband was an invalid and knowledge of the debt might kill him. The lawyer suggested she have the income from the trust set aside at Reynolds's bank to pay the debt. Oh no, she couldn't do that, she said, she didn't want Reynolds to know her situation. "I would not have him know of it for the world," she said.[37]

After a couple of more visits with the New Yorker, Mrs. Chadwick asked him to raise $200,000 for her collateralized by a claim against the Reynolds securities. Cassie said that Reynolds was a reputable man in Cleveland and she could prove to anybody that the loan would be "absolutely safe." She said she would pay a large bonus—a well-established part of Mrs. Chadwick's modus operandi—to any lender. The attorney told her that her request was impossible without better collateral. She tried to negotiate, but the interview ended when Cassie was told that even $30,000 was out of the question. She never sent her jewelry to Pittsburgh.[38]

In June, Mrs. Chadwick arranged an appointment with a Pittsburgh lawyer, Willis McCook, who was also the attorney for former Carnegie partner Henry Clay Frick. She asked McCook to use his contacts to obtain an immediate $200,000 loan in return for a fee of $50,000. She bolstered her claim to a Carnegie connection with a copy of the trust agreement and other documents. According to McCook, "When she came to me, she had several documents to back up her story. I saw at a glance that they were the work of a very able lawyer, one familiar with big affairs." However, suspicious of the ridiculously high fee, McCook asked what collateral she could provide. She told him she had $5 million in securities that were "first class in every respect." The paper was held, Cassie told McCook, by the well-known Moore Brothers investment firm in Chicago. She promised she would prove to any lender, in writing, that the securities existed. A cautious McCook demanded to see them, and Cassie conceded she could not produce them. "I laughed at her when she couldn't produce the papers," McCook later recalled. Cassie's days of borrowing money in Pittsburgh were at an end. Some of the Pittsburgh debts were repaid, but most were not. Friend himself held diamond jewelry now valued at $79,000. The rest of the Pittsburghers, it was believed, lost the unpaid balances. Just one lender, unafraid of the embarrassment of being outsmarted by a woman, sued in the spring of 1904 for $25,000 and settled for $15,000.[39]

CHAPTER ELEVEN

H. CLARK FORD AND THE
OBERLIN COLLEGE LOANS

Cassie Chadwick understood that having a well-known and respected attorney as the front man for her loans gave her an added layer of credibility and respect that as a woman she might not be granted. By chance or design, Mrs. Chadwick became acquainted with a fellow Euclid Avenue resident, H. Clark Ford, a forty-seven-year-old corporate lawyer, businessman, and financier. Ford, whose father was an early developer of Cleveland real estate, was wealthy in his own right and had married money as well. Ford's family and Elihu Chadwick were acquainted. Ford was a founder and president of Garfield Savings Bank and a director of the Cleveland Trust Company. In 1900, Ford formed the syndicate that built the Williamson Building, Cleveland's most luxurious office space and where Ford had his law office. Ford had social and business connections to moneyed Clevelanders and a sterling reputation. He was exactly the kind of attorney Cassie Chadwick sought out.[1]

In April 1903, Ford arranged an $85,000 loan for Mrs. Chadwick from a wealthy Elyria man, W. V. Coons, a onetime oilman now prospering in what he described as the "investment securities" business. Coons's investment vehicle was his former oil company, the Producer's Oil Company of Findlay, Ohio. Cassie paid Coons a $12,500 commission and something more than the legal 6 percent rate of interest for the loan. Although Coons was a former oilman and no stranger to risk, he wanted Ford to guarantee the collateral—a $150,000 charge against the unseen Chadwick securities at Wade Park Banking. Ford declined, but instead he suggested to Coons that he would cover half of any losses or take half of any profit Coons made on the loan. The two men had been in the habit of splitting the commissions, but Ford offered to decline his half on this occasion also. Ford later claimed he didn't make $5,000 on the deal. However, when Iri Reynolds, who knew Ford, told Cassie of her attorney's arrangement with Coons, Cassie canceled payment on an unsolicited $6,000 bonus she had sent Ford for arranging the loan.[2]

On May 29, 1903, Ford arranged a loan of $15,000 through his own bank, Cleveland's Garfield Savings Bank. The loan was due August 21. Apparently pleased with Ford's efforts thus far, the Chadwicks' negotiated a retainer agreement with Ford that would pay him an astounding $25,000 a year—well over half a million in 2020—to manage the Chadwicks' financial affairs. This was an amount that would get the attention of any man, even a wealthy and successful attorney like H. Clark Ford.[3]

Ford had a close relationship with Oberlin College's treasurer, a flinty fifty-seven-year-old Vermonter, James R. Severance. Ford, who had attended Oberlin College, and Severance had a history of financial dealings. Ford was an Oberlin trustee and member of the finance committee and had arranged private loans paying excellent interest from the college's endowment in the past. Ford proposed that the endowment fund loan to the Chadwicks. The securities held by Iri Reynolds would serve as collateral. One of the college's more cautious trustees went to Wade Park and asked to see the actual securities. Although Reynolds admitted he held "certain securities" of Mrs. Chadwick's, he declined to show them to the man. Reynolds did take the extraordinary step of cautioning the college trustees to "go slowly and look carefully" before lending money to the couple. Had Reynolds developed doubts about his old friend's wealthy wife?[4]

Nevertheless, on June 2, 1903, Oberlin College loaned $60,000 to the Chadwicks at 6 percent interest for one year, collateralized by the securities Reynolds claimed to hold. For this loan, the Chadwicks would pay Oberlin College and Garfield Savings Bank a $5,000 commission, equally divided and up front. The college would disguise their $2,500 share by depositing it in the $500,000 endowment fund campaign as a gift, not a commission, from the generous Chadwicks. Of the remaining $55,000, a portion was used to pay off Garfield's previous $15,000 loan to the Chadwicks. The remaining $40,000 was issued in four bank drafts to the couple—two for $5,000, one for $10,000, and one for $20,000—drawn on the Bank of America in New York but charged to the New York bank's Cleveland partner, the Garfield Savings Bank. A cooperative Reynolds would record that Dr. Chadwick, not Garfield Savings Bank nor Oberlin College, had a claim for $60,000 against the securities. The only other claim against the securities at the time was $10,000 charged to Dr. Chadwick. Ford had disguised the transaction to appear to be a loan from Garfield Bank. Why the subterfuge was undertaken remains a secret. It can only be surmised that the college didn't want it to be public knowledge that it was making private loans to wealthy Clevelanders, which some in the college community might find inappropriate. Ford personally received no commission.[5]

At the end of June, Ford's quarterly retainer payment was due, and Cassie sent him a note indicating she was leaving for her brother-in-law James Chadwick's funeral in Franklin. She offered Ford $1,000 cash immediately if he would push the payment date back to July 5 at which time she promised to pay in full. Ford agreed.[6]

Typical of her methods, Cassie Chadwick continued to search northeast Ohio for loans despite having H. Clark Ford on retainer. In the summer of 1903, Cassie arrived unannounced at the only bank in the tiny Portage County crossroads of Mantua, south of Cleveland. She went straight past the tellers' cages to the president, W. E. Crafts, who was also the county's representative in the Ohio legislature. She told Craft she wanted to borrow $15,000 and offered several promissory notes as security. Mrs. Chadwick was unknown to Craft, and he told her he would have to make inquiries regarding the collateral. Cassie tried to deflect this line of questioning by reducing the loan to $10,000, then $5,000, but Craft still refused a loan without doing his due diligence first. She left empty-handed but determined.

Mrs. Chadwick returned to Mantua some weeks later. This time Cassie told Craft she wanted to open an account and put a heavy valise filled with cash on the desk. A teller tallied $15,000, exactly what Craft had refused to loan. Over the next several months, Mrs. Chadwick slowly withdrew the money. When it was exhausted, Craft's bank received a telegram from a New York bank indicating that Mrs. Chadwick had deposited $15,000 there to the Mantua bank's credit. Shortly thereafter, Cassie appeared in Mantua, and requested withdrawal of the full $15,000. Suspicious, Craft wired New York, and discovered that the $15,000 was indeed there. Mrs. Chadwick left Mantua with the $15,000. A few months later, another telegram arrived in Mantua stating that Cassie had deposited $50,000 in New York to the Mantua bank's credit. It wasn't long before she arrived in town and asked to withdraw the $50,000. President Craft sent an immediate telegram to New York for confirmation, but Mrs. Chadwick became indignant at the affront to her integrity and left before a reply was received. When the response arrived by telegram, it revealed that Mrs. Chadwick didn't have even a dollar to her credit at the New York bank. President Craft's prudence had saved his bank from failure. This attempted swindle became yet another banker's secret, of which Victorian bankers seemed to pride themselves, tucked away, rarely discussed, and never passed along to the authorities.[7]

In July 1903, Mrs. Chadwick tried to persuade a prominent Akron attorney to secure funds for her to cover another loan in which securities had been given as collateral. She told the attorney she had an "immense" estate but could not touch it without court action, which would trigger "large sums" in back taxes. She wanted to borrow $30,000 and offered gems valued, in her estimation, at $50,000 to $75,000 as security, but to no avail. Four months later, Cassie went to an Akron jewelry store wishing to borrow $60,000 on the same pieces, which had been appraised at only $20,000. There was no loan.[8]

Ford contacted Mrs. Chadwick, who was in New York City, on July 23 concerning some of her checks that had been returned for lack of funds—"contested" in the banking terminology of the day. She brushed the matter off in a note to Ford the next day, calling it a "little matter," and thanked him for his "frankness" in bringing it to her attention. She closed her note with a vague reference to a "matter" submitted to her that she considered "very good" and had decided to act upon. Whatever the "matter" was, Cassie was unwilling to share it with Ford.[9]

On August 1, Ford wrote to treasurer Severance's brother, L. H. Severance, at the Waldorf-Astoria Hotel in New York. Severance was a professional investment adviser and member of the college finance committee. Ford informed Severance that Mrs. Chadwick would like to extend the first loan and borrow another $85,000 from Oberlin College, this time giving $12,500 to the endowment fund. The new loan for $145,000 would be due in August 1905 and pay 6 percent interest. Security would be $300,000 in US Steel gold bonds—nicknamed "Carnegie" bonds—which Iri Reynolds would hold for three weeks before delivering them to the college treasurer. The $12,500 gift would be paid by January 1, 1904. Ford noted that the earlier $2,500 gift had been received. According to Ford, the college treasurer favored the deal, but another trustee was opposed. Severance favored the arrangement because the collateral would be delivered to the college treasurer instead of being held by Reynolds. As he wrote Ford on August 3, "I don't like the third party business." Severance was also pleased the loan was less than half the value of the securities.[10]

The copy of Mrs. Chadwick's trust agreement shown to Iri Reynolds was to have expired in August 1902. Cassie, without elaboration, told Ford that the agreement had been extended until July 1, 1903. Also, according to Cassie, a Pittsburgh banking firm now held a power of attorney over the trust and was demanding $750,000 to relinquish the assets—one year's income by Mrs.

Chadwick's calculation. Through some negotiation process—she was vague about this—the Pittsburgh bank agreed to reduce their demand to $500,000.[11]

Ford was kept out of the loop where these negotiations with the Pittsburgh bank were concerned. A Chadwick letter to Ford on July 24 revealed Cassie's desire that the attorney find her $500,000 for what she vaguely described as a "very good matter." A week later, Ford informed her that without better collateral than her personal note, a loan of that size was impossible. On August 4, Cassie sent Ford a message complaining that she was "so distressed this AM that I am hardly able to be on my feet" because of Ford's failure to find the money. She closed the note by asking Ford for a personal loan of $5,000, likely hoping that she had made Ford feel guilty enough to loosen his personal purse strings.[12]

The Pittsburghers, according to Mrs. Chadwick, were willing to loan her the $500,000 if she could raise $100,000 as a down payment. She wrote Ford on August 6 that she had thought the matter over all night, and this would be her "last appeal." She would give Ford an order against Reynolds's securities for $150,000 if he could arrange a loan of $100,000 by 3:00 P.M. that same day. She didn't want Oberlin College, whose second loan deal was now pending, contacted. Cassie promised she would give Ford full payment of the $150,000 on August 20, 1903. Ford was instructed to do this quietly and, most importantly, without the use of her name. If he could do it, "and I am sure you can," she wrote, Ford could keep an astounding $50,000 as a commission. Mrs. Chadwick considered the proposed commission "very cheap."[13]

Despite the offer of a huge commission, Ford knew it couldn't be done and said so in a message later that afternoon. Mrs. Chadwick thanked Ford for his prompt and faithful service before complaining about how emotionally invested she was in the whole idea of moving her trust. "To think," she chided Ford that evening for being unwilling to personally give her the money, "you are worth so much and cannot obtain so small a sum which meant so much to me, was crushing." She went on to write that she admired faithfulness and loyalty above all else. As for the former trustee who had placed Cassie's trust with the Pittsburgh firm, she wrote that she could not herself be faithful or loyal to him.[14]

Cassie told Ford that she had authorized Iri Reynolds to make a charge against the securities for $500,000 "as the best and only I can do." She also explained that she hadn't asked Reynolds to speak to Dr. Chadwick—falling back on her husband as head of household when it suited her—nor would she after Ford received the letter. "You will be able to advise best what is to done," she told Ford. "We seem to have been defeated." The Oberlin bankers, Beckwith and Spear, who were anxiously awaiting control of the trust, were informed that the demands of the Pittsburghers would require some time to straighten out.[15]

Did Cassie Chadwick really have a trust in Pittsburgh or was the money needed to quiet her Pittsburgh creditors? None of the experienced money-men who were involved with the woman had ever seen anything other than the circumstantial evidence provided by the trust agreement signed "Andrew Carnegie." That not one man ever contacted Carnegie regarding the authenticity of the papers says something about Carnegie's stature, the bankers' and lawyers' greed, and Mrs. Chadwick's persuasiveness.

Coons's $85,000 loan against Reynolds's attest was due August 21, 1903. When the loan was made, Cassie made it clear that she wanted Coons to keep her finances confidential. As the due date approached, she told Ford on August 13, "Now I want you to caution that gentleman [Coons] *not* to speak of the amount of the estate [her trust] or the bank [in Pittsburgh] that holds it." Complaining of recent defeats in her efforts to raise more cash, she told Ford she had written Oberlin's treasurer Severance, explaining a loan proposal she had made to Ford. Not receiving a positive response, or perhaps no response at all, she admitted being resigned to failure. "So I guess it will all fail as usual."[16]

Mrs. Chadwick met with Ford during the morning of August 16. Ford was angry, perhaps because she approached Oberlin College behind his back. She tried to soothe it over in a note sent that afternoon. Claiming to "fully appreciate your feelings," Cassie told Ford, "I hope I have said not one word for you to grieve over." That said, she quickly turned to her need for money. Mrs. Chadwick proposed to Ford that she give him a note against Reynolds's securities for him to endorse—cosign—and she would use it to find her own lender. Furthermore, she was enclosing a personal note for $1,000 for which she wanted Ford to send her his check for the same amount. "What do you think of this proposition?" she asked.[17]

Ford had cosigned Mrs. Chadwick's loans before, but half a million dollars was too much for him. He sent her some money on her personal note, later admitting to loaning her no more than $2,000 from his own purse in total during their business relationship. Ford persuaded Coons to extend his loan for five days for a $12,500 commission, making the Chadwicks' indebtedness to Coons $97,500. Ford arranged a $25,000 loan on a valuable necklace. Furthermore, Ford asked Dr. Chadwick to cosign on all of his wife's loans. This prompted a terse response from the doctor on August 18. "I have signed the note," Dr. Chadwick wrote in a clear bold hand, "and other paper you requested and feel that you are asking a great deal under the circumstances, and I will not give my consent for anything further." Had Dr. Chadwick finally developed doubts about his wife?[18]

Cassie herself had developed a fondness for New York City's merchants and luxury hotels—the Breslin, New Amsterdam, and the prestigious Holland House—where she and a maid or two would take up residence for three or four days at least once a month in a suite of luxury rooms. The Holland House staff found Mrs. Chadwick a difficult guest, but the management was encouraged by her frequent hints that she might take up permanent residence in their establishment. The Holland House, like many New York hotels, had many older, wealthy women residents. When Cassie was in residence, she was inclined to sweep into the lobby or dining room wearing costly gowns, which were not always designed in the best taste. Cassie was usually bedecked in too much expensive jewelry. Her appearance invariably resulted in hushed, unflattering whispers among the wealthy older society matrons present.[19]

Despite her whining about his failures to raise funds, Cassie Chadwick indicated her satisfaction with H. Clark Ford on August 18 by extending his retainer agreement until May 18, 1907. If for any reason Ford and the Chadwicks parted company in the meantime, Ford would still be paid in full. This was an extraordinary windfall for any attorney, even a wealthy one. The reason for this extension, according to Mrs. Chadwick, was that Ford "personally made advancements of money to me, has secured for me large loans . . . and has obligated himself for me as endorser and otherwise."[20]

Mrs. Chadwick and Ford met again on August 24 in Cleveland. She was scheduled to leave for New York the next day. On August 25, she wrote to Ford asking him to cancel and return some expired promissory notes and orders of hers on the pretense that if Ford died suddenly, "it might complicate matters" if someone saw the papers. She apologized for the request, writing *"you must not take offense."* Mrs. Chadwick said she would send one of her "girls" to his office to pick them up.[21]

Outstanding promissory notes, or even canceled ones, could complicate a man's estate, prove embarrassing, and lead to public litigation. Former US House of Representatives Speaker Thomas B. Reed had passed away suddenly in December 1902. On that occasion, Andrew Carnegie, then well into his sixties, had expressed the belief that he might die similarly. If the iron-master did die suddenly, what would happen to the $5 million promissory note purportedly bearing Carnegie's signature that Iri Reynolds held for Mrs.

Chadwick? Would she have a legal claim? Would the estate of Andrew Carnegie quietly pay her off to avoid besmirching the man's carefully guarded
reputation? Was it possible that part of Cassie's scheme was to hope for the
man's death so she could present the note? It was a plausible scenario.[22]

After consulting with Ford on August 24, Mrs. Chadwick took the train to
Oberlin, where she asked Citizen's National's cashier, Arthur Spear, to certify
a check, payable to herself, for $12,500. National bank regulations required
that the check's maker have sufficient funds present and entered in the proper
bank ledger on the date of the check. These regulations were not strictly followed or enforced. Bookkeeping errors—not having the funds entered in the
correct bank ledger—were commonplace, especially when large banks and
brokerages handled the sale of securities. In fact, Mrs. Chadwick did not have
the funds at Citizen's National correctly credited to her, if she had any funds
at all. When Spear wrote "Good when properly endorsed" on the check and
signed his name, he was in technical violation of the Banking Act of 1882.
However, the crime was only a misdemeanor, and it was rarely prosecuted if
the check's maker was credited with the funds in a day or two.[23]

Dr. Chadwick spent much of the latter half of 1903 in Europe—Belgium,
France, Italy, and Britain—and away from Cleveland and his wife. Mrs. Chadwick supplied the funds for Leroy to enjoy life among American expats abroad.
In the summer of 1903, Mrs. Chadwick opened an account at Cleveland's Pru-
dential Trust Company in the name of Cassie L. Chadwick and C. L. Shippen,
each to be honored individually. Shippen was Leroy's middle name. Three separate deposits were made for $12,500, $50,000, and $30,000. By October 1903,
her balance was $92,500, over $2 million today. A rumor later circulated that
Cassie gave her husband $2.5 million to cover his expenses. Both Chadwicks
denied it. Where the $92,500 went is unknown.[24]

The Coons loan was once again coming due, and Ford decided to let his
two clients argue it out without his intervention. From Cleveland on September 16, Mrs. Chadwick wrote Ford that it was "embarrassing" for her to have
to "adjust this matter with Mr. Coons alone." Although Ford was obviously
no longer comfortable with Mrs. Chadwick, he eventually concluded that he
needed to mediate this dispute. Cassie wrote thanking Ford on September
18, noting that Coons had agreed to extend the loan for a few days—there
would be two extensions until mid-October in return for fees amounting to
$24,500. But, she said, extensions would not suffice; she wanted to roll the
loan over. Whining as usual about her delicate female psyche, Cassie told
Ford she was very disheartened and dismayed. With resignation, she told

Ford she would "place the matter with the Doctor" in a few days—a seemingly threatening statement that anyone who knew Leroy Chadwick would find amusing. She alluded to the only one course of action that remained open to her, but she failed to elaborate. She concluded the letter to Ford with a tagline of questionable veracity: "It matters not to me what comes so long as I know I pay everything I promise to pay."[25]

H. Clark Ford met with his client on September 28 to try yet another angle to bring some order to Mrs. Chadwick's indebtedness. The first Oberlin College loan to Cassie and its "donation" had been paid, and the college was open to new terms—so long as they included real collateral, not promissory notes or claims against the unseen securities. Cassie offered another "donation" to sweeten the deal. She knew that Ford no longer approved of the fee disguised as a donation, but she assured him that Mr. Severance, the college treasurer, had not solicited it. In fact, Severance had generously suggested delaying any fee until Mrs. Chadwick was financially sound. She told Ford, "You don't worry about anyone ever saying that the College done anything wrong." Ford, the attorney and Oberlin trustee, could appreciate that there was plenty to worry about. Still, a loan was made for $75,000 at 6 percent interest and for a $5,000 "donation" to the college endowment fund, payable when the loan matured. The securities meant to collateralize the loan—real stocks and bonds—failed to materialize in a timely fashion. Within days, the Oberlin College trustees began to agitate for their security and doubt their wisdom in making the loan. Elyria attorney W. L. Fay learned of the loan and commented, "You cannot make me believe that the Trustees of Oberlin College loaned Mrs. Chadwick without ample security. There are too many wise men on the board to do that." In fact, the trustees had done exactly that.[26]

The next day Ford received a message from Mrs. Chadwick apologizing for not offering Ford a fee for assisting with the Oberlin loan. "Anything you do for me will not be forgotten," she wrote. "I regard a sacred confidence more than money." It appears that there were discussions between Ford, Coons, and Cassie for a loan in the $350,000 range. As collateral, she was offering $500,000 in full value, not discounted, securities to be held by Ford. These loans were to be arranged without mentioning Mrs. Chadwick's name. In her letter, she suggested that if Ford and Coons could arrange this without *any* security, the men would receive a fee of $25,000 each. "This ought to be a fair figure," she said. Furthermore, she wanted $100,000 in a matter of days, after which she could raise the balance "at leisure" by October 15.[27]

Two days later on October 1, Mrs. Chadwick informed Ford that she required more money. She wanted the original $100,000, plus the amount of Coons's loan, $85,000, all in cash. She still wanted the $100,000 "at once," and each man would receive $25,000 if this could be done in less than a week. Lastly, she wanted $10,000 from Ford tomorrow "if all right." She reminded Ford that he was not to mention their fees to anyone. Ford would be delivered the collateral in cloak-and-dagger fashion at a place to be determined later. The security/collateral was to remain in Ford's hands and not be physically given to anyone. In her scrawling and careless hand, Mrs. Chadwick reminded her attorney that she was placing more confidence in him than he was aware of. Should this loan fail to materialize, Cassie hoped to make Ford feel he had let her down and had to draw on his own personal fortune to make amends.[28]

A scribbled note in pencil on scrap paper arrived at Ford's office on October 2, 1903, from Mrs. Chadwick with the details of what amounted to a loan consolidation plan. She wanted to borrow $350,000 until March 1, 1904. She intended to use the money, she told Ford, to take up what now amounted to $230,000 in orders against the securities Reynolds held. In addition, she wanted to acquire sufficient commitments of funds to cover the debts to W. V. Coons and Oberlin College, totaling $165,000. She admitted an outstanding $100,000 debt to Oberlin's Citizen's National Bank, but this was not included. When the first two debts were subtracted from the $350,000, the balance was $185,000. This she wanted in cash. She wanted $115,000 in cash by October 5 and the remaining $70,000 by October 15. The loans would be covered by collateral—Cassie's favored term was always "security"—including the commissions. She promised that this would be all she would ask of Ford until March. At the beginning of the twentieth century, very few people in America could borrow $350,000, in excess of $8 million today, on unseen collateral, and Mrs. Chadwick wasn't one of them. Thinking she could was simply delusional.[29]

Still, Ford and Coons had arranged over $250,000 in loans for Mrs. Chadwick in a matter of months. Perhaps it was not so much the dollar amount as the impossible timeline she set. It is conceivable that she was attempting to persuade the two men to dip into their own personal fortunes. If this was her true motive, Cassie failed because neither man was so under her spell that he personally loaned her more than he made in commissions and fees. H. Clark Ford was one of those rare men who profited from his association with Mrs. Chadwick.

While Cassie played her game with Ford and Coons, she still needed money. She went again to Spear, Citizen's National's cashier, to certify another check on October 2. One of Fay's clients had loaned Mrs. Chadwick $2,400, and a payment was due. On October 2, Spear certified a check for $2,400, and as previously, Mrs. Chadwick had no credit on the bank ledgers.[30]

The woman's indebtedness to Citizen's National Bank on October 2, 1903, by her accounting, was $100,000. National banks were permitted to loan no more than 10 percent of their capitalization to one person. This was $6,000 in the case of the Oberlin bank, yet Mrs. Chadwick's loans far exceeded that amount. Why had Beckwith and Spear loaned Cassie so much? Beckwith accepted Iri Reynolds's receipt as an attest and proof of Mrs. Chadwick's wealth, trusting another banker's word implicitly at a time when changing business practices made this unwise. Beckwith and Spear received generous commissions for arranging the loans. Beckwith, blinded by greed and swayed by Cassie's persuasiveness, trusted his own instincts about Cassie despite the concerns expressed by attorney and bank trustee W. B. Bedortha about the woman in 1901. Contrary to usual practice, the bank's directors were not informed of the large loans to Cassie. Citizen's National was audited by a federal examiner twice a year, and a routine audit in October 1903 revealed no loans to Mrs. Chadwick. "We did not carry an open account with her," Beckwith would later admit, "but kept it off the books and carried it secretly."[31]

The Elyria moneymen, Wurst and Fay, were still Chadwick creditors in October 1903. Henry Wurst, a clever fellow, had developed a scheme to borrow from Citizen's National at the usual interest rate, turn around and loan the money to Mrs. Chadwick at a higher interest rate, and pocket the rate differential and a handsome commission, in turn denying Beckwith and Spear a commission. In early October, one of these loan payments was due, and the woman didn't have the funds. Cassie wrote to her Oberlin bankers with an intricate plan to cover the loan from Wurst. Spear would certify her check for $15,600, payable November 1. She would tell Fay the money came to her in connection with a loan from Oberlin College that had gone through Citizen's. This was technically correct because Oberlin College's loan had gone through Citizen's—college treasurer James R. Severance was a stockholder in the bank. Mrs. Chadwick also assured the bankers that "if they [Oberlin College] help me in the future, it will be through you." She thought it best not to let Wurst and Fay know that the money to pay off the loan had come from the bank that made the loan to Wurst in the first place. This subterfuge would allow Mrs. Chadwick, she told the Oberlin bankers, to "get the funds on the goods in the East to meet the check, and you would not be anything out." Cassie's obsession with secrecy meant her correspondence could be maddeningly vague. But in this case, the "goods" were likely gemstones she was going to use as collateral for a loan from Ludwig Niessen, a New York jeweler. She apparently preferred not to give Wurst the jewelry. Niessen subsequently loaned her $29,000 for which he was given $30,000 in jewelry as security.[32]

Cassie wrote to Spear, "Please don't be afraid to do this because I will be most careful over this." Which meant that she would not fail to cover the check on November 1. For this check-certifying accommodation when she lacked deposits to cover the check, Cassie promised, "I will pay you and Mr. B well for this favor." On October 2, Spear certified Cassie's check to Wurst, which would not be payable until November 1, 1903. In the convoluted banking rules of the day, this transaction was later considered a loan and the check a promissory note because of the four-week time frame. Whether Mrs. Chadwick covered the check or treated it as a loan from the bank is not known.[33]

A day or so later, Mrs. Chadwick, in a second letter to Spear, said she had given the check to Fay, who indicated that Wurst would extend his loan to her until November 1, if she would provide her personal note as security. She told the Oberlin bankers to expect Fay first thing in the morning with the check. She did not want Fay told anything except that Citizen's would extend the loan to Wurst on the strength of the check not being payable before November 1. Mrs. Chadwick informed the bankers that Fay had said they would be surprised to see him with the check. After all, the game Wurst and Fay were playing was supposed to be kept secret from Beckwith and Spear. She instructed the cashier, "So you better be surprised, if you don't say it, you can look it." She enclosed with the letter her personal note to secure the certified check and "a small commission for your kindness." Cassie wrote in closing, "If you can do this, I save. What I save, I give you." Cassie Chadwick was clearly capable of scheming and plotting on a level on par with some of the shrewdest money-men of the day who regularly underestimated her abilities.[34]

On October 14, 1903, and December 7, 1903, cashier Spear certified $5,000 checks for Mrs. Chadwick, payable to her. Spear certified both of the checks, although he knew Cassie had no funds in the bank. She had unilaterally decided to treat the checks as loans contrary to established banking regulations and practice. Spear had certified all of Mrs. Chadwick's checks thus far and knew that what he was doing was illegal. He would not have acted without Beckwith's knowledge. It was also Spear, with his bookkeeping expertise, who falsified the bank's ledgers.[35]

CHAPTER TWELVE

THE CARNEGIE NOTES

By November 1903, the Ford-Chadwick relationship was strained. Since April, a little over six months, Ford and Coons had negotiated, by their accounting, $258,000 in loans for Cassie Chadwick. But Oberlin College had yet to receive the actual stocks and bonds they were promised as collateral for their $75,000 loan. H. Clark Ford had made it clear that his first allegiance was to the college, and Mrs. Chadwick decided she required a new attorney to negotiate on her behalf. Learning that attorney and former New York governor Frank S. Black was staying at her New York hotel, she sent her calling card to him requesting a meeting. A Republican, Black had been governor from 1897 to 1898 and had become a prominent barrister with excellent political connections. Black was an old-school Victorian gentleman who was surprised and taken aback when the client who met him in the lobby—the calling card read "C. L. Chadwick"—turned out to be a woman. Cassie paid Black $50 for an hour's discussion about her financial affairs.[1]

Iri Reynolds was never far from Mrs. Chadwick's thoughts. Late in 1903, to show her gratitude for his services, she offered to give him, no strings attached, four of her personal promissory notes totaling $100,000. Cassie assured Reynolds the notes were good as gold, and he believed she would honor the notes as she had similar ones given to Cleveland banks. Yet Reynolds declined the gratuity, explaining that because he was an officer of the bank, accepting it would be unethical. Reynolds's honesty likely saved him from future grief because it would be true to form for Mrs. Chadwick to have used him as front man to raise cash for her on the notes much as poor Joe Lamb had.[2]

In late 1902, Mrs. Chadwick had been a suspect in a $200,000 smuggling scheme that was investigated by the New York customhouse. Nothing came of the investigation. However, in December 1903, a New York treasury agent seized a costly necklace from Cassie when she returned from Europe on the assumption that she had purchased it overseas and not paid the duty on it upon her return to the States. Ohio senator Mark Hanna's office intervened by sending a letter to the customhouse stating that the woman was "thoroughly reliable." The necklace was returned to Mrs. Chadwick when she provided proof that she had taken the piece to Europe with her. Despite Hanna's intervention, the woman remained on Customs' watch list.[3]

With Mrs. Chadwick's written promise to move her considerable trust to Citizen's National broken, Beckwith and Spear found themselves with no solid collateral for the loans they had made to her. The bank's only collateral amounted to the woman's promissory notes backed by a claim made against the unseen securities held by Iri Reynolds. Beckwith, who had thus far concealed the loans from his board of directors, was desperate for something more tangible. Mrs. Chadwick doubled down on her carefully concocted Carnegie connection, and in mid-January 1904, she provided Beckwith with a promissory note for $250,000 purportedly signed by Andrew Carnegie. Written in a somewhat feminine longhand on a simple stationery store blank note, it was illustrated with a hound's head motif, which was meant to convey a sense of security similar to a stock certificate. The note was simple and to the point. It read "New York. January 7, 1904. One year after date, I promise to pay to the order of C. L. Chadwick two hundred and fifty thousand dollars at my office New York City. Interest 5%. Andrew Carnegie." This new note with the Carnegie signature was given to Beckwith as secondary security for the $102,000 Cassie had borrowed personally from the banker. He ignored any doubts he harbored and accepted the note as temporary salvation.[4]

In late March, Cassie Chadwick gave a $500,000 Carnegie note to Beckwith and Spear to backstop her indebtedness to Citizen's National. The two notes were identical except for the amounts. On March 14, 1904, Cassie assigned the $250,000 note to C. T. Beckwith personally in a handwritten document witnessed by Spear. A month later on April 12, she assigned, in a document written by Spear and witnessed by a bank employee, the $500,000 note not to the bank to whom she owed about $225,000 but jointly to Beckwith and Spear. The two men squabbled over who should hold the last note. Unable to agree, they decided to put it in an envelope, seal it, and give it to C. K. Whitney, the township treasurer. His father, L. T. Whitney, was a bank director, and his business was one of the bank's largest depositors. Beckwith and Spear's plan, if Cassie's loans were not paid, seemed to be to redeem the notes in January, pay off the bank loans, and pocket the rest. Whether or not both men truly believed Mrs. Chadwick's Carnegie story, they were now fully entrapped in her web of deceit.[5]

Why did Beckwith, Spear, Reynolds, Friend, Ford, and others accept Cassie Chadwick's claim of a Carnegie connection so readily? All of them were rational and experienced businessmen. Each man had his own reasons for preferring to believe that Carnegie was just another Gilded Age millionaire businessman with illegitimate offspring he preferred not to publicly acknowledge. Much of Cassie's success depended on the huge fortune she claimed—an amount so large and audacious as to overcome common sense. But it was her uncanny ability to find the weakness in each man and her exceptional persuasiveness that was the hallmark of her success.

Back in New York on March 2, 1904, Mrs. Chadwick had a second consultation with former governor Frank Black. They were joined by former judge William M. K. Olcott, Black's partner. Olcott, a native New Yorker, was a former alderman and district attorney whom Black had appointed as a judge in 1898. Mrs. Chadwick wanted Black to negotiate with Oberlin College, which was threatening to place an attachment on her home—it was already mortgaged and Cassie wanted to avoid the embarrassing consequences—because she had failed to provide the promised securities as collateral. Cassie wanted Black to go to Ohio and negotiate with the college. According to Olcott, Mrs. Chadwick "drew from her reticle $1,000 and laid it in front of Governor Black for his expenses to Cleveland." Olcott continued, "Mrs. Chadwick, in that slow impressive manner of hers said to Governor Black, 'I am a very rich woman. I have $5 million in a trust fund.'" At this statement, the two men glanced at each other and, in Olcott's words, "we were naturally impressed." As proof, Cassie produced Iri Reynolds's receipt and the Carnegie trust agreement. Olcott said, "This naturally led us to believe that the woman spoke the truth." Nevertheless, Black declined to go. Olcott agreed to go instead for a $500 fee. The forty-two-year-old Olcott, sporting a handlebar mustache and New York accent, was described as a "small spare man of nervous temperament and a capacity for work that made him a terror."[6]

Cassie impressed upon Olcott the urgency of the matter, and he left March 3 for Cleveland. The next day in northeastern Ohio, Olcott met Mrs. Chadwick and asked to see the securities before meeting the Oberlin men. Cassie deftly stalled Olcott with the tale that Reynolds was ill. Olcott went to Oberlin College and met with treasurer Severance and a bevy of lawyers. Olcott asked what terms Oberlin College offered to settle the loans. The Oberlin men bluntly asked Olcott if he had any concrete proof of Cassie's wealth, and

Olcott admitted he did not. "You don't know any more about this case than we do," one lawyer told a chagrined Olcott. The New Yorker admitted, "as far as my accomplishing anything with Mrs. Chadwick and with the Oberlin people was concerned, my visit was futile." That evening back in Cleveland, Cassie got Reynolds on the telephone, and he confirmed to Olcott that he had the securities. But Reynolds conceded he had never actually seen them. All Reynolds had seen, he told Olcott, was the $5 million note that indicated Carnegie held the securities. Pressed by Olcott to see the actual stocks and bonds, Reynolds was evasive, saying they were in sealed envelopes in his office safe and the bank was closed for the day. As Olcott prepared to leave Cleveland in this failed bid, Mrs. Chadwick told him that she was short of ready funds and asked him to loan her $1,500. Olcott, perhaps feeling guilty over his failure in Oberlin, gave the woman a personal check on her solemn assurance that she would repay him in two days. Olcott returned to New York. Mrs. Chadwick cashed the check at Wade Park Banking the next day.[7]

March 6 came and went without Olcott receiving his money. "I then became somewhat suspicious, but not entirely so," Olcott said. "I still had confidence in her and would probably have believed her to this day had it not been for the fact that I heard from Cleveland that she had been representing about town that I was Mr. Carnegie's representative." Olcott's faith in his new client shaken, he vowed to "get my money back."[8]

A determined man not to be trifled with, Olcott boarded a westbound train headed for Cleveland on March 15. Confronting Mrs. Chadwick at her home, Olcott demanded immediate payment of the full $1,500. Cassie feigned illness. "Why, I am a sick woman, and I cannot pay you today," she told the lawyer. But Olcott was blunt: "I told her that I had come to Cleveland to get that money, to get it that day and I would not leave without it." To back up his claim, Olcott threatened legal action. Mrs. Chadwick relented and told Olcott she would have his money inside of two hours. The New Yorker calmly went to dinner at his hotel. Upon the expiration of two hours, Olcott presented himself to Mrs. Chadwick and was given fifteen new $100 bills. According to Olcott, that "terminated" his law firm's representation of Mrs. Chadwick.[9]

Despite getting off on the completely wrong foot with Black and Olcott, Cassie continued in the coming months to attempt to retain them as her attorneys. They refused. Nevertheless, Black and Olcott remained impressed by the reasons for the trust fund, later suggesting that there were untold secrets of great import. Less impressed was a member of Black's law firm, Abraham Gruber, who said that Mrs. Chadwick reminded him of Bertha Heyman, the famous New York confidence woman who made headlines twenty years ago. Bertha swindled a stockbroker by telling him that she had $87,000 in stocks and bonds in a sealed envelope locked in a hotel safe. Bertha succeeded in getting almost $500 and a diamond pin from the man before she was arrested in July 1883. The package of securities was found to contain wastepaper. The police and press in New York had nicknamed Bertha "the Confidence Queen." New York City chief of detectives Thomas Byrnes said of Bertha in 1886, "She possesses a wonderful knowledge of human nature, and can deceive those who consider themselves particularly shrewd in business matters."[10]

Beckwith and Spear continued to certify checks for Mrs. Chadwick. On February 11, 1904, Spear certified a $10,000 check payable to W. L. Fay on March 1. Fay successfully cashed the check at the Oriental Bank in New York on March 1. A short time later, the woman missed another payment to Henry Wurst, who demanded his money immediately or else he would sell the jewelry he held as collateral. Cassie went to Beckwith with her concern that a public sale would cast doubt on her creditworthiness and, by extension, Citizen's National. Spear certified a $10,000 check for Mrs. Chadwick, payable to Wurst in thirty days. Wurst tried to cash the check immediately at an Elyria bank, but the bank's officers refused because of the long postdate. Beckwith and Spear personally went to Elyria to ask the bankers to honor the check. The Elyria bank steadfastly refused. In the end, Beckwith gave Wurst his personal note as payment on the loan to Cassie and later redeemed it with cash.[11]

Late winter of 1904, Mrs. Chadwick took the train into Ravenna, Ohio, a short distance south of Cleveland. At a grocery store she asked for the most responsible attorney in town. By consensus, she was directed to L. T. Siddall, whom she retained to arrange a loan of $15,000. Mrs. Chadwick told Siddall that she was wealthy but had endorsed the promissory notes of a well-known Cleveland businessman who fell on hard times, requiring her to cover his notes. She admitted she was now temporarily short of funds, and she desperately needed cash to send her invalid husband, who was convalescing in the dry mountain air in Carlsbad, New Mexico. Siddall took her to the Second National Bank and its president, C. G. Bentley. Both men decided to go to Cleveland to make inquiries about Mrs. Chadwick. She arranged for a well-appointed carriage to chauffeur them to various local banks. Their inquiries complete, the two men went to the Chadwick home on Euclid Avenue, where Bentley declined to loan her the money. "You are the only man who ever doubted my honesty and integrity," Cassie scolded Bentley. The banker replied, "Mrs. Chadwick, it is my business to doubt people."[12]

Mrs. Chadwick's difficulties with Oberlin College were finally settled on March 24, 1904. In the end, it wasn't attorneys who saved her but Charles Beckwith. Cassie was desperate to avoid legal action, and Beckwith negotiated a settlement in which the college got its money in return for dropping the endowment fund "donation." Rumors flew around Oberlin regarding the settlement. A director from another bank in town had been gossiping about the loan with local residents, and Beckwith confronted him, demanding to know what the man knew. "I know that a $75,000 deal of that kind is rather unusual for a town the size of Oberlin," the man said. "Well, I will tell you something," Beckwith shot back, "I took up that loan. Mr. Severence, treasurer of the College, lost his nerve. Yes, sir, I took up that loan and made $6000 on the deal." Beckwith bragged. "The college was paid in full and was happy to get it." In a cooler moment, he admitted that he had not repaid the loan personally. Instead, "Mrs. Chadwick furnished the means in good hard cash." Where the woman got the money is unknown; however, Beckwith's $6,000 might have been a fee or commission for helping Cassie secure the funds.[13]

Mrs. Chadwick's failure to fully repay the loans arranged by W. V. Coons and H. Clark Ford in a timely manner ultimately led to legal action. In early 1904, Coons took her to court in Findlay to avoid undesired publicity in Cleveland. Coons's Producer's Oil Company won a judgment against Mrs. Chadwick for $25,310. Coons received a combination of cash and jewelry as settlement. At the same time, another Cleveland man and Fay client, E. C. Vermilion, sued for an overdue loan and was awarded $28,808, which was later settled for $15,000. Charles Beckwith raised the $15,000 to cover the judgment, which Mrs. Chadwick wanted resolved quickly. "If she had only given me a little more rein, I could have settled the judgement much cheaper," Beckwith later complained, "but she was in a desperate hurry for the money, and no wonder, she was being hounded to death by sharpers."[14]

Having satisfied their biggest creditors, the Chadwicks left for the Continent early in 1904. Before they left, Mrs. Chadwick left some insurance against any needs that might arise with the reliable Iri Reynolds. She struggled into Wade Park Banking one afternoon with an armful of envelopes that she said contained US Steel bonds. She asked Reynolds to store them in the vault while she was abroad. There they remained, undisturbed, until she returned from Europe when she retrieved the fortune. An unnamed attorney had suggested, she said, that the securities be placed in a stronger vault. Reynolds quietly accepted this explanation and took her to mean in New York or Pittsburgh.[15]

In April 1904, Citizen's National Bank's books were again inspected by a federal bank examiner. This audit uncovered Mrs. Chadwick's indebtedness to the bank in the amount of $227,566. The examiner faulted the bank's officers for exceeding the $6,000 loan limit. However, the examiner, after seeing the Carnegie note, Reynolds's receipt, and a copy of Cassie's trust agreement, expressed the opinion that the bank had excellent security. He also later claimed he saw outside securities held by another trustee, which is doubtful. In the end, the examiner concluded that Mrs. Chadwick was worth $4 to $5 million. Following this audit, the bank was directed to reduce their loans to her immediately, and the examiner was assured by Beckwith and Spear in April that the lady was in New York raising money to do just that. The 10 percent rule was a regulation, not a law, and federal bank examiners in 1904 had no legal power to enforce it. However, the stockholders were liable for any losses above the limit, a penalty believed to be a sufficient deterrent. None of the directors or the stockholders of Citizen's National were informed of this "overloan" and any steps being pursued to correct it.[16]

The Chadwicks were in Europe in April 1904. On April 12, Mrs. Chadwick bought $242 worth of knickknacks from a retail establishment, Kneim-Coutille, in Brussels, Belgium. She paid with an Ohio bank check, which was eventually returned for lack of funds. The Brussels merchant sent the check to a New York law firm for investigation but not collection. It was early September before the check caught up with Cassie, who promised to give it immediate attention, but she never did. A lawsuit was later filed in Cleveland.[17]

Mrs. Chadwick was back in the States in the late spring of 1904. She approached Rev. Dr. Charles Eaton, the nationally prominent pastor of Cleveland's Euclid Avenue Baptist Church. Eaton had been John D. Rockefeller's pastor when the oil magnate resided in Cleveland. Cassie was not a member of Eaton's church or any other church for that matter. She had never attended even one service there or dropped a penny in the collection plate. This did not prevent her from approaching Reverend Eaton with a tale of temporary financial embarrassment. Eaton's fame meant hundreds of strangers approached him for help, and, being the good clergyman he was, Eaton tried. To establish credibility, Cassie carried Iri Reynolds's receipt. Reverend Eaton knew Reynolds as secretary-treasurer of Wade Park Banking Company whose president was John D. Rockefeller's brother, Frank. Reverend Eaton was perplexed by this woman who sought his advice. He was not a financial man and logically suggested Cassie go to a local bank. But Mrs. Chadwick said she preferred not to have local people know of her financial embarrassment, not an uncommon sentiment for a wealthy woman with a Euclid Avenue address. "You came from the East," she told Eaton. "Do you know some person there who will loan me several thousand dollars? I will pay them back and reward them much." In the face of Mrs. Chadwick's persistence, Eaton surrendered. Somewhat reluctantly, he recommended some firms and gave her a letter of introduction. One of those was the law firm of his cousin, Boston attorney John Eaton. Reverend Eaton was careful to mention in his letter that his endorsement was dependent upon verification of Mrs. Chadwick's wealth. He ended the interview by telling Mrs. Chadwick to place her affairs in the hands of a reputable lawyer or businessman.[18]

Cassie hastened to Boston to see John Eaton, armed with a $500,000 Carnegie promissory note—like the one at Citizen's National—and Reynolds's receipt for $5 million in securities. Carnegie's signature was not verified, but Reynolds's standing in the community was confirmed by Reverend Eaton, who spoke highly of Reynolds's honor and integrity. John Eaton contacted Reynolds and confirmed that he signed the receipt.[19]

With this background check, John Eaton took the Carnegie note and list of securities to his law firm's banker, John Graham, president of the Boston-based International Trust Company. Eaton said he was acting as agent for a Cleveland woman who wished to borrow $200,000. Graham was a gruff Scot who doubted that fellow Scot Carnegie would sign a $500,000 personal note. After reviewing the list of securities, Graham decided he would have none of it.[20]

Cassie's offer of a substantial fee and her persuasiveness kept Eaton in the game despite Graham's rejection and reservations. John Eaton next approached Herbert Newton, a forty-three-year-old Brookline, Massachusetts, coal and coke wholesaler. Newton was a religious man and devoted father of six. Although a strict Episcopalian, Newton nevertheless knew Rev. Charles Eaton as a prominent Cleveland clergyman who occasionally preached in Boston. In fact, Newton had once enjoyed an Eaton sermon. Like many modestly wealthy men, Newton was looking for investments less risky than stocks and more profitable than bank interest. He was just the sort of man who suited Cassie Chadwick's needs, although her initial approach of Reverend Eaton might have been aimed at John D. Rockefeller himself.[21]

Newton and Mrs. Chadwick met in attorney Eaton's Boston office. Cassie told Newton of her temporary financial shortfall, practically pleading for assistance. She told Newton she was "a person of large wealth," that her income was $175,000 every six months, and that she had at Wade Park in Cleveland $5 million in gilt-edged securities in the form of US Steel gold bonds and Scottish

Caledonian railway stock—both securities were associated with Carnegie. Newton was shown a $500,000 Carnegie note, which Mrs. Chadwick said she was given because Carnegie was selling her Caledonian railroad stock in Scotland, where it would fetch a better price than in New York. When the meeting ended, Newton was interested but not convinced.[22]

Mrs. Chadwick left Parker House in Boston and returned to Holland House in New York. Immediately she wrote a long pleading letter to Newton in Boston. The Boston man was moved and without telling his attorneys, who were opposed to a Chadwick loan, went to Holland House. When he returned to Boston, Newton's attorneys scolded him, but he had already decided to make a loan. First, however, Newton had Reverend Eaton vouch for Reynolds's signature on the receipt. Next, he talked to Iri Reynolds personally, who confirmed the receipt. Was it a receipt or an attest? Reynolds let the confusion continue, but to Newton, it was an attest. Quietly, Newton checked Reynolds's Cleveland reputation and found "a man of the highest integrity and honor." Nobody made any attempt to verify Andrew Carnegie's signature on anything. Satisfied, Newton gave John Eaton a check for $14,000. Eaton gave Mrs. Chadwick his check for the same amount. Newton didn't request any collateral, but someone likely got a decent fee or commission.[23]

Cassie wasn't about to let Newton slip away and pressed for more loans. The New Englander was invited to Cleveland, where he was wined and dined. Dr. Chadwick himself drove Newton down Euclid Avenue, Cleveland's millionaire's row, in his motorcar. Later, for after-dinner entertainment, the doctor displayed his musical talent on the Chadwicks' magnificent pipe organ. Newton left Cleveland suitably impressed.[24]

L. S. CHADWICK

Left: Andrew Carnegie in 1905 (Courtesy Library of Congress, LC-USZ62-88699). *Right:* Dr. Leroy Chadwick, late 1890s (Cleveland Public Library).

Andrew Carnegie's mansion on New York's Fifth Avenue in 1907 (Courtesy Library of Congress, LC-DIG-det-4a10976)

The Chadwick family mansion on Cleveland's Euclid Avenue, circa 1905 (Cleveland Public Library)

Cassie Chadwick (*far right*) with son, Emil (*far left*), and stepdaughter, Mary Chadwick (*center*), circa 1903 or 1904. The cyclist is unknown. (The Western Reserve Historical Society, Cleveland, Ohio)

The library in the Chadwick mansion, 1904 (Cleveland Public Library)

Above: Betsy Bigley, mid-1880s (Cleveland Public Library)

Right: Cassie Chadwick in 1904 (Cleveland Public Library)

MRS CASSIE L. CHADWICK

Ohio Penitentiary mugshots of Madame Lydia Devere in 1891 (*left*) and Cassie Chadwick in 1906 (*right*) (Cleveland Police Museum)

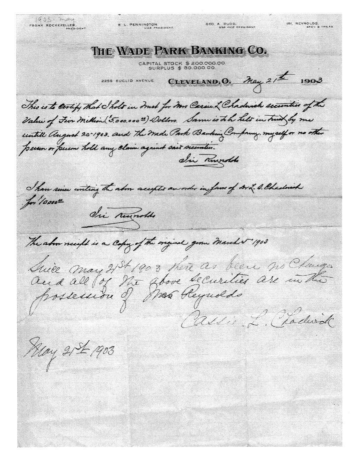

The infamous receipt from Iri Reynolds that Cassie Chadwick used to procure hundreds of thousand of dollars in loans (The Western Reserve Historical Society, Cleveland, Ohio)

The $5,000,000 promissory note bearing Andrew Carnegie's forged signature that was the basis for Iri Reynolds's receipt (The Western Reserve Historical Society, Cleveland, Ohio)

CHAPTER THIRTEEN

FRENZIED FINANCE

Rumors in Cleveland and Boston during the winter and spring of 1904 suggested that Cassie Chadwick had used two promissory notes as loan collateral in Boston that bore the signature of Mark Hanna, an Ohio senator and wealthy Cleveland businessman. The senator passed away on February 15, 1904. Mrs. Chadwick was acquainted with Hanna, who resided on Euclid Avenue and had assisted her with a New York customhouse matter. Hanna was a powerful Republican fundraiser and known as the man who made William McKinley president in 1894. The notes were for $100,000 each and were dated January 2 and January 5, 1904, payable in twelve months and eighteen months, respectively. If the story was true, the notes would be a thorny issue for Hanna's estate. However, the newspapers later reported that the holders of the notes "will pocket their loss and say nothing to avoid damage to their reputations." The holders went unidentified, and the story died unconfirmed.[1]

Cassie had persuaded a New York jeweler, Ludwig Niessen, to loan her $29,000 on pearls valued at $30,000. On April 20, 1904, she sent Niessen a $10,000 check drawn on Citizen's National as partial repayment. The check arrived back in Oberlin for settlement on April 26. Mrs. Chadwick had no cash or credit of record at the bank, and Beckwith and Spear were out of town. Citizen's assistant cashier, Harry Avery, refused to honor the check. However, he knew that Mrs. Chadwick was an important customer and chose what he believed was the safest course of action. Instead of refusing to honor the check for lack of funds, Avery listed as his reason as "not sure of the genuineness of the signature." This would buy time until Beckwith or Spear returned to Oberlin.[2]

Cassie was in Oberlin just days later and convinced Beckwith to approve the check to prevent the pearls from being sold by Niessen. This check was remarkable because the bank's directors were informed, making it the only

Chadwick transaction of which they were made aware to date. Avery's involvement was the catalyst since his knowledge made it impossible for Beckwith and Spear to conceal the transaction. Cassie never fully repaid Niessen, who had intentionally undervalued the collateral and eventually sold the pearls for a reported $60,000. Shortly thereafter, Beckwith told the bank's attorney and director, W. B. Bedortha, about the Chadwick loans made despite the attorney's reservations about her. It would be June before Beckworth let Oberlin mayor and director O. Frank Carter in on the secret.[3]

In New York that spring, Mrs. Chadwick deposited $100,000 in the Lincoln National Bank. This deposit was so large, according to one source, as to mark her as one of the country's "women of considerable wealth." Cassie also displayed letters of introduction from local men and Iri Reynolds's receipt. Other deposits were made that were followed immediately by rapid withdrawals at such a pace that it was difficult for Lincoln National's bookkeepers to track her account balance. At one time Mrs. Chadwick wrote a check for $150,000—at least $3 million today—on her account at Lincoln payable to Citizen's National in Oberlin. In reality, Mrs. Chadwick had less than $5,000 on deposit at Lincoln. Believing Mrs. Chadwick to be a very wealthy woman for whom an overdraft would not be uncommon, the New York bankers did not immediately contest the check, but instead they contacted Charles Beckwith. The Oberlin banker asked Lincoln to hold the check a few days to await a deposit from Mrs. Chadwick. A deposit never appeared. Beckwith and Spear sent the worthless check back to New York. By now Citizen's National was in too deep with Mrs. Chadwick to consider any sort of legal action.[4]

Having succeeded in writing one large bad check with no consequences, Cassie doubled down. A short time later, a Lincoln National check of hers for $300,000 was presented for payment at a Boston financial institution. She had nowhere near that amount on deposit. Officials at Lincoln concluded that two massive overdrafts were no coincidence but rather the act of someone either delusional or criminal. The check was sent back to Boston for insufficient funds, and Mrs. Chadwick was instructed by the management at Lincoln National to take her account elsewhere. She erupted in a great show of indignation, but the bankers were unmoved. The overdrafts remained yet another banking secret.[5]

The men at Lincoln National suspected that Cassie was, in banking vernacular, "kiting" checks. In 1904, checks took days, even weeks, to clear—known as settlement delays—and it was possible to take advantage of the delay to use funds credited to an account in one bank to open an account at another bank before a bad check was returned to the first bank. A clever operator could then borrow or even withdraw against those accounts. Kiting was illegal and required an elementary knowledge of banking procedures, which was no problem for a woman of Cassie Chadwick's ability. It appears she adroitly manipulated her funds in Ohio and New York banks to her advantage by exploiting settlement delays. She treated overdrawn accounts and overdue loans as additional loans. The sheer size of her deposits, her audacity, gave them unwarranted credibility. Although Cassie had been asked to leave Lincoln National, where the total for the attempted overdrafts reached $600,000, no one there was willing to accuse her of having "that malice which is the essence of crime."[6]

For the past two years, Mrs. Chadwick had occasionally borrowed small sums of money from Wade Park Banking, always giving sealed envelopes, which she claimed held valuable securities, as collateral. Once she had been so bold as to provide the bank's loan committee with a written statement indicating she had $2 million in bonds in a safe deposit box in the bank's vault. Cassie was a shareholder in Wade Park, and the officials there had given her more leeway than the average customer might receive. In the spring of 1904, Mrs. Chadwick approached the always sympathetic Iri Reynolds and told him she had a $12,000 note due but lacked the funds to repay it. She assured Reynolds that if he gave her the money, she would provide steel stocks and bonds as collateral. Her intention was to have Reynolds dip into his personal funds, but instead he went to Wade Park's loan committee. They agreed to a loan. The next morning, Cassie delivered a sealed package that she claimed held $250,000 in steel securities whose origin she declined to divulge. Wade Park reluctantly accepted the unseen collateral.[7]

Never satisfied by a single loan from a willing lender, Mrs. Chadwick soon returned to Wade Park for another loan. The bank declined, saying they had been "somewhat lenient" in the past but would no longer loan to her unless she could provide "satisfactory collateral," which meant no more purported securities in sealed envelopes. Feigning astonishment, Cassie looked the banker in the eye and said, "Why this is ridiculous." Her indignation rising, she lectured the man: "You refuse to let me have a paltry few thousands of dollars. The day before yesterday, I was paid $3 million and now you hesitate to trust me." As Cassie's response circulated among the bankers, one of them summed up the reasoning at Wade Park when he questioned how someone paid $3 million two days ago could need money.[8]

Reynolds and Wade Park Banking wanted to be free of Mrs. Chadwick after this episode, but she stalled at every turn. In May 1904, Reynolds went to

New York City in hopes that she would settle her accounts with him and the bank and relieve him of the envelopes in his safe. He sought an audience with her at Holland House. After waiting two days in New York, Reynolds left, never once being acknowledged. The Chadwick method was to plead and persuade when she wanted something, but once she had her man hooked, she treated him with disdain. Joe Lamb, if he were still alive, would sympathize with Reynolds.[9]

In the spring of 1904 Cassie took a diamond necklace with sixty stones to a private lender in Akron, L. C. Miller. She wanted a $20,000 loan. The necklace was appraised locally at $10,000 to $20,000. Miller offered $15,000, but Mrs. Chadwick declined. Miller later regretted not taking the deal as he personally believed the appraiser intentionally undervalued what was in reality a $30,000 necklace.[10]

In the summer of 1904, Cassie Chadwick was injured when her carriage collided with a streetcar. She was confined to bed for some time by her injuries. Dr. Chadwick was in Europe showing a decided lack of urgency to return to Cleveland. While Mrs. Chadwick was recovering from her accident, a New York loan for $53,000, collateralized by $98,000 in jewels, came due. Cassie asked Iri Reynolds to travel to New York to arrange for payment. He succeeded in having the loan extended by agreeing to personally cosign for it. Cassie did eventually repay the loan and retrieve the jewels.[11]

Back on her feet after her accident, Cassie took a summer trip to Canada to visit family. While in Ontario, she took a side trip to Brantford, the location of some of her youthful misdeeds. She tried to find an accommodating bank for a loan but failed. Her inquiries brought her to the attention of Thomas Woodyatt, the local police magistrate.[12]

While Cassie was out of Cleveland that summer, a letter for her arrived at Iri Reynolds's home. When she returned and retrieved the letter, Mrs. Chadwick showed Reynolds the contents—a $60,000 check bearing the signature "Andrew Carnegie." This did not seem overly strange to Reynolds, who was convinced that Carnegie stood behind Cassie in all her financial transactions. Reynolds later said he did not know what became of the check. In fact, despite being a critical part of Mrs. Chadwick's financial activities, Reynolds knew very little of Mrs. Chadwick's business. "I know as little of her affairs as any man living," Reynolds once admitted. It was likely true. He was just an honest, simple man who automatically gave his old friend's second wife the benefit of the doubt. Cassie spread her business across multiple banks, lenders, and lawyers. She gave information sparingly and convincingly in hushed tones and swore everyone to secrecy in an era when secrets were kept. Furthermore, she had endeared herself to Reynolds and his family to such an extent that, according to Reynolds, "My child loved her like a mother."[13]

Mrs. Chadwick dealt with dozens of banks, and the vast majority were able to remain mum about their business with the woman. One bank that couldn't remain quiet was the Euclid Avenue Trust and Savings. Mrs. Chadwick had what were described as "many mutual business dealings" with the bank. Euclid Avenue Trust had failed, and Mrs. Chadwick's loan was in default. F. H. Ginn, the receiver for the defunct bank, filed a lawsuit against her in Cuyahoga County Common Pleas Court to collect. The court found that Mrs. Chadwick owed the receiver $38,231. She disputed the amount, declined to pay the judgment, and threatened to appeal. The astronomical bonuses and fees she paid for loans were usually rolled into the loan and these, along with interest, provided a sure means to dispute any lender's demands.[14]

After the April 1904 audit of Citizen's National, Charles Beckwith became increasingly frantic to collect the money Cassie Chadwick owed the bank. In June 1904, Beckwith secretly informed Oberlin mayor and director O. Frank Carter of the Chadwick loans. After W. B. Bedortha, Carter became the second director to share Beckwith's terrible secret. The banker's explanation for not telling the entire board was a lesson in small-town life. "Eight directors with their eight wives would do a lot of gossiping," Beckwith reckoned.[15]

Mrs. Chadwick brought two bank drafts, totaling $80,000, drawn on Importers and Manufacturers National Bank of New York to Citizen's National on August 24, 1904. Cashier Spear credited her with the $80,000 and then certified a check for her for $12,500. Technically, she didn't have any money in her account at Citizen's because the New York checks had not yet cleared. Nevertheless, with some imaginative bookkeeping, Spear manipulated the bank's ledgers to indicate the funds were in Mrs. Chadwick's account. This was an instance of Cassie kiting checks—depositing New York checks in Ohio and withdrawing funds against them before the checks had a chance to clear the East Coast bank. Despite the illegality of actual check kiting, this tactic of playing the float as checks cleared was commonplace.[16]

This was hardly Spear's first effort at creative accounting to cover Cassie's withdrawals. On February 9, 1904, Spear manipulated the books to show a positive balance of $6,846 with the Colonial National Bank when the actual balance was $1,796. On March 1, 1904, Spear recorded the day's deposits as $18,900 when the actual amount was $8,900. In July 1904, Citizen's National's books indicated a positive balance with Cleveland's First National Bank when in reality, Oberlin was overdrawn by $12,000. These three episodes represented only the tip of the iceberg.[17]

On August 26, Mrs. Chadwick sent a telegram to Beckwith indicating that she was ready to settle her account with Citizen's National. A second telegram on August 27 confirmed that the matter was all arranged. August 28 brought a third telegram stating that Dr. Chadwick, who was at sea returning from Europe, would take up the Carnegie notes if Beckwith would come to Cleveland on September 3. At that very moment on the voyage home, the doctor was aware that the family finances were teetering on the brink of collapse. Before reaching the States, Chadwick took Emil aside and, without explanation, warned him to be careful how he spent his money.[18]

An eager Charles Beckwith arrived at the Chadwick home at 4:00 P.M. on September 3. Dr. Chadwick had just returned from Europe at 2:00 P.M. that very afternoon. The doctor told Beckwith that he had just arrived, was tired, and it would be impossible for him to raise the funds until the first of the next week. Beckwith was adamant that he must have something immediately. "Well," Chadwick responded, "I can give you $20,000 now and next week I will send you some more, which will help you out." The doctor gave Beckwith two personal checks for $10,000 each to cover two promissory notes his wife had given Beckwith that were overdue. The doctor knew his checks were worthless. There would be no relief for poor Beckwith, who, when he discovered the checks were bogus, insured his life for $40,000.[19]

Having failed in her numerous overtures to Black and Olcott, Mrs. Chadwick retained New York attorney Edmund Powers in September to represent her. Powers would prove a staunch defender, willing to say whatever was necessary. One of his first tasks was to reassure those nervous fellows at Citizen's National. Powers went to Oberlin and/or Cleveland six times. "Yes, I met Mr. Beckwith and Mrs. Chadwick, the whole lot, in fact," Powers later admitted. He never went with Mrs. Chadwick to Oberlin, he said, but saw Beckwith there twice and several times in Cleveland. Powers assured everyone that Mrs. Chadwick was "worth millions." According to Powers, "I have known her several years, and I know that she is absolutely honest, although she may be a little lax in business methods." Powers said she gave her husband $2 million three years ago. The attorney was adamant that this was "true from first to last. There are witnesses who saw her give him the money . . . and they are upright and reputable men." It was all lies. Powers further urged the Oberlin men to have patience and give Mrs. Chadwick time to adjust her financial affairs.[20]

On one of his trips to Oberlin, Powers perused Citizen National's ledgers with, he claimed, an eye to moving Cassie's trust to the Oberlin bank, dangling that old pot of gold before the desperate bankers. Beckwith, less enamored than before and suspecting the worst, asked Powers if the Carnegie promissory notes were good. Mrs. Chadwick had, according to Beckwith, sworn repeatedly to him and to Spear that she had witnessed Andrew Carnegie sign the notes. Powers replied that in his opinion, the notes were genuine, "but Mrs. Chadwick ought not to use them." Why not discount them to raise funds and pay the bank, Beckwith wanted to know. Powers refused to elaborate, but his reasons "were sufficient for me." The New Yorker pressured Beckwith not to take any legal action on Cassie's overdue loans and avoid publicity, anything that would "throw the whole thing up in the air."[21]

The Oberlin men came away from their meetings with Edmund Powers with the belief that he was indeed Andrew Carnegie's representative. How they got that impression isn't clear, and Powers belatedly denied any connection to Carnegie—one of the few honest statements he made. Still, the impression, erected on a foundation of hope, persisted. The director, W. B. Bedortha, had met with Powers and had been skeptical. His health was failing, and the secret of the Chadwick loans made him worse. Bedortha took to his bed in late September. During the first week of October, he summoned three fellow bank directors to his deathbed and told of the concealed Chadwick loans. He died on October 12, 1904, his death later attributed in part to Mrs. Chadwick.

Arthur Spear was out of town on October 12, 1904, and Cassie Chadwick asked Charles Beckwith to certify a check she had written to herself for $15,000. Beckwith did—the only Chadwick check Beckwith personally certified. Cassie wanted to deposit it in Cleveland's First National Bank, where she was acquainted with A. B. Marshall, the bank's vice president. Marshall had almost three decades in banking and had known Beckwith and Spear for ten years. Since August 1903, Mrs. Chadwick's deposits in Marshall's bank totaled $105,000. From her home on Euclid Avenue, Cassie telephoned Marshall on October 13 and asked him if he would give her the $15,000 cash but not send the check back to Oberlin until October 19. Marshall made it clear that this could be done only on Charles Beckwith's authority. This would be the second time that Cassie had requested Marshall hold a Citizen's National check. The first was for just a single day. Marshall knew that holding these checks was "unusual" and that he had no obligation to do so. According to Marshall, "It is customary to use due diligence in getting a check to its destination." Beckwith was at Mrs. Chadwick's elbow and got on the telephone. The two bankers agreed that Marshall, as a favor to Beckwith, would hold the check if the Oberlin banker would write a letter certifying the check on a future date.[22]

The following day, Beckwith called Marshall from the Kennard House hotel in Cleveland and read the letter over the telephone. "Oberlin, Ohio. October 13, 1904. To A. B. Marshall, V. P. You are hereby authorized to hold a check signed by Mrs. C. L. Chadwick on my bank and certified by me October 12, 1904, until Wednesday the 19th, or such time that Mrs. Chadwick may order you to put such cheque through. Yours truly, C. T. Beckwith, president." Beckwith said illness prevented him from coming personally to First National—a lie—so he sent the letter and check over by messenger. At Beckwith's request, Marshall then personally brought the cash to the hotel, where Beckwith and Mrs. Chadwick were waiting. After politely inquiring after Beckwith's health, Marshall turned over the cash. Marshall was true to his word, and First National held the check until October 19 before sending it back to Oberlin for settlement.[23]

The real purpose for holding the $15,000 check in Cleveland was to keep it away from Oberlin while the federal auditor was performing his semiannual audit. As usual, Mrs. Chadwick had no funds on deposit at Citizen's National. Beckwith understood that if Mrs. Chadwick's finances were in any way questioned, the publicity could ultimately shake public confidence in Citizen's National Bank. Before the advent of deposit insurance, the loss of depositors' collective confidence in a bank could result in catastrophic consequences. The auditor noted the unresolved large loans to Mrs. Chadwick but took no further action.[24]

Beckwith asked two directors, Oberlin Mayor Carter and J. F. Randolph, to accompany him to New York in September on the pretense that he needed their input on some bank business. Actually, Beckwith was going to meet Mrs. Chadwick and attorney Powers in her five-room suite at Holland House to negotiate a settlement of the woman's loans. When the trio arrived, Powers said that arrangements for the cash to pay off the loans had been made and that it would be available tomorrow. He suggested that the directors return home and let Beckwith pick up the money. But when Beckwith arrived at Holland House the next morning, Powers was nowhere to be seen and Cassie said that Dr. Chadwick, who was in Europe, had certain documents necessary to complete the transaction. There would be no money today. Poor Beckwith, with the memory of Dr. Chadwick's worthless checks still fresh, was crushed and saw clearly that he was being played.[25]

Beckwith and Spear were in a tight place. Citizen's National badly needed the funds that the Cassie Chadwick and Andrew Carnegie promissory notes represented. After some inquiries, Beckwith found a Cleveland bank willing to consider negotiating the Chadwick and Carnegie notes. Which Cleveland bank was involved and what inquiries into Mrs. Chadwick it made were known only to Beckwith, Spear, and the Cleveland bank. Nevertheless, the bank gave Beckwith tentative approval for the transaction, $240,000 in cash.[26]

Beckwith walked into the Cleveland bank on the day and time he was to receive the funds. The Oberlin banker was stunned when the Cleveland bank's president, one president to another, apologized because the bank's loan committee had decided to reconsider the loan. The man told Beckwith there would be no money today. Beckwith, with years in the banking business, knew what it meant to tell a borrower their loan was reconsidered. The old man went back to Oberlin in a daze. His seemingly last avenue of escape had closed.[27]

Unfazed by her debt in Oberlin, Mrs. Chadwick continued her search for loans right in Citizen's National Bank's backyard, Lorain, Ohio. Cashier A. B. Taylor of Lorain County Banking Company met her in Cleveland in the fall of 1904. She offered him securities he considered "doubtful" for collateral and nixed the idea of a loan. "Mrs. Chadwick," Taylor remarked, "I am too young a man to take a chance like this." Cassie next approached the cashier of Penfield Avenue Savings Bank in Lorain, brandishing a canceled promissory note as proof of her creditworthiness, but she was again rebuked. She left the man $10 for his time. She returned to the Lorain County Banking Company and asked the president, Parks Foster, for a personal loan of $30,000 in return for a $1,000 fee. Foster wasn't interested.[28]

The Boston man, Herbert Newton, had come away from his springtime visit to the Chadwick home in Cleveland impressed. In return for a high rate of interest and large fees, Newton agreed to more loans. In New York on May 11, 1904, Mrs. Chadwick persuaded Newton to give Clevelander E. E. Williams two $15,000 notes payable November 3. Williams was cashier of the Elyria National Bank, which had refused Mrs. Chadwick a loan, but he had been sufficiently enticed by a sizable bonus to act as a broker for a private $30,000 loan. Williams demanded that Mrs. Chadwick endorse the notes, and he negotiated them for cash for Mrs. Chadwick. Newton also gave Mrs. Chadwick two of his $10,000 notes, also due November 3. One, dated August 26, 1904, was negotiated by Mrs. Chadwick at the Corn Exchange Bank in New York for her "accommodations"—that is, to pay her living expenses in New York. Mrs. Chadwick lamely told Newton she had "misplaced" the second $10,000 note, dated August 27, when in reality she had given it to Citizen's National in Oberlin. By late October, Newton calculated he had given Cassie a total of $90,800 in various small loans. Fifty thousand dollars was due November 3, and the remaining $40,800 was due December 15.[29]

Newton had seen a Carnegie signed note for $500,000 and Reynolds's security receipt, which reassured him sufficiently, and his initial loans had been made without any more solid collateral than a charge against those sealed securities at Wade Park. Now he wanted something more substantial. Dr. Chadwick agreed and gave Newton two of his wife's promissory notes for $25,000 each, due November 7 and 14, respectively.[30]

In October 1904, Cassie missed a payment on the Williams loan of $30,000. On October 25, a nervous and impatient Williams asked Newton to pay up on his notes, although they weren't due until November 3. When this information made the short trip from Elyria to Oberlin, cash-strapped Citizen's National demanded repayment of the $10,000 Newton note it held also.[31]

Newton refused to accept responsibility for any of the notes he had given Mrs. Chadwick, arguing that she had endorsed them, so she should pay them. The first week of November, Newton confronted Mrs. Chadwick in New York at Holland House about missing Williams's payment and presented her with the three notes due on November 3. Dr. Chadwick stepped in on his wife's behalf and offered Newton two postdated personal checks from a Wade Park account for $25,000 each and a paltry $300 in cash. When the first check was presented to Wade Park on November 10, it came back to Newton marked "no funds." The second check was likewise returned.[32]

Citizen's National's directors were uneasy and asking embarrassing questions about the bank's stability. Why was the bank short of ready cash? Beckwith said the large cash deposits were kept at other banks when in fact all the cash reserves had gone to Mrs. Chadwick. The aged banker knew assurances from the Chadwicks that a settlement was at hand were false, but he could do nothing. The bank's precarious situation demanded instant action. In a meeting at the Chadwick residence attended by Beckwith, Spear, and two directors, the old banker began the meeting by chiding Cassie for her lax business methods. "You have attorneys all over the country, why do you not put all your affairs into the hands of one attorney save the expense and in addition have your matters handled in better shape?" he asked. Mrs. Chadwick became emotional, burst into tears, and agreed that she would.[33]

Cassie placed her visitors in separate rooms to continue the discussions. She promised each man "rewards" for his past efforts to accommodate her needs.

In a bit of prearranged theater, a maid would announce every few minutes a telegram or phone call calculated to allay suspicions and bolster hope that relief was in sight. At her most persuasive, Cassie artfully explained that to rush things might spoil everything, which meant that her finances, built solely on debt, would collapse if word got out. Beckwith, almost on his knees, pleaded with Cassie. Although he had personally loaned Mrs. Chadwick over $100,000, Beckwith implored her to pay the $240,000 she owed the bank. Cassie rushed from the room in a fit of hysteria, claiming that the banker had a revolver and bottle of poison and was threatening suicide. If Beckwith died, all would be lost, she wailed. One of the directors went to Beckwith, who was excited but said he meant nothing by the threat. Likewise, nothing came of the meeting.[34]

A few days later, at yet another meeting, a deflated Beckwith pleaded with Mrs. Chadwick. If he didn't get some money immediately for the bank, public exposure was sure to follow to the detriment of all involved, he said. Mrs. Chadwick gave him $50,000 in checks of which only one for $15,000 was good, and it was held up at the bank it was drawn on. These bad checks were followed by two $25,000 checks. However, the next day a messenger from Cleveland told Beckwith to hold those until Cassie had funds to cover them. That notice never came.[35]

Herbert Newton was responsible to Williams for his notes, but so was Mrs. Chadwick because of her endorsement. According to Williams, Newton "seemed to think he was not liable." This prompted Williams to file a lien on Newton's property in Sussex County, Massachusetts. On November 12, Newton's attorneys retaliated by filing a legal action in New York to compel Mrs. Chadwick to reveal exactly what securities Iri Reynolds held in Cleveland and to prevent Reynolds or Wade Park from disposing of them.[36]

Within days the parties met to discuss their various demands at Holland House. Cassie; her newest lawyer, Judge J. W. Albaugh; Herbert Newton; and two of his lawyers began a marathon negotiating session to forestall a trial, which kept them talking from noon until midnight. Albaugh was another prominent Ohio attorney, this time from Canton, retained by Mrs. Chadwick. She had selected him for his involvement in the acquittal of Anna George, a married woman accused of killing a philandering in-law of President McKinley in 1899. Judge Albaugh had seen a $500,000 Carnegie note because Cassie had retained him to assist in obtaining a $300,000 loan in Canton, presumably to cover her indebtedness in Oberlin. On this day, the judge was ill and remained in Ohio, participating by telephone. In what was described as a "lively" session, Mrs. Chadwick informed Newton that the securities in

Reynolds's possession were already assigned to another lender as security for a $300,000 loan, and that lender demanded $800,000 to release them. Newton's attorneys declared this was a bluff. She also claimed that Dr. Chadwick had gone to Europe to sell the Scottish railway stock and would soon wire the proceeds. This was greeted with skepticism. One of Newton's attorneys told Mrs. Chadwick that the doctor's bad checks had been sent for collection to a Cleveland law firm, Carr, Stearns, which was, ironically, in the same Williamson office building as H. Clark Ford. Mrs. Chadwick became very agitated and declared such an action would ruin her. Newton demanded that Mrs. Chadwick assign all her securities to him, and she eventually agreed if the check collection in Cleveland was halted. Newton had his lawyers draw up the papers. Since Judge Albaugh was not present to review them, it was agreed that Mrs. Chadwick would arrange a meeting in two days to sign the papers. She failed to arrange a meeting.[37]

The following Monday, November 14, Newton's lawyers went to Cleveland to see Iri Reynolds and examine the securities. Reynolds refused their request and admitted that even he had not seen them. Instead, he gave the lawyers a list of what Mrs. Chadwick had told him was in the envelopes. Reynolds said that if Mrs. Chadwick would provide her notarized consent, he would not object to the envelopes being opened.[38]

In a last-ditch effort to avoid litigation, Newton's lawyers decided to pay one more visit to Cassie while in Cleveland. Threats in New York had failed. Flattery would be the strategy of the day. That attempt failed. Newton's attorneys came away with a paltry $50 in cash, which Cassie made a grand show of presenting them, barely enough to cover their actual expenses. Newton had a choice to make: he could continue negotiations that were going nowhere, or he could sue and hope the leverage of a lawsuit would work to his advantage.[39]

After rebuffing Newton's attorneys, Mrs. Chadwick departed Cleveland on Friday, November 18, with her personal maid and nurse for somewhere on the East Coast. Her departure raised concern in Newton's camp that she might flee to Europe to join Dr. Chadwick, whose precise whereabouts were likewise unknown. In Europe, she would be "beyond the reach of U.S. courts." Newton sent private detectives to search for his wayward debtor. Servants at the Chadwick home said it was not unusual for Mrs. Chadwick to take frequent trips. This was no assurance for nervous creditors.[40]

Cornered and pushed to the breaking point, Charles Beckwith tucked the $250,000 Carnegie note, endorsed by Mrs. Chadwick to him, in his pocket and boarded a train to New York. The Oberlin banker had every intention of raising

money on the note from some New York bank. Beckwith no longer believed
in Mrs. Chadwick, and deep inside he questioned the genuineness of the note
bearing Andrew Carnegie's signature. When he reached New York, Beckwith's
conscience restrained him. "My heart failed me, for something kept telling me
that all was not right," he later admitted. "I came back home without making
any attempt to raise money on the note." Passing a forged promissory note was
illegal and a state crime everywhere. Trapped in a web of deceit in a rapidly
deteriorating situation, Beckwith was still, at heart, an honorable man.[41]

CHAPTER FOURTEEN

ABSURD!

Herbert Newton had little recourse if he wanted his money. On Monday, November 21, Newton's lawyers filed a lawsuit in Cuyahoga County to recover the $190,800 he claimed Mrs. Chadwick owed him. Wade Park Banking and Iri Reynolds were named codefendants. The legal documents that supported Newton's lawsuit were described as "voluminous," although there were few truly factual documents attached. The court filing was kept off the official court docket initially—"held for service" in legal parlance—in an attempt to keep it secret as long as possible. Newton's attorneys held out hope for a quiet settlement, but they wanted some leverage. No doubt Newton preferred not to have it known that he was dealing with a woman who was proving to be cleverer than he was.[1]

That same day, Cassie Chadwick was in the Mahoning Valley, one of the few places in northeast Ohio where she had not tried to float a loan. It had been the home of Youngstowner Richard Brown, one of Madame Devere's Toledo victims. Brown had died in September 1903 and perhaps as a sign of her increasing desperation, Mrs. Chadwick went to Warren. After visiting two banks and a local attorney unsuccessfully seeking a $50,000 loan, she left town empty-handed.[2]

Unfortunately for Mr. Newton, the Cuyahoga County clerk of courts office was not a place where secrets were kept. Newton's legal action remained under wraps for all of twenty-four hours before one of those enterprising reporters who seemed to practically live at the courthouse sniffed it out. As would be expected of a woman with a seamy past, questionable ethics, and larceny in her heart, Cassie Chadwick avoided publicity. Imagine her chagrin when a creditor's lawsuit became front-page news in a penny daily newspaper like the *Cleveland Plain Dealer*. On Tuesday, November 22, 1904, two days before

Thanksgiving, the newspapers in Cleveland announced that a Brookline, Massachusetts, coal and coke wholesaler, Herbert B. Newton, had filed a lawsuit against a Euclid Avenue resident, Mrs. Cassie Chadwick, for defaulting on loans totaling $190,800.[3]

The financial affairs of the social class to which Cassie Chadwick aspired were rarely discussed in the newspapers, and the Newton lawsuit was extraordinary because of the amount of money involved and the sex of the defendant. Everyday Clevelanders, like all Americans, loved a story about upper-class financial scandal and skullduggery. Newspaper sales were brisk. The *Cleveland Press* was the city's largest daily, and its aggressive editor smelled a profitable story in Newton versus Chadwick. Whispered rumors of a dark past had swirled around Mrs. Chadwick for years. Newspaper reporters across the city fanned out to trace the woman's history in a repetition of the press frenzy that had surrounded Madame Devere in Toledo fourteen years ago. Soon facts about Mrs. Chadwick began to flow through their pencil points. Within a week, the story would be on the front page of the *New York Times*.[4]

Word of the suit reached Charles Beckwith in Oberlin on November 23, and he immediately went to Cleveland to see Mrs. Chadwick. "I do not care for myself," Beckwith told her. "It is not my fortune I am trying to retrieve now, but my honor." Why could she not give Beckwith the money owed the bank, he asked, so he could "put it where it belongs"? For her part, Mrs. Chadwick kept repeating, "I cannot pay now." Despite Beckwith's earnest pleading, Cassie was unmoved and promised, once again, that all her obligations would be met. Beckwith realized that all was lost.[5]

Earlier in the year, Mrs. Chadwick had given Iri Reynolds a sealed package of securities as collateral for a $12,000 loan from Wade Park Banking. Reynolds was to hold this package, as he did the other, in trust for her. According to Cassie, the package contained $200,000 in US Steel bonds and a $250,000 certificate. Since Newton's lawsuit sought an injunction to keep Wade Park from disposing of the Chadwick securities, the bank's officials believed they were justified in opening this package. As several bankers held their collective breath, the envelopes were opened. There were bonds and certificates inside—five $1,000 bonds of the Home Telegraph Company of Niagara, New York, and six certificates of the Buckeye Fish Company. The Wade Park men looked at each other and quietly took a vow of silence. Reynolds called the discovery of this Chadwick deception "a little banking secret."[6]

Thus far in 1904, Newton had received a mere $350 cash from the Chadwicks on the debt. "I am not alone concerned in this matter," Newton told reporters of his status as an unpaid Chadwick creditor because he discovered that Mrs. Chadwick was "largely indebted to many persons" whom he declined to name. Newton, like Youngstown industrialist Richard Brown, was proving that he was a man not to be crossed. His Boston attorney was Percy Carver, whose law firm's motto said something about the lawyer's approach to legal disputes: "Fight to the limit and never say die until you are dead." Carver explained to the press why his client had loaned to Mrs. Chadwick. "Mr. Newton alleges that as an inducement for him to loan Mrs. Chadwick $190,800, Mrs. Chadwick showed him a note for $500,000 which was signed by a man whom Newton believed to be fully responsible." Carver refused to name the man publicly but said he would not contradict the idea that it was Andrew Carnegie. While Newton played the wounded party, he could only produce proof that he loaned $90,800. The additional $100,000 was comprised of unpaid bonuses, interest, and wishful thinking.[7]

Newton had lawyers and private detectives investigating Cassie Chadwick in Cleveland and New York. "I made the loans on the strength of a statement of Mrs. Chadwick that she was a woman of wealth and owned securities sufficient to warrant the loans," Newton told the press. "We propose to find out whether her assertions were true." Hinting that he knew more than he was telling about the woman, Newton warned, "There may be some interesting facts made public a little later."[8]

Mrs. Chadwick was back in New York after Thanksgiving, and reporters from New York's highly competitive press located her. Cassie was forty-seven years old in 1904, but she looked ten years older. This would be the New Yorkers' first hard look at the woman. The newsmen were impressed by her large, soft, "superb" brown eyes and her "wonderful" complexion for a woman of fifty. Her hands, they suggested, were "well shaped" and "naturally delicate." They were less kind about her voice, describing it as possessing the "rasping tones of plebian origin." As for her speech, the New Yorkers complained of a "disregard for the easiest principles of grammar." There was no mention of a lisp. Clevelanders rounded out the description. While past her physical prime, mentally she was described by one Cleveland attorney as "clever beyond a doubt" with a droll, self-deprecating humor. Cleveland acquaintances told reporters that she was reserved, but with an air of power. They described her as tall for a woman of her time—she was five foot seven—with traces of her earlier beauty visible and a well-preserved figure. Cassie was known for wearing fashionable, well-fitting, and exquisite clothes. It was common knowledge that she was almost deaf, especially when it suited her.[9]

Women of the Victorian era were not expected to have any financial knowledge. The men in their lives were expected to handle their finances, or an agent was engaged for that purpose. That a woman would directly participate in transactions totaling nearly $200,000—about $5 million today—was extraordinary. If the average American could name any woman capable of transactions of that magnitude, it would be New York's Hetty Green. The independent Mrs. Green was as well known for her parsimony as her conservative investment strategy, which required patience—the opposite of Cassie Chadwick.

Newsmen searching the Cuyahoga County courthouse records uncovered three additional lawsuits for overdue loans. The receiver for the defunct Euclid Avenue Savings and Trust Company, F. H. Ginn, was suing for $38,231.32, while the American Exchange Bank was demanding $28,808.25. Also, the Savings Deposit Bank and Trust of Elyria claimed that, of the $44,500 Mrs. Chadwick had borrowed, a $10,000 loan was past due. Only the Elyria bank had solid collateral in the form of a mortgage on the Chadwick house and personal property. The extensive inventory list of personal property attached to the mortgage by the bank indicated that Cassie had even mortgaged her bed sheets.[10]

Newton's $10,000 note held by Citizen's National Bank was disclosed to the press on November 23. It was reported in the Cleveland papers, and depositors in Oberlin became alarmed as rumors spread that the bank held more notes related to Mrs. Chadwick. The bank was open Saturday evening, November 26, as usual from 6:00 to 8:00 P.M. to receive deposits from businesses and workers. The finance industry in Victorian America was plagued by bank failures, and depositors were forever on a hair trigger to pull their money from any bank at any hint of trouble. Andrew Carnegie had labeled the US banking system "the worst in the civilized world," which was a stinging indictment from one of the wealthiest men in America. Nervous depositors flocked to Citizen's National to withdraw their money, a classic bank run that was every banker, bank director, and bank stockholder's worst nightmare. To make matters worse, an unsubstantiated rumor that bank insiders had forewarned friends and family to pull their deposits spread like wildfire. The bank had only $12,000 cash on hand, and this was quickly depleted. Citizen's accounts at its Cleveland repositories were uncharacteristically empty, so efficient had been Mrs. Chadwick's pillaging. Prospects for obtaining more cash quickly were slim. After almost fifty years, Citizen's National Bank closed its doors. At a hasty meeting late Saturday with the board of directors, Charles Beckwith admitted loaning Mrs. Chadwick in excess of $240,000 of the bank's money—four times the amount of the bank's capital stock and forty times the allowed limit of $6,000. The bank loans—rolled over, consolidated, and renegotiated—were due January 1, 1905. Beckwith had also loaned Mrs. Chadwick $102,000 of his own funds. Without an immediate infusion of cash, Citizen's National appeared doomed.[11]

On Sunday, a national bank examiner, L. L. Miller, arrived and huddled with Beckwith, Spear, and the directors. Miller quickly determined that the bank was insolvent. Sunday evening, November 27, the directors voted to close the bank. After facing the examiner and the directors, Beckwith admitted to reporters, "Yes, I did loan Mrs. Chadwick money. But why not? She is an honest woman and I know I will get my money back." Beckwith publicly downplayed the $240,000 in bank loans made to Mrs. Chadwick, commenting, "It will not reach quite that amount." The loans were backed by two notes signed by one of the wealthiest men in America, he said. Beckwith denied it was Andrew Carnegie. "All her troubles have been brought on by her foolish business methods," Beckwith said. "I have known all about her transactions for years." The banker had also personally borrowed $102,000, which he loaned to the woman. To cover these loans, he had quietly sold property he had in Oberlin, including lucrative holdings that included the $13,000 village post office and stock he held in electric and gas utilities in town. Beckwith sounded confident that his loans would be repaid soon. "Personally, I have no fear," he told newsmen. It was a good show on Beckwith's part, but driven by greed and under the spell of a persuasive woman, he had allowed himself to be swindled. Deep in his heart, he knew it too. After this interview, Beckwith took to his bed, ill.[12]

Monday morning, November 28, Oberlin residents crowded the sidewalk to read the notice posted on the bank's door indicating that the bank was in the hands of the examiners and would remain closed indefinitely. Even more startling were the press reports of Beckwith's admission that Citizen's National had made enormous loans to Cassie Chadwick. Unless one of her agents—the most often cited white knight was Canton attorney J. W. Albaugh—arrived immediately with $300,000 to cover the loans, all would be lost, Beckwith said. Bank vice president M. M. Squire, who owned $10,000 in stock, also added to the sense of doom. "It is only a hope that we will secure assistance from New York," he told the press. Stockholders of national banks in 1904 were personally responsible for any bank losses that exceeded 10 percent of capitalization, $6,000 in Oberlin's case. All the directors were stockholders. Squire, stone-faced, said, "The amount is so vast that it could not possibly be shouldered by the directors."[13]

Citizen's National Bank was "hanging by a thread," one of its directors, J. F. Randolph, admitted. Another director, Mayor O. F. Carter, who, like Randolph, had known of the Chadwick loans since early fall, tried to spin the examiner's appraisal, saying in all sincerity, "The bank is in splendid condition save for a heavy overloan on the paper of Mrs. Chadwick." Squire told the press that the loans were made by Beckwith and cashier Spear without consultation with the bank's directors. The directors had been led to believe that all the Chadwick paper held by the bank was that single Herbert Newton note for $10,000. Only recently had Beckwith come clean with his board. "It is asserted by the president of the bank," Squire told reporters, "that he had two notes in the bank as security for a loan made to Mrs. Chadwick, one for $500,000 and the other for $250,000, which we supposed were gilt-edged."[14]

To protect the economy in Oberlin, the town's two remaining banks received an infusion of $60,000 in cash from Cleveland to prop them up should they experience a run by their depositors.[15]

That Monday as the depositors read the terrible news about the bank, Beckwith lay in his bed, exhausted from nervous tension. In addition to the bank's failure, Beckwith faced a personal financial crisis. He had loaned most of his personal fortune to Mrs. Chadwick and was a bank stockholder. That evening he was physically unable to make his final report to the directors in person, instead giving it over the telephone to Frank Carter, Oberlin's mayor, who relayed it to his fellow directors. When the brief conversation concluded, the banker quietly said "good-bye." Mayor Carter observed, "Somehow it seems to me that his good-bye was significant."[16]

Bank director and businessman L. T. Whitney was perhaps the largest single depositor. His son, C. K. Whitney, was a township official responsible for $2,700 in township funds deposited in the bank. The elder Whitney told the *Cleveland Plain Dealer* that the loans to Mrs. Chadwick were made without consulting with the board. Instead, Whitney said, the loans were "purposely concealed." He concluded with emotion, "This matter is awful."[17]

Tuesday morning, November 29, a *Cleveland Plain Dealer* reporter found Beckwith seated in an armchair in his parlor. His face was ashen, and he was barely in control of himself. Beckwith sent mixed signals regarding Citizen's National's future but tried to be optimistic. "I believe the indebtedness to the bank will be paid shortly, possibly tomorrow," he told the reporter. But if not, "then the real break will come." Did he have two gilt-edged personal promissory notes as collateral as rumored, the newsman wanted to know and, if so, who had signed them? "That will never be known, not from me," Beckwith defiantly declared. Admitting that others had seen the notes, Beckwith stuck resolutely with his banker's code: "They may tell, but I, never. I am bound by an oath that I cannot break!" Beckwith accepted the responsibility for his bank's failure: "It is all my fault anyhow. I simply made an overloan." He concluded by reserving some of the blame for New Englander Herbert Newton, whose very public lawsuit had destroyed any chance of a negotiated settlement with Mrs. Chadwick. "If it had not been for Newton of Boston suing for his claim, this would not have been made public."[18]

Reporters located cashier Arthur Spear in the village. He refused to comment, except to say that he was under the "strictest kind of orders" to say nothing until the examiner had concluded his work. "And I intend to obey the orders," Spear emphatically told the press.[19]

The *Cleveland Plain Dealer*'s reporter, Ben Allen, was in Oberlin and observed that "the grief of many depositors of the bank was distressing." One old hack driver, Charles Mason, who charged twenty-five cents a fare, had managed to save $3,000 for retirement over decades of work. This nest egg had been on deposit in Beckwith's bank. College students were some of the most severely affected. Many of them had every cent saved for their education in Citizen's National, Allen wrote. When the news of the bank's closure reached them, many, in Allen's words, tearfully asked their professors, "What in the world shall we do?"[20]

Newsman located numerous members of the Cleveland financial community who had seen the $500,000 note and were willing to talk about it. All agreed the note bore the purported signature of Andrew Carnegie. J. F. Randolph, one of Citizen's National's directors who had seen one of the notes, dismissed Mrs. Chadwick's collateral, saying, "I do not think the notes [are] worth anything now." Some bankers also claimed that Mrs. Chadwick had shown them papers indicating she had $5 million worth of US Steel bonds and Caledonian Railway of Scotland stock, which she offered as collateral for her loans.[21]

From his home in New York City, Andrew Carnegie issued a one-word response to the idea that the promissory notes were signed by him: "Absurd!" His private secretary informed reporters that his employer "will not discuss the matter." But Carnegie did give his secretary a written statement to read. "Mr. Carnegie has never met Mrs. Chadwick to his knowledge and does not know her. He has for a number of years made a practice of never giving his signature to notes of any description. He is certain it is not on these notes."[22]

One banker who was familiar with Mrs. Chadwick commented on the "preposterous" idea that Andrew Carnegie would give any woman a promissory note. "Well, it does sound ridiculous to say that Carnegie would give anyone, much less a woman," the banker said, "a note . . . but it beat the deuce where this woman gets her securities from. Why, she once had in a safe deposit box in my bank $20,000 worth of United States steel securities, and she told me they came from the richest man in Pittsburgh." Carnegie was living in New York by then, but James Friend was in Pittsburgh.[23]

Where was Mrs. Chadwick, the press wanted to know. Had she fled to Europe, beyond the easy reach of US courts? Actually, she wasn't hiding at all; she was at her favorite New York haunt, Holland House. She sent a reassuring telegram to the *Cleveland Plain Dealer*. "Please deny report that I am going to Europe. Will return to Cleveland and settle all claims in a few days." On the evening of November 29, Holland House was thrown into confusion when police arrived on a tip that Mrs. Chadwick had committed suicide. Hotel staff scurried throughout the building before management pronounced the rumor false. Reporters were told the next day, November 30, that Mrs. Chadwick had left for Cleveland and the *Cleveland Plain Dealer* received a telegram from Cassie Chadwick that read: "Please deny reported suicide. Nothing in my affairs would warrant anything rash."[24]

During the morning of November 30, a "richly gowned" woman appeared at Holland House's front desk, asking for Mrs. Chadwick. Informed that Cassie was out, the woman turned to leave when a reporter hanging around the lobby asked her business. The woman, who would only identify herself as "Mrs. Smith" because "I do not wish to be dragged into this case," said that she was a friend of Mrs. Chadwick for many years and wished to offer her support. Mrs. Smith said she knew that Mrs. Chadwick was not Madame Devere and that she was "amply able to meet all her financial obligations." Then Mrs. Smith offered a new explanation for Mrs. Chadwick's woes. "She is being persecuted by a prominent Republican office holder in Ohio," the woman stated. "Mrs. Chadwick," Mrs. Smith asserted, "would vindicate herself absolutely when the proper time comes." The woman departed, saying no more, and this accusation of persecution died with her departure.[25]

Phillip Carpenter, a former assistant district attorney and Edmund Powers's law partner, was one of Cassie's New York attorneys. She had met Carpenter when she retained him to secure a $200,000 loan. Carpenter was unsuccessful. Speaking to reporters, he assured them that Mrs. Chadwick was "a woman of the highest sense of honor and her dealings which came under my observation were all open and above board. I believe her to be an honest woman."[26]

Newton's lawyers, despite all of Mrs. Chadwick's hollow promises, were optimistic that the matter could be settled amiably. After more negotiations at Holland House on November 30, George Ryall, Newton's counsel in New York, continued posturing by issuing a statement proclaiming that Mrs. Chadwick would pay the full $190,800 in cash. The woman's attorney, Powers, agreed that a settlement was in the offing. However, Mrs. Chadwick would pay $78,000 at once and $50,000 when the remaining notes fell due at the end of the 1904. Commissions and bonuses remained in dispute. Although negotiations continued, Herbert Newton was realistic and privately he admitted he would be lucky just to get his principal back. Even that was a faint hope.[27]

Newton's lawyer, Ryall, sounded a note of optimism the evening of December 1. Mrs. Chadwick left Holland House before lunch and went to the Central Trust Company on Wall Street. A bank officer took her upstairs to the sixth-floor law offices of Butler, Notman, Joline, and Mynderse, who represented both Andrew Carnegie and James Friend. A four-hour conference took place over lunch. A bold hound dog of a reporter walked straight into the law office. In the conference room, the scribe believed he saw Mrs. Chadwick talking with two unidentified men in front of a paper-strewn table. The newsman also noticed an unknown middle-aged woman seated at the table. On a leather couch against the wall was a second woman, dressed in black with her face buried in a pillow, sobbing. In the next office was Mr. Joline, Carnegie's attorney. What was happening in the conference room, the newsman wanted to know. Joline denied any connection to Mrs. Chadwick and any knowledge of the conference next door as he showed the reporter out. The women in the conference room were a mystery, identified in the papers as possibly some influential friends of Mrs. Chadwick. It was later determined that Cassie was actually in the law office meeting with James Friend and not receiving cash from Andrew Carnegie.[28]

During the meeting at Butler, Notman, James Friend couldn't resist taking a swipe at his old business partner, Andrew Carnegie. "I know that this woman is the daughter of Andrew Carnegie," he told Cleveland attorney Andrew Squire, representing some of the Pittsburgh creditors, in Cassie's presence. "He [Carnegie] has told me so himself." Carnegie, naturally, wished to keep this fact a secret, Friend confided to Squire. To convince him, Friend covered the lower half of Mrs. Chadwick's face with his hand and asked, "Whom do you see here?" The attorney answered honestly, "Mrs. Chadwick."

Friend exclaimed, "I see Andrew Carnegie!" Squire found this neither funny nor convincing and was unmoved.[29]

Attorney Ryall told reporters a day later that a New York society woman of power and influence would provide money for a settlement with Herbert Newton. The woman's name, he said, would be familiar to newspaper readers and her fortune was multigenerational. According to Ryall, the woman met Mrs. Chadwick while traveling. This mystery lady had been short of cash, and Cassie gave her some money. As a result, the New York woman told Mrs. Chadwick that if she ever needed help, she could count on her assistance. Ryall said that this unidentified woman would give him cash to pay the full $190,800, which he would pass on to Newton. Pressed by reporters, Ryall said, "I cannot reveal the identity of Mrs. Chadwick's friend." Not even Newton would know who paid the debt. The newspapers widely reported this story and speculated that Mrs. Chadwick's rescuer was one of the women in the conference room seen by the nosy reporter.[30]

Another potential savior for Mrs. Chadwick was purported to be the estate of a wealthy Pittsburgher, Mary Elizabeth Schenley. The *Cleveland Plain Dealer* reported a rumor that the late Mrs. Schenley had done business with Cassie and had some of her notes stored in a New York bank vault. The trustees of Mrs. Schenley's estate were adamant that they held no securities or notes relating to Mrs. Chadwick.[31]

Back in Ohio, Canton attorney J. W. Albaugh was rumored to have secured a $300,000 loan for Mrs. Chadwick and would deliver the money to Oberlin any day to save Citizen's National. A couple days into December, he quashed the rumors. "I have no securities to take to the Oberlin bank," he told reporters. "The people of Oberlin, if expecting me there, jumped to conclusions." Albaugh acknowledged several telegrams from Mrs. Chadwick but declined to give details. He said he was no longer under retainer to Mrs. Chadwick and distanced himself from the Oberlin mess: "I am busy in court with other matters." That Albaugh no longer felt obligated to assist Mrs. Chadwick might have had something to do with a $5,000 retainer or fee that he never received.[32]

In Cleveland, the fact that the Chadwick saga involved Wade Park Banking was not lost on its depositors. When the Newton lawsuit made headlines, more than a few Clevelanders with deposits in Wade Park made withdrawals. This activity did not rise to the level of a bank run like Citizen's National experienced, but it was worrisome for its management and directors. Wade Park was a fairly strong small bank with $1.5 million in deposits and $1.8 million in total assets. However, its directors decided to invoke the so-called "sixty-day rule" on November 29. Depositors wishing to withdraw funds would have to make a request in writing and then wait sixty days to receive their money. Bank customers were assured that despite Iri Reynolds's involvement with Mrs. Chadwick, the bank had only a single $12,000 loan outstanding to her for which it held "the best of collateral," which was, in fact, her thirty-odd shares of the bank's stock. Lastly, to reassure its customers, the directors decided to employ an independent accounting firm to examine the condition of the bank. All these measures were meant to convey the impression to the community of a sound bank.[33]

Any suspicion that a bank had Chadwick loans outstanding could be devastating. Two weeks after the Oberlin bank closed, the First National Bank of Conneaut, located on the Lake Erie shore, was shuttered. A rumor had spread through Conneaut that First National held some of Mrs. Chadwick's notes. It was eventually determined that this was untrue, but this was not before panicked depositors had jammed the lobby, attempting to withdraw their funds. An infusion of cash proved insufficient, and the bank closed. Too late, it was discovered by examiners that skullduggery by some of the bank's officers had been the real catalyst for First National's demise—no assistance from Mrs. Chadwick had been required.[34]

Herbert B. Newton's lawsuit against Cassie Chadwick understandably unnerved her creditors. George Couch, a Cleveland livery operator, filed a legal action against Cassie, who owed him $215.50 for carriage hires dating back to July. But the spark that initiated the collapse of the Chadwick house of cards came not from a creditor to whom she owed tens of thousands of dollars but from one owed just $600. James Krakauer, a New York City linen merchant on Fifth Avenue, instructed his Cleveland attorneys to investigate Cassie's finances based on rumors circulating in New York. "Mrs. Chadwick has an account with us and has always been prompt in settlement . . . when her present difficulties became known I followed the usual business custom of having my attorneys in Cleveland look out for my interests," explained Krakauer. Based on Mrs. Chadwick's missed mortgage payments to an Elyria bank in July, Krakauer's attorney, Louis Grossman, decided to file a petition of involuntary bankruptcy in Federal Court in Cleveland on December 2, 1904. Bankruptcy laws in 1904 permitted unpaid creditors to force a borrower into bankruptcy to collect. The Chadwicks had dodged this bullet back 1903, when they failed to repay the loan from James Chadwick. Krakauer's action was joined by a New York City liveryman and another city merchant whose claims totaled just $1,100. Krakauer didn't wish to appear hard-nosed and told newsmen that he had not instructed his attorneys in Cleveland to force Mrs. Chadwick into bankruptcy. "I believe she has plenty of money," he told the press. If Krakauer had not wanted the petition, why had his attorney, Grossman, been so quick to file one?[35]

Before the close of business on December 2, the Federal Bankruptcy Court in Cleveland had appointed a receiver, Nathan Loeser, who was granted dictatorial control over all of Dr. and Mrs. Chadwick's property. Loeser, thirty-five, was a Cleveland attorney who, not by coincidence, happened to be associated with Louis Grossman. Loeser posted his required $10,000 bond and got down to business. As the New York Times explained it, "The adjudication under bankruptcy law of Mrs. Chadwick's affairs will mean their full closing up. It will force a settlement and a complete estoppel of further operations by Mrs. Chadwick and involve a complete investigation, exposure, and final distribution of her property among various creditors."[36]

The Bankruptcy Court referee was Harold Remington, a position akin to a judge in a criminal court. He explained to the press that the bankruptcy petition was meant to protect small creditors from large ones and ensure an equitable settlement for all creditors. If the large creditors did not press for a quick settlement, little would happen in the near term, he said. Remington stressed that this bankruptcy action did not preclude a settlement between Mrs. Chadwick and Herbert Newton.[37]

On December 4, six of Citizen's National's directors met in Mayor Carter's office to review their options and, in the words of one, "to brace each other up." If the stockholders were forced to cover the losses, it could be devastating to the village. "To Oberlin this will mean a solid year of night with no ray of light anywhere breaking the gloom," was the assessment of one director. The directors were free to meet, but the US Treasury was now in control of the bank. The federal bank examiner bluntly told the directors as much: "Gentlemen, this matter is now in the hands of the government. Until we get through, you can do nothing." Cashier Arthur Spear was cooperating with the examiner, trying to make sense of the bank's ledgers. He knew more than anyone about those ledgers, but he refused to talk to reporters. "I have sealed my lips and no one can pry them open." Spear's wife had suffered a nervous breakdown and was now with her parents in Pennsylvania.[38]

Citizen's National was the depository for village and township funds totaling $28,000. Jud Stone, village treasurer, and C. K. Whitney, township treasurer, would be held personally responsible for those public funds. They clung to the forlorn hope that their representative in the Ohio legislature could push through a special relief bill and have the state make them whole again. This was unlikely because Ohio's political leaders took a dim view of this kind of bailout.[39]

The New York press had all of Cassie Chadwick's known haunts under scrutiny. When it was discovered that Coleman Carnegie had attempted to see Mrs. Chadwick at Holland House, a new round of Carnegie speculation was ignited. The twenty-four-year-old Carnegie was the son of Andrew's deceased brother, Tom, and was said to be the ironmaster's favorite nephew, having been instructed by Andrew himself to become laird of his Scotland estate. Coleman's mother was Lucy Coleman Carnegie, heir to a sizable fortune in her own right as the daughter of William Coleman, a wealthy former Pittsburgh neighbor of Andrew Carnegie. Coleman Carnegie was an avid outdoorsman with a $125,000 annual allowance that enabled him to pursue hunting and fishing full time. Lucy Carnegie was active in the New York Yacht Club, and her son kept a bachelor apartment in the city not far from Holland House. The reason for Coleman Carnegie's desire to meet with Cassie Chadwick was never determined. After a 1905 auto accident in which Coleman refused to pay $3,000 in damages, he disappeared from public view. He died of pneumonia in 1911. His appearance, however brief, in the Chadwick saga would remain a matter of speculation and an enduring mystery.[40]

No one suggested that Coleman Carnegie was at Holland House to pay off his uncle's notes. The *New York Times* calculated that Carnegie's name had been forged to $16 million's worth of bogus paper. In addition to using that paper as collateral for loans, the *Times* suggested that "she banked all on the death of Carnegie, hoping to stay matters by continually borrowing until the steel king had died, when she hoped to prove the notes and papers genuine." What if Carnegie, sixty-nine, had died suddenly? The holders of the forged Carnegie notes would demand payment. The ironmaster's estate might quietly pay up to avoid any stain on Carnegie's good name. This was not an implausible scenario and was one worthy of consideration. Cassie remained silent on the subject.[41]

CHAPTER FIFTEEN

A Most Unpleasant Duty

As the directors of Citizen's National contemplated a dark financial future, the long arm of the law was reaching out for Charles Beckwith and Arthur Spear. An afternoon meeting on December 4 of federal bank examiners and Treasury agents in the office of US district attorney John J. Sullivan in Cleveland's federal building concluded at 8:00 P.M. with the issue of arrest warrants for the Oberlin bankers. US marshal Frank Chandler, a deputy marshal, and a contingent of newsmen immediately left on a train for Oberlin, arriving at 11:00 P.M. After meeting the town marshal, the lawmen proceeded to a home on East Lorain Street, where Spear was staying with a friend. He surrendered peacefully and was, according to the *Cleveland Plain Dealer*, "very cool when arrested." Chandler offered the cashier a choice of confinements: a hotel room shared with the marshal or the village jail. Spear replied, "I'd a good deal rather go with you to the hotel than go to the lockup."[1]

From East Lorain, the marshals proceeded to Beckwith's North Pleasant Street home, arriving at midnight just as the village lights went dark. With some effort, the lawmen succeeded in rousing Beckwith's daughter-in-law from among the sleeping household. They demanded to see the aged banker, but she refused until they identified themselves as US marshals. Upon entering, Mrs. Beckwith, previously her husband's source of strength, collapsed in tears. Charles Beckwith wasn't in much better control of himself. Weak, drawn, and appearing to have aged ten years in a week, he had been bedridden much of the time since the crisis broke. Crushed by the prospect of arrest, Beckwith was in no condition to leave his home that night. He remained there, guarded by the deputy marshal.[2]

The following morning, reporters found Marshal Chandler and Spear calmly eating breakfast in the hotel. Beckwith arrived after a tearful parting from his wife and was too distraught to eat. Beckwith and Spear talked quietly for half an hour as a crowd gathered. Finally, the marshals and their prisoners boarded a train for Cleveland, where they would be arraigned. Spear read a newspaper, occasionally speaking to Beckwith, who seemed completely befuddled. Arriving in Cleveland, Beckwith was met at the station by his son, Charles. Once in Federal Court, the judge explained what was transpiring. The two bankers were charged on warrants initiated by Citizen's National's federally appointed receiver, Robert Lyons, with violating the federal banking statutes pertaining to the certification of checks. Specifically, Beckwith for certifying a $15,000 Chadwick check, dated October 12, 1904, and Spear for certifying one for $12,500, dated August 24, 1903. Both men, it was alleged, knew Mrs. Chadwick had insufficient funds to her credit to cover the checks. Each man could face up to $5,000 in fines and five years in prison.[3]

Beckwith asked prosecutor Sullivan if there would be more charges forthcoming, and the answer was yes. The bank president was also ordered to produce the Carnegie notes. One was in the bank, and a director's son, C. K. Whitney, had the other. The two notes had been assigned by Mrs. Chadwick to the bankers. The notes would be important evidence in any criminal proceeding. A note similar to the $500,000 one that Whitney held had been used to convince Newton to loan Mrs. Chadwick money. Its whereabouts was unknown.[4]

Bail for both bankers was set at $10,000. Spear, in anticipation, had already made bail arrangements. According to the Cleveland Plain Dealer, Spear had also begun collecting photographs of himself from friends in Oberlin several weeks ago, and now the press could find none. Poor Beckwith had to wait until evening in the prosecutor's office in the federal building for his bail to arrive. He confessed to curious newsmen while waiting: "I am either an awful dupe or terrible fool. . . . I do not propose to be made a scapegoat to shield the sins of others . . . one of those whose answer must be had is Mrs. Cassie L. Chadwick." The distraught Beckwith described his dealings with Mrs. Chadwick as a "tale of transactions and torture covering a period of over a year." The banker's bond was finally posted by three wealthy Cleveland businessmen.[5]

Both men returned to Oberlin. Spear was said to be in good spirits. Pressed by reporters, Spear said, "I have nothing to say. . . . Newspaper correspondents are a terror to me, and I desire no further conversation." At the Beckwith home, Mrs. Beckwith answered a newsman's knock at the door. The brave old woman stated emphatically, "We have been hounded to death by newspaper correspondents who have grossly misrepresented things," and slammed the door. That evening, in downtown Oberlin, a hopeful crowd gathered outside the padlocked bank in response to an unfounded report that the vault, possibly containing some forgotten cash, was to be blown open at midnight. Midnight came and went in silence.[6]

Optimism rose in Oberlin when former Citizen's National assistant cashier Harry Avery said he believed the Chadwick notes would be settled. It turned to pessimism when out-of-town speculators descended like vultures on Oberlin, offering forty cents on the dollar to Citizen's National depositors. There were few takers. Village residents were asking how much of a bonus Cassie Chadwick paid Spear and Beckwith for the loans. A close friend of Spear suggested that the pair received about $50,000. It was merely a guess. No one really knew.[7]

As the drama in Oberlin proceeded, Cassie Chadwick quietly returned to New York. Before she departed, she induced Wade Park Banking to cash a $300 check. The check was later returned from New York with the notation "account closed." The ever-loyal Iri Reynolds replaced her check with his own. It was money he would never see again.[8]

While Beckwith and Spear faced the bleak prospect of prison, Cassie Chadwick was resting comfortably in her luxury suite at New York's Holland House, tended by her personal Swedish nurse and French maid. The hotel was located on Fifth Avenue at 30th Street. When it opened in 1891, the eleven-story, 350-room Holland House was New York's most luxurious hotel. The walls of the main lobby were Sienna marble, and the main staircase was carved marble with a silver ceiling. The café featured electric lights in crystal globes hanging from silver chandeliers above every table. The *New York Times* in 1891 praised the hotel as "beautifully furnished and decorated." A staff of 180, attired in simple dark-blue uniforms, attended to guests. In 1893, Holland House was eclipsed by the Waldorf-Astoria, but it remained one of the city's best hotels. It was a prestigious lodging and home to many moneyed New Yorkers. The hotel suited Mrs. Chadwick.[9]

New York reporters asked the woman to comment on the failure of Citizen's National. "It was a dreadful shock to me," she claimed. "Every dollar of that money shall be paid depositors." One of her attorneys in New York, Edmund Powers, said the bank's failure was not Cassie's fault. National banks do not fail if managed strictly in accordance with national banking laws, he snorted. The officials of the bank were responsible, not his client, Powers insisted, who merely borrowed from the institution and could not be expected to know the details of banking regulations. Powers had a point.[10]

Mrs. Chadwick was not acting in the least like a woman the papers speculated might be bankrupt. Instead of being embarrassed, she was full of fight.

In briefly discussing the Newton matter, she was, the *Cleveland Plain Dealer* noted, "very cool, entirely self-possessed." Her comments regarding Newton's suit were offered in a "somewhat desultory manner." She was confident, telling newsmen, "I expect everything to be adjusted within the course of the next few days, but I cannot say the matter will not go to the courts." Regarding the lawsuit by the receivers of the defunct Euclid Avenue Savings and Trust Company with which she had "many mutual business dealings," Mrs. Chadwick said she owed it nothing because the bank's accounting was incorrect. Additionally, she claimed she held the $50,000 personal note of an unnamed official of the defunct bank that would cover any debt.[11]

A frenzied press in Cleveland and New York was hounding Mrs. Chadwick, but she was not giving reporters much. She told a *Cleveland Press* reporter that her lawyers advised her not to talk to reporters because women, her attorneys advised, talk too much. *Cleveland Press*'s man sarcastically responded that her lawyer needn't worry. Unhappy with her press coverage, Cassie sent a telegram to the *Cleveland Plain Dealer,* declaring its reporting to be "wickedly false," and threatened to sue. She instructed one of her New York lawyers, Phillip Carpenter, Powers's law partner, to issue a written statement complaining that she was plagued by inaccurate press reports and denying any association with Andrew Carnegie. Furthermore, Cassie denied any connection to Madame Devere, any clairvoyant powers, and any previous criminal convictions. Exhausted, Mrs. Chadwick retreated to her often-employed claim of illness. She promised that once she had recovered, she would provide a full outline of her career.[12]

In contrast to his wife's visibility, Dr. Chadwick was practically hiding in Paris. A Cincinnati businessman and acquaintance told reporters that the doctor lived luxuriously in France. Chadwick spent much of his time at the Paris branch of the YMCA, according to the businessman, reading the latest American newspapers and impatiently awaiting the daily arrival of the mail from America. Dr. Chadwick never explained his interest in the mail.[13]

Mrs. Chadwick was now the center of a financial scandal that stretched from the shores of Lake Erie to Boston. How she could have borrowed so much on so little from normally cautious lenders was a source of amazement to bankers everywhere. The *Cleveland Press* suggested to its readers that "The mere fact of a woman being able to borrow such money is in itself interesting and unusual. When it is known that she borrowed the money vast sums, on personal notes giving no security but her promise to pay, the case becomes extraordinary and unprecedented in the history of local finance."[14]

The unpleasant specter of Madame Devere haunted Cassie at every turn. It was only a matter of days after the Newton lawsuit was filed before she was accused of being the Toledo swindler. Joe Lamb's defense attorney, Irving Belford, now clerk of the Federal Court in Cleveland, was free with his opinions to reporters. Belford called Madame Devere a woman who "will be remembered by men who wish to forget," and said he personally found her "fascinating to the degree that she caused men to lose their heads."[15]

Because of Mrs. Chadwick's possible connection to Madame Devere, there was speculation that hypnosis was the basis for Cassie's power. It had proven to be a successful defense for Joe Lamb. Charles Beckwith issued an indignant denial. "I am 65 years old, and have been in this business since I was 18. I know people pretty well, and I tell you this woman has not hypnotized me." One of Newton's attorneys had this to say about hypnotic influence: "You may call it what you will. The loan was made [by Newton] and there was no security given. Personally I do not know of hypnotic force." A. B. Taylor, cashier of the Lorain County Banking Company, met Cassie in Cleveland in 1903. Her subsequent pleading for a loan led Taylor to suggest, "I can readily imagine that she might have hypnotic influence on some people." Tom Porter, a former deputy hired to guard the Chadwick home, had known Mrs. Chadwick for some time. He toyed with the reporters, saying of Mrs. Chadwick, "I'll tell you I can't understand those eyes . . . I began to blink and blink under the piercing gaze . . . I grew dizzy from the effect." On November 30 the *Cleveland Plain Dealer* poked fun at the hypnosis theory by printing a large cartoon on the front page titled, "Svengali Up to Date." Plump, well-dressed, goggle-eyed bankers with gold watch chains were depicted in a trance, throwing money at Mrs. Chadwick while she, with outstretched arms, cast a spell upon them. For the newspapers, Cassie Chadwick was proving to be great copy.[16]

The hypnosis theory didn't last. A journalist, Jay Ford Laning, nicknamed Mrs. Chadwick the "Queen of Finance" and shared his thoughts on her methods. "At the outset, it was intimated that it might have been hypnotic influences that made her successful," Laning wrote. "She did not use occult powers to win moneyed men. . . . She simply flashed collateral that made even the big banker dizzy and paid such large interest, and in many instances such handsome bonuses, that the men who handle money to make money did not resist the flattering propositions."[17]

Despite his present difficulty with the Chadwicks, Herbert Newton told reporters he did not blame Rev. Charles Eaton or his cousin, John. "I believe that both Eatons acted in perfect good faith in the introduction [of Mrs. Chadwick] and their confidences were abused."[18]

When the story broke, Reverend Eaton was preaching in Louisville. Lest he be tainted by the blossoming affair and press innuendo, he sought to explain his role. He stated that Mrs. Chadwick had no connection to his church, and that he had recommended she place her affairs in the hands of one of the reputable agents on a list he provided her. Beyond that, Reverend Eaton said he knew only what he had read in the papers. Once back in Cleveland, Eaton took to his bed, claiming fatigue, but mainly it was to avoid the aggressive newsmen. Eaton's statement touched a nerve with Newton. "I don't see why," Newton huffed, "simply because a man happens to be a minister of the gospel, he should not step forth in man fashion and take his medicine like the rest of us." Newton believed he had been swindled and Eaton should admit he had been duped. There was speculation in the newspapers that John D. Rockefeller would step in and settle the Newton lawsuit to protect Eaton, his favorite Cleveland Baptist pastor, from unpleasant notoriety. Newton himself nixed the idea, saying he had hopes for a settlement, "but not through Mr. Rockefeller." Asked if he bore Mrs. Chadwick any bitterness, Newton was magnanimous: "I can truthfully say I do not. . . . I pity her from the bottom of my heart."[19]

Pittsburgh reporters sought out Reverend Jolly, the Chadwick cousin who presided at the couple's first marriage ceremony. Jolly defended his cousin's wife: "If she did wrong, the Cleveland bankers are to blame. They must have had knowledge of her assets or else they would not have recommended her and introduced her to bankers of other cities."[20]

Reporters in New York asked attorney Edmund Powers if Mrs. Chadwick's outstanding debt exceeded $1 million. "You may put it at that sum," Powers agreed, then contemptuously said that only legitimate debts would be paid and those amounted to $600,000. That creditors were inflating their claims was understood. Powers defended his client, saying, "Mrs. Chadwick is an honest woman, and will pay all she owes. It is nothing unusual that a very wealthy woman gets money by pledging securities. Why shouldn't she?" Powers went on to point out that Mrs. Chadwick was known as one of Cleveland's wealthiest women for the last seven years. Powers pegged her fortune at $4 million with $2 million available to meet her immediate needs, which was pure fiction. Powers said he had known Cassie Chadwick for years—more fiction—and was convinced of her honesty, although he conceded that "she may be a little lax in business methods." Had Powers been the attorney who told the Oberlin bankers the Carnegie notes were genuine, a reporter inquired. He adamantly denied it. "No, no. Certainly not." Powers did admit telling the Oberlin men that the lady was worth millions. He went on to say that the rumor that his client was Madame Devere was incorrect. "Would this [Mrs. Chadwick's fortune] have been possible if she had been charged with a crime and imprisoned until 1893?" he asked. "I believe then, and I believe now that she is worth millions," Powers averred. "I still believe that every creditor of Mrs. Chadwick will get every cent that is due." After this interview, the *Cleveland Plain Dealer* rhetorically asked its readers, "Where did Mrs. Chadwick get the vast sum of $4,000,000?"[21]

In New York, Cassie Chadwick was a celebrity in a city with a highly competitive press. If she took a carriage ride anywhere in New York, it was attended by a crush of cabs carrying newsmen intent on getting a picture or hearing an unguarded word. To thwart them on December 2, the day she was forced into bankruptcy, she engaged in a clever ruse quite uncharacteristic for a Victorian woman. She took a closed cab to Wall Street, supposedly for a conference pertaining to the Newton lawsuit. She arrived at 54 Wall Street, home of the Central Trust Company. Cassie entered the company's offices escorted by two bodyguards and went straight to the elevator. As word of her appearance spread, a crowd of Wall Street clerks, brokers, and messenger boys grew outside the trust company to almost a thousand. Police were summoned to preserve order.[22]

Anxious reporters badgered trust company employees, who denied knowing Mrs. Chadwick. A building employee said she went to the law offices of Butler, Notman, Joline, and Mynderse on the sixth floor. However, all four partners were unavailable when reporters and private detectives on her trail arrived on the sixth floor. Speculation reached a fevered pitch when it was learned that one of the partners, Joline, had done work for Andrew Carnegie. A junior member of the law firm later said, "At first these rumors about Mrs. Chadwick's visiting here were amusing to us. Now they have become annoying."[23]

Finally, after four hours, a police captain announced Mrs. Chadwick was gone, but he declined to elaborate. Actually, Cassie, dressed in a formfitting brown gown, had slipped out a rear window of the law office and down a fire escape to a roof extension. From there she crossed to a narrow ledge, following it to a rear window of a neighboring building before exiting on Pine Street, where a cab was waiting for her. With this bit of daring, Mrs. Chadwick had given the press and Newton's detectives the slip.[24]

Attorney Phillip Carpenter later admitted the visit to Butler, Notman, but said Mrs. Chadwick had been a client of the law firm for years. When asked the purpose of the visit to Wall Street, he sarcastically replied, "Some newspapers say she lost a lot of money in Wall Street. Maybe she went down there to get some of it back."[25]

Before steaming for France aboard the *Savoie* on November 3, Dr. Chadwick had attended a conference with Newton's attorneys. Once the story broke, the doctor cabled a New York lawyer, not his wife, offering to assist in any settlement. Dr. Chadwick seemed unconcerned that his two previous $25,000 checks had been returned for lack of funds. Chadwick's whereabouts were unknown, and unless he surfaced somewhere soon, federal authorities hinted at international legal action.[26]

Creditors continued to emerge. On November 16, Mrs. Chadwick gave a New York dressmaker, Louise and Company, a check for $1,357, postdated to December 1. Louise and Company was an exclusive retailer requiring an introduction to do business, and Mrs. Chadwick had been a client for two years. The dressmaker often accepted postdated checks from wealthy clients. When news of Cassie's financial troubles became public, Louise and Company took the check to the bank. Wade Park Banking returned it for lack of funds. When the head saleswoman at the dressmaker attempted to see Mrs. Chadwick at Holland House, she was rebuffed. Immediately the dressmaker filed for a foreign attachment on Mrs. Chadwick's luggage at Holland House. A foreign attachment was a legal device used by New York City merchants and hotels when they thought that a visitor might leave town without paying his or her bill. A deputy sheriff was sent immediately to serve Mrs. Chadwick with the papers and to inventory the baggage. The deputy strode boldly to the elegant Holland House front desk and demanded Mrs. Chadwick. At that moment, the lobby was filled with aged society matrons, including a "Mrs. Vanderbilt," preparing for an evening out. A collective gasp arose from the ladies, one dropped her gold-encrusted handbag, and another reached for her smelling salts, exclaiming, "Gracious, this is terrible."[27]

When the deputy arrived at Mrs. Chadwick's door, her nurse Freda briefly blocked it, claiming her mistress was ill. Undeterred, the deputy pressed ahead and found his quarry on her large brass bed, wearing only a long silk kimono. Cassie appeared pale and haggard, and the nightstand was covered with vials of medicine. The deputy found only two small pieces of luggage and three trunks in her room at Holland House. It was said that she had arrived in New York with twenty-eight heavy trunks, a falsehood that originated with the hotel's chief porter. Holland House laid claim to those pieces for unpaid hotel bills. The hotel doctor was summoned for Cassie and diagnosed her as suffering from nervous exhaustion and ordered her to remain in bed. The doctor said she was genuinely ill and shouldn't be moved for three or four days. The next day a medical specialist examined Mrs. Chadwick and declared her organically fine but very agitated. The specialist speculated that she might have to remain in bed for up to two weeks.[28]

While the woman was confined to her bed, Andrew Carnegie's daily walk in Central Park was interrupted by an eager reporter. Asked about his willingness to talk to federal banking officials regarding the Chadwick promissory notes, he gave a generic answer, saying any official would "receive a very gracious reception" from him.[29]

Wall Street bankers, feeling a bit superior to their Cleveland colleagues, wondered aloud why those Ohio bankers had loaned Mrs. Chadwick money without knowing how and where it would be used. Many New York banks had an unwritten policy of not loaning to women at all. Loans were rarely made to women for real estate, and under no circumstances could they be used for stock speculation, which was rumored to be Mrs. Chadwick's downfall.[30]

Herbert Newton had Pinkerton detectives following Cassie. They were joined on December 5 by Treasury Department secret service agents, who stationed themselves on the same floor as Mrs. Chadwick's rooms. The government surveillance was in response to her request for Mexican tourist guides and timetables from the Holland House concierge. It was falsely reported that President Theodore Roosevelt had assigned secret service agents to *protect* Andrew Carnegie.[31]

Nineteen-year-old Emil Hoover was also under scrutiny. Was he really Cassie Chadwick's biological son? His last name was always given as Hoover, a source of confusion. Employees at Holland House knew Emil as Cassie's son. Yet rumors circulated that he was her stepson. Even her attorney, Phillip Carpenter, was confused. Asked Mrs. Chadwick's son's age, he exclaimed, "Her son, Emil? I didn't know Emil was her son!" Mrs. Chadwick defended Emil, saying, "He has looked out for me at every turn, and has thought of me always before himself."[32]

Even more fantastic rumors suggested Emil possessed $7 million in securities, or was conspiring with Charles Beckwith in Oberlin, or sending secret telegrams. Only the last was true. A New York telegrapher was only too happy—likely for a small bribe—to report that Emil had sent a message to a Cleveland attorney for his mother using a fictitious name. The telegram read, "I must know the conditions in Oberlin. Is there likelihood of an arrest? Telegraph answer to me without fail today."[33]

Emil Hoover abruptly left New York City on December 5 and arrived in Cleveland the next morning. Once in Cleveland, young Hoover gave reporters the slip. Inquiries at local hotels and at his home failed to locate him. It was subsequently reported that he was staying with friends on the city's east side. An unidentified source close to the Chadwick saga said that two of his mother's steamer trunks, containing clothes and jewels, had been shipped by train to Cleveland to avoid seizure by creditors in New York. Emil, so the rumor went, had taken the claim checks to collect the trunks in Cleveland and hide them. Emil was back in New York a day later. His mother defended him. "I wish to deny," she said to no one's satisfaction, "the false rumors set afloat that my son has run away with my jewels. I have no jewels here, nor anyplace else, therefore it would be an impossibility for my son to run away with them."[34]

As creditors closed in and the press grew hostile, Dr. Chadwick sent a telegram to the New York lawyer, Phillip Carpenter, asking him to deny the negative statements published in the newspapers regarding his wife. According to the doctor, "they are absolutely false" and her family "stands behind her."[35]

Like birds of prey circling their quarry, federal officials tightened their net around Mrs. Cassie Chadwick. She departed Holland House for refuge at the New Amsterdam Hotel, which lacked telephones in the rooms, on Tuesday night, December 6, and then fled to the Hotel Breslin, which had telephones, on Wednesday. Holland House was not sorry to see her go because her suite and the four lawmen watching her were visible from the street, making the hotel a stop on the regular city tourist route. The departure from the New Amsterdam was intended to be clandestine, but hotel clerks' tongues were easily loosened by coin. Within minutes, a dozen cabs carrying reporters were waiting in the street to follow her as she relocated. At 2:00 P.M. she exited, followed by the secret service men, and entered a cab. Her cabbie decided to make a race of it. He won but was chastised in the *New York Times* for "whipping his horses savagely." At the Breslin, Emil paid $100 to reserve a suite of three rooms and a bath for five days. Cassie's Swedish nurse, Freda, described by reporters as "neat looking," accompanied her.[36]

Cassie Chadwick potentially faced both federal charges for her role in the Oberlin bank demise and state charges in Ohio for forging and passing the fraudulent notes bearing Andrew Carnegie's signature. Neither jurisdiction had a strong case. Any federal charge would involve conspiracy, based on banking technicalities, which would be difficult to prove. A state case would rely on proving Cassie had forged the notes and then attempted to pass them, even if by proxy. She had merely used the forgeries as collateral for loans rather than negotiating them directly. Nevertheless, the nationwide publicity would force one or both jurisdictions to act soon. As it stood now, Mrs. Chadwick was free to go wherever she desired, be it Cleveland, Mexico, or Europe. .

The press learned that federal authorities in Cleveland were preparing to issue an arrest warrant for Mrs. Chadwick for conspiring with Beckwith and Spear to defraud the Oberlin bank. With the woman's arrest imminent, New York's endless supply of spectators crowded the lobby of the Breslin, and secret service agents maintained a surveillance outside her hotel room. There could be no escape.[37]

The wheels of justice slowly began to turn on Wednesday, December 7, when the Cleveland arrest warrant reached New York. The US marshal for New York City, William Henkel, and five deputies and secret service men burst into the Chadwick suite around 2:30 P.M. and brushed past Freda, who kept repeating, "Madam is ill!" Emil wisely melted away from his post at his mother's bedchamber door in the face of the federal onslaught. With Henkel in the lead, the posse marched straight to the large brass bed. Propped up by two pillows and wearing a plain white nightdress, Cassie Chadwick betrayed no emotion. Although they had been shadowing her for days, the secret service men got their first real look at the woman the newspapers were calling an adventuress, an unscrupulous schemer. Instead of a hardened criminal, one of the lawmen later remarked on her beauty; her clear, wrinkle-free complexion; her big dark eyes; and hair that was almost snow-white. One secret service agent later remarked, "The kindliest, gentlest face one would ever want to see. Just such a one as you or I'd like to see in our own family."[38]

The hulking Marshal Henkel called it "a most unpleasant duty" as he arrested her. She was specifically charged with conspiracy to embezzle funds from Citizen's National based on a certified check for $12,500, dated August 24, 1903. Cassie's lips trembled, and she began to sob. Henkel was almost apologetic, saying, "I regret it, madam." Cassie made a gesture with her right hand as if to dismiss the marshal and repeated over and over, "I don't want to hear it!"[39]

As this drama unfolded, a small wizened-faced bald little man with a fringe of gray hair and small glittering eyes sat nervously in her bedroom, tapping the arms of his cushioned chair with long thin fingers. Somehow the old man had slipped past the secret service agents, and his presence was an embarrassment to the lawmen. Henkel asked if the man was her lawyer. "I decline to say who I am," he snapped. "All right," said the marshal evenly, "You don't have to . . . now."[40]

One of the agents suggested that Freda be present to console Mrs. Chadwick should she break down as the warrant was read to her. Freda returned, but before Marshal Henkel finished one sentence, the nurse screamed, threw herself across Cassie's chest, and sobbed hysterically. A secret service agent gently relocated her to a chair.[41]

The mysterious stranger rose from his seat. Agreeing to act as her legal counsel, he said, "I guess I'll do for the present." He spent the next five minutes silently reading the marshal's papers and then explained the charges to Cassie while reassuring her. "Be perfectly calm, Mrs. Chadwick. It is not a serious charge. This merely outlines the pretext on which you are being hounded. Of course, if these men have any consideration for the sick, they will leave you here tonight." Unwilling to accept her as a client, the mystery lawyer offered to take a message to one of her New York lawyers.[42]

Marshal Henkel agreed to let Mrs. Chadwick stay in her suite, but he would leave men to guard her. She asked the marshal, "I hope you will let me consult with my friend in private for a moment." Everyone withdrew, except Henkel. The stranger asked for further privacy, which agitated the marshal, but he did leave.[43]

The mysterious visitor in Mrs. Chadwick's bedroom might have been unknown in New York City, but he was well known in Cleveland legal circles. Virgil P. Kline, sixty, was Dr. Chadwick's legal counsel and, on occasion, John D. Rockefeller's. Kline was in New York representing some of Cassie's creditors. Mrs. Chadwick learned of his presence and asked him to call. Kline was a bit surprised since he had objected to her use of a falsified receipt from his office for legal services amounting to $30,000. Cassie used the receipt as proof of wealth in an attempt to borrow $50,000 from a Mansfield, Ohio, bank in early 1904. The bank refused to consider a loan for which a paid receipt was the only collateral. The crusty Kline forcefully denied ever receiving that high a fee from her and labeled the receipt a forgery.[44]

Yet here was Kline conferring with Mrs. Chadwick. He felt that the federal presence was heavy-handed for what was, to him, a trivial charge and said so. Mrs. Chadwick was sick in bed, several floors above the street, and the corridor outside her room was filled with vigilant newsmen. He did not believe she was a flight risk. Apparently, Henkel did and announced that one deputy would remain in Mrs. Chadwick's bedroom at all times. To reporters clogging the hallway and clamoring for a statement, one deputy marshal remarked, "They found a charge on which to catch her. Now they have more time to investigate the other matters." According to the New York Times, when the stranger went to depart, one of the lawmen asked his name. "I'm Mr. Thompson of Paris," was the obviously false reply. "Who are you?"[45]

At around 8:00 P.M., callers began sending their cards up to Mrs. Chadwick. Attorney Andrew Squire of Cleveland, representing Wade Park Banking, was admitted for a conference. Squire was a respected corporate attorney, a staunch Republican, and acquainted with President Roosevelt and Mark Hanna. Squire doubted her arrest would have any effect on Wade Park. Asked by newsmen about the Carnegie notes, which he had seen and considered suspect, he dead-panned, "They stand for what they are worth." After Squire, Cassie and one of her New York lawyers, Phillip Carpenter, conferred for half an hour. He told the press that due to the public outcry in Ohio, Mrs. Chadwick's arrest was not unexpected. Carpenter caused a burst of excitement when he was asked if the woman had been in contact with Andrew Carnegie, and he answered, "She hasn't been in communication with him today." Did that mean Carnegie and Mrs. Chadwick were talking? Carpenter only laughed in response. Lastly, Mrs. Chadwick refused to see C. K. Whitney, son of a director of Citizen's National.[46]

Andrew Carnegie was asked by reporters the day Mrs. Chadwick was arrested if he intended legal action against her. "Why, no. Why should I?" Someone suggested that it was his civic duty to press the issue. The ironmaster, with a twinkle in his eye, laughed, "Wouldn't you feel rather honored if somebody could go around and get together a million or so by signing your name to a piece of paper?"[47]

The morning of December 8, Henkel collected Mrs. Chadwick, who had slept little, at 8:00 A.M. Cassie, Emil, Freda, and the marshal all entered a carriage for the trip downtown to the federal courthouse. She told Henkel, "The time will come when people will see that I am very much maligned." Mrs. Chadwick wanted to consult Virgil Kline. Emil left a note at Kline's hotel at 7:30 A.M. and later placed a call to Kline. When there was no response, his mother cried, "Why doesn't Mr. Kline come to my assistance?" Kline was conveniently on a train to Chicago.[48]

Outside the courthouse, over fifty photographers waited to ambush Mrs. Chadwick, and beyond them a crowd of everyday New Yorkers jostled around for a look at the creature who was either Andrew Carnegie's illegitimate daughter or one of the country's biggest imposters. One round of camera flashes so startled her that she fell to her knees. She was physically carried into the courtroom by her attorney Carpenter and Henkel, her eyes closed as she occasionally sighed dramatically. She was wearing a brown cloak, fine fur about her neck, and a stylish hat. She was seated so that her stone-deaf right ear was facing away from the presiding officer. Carpenter said she had nothing to say and commenced the argument over bail, which was fixed at $15,000. Carpenter pointed out that the amount exceeded the $10,000 Beckwith and Spear had posted in Ohio. This argument carried no weight, and Carpenter went looking for a bondsman. The marshal kindly agreed to let Mrs. Chadwick wait in his office while her attorney sought bail. Cassie noticed an open safe. "You oughtn't leave a safe unlocked when a woman like myself is around," she told Henkel.[49]

While they waited, the loyal Freda remarked that a steamship painting on the wall resembled the one she had come over on from Sweden. This prompted Mrs. Chadwick to reply, "Yes, I wish we were on it now." Freda Svensson was a Swedish national and a graduate of a nursing program in Stockholm. She bristled at the insinuation she was a French maid. She had been in the United States for seven months, six in Mrs. Chadwick's employ. Male reporters found her Scandinavian beauty appealing. Freda took her duties seriously and was loyal to her employer.[50]

A 5:00 P.M. deadline for bail passed in silence. Federal authorities agreed to extend it until 9:00 P.M. Marshal Henkel, stung by Virgil Kline's earlier attacks on his methods, announced to reporters that he was "a man with a heart" who magnanimously volunteered to personally stay until 9:00 P.M. Mrs. Chadwick did her part in the drama by lying on a sofa with a handkerchief over her face, breathing heavily while Freda quietly sobbed.[51]

At 8:10, Carpenter returned to admit defeat in his search for bail, a situation reminiscent of Toledo. Mrs. Chadwick, accustomed to the finest New York hotels, would have to go to the infamous Tombs prison like any common criminal, except she had to pay for the cab that transported her there. With Emil on one arm and Henkel on the other and Freda bringing up the rear, they left the marshal's office. Henkel sternly forbade any flashing camera lights and no riders in the elevator, except the four principals. After an uneventful carriage ride, the entourage arrived at the Tombs at 9:02, where about a hundred onlookers milled around. Marshal Henkel and some of the turnkeys forced the crowd aside. In the warden's office, Cassie collapsed into a chair as Henkel formally turned her over to the jailers. He asked for consideration on account of her illness. Mrs. Chadwick embraced her son for a few minutes, both weeping. She was not allowed to keep a small medicine chest after she was turned over to the jail matron. She was isolated in a cell, which certainly brought back unpleasant memories, and would remain there except for meals. At the Tombs, Cassie would briefly eclipse the lockup's most famous female inmate, Nan Patterson, just a few cells away. Miss Patterson, a showgirl, was enduring a second murder trial in the death of her gambler boyfriend and was front-page news across the city.[52]

New York authorities were concerned about Cassie's mental state. Denied the use of a knife or fork, she was reduced to eating her lamb-chop dinner with a spoon after it was precut. Asked if Mrs. Chadwick would be examined for insanity, her attorney Edmund Powers replied, "It would make a pretty good defense in a criminal action wouldn't it?" Mrs. Chadwick waived the exam by saying if bail was not forthcoming, she would return to Cleveland voluntarily, disregarding her attorneys' advice. The *Cleveland Plain Dealer* asked, "Is the woman simply a brilliant lunatic, with a monomania for lavish financial dealings and no conscience?" The newspaper believed that the case for insanity was undermined by the cleverness of the documents she was alleged to have created.[53]

George Ryall, one of Herbert Newton's attorneys, was surprised at the arrest. He offered his sympathy to Mrs. Chadwick and said he remained hopeful that a financial settlement could be arranged. After all, he said, "In this case anything is possible."[54]

Prior to her arrest, Cassie Chadwick had telephoned Iri Reynolds and summoned him to New York for a conference. This request was reenforced by a visit to Reynolds by Emil Hoover, who was well liked by the man. Reynolds and attorney Andrew Squire, representing both Reynolds and some of the Pittsburgh lenders, went to New York the evening of Monday, December 5. Reporters descended on Reynolds's home, and his wife would only say that her husband was "very tired and worn" and had gone out of town for a rest. It was a ruse. Reynolds and Squire met with federal authorities and Chadwick creditors, including Citizen's National's examiner Robert Lyons and bank director L. T. Whitney, in New York on the morning of December 7.[55]

Newsmen in New York discovered Reynolds as he departed the meeting and pressed him for a statement. He remained silent. He went by Holland House and saw the crowds of rowdy onlookers and learned that Mrs. Chadwick was no longer there. At 5:30, Reynolds quietly boarded a train for New Jersey. When discovered, his disappearance caused a minor stir in the press. Back in Cleveland, his wife admitted that she had not heard from Iri since he left, making creditors and federal authorities uneasy. What if the "securities" weren't worthless and Reynolds had, very uncharacteristically, absconded with them?[56]

Reynolds arrived in Jersey City and spent the night in a cheap local hotel. The next morning, December 8, he went directly to a local bank, where some

weeks ago he had secretly deposited Mrs. Chadwick's precious envelopes in
the vault to prevent creditors from seizing them. As additional protection,
a Cleveland lawyer was given power of attorney over the supposed securities to prevent creditors from negotiating them. It seems unlikely that this
was Reynolds's idea, so whose was it? Mrs. Chadwick, the doctor, Wade Park
Banking, or some unknown operator? The answer is open to speculation.
Courts in Cleveland ordered Reynolds to produce the Chadwick securities
the following week, so he retrieved them. He was back in Cleveland in his office early on December 9, where he could see a *Cleveland Plain Dealer* headline that read, "No Word of Reynolds." The strain was beginning to tell on the
man. By the next edition of the *Plain Dealer,* the paper could report that he
was back in the city, but "his face is thin and haggard and is deeply marked
with lines of care and worry." Despite the mounting pressure, Reynolds continued his silence.[57]

CHAPTER SIXTEEN

SIMPLY A SUCKER

While a settlement of Mrs. Chadwick's debts remained a faint hope, future indictments were a certainty. Federal bank examiners in Ohio wanted forgery charges. A state grand jury in Lorain County, Ohio, which had jurisdiction over Oberlin, was questioning a talkative Arthur Spear, the former cashier of Citizen's National. Upon receiving a summons to testify before the Cuyahoga County grand jury, Spear lightheartedly said, "I seem to be mighty popular these days." The Lorain grand jury, whose foreman was a director of the bank that held the mortgage on the Chadwick home, voted to indict Mrs. Chadwick on a charge of obtaining money under false pretenses.[1]

Secret grand jury testimony leaked to the press suggested that Mrs. Chadwick was not the forger of the Carnegie notes. According to the *Cleveland Plain Dealer*, the actual forger was the scion of a wealthy family, as yet unnamed in the case, who several years ago was very close to Cassie Chadwick. "It is understood that the disclosure of his identity," the paper reported, "and perhaps his arrest, is the big and overshadowing sensation which attorneys have been promising for several days." Nothing came of the story.[2]

Enterprising reporters found Cassie's now widowed sister, Alice M. York, in San Francisco. Alice admitted that she was Mrs. Chadwick's sister, confirmed her sister was Canadian, and said her real name was Elizabeth Bigley. According to Mrs. York, young Elizabeth was not unusual as a child, except that she was a "deep thinker," who occasionally descended into a trancelike state lasting hours from which she awoke "bewildered." Alice, either confused or simply lying, told reporters that Mrs. Chadwick was either thirty-eight or forty-two and in 1880 had married C. R. Hoover from Cleveland. Hoover died in 1887, so Alice said, leaving his wife $50,000. Cassie subsequently traveled as an agent for a millinery establishment. Mrs. York refused to comment on any problems her sister had with the law, simply saying, "There was some trouble." Mrs. York said she knew nothing of Andrew Carnegie but felt her sister had sufficient money to solve her problems. As for Madame Devere, Alice replied, "Not one of our family ever posed as a medium," which was true. Two days later, Mrs. York was tricked by skeptical reporters into identifying a newspaper photo of Madame Devere as her sister, Mrs. Cassie Chadwick.[3]

Emil Hoover's welfare was a concern for the New York Society for the Prevention of Cruelty to Children, which was worried about the lad's exposure to the evil influences in the Tombs prison. The devoted Emil stayed in his mother's suite at the Breslin with Freda but visited his mother frequently at the Tombs. Unfortunately, no one could protect Emil from the New York reporters lingering on practically every corner. Emil told one group, "I don't believe my mother ever borrowed any money she can't repay." He called the charges against his mother "all lies." The lad was asked by newsmen as he left the Tombs about Mrs. York's statement in San Francisco. Emil's carefully worded reply regarding Mrs. York was odd. "It is true that I have stayed at her house," Emil admitted to reporters, "and that I was taught as a boy to call Mrs. York's boy my cousin." When Cassie Chadwick herself was asked about Mrs. York, she said that they were not in any way related, but they were raised together, which was consistent with her illegitimate Carnegie daughter story.[4]

Jailers at the Tombs had confiscated Cassie Chadwick's medicines, so she sent Emil, who had a jail pass, to a local saloon to acquire a favored brand of liquor. The bartender offered Emil a bottle for $2. "But I only want a quarters' worth," Emil protested. The saloonkeeper refused to open the bottle amid hoots and catcalls from the patrons. Emil, a slightly built youth with wire-rim glasses, wisely departed. Upon hearing the story later, one jailer suggested that a quarter was all the money the boy had, but another was certain that Cassie had given him a sizable wad of cash. Whichever was true, Emil seemed to never lack for money. The lad was popular among the jailers for his devotion to his mother and his intelligence. A *New York Times* reporter described Emil as "a slender, rather pale chap with a quiet manner that immediately attract one."[5]

Herbert B. Newton had loaned Mrs. Chadwick a large sum of money without receiving any significant collateral. What he had received was a written assurance that Mrs. Chadwick was worth millions from that impeccable Cleveland banker, Iri Reynolds, for whom the Reverend Eaton had vouched. Newton's attorneys naturally laid some of the blame for his predicament on Reynolds's doorstep. One of Newton's first legal actions had been to ask the

Cleveland court to restrain Reynolds or Wade Park from disposing of any of the Chadwick securities.[6]

Until Cassie's arrest, Reynolds had insisted that the securities were genuine. "I know they are good—I know it. Mrs. Chadwick, I am sure, will pay everything." His refusal to show anyone the contents of the sealed envelopes was making him look like a coconspirator or that he was acting under instructions, perhaps, it was speculated, from Carnegie himself. As for rumors that the securities had already been examined and were worthless, Reynolds bristled and told reporters, "There is no possible means whereby any information in regard to the genuineness of the securities I hold of Mrs. Chadwick's could have become known." As for the certificate he had signed, Reynolds declined to discuss it. His colleagues at Wade Park did not share his faith in Mrs. Chadwick. One unnamed member of the bank's board, with the benefit of having seen the contents of one package, told reporters, "From what I know of these securities, I wouldn't give a snap of my finger for the whole package."[7]

The *New York Times* estimated Mrs. Chadwick's borrowing had reached $2 million over the last three years. The *Cleveland Plain Dealer* put the grand total of the Chadwick paper bearing Andrew Carnegie's signature at $13,750,000. The newspaper also calculated that from September to December 1904, $100,000 of Mrs. Chadwick's checks had been returned for lack of funds. The bad checks came from all over the map. One for $16,000 had been given to a New York rug merchant and another for $10,000 to a Detroit jeweler. Finally, there were two $15,000 checks given to a merchant in Paris, where the Chadwick saga was attracting interest because of similarities with the Therese Humbert swindle.[8]

After the media frenzy caused by Reynolds's brief disappearance following his trip to New York, the Cleveland papers reported without fanfare that Reynolds and Squire were hard at work in their respective offices the afternoon of December 9. Reynolds was said to have gone home at 3:00 P.M. to rest. However, there was subterfuge afoot. Reynolds, Squire, and a second attorney, A. A. Stearns, representing Newton, quietly gathered at the bank, where they intended to examine the Chadwick securities now that Reynolds had retrieved them from the New Jersey bank. The small bundle of three sealed envelopes held together with paper tape was labeled "papers of Cassie Chadwick for safe keeping only." The tape was signed and dated, but the envelopes were devoid of any clue to their contents. Stearns and Squire both signed the wrappers as witnesses to the proceedings. The first envelope opened contained the $5 million promissory note dated May 1902 and the trust agreement, both signed "Andrew Carnegie." The second envelope held a copy of the trust agreement, identical except for a different date. The last envelope held a mortgage on the home of Mrs. Chadwick's sister Emily Pine for $1,800. Quick calculations revealed that the total amount represented by the documents was $15,248,000 of which only the Pine mortgage represented real value. Reynolds had known what was in the envelopes and likely confided in Squire. Stearns had been forewarned, yet he harbored hope for his client. After examining the documents, Stearns left the bank to call Boston with the bad news. He later told the press of the envelopes' contents: "It is my candid opinion that the securities on which my client and many others have been basing their hopes are not worth a cent."[9]

The contents of the packages were crucial evidence for any criminal proceedings. State officials were alerted by Newton's camp that the packages were being examined. Likewise, someone alerted federal authorities. A state official arrived at Wade Park with a court order thirty minutes ahead of a federal marshal, and Reynolds surrendered the papers he had guarded so zealously to him.[10]

After learning the contents of the envelopes, Newton still believed that "certain influences," whom he declined to discuss, were working toward getting him a full settlement. Newton seemed to think that his last chance of a settlement rested with Dr. Chadwick, although the doctor's two previous $25,000 checks had proved worthless. Those checks Newton blamed on Mrs. Chadwick, and he held out hope that rumors of the doctor being given $2.5 million were true. Newton was angry at those merchants who forced the Chadwicks into involuntary bankruptcy. "If the woman had not been driven to bay so quickly," he complained, "I should have received my money." Insinuating that his lawsuit had been a negotiating tactic, Newton pointed out that Mrs. Chadwick had been sued before and the threat of public exposure had induced her to settle. Newton also attacked Iri Reynolds. He called the circumstances under which he made loans to Mrs. Chadwick a "miserable fabric of falsehoods. Had I not been given a sworn statement by Iri Reynolds to the effect that he had in his possession $5 million worth of collateral . . . I would not have loaned her money." Newton reached the same conclusion as state and federal prosecutors. "I do know that she could never have borrowed the money she did in the manner she did without someone as an accomplice." Who was that coconspirator? Her husband, Reynolds, attorney Powers, or some shadowy operator pulling the strings in secret? A mere woman couldn't be that clever, could she?[11]

After the packages were finally opened, Reynolds no longer felt constrained by confidentiality and spoke publicly for the first time. "[Mrs. Chadwick] told me she was the illegitimate daughter of Andrew Carnegie," he told Cleveland reporters, "and I believed her." Reynolds claimed that Dr. Chadwick was present when his wife revealed her Carnegie connection. "I never doubted her story until on the occasion of my last visit to New York when Mr. Squire came to me and declared that all the securities she had given me as notes of Andrew Carnegie were worthless." Reynolds declared, "I have not done a single crooked thing in this whole matter." He denied suggestions he was hypnotized by Mrs. Chadwick. "She fooled me and many men smarter than me," Reynolds said. "I guess I was simply a sucker." Reynolds dashed Newton's hopes of receiving money from the doctor while showing attorney Edmund Powers to be a liar when the old banker stated that Mrs. Chadwick never gave her husband a large sum of money. If anyone was in a position to know, it was Reynolds. In truth, the doctor, who was in Europe, was reported to be penniless.[12]

Cassie Chadwick's clever claim that she was Carnegie's daughter had helped erect a barrier between her victims and the ironmaster. Many of Cassie's creditors considered it plausible that Carnegie, like so many other wealthy Victorian men, had an illegitimate child he wished to keep secret. Those creditors were reluctant to expend even a two-cent stamp for a letter to Carnegie to verify his promissory notes for fear of upsetting the man, who might then disavow the notes. No one would profit from a disavowal. Mrs. Chadwick's carefully crafted tale also appeared to explain away any inconsistencies in her previous explanations of her finances. While design and luck were factors in the success of the scheme, most certainly it was Cassie's audacity and persuasiveness that made the swindle work.[13]

Cassie's brother-in-law, Daniel Pine, was cornered by newsmen since the only legitimate asset in the packages was the $1,800 Pine note. Daniel and Emily Pine had purchased a home valued at $3,400 in 1902 with the assistance of Mrs. Chadwick. Since then, they had made no payments. Publicly, Pine lied to distance himself from Cassie Chadwick. "I really do not know if Mrs. Chadwick is my wife's sister or not. . . . Nor could I swear in regard to the relationship of Mrs. York." According to Pine, Dr. Chadwick had been the Pine family physician, and that was how the doctor and Cassie's relationship began. Pine readily admitted to having engaged in several small business deals with the woman. Referring to the lack of payments on his mortgage, reporters sarcastically remarked on Mrs. Chadwick's generosity. Pine sharply rebuked them. "I have heard a lot about pianos and automobiles being given away, but I don't see any around this place. I would hardly call it generous to keep that mortgage against us in the bank there, when she was giving away more expensive presents." It was rumored that Cassie had given away French motorcars as wedding gifts. Both Pine and his wife were surprised by recent revelations about Mrs. Chadwick. According to Daniel Pine, they had no idea she was involved in such high finance.[14]

Pine also denied any knowledge of Toledo's infamous Madame Devere. As it turned out, there were men from the Toledo days who were eager to talk. The list included Irving Belford, Joe Lamb's attorney; an 1890 express company employee from Toledo; and a Toledo banker. Former Toledo police detective John Manley volunteered that "I would know her anywhere." Same for his old police chief in 1890, who said, "I would know her if I saw her again." James Southard, the former prosecutor in Toledo, was now a congressman. "I am led to believe that Mrs. Cassie L. Chadwick is none other than Madame Devere," he said. "Mrs. Chadwick's illness is one of the ruses which the Devere woman manipulated to secure her parole." This certainty was contradicted by a coroner in Anderson, Indiana. He identified a recent suicide in his jurisdiction who had been posing as a palmist as Madame Devere based on newspaper photographs. The current warden of the Ohio Penitentiary offered to send prison employees who had had contact with Madame Devere during her incarceration to Cleveland. Federal officials went to Toledo on December 7 to gather police records on Madame. On December 10, Lydia Devere's description from the prison record was published in the newspapers. The only unique detail matching both women, however, was a burn scar on the right elbow.[15]

Cleveland attorney John Smith was now representing creditors in the bankruptcy proceedings. Smith had followed Mrs. Chadwick's career for years and once threatened to expose her as Madame Devere over a bank loan. But Smith did not go public with the information at the time. "I did tell a number of people," Smith said in his defense, "and many of the banks have refused to have any dealings with her." Smith was also familiar with a couple of nearly decade-old blackmail cases involving the then Mrs. Hoover, which were settle out of court. Smith said of Mrs. Chadwick, "She was the greatest adventuress in the world, I believe, and had 'Becky Sharp' of *Vanity Fair* outsharped. It is truly laughable to think of such a woman as she was getting ahead of a lot of hard-headed bankers." Becky Sharp was a character in the

1848 satirical novel *Vanity Fair*. She was a cynical social climber and charming seducer of upper-class men. The name Sharp had become "sharper," a nineteenth-century slang term for a con artist. The Becky Sharp character became a hero to lower-class readers.[16]

The involuntary bankruptcy proceeding against Mrs. Chadwick began Monday, December 12, and Iri Reynolds was the first witness. The banker had been under great strain, and although only in his early fifties, he looked older. Reporters noted his stooped posture, the dark rings under his eyes, and the persistent nervous tremor. His eyes darted about, and his fingers nervously drummed whatever they rested upon. Andrew Squire was his attorney. Reynolds would be interrogated by Louis Grossman, who had initiated the proceedings and now fulfilled the role of prosecutor in Bankruptcy Court. Grossman's law partner, Nathan Loeser, had been appointed bankruptcy receiver. Grossman was assisted by attorney Smith, who brought his vast knowledge of the woman's past to the proceedings.[17]

Grossman first attempted to induce Reynolds to admit an affair with Mrs. Chadwick but retreated under attorney Squire's strenuous objections. Next, Grossman tried to demonstrate a conspiracy between Reynolds and Newton to keep the Chadwick "securities" out of federal hands. The Bankruptcy Court believed it was entitled to them. State prosecutors, however, had possession and refused to relinquish the papers. Reynolds defended himself by pointing out that he had faced a state court order to surrender the evidence. Grossman moved on to questions about Mrs. Chadwick's dealings with other local banks, again in the quest for assets. Reynolds's lips trembled as he answered that he knew "as little of her affairs as any man living. She always swore everybody she dealt with to secrecy. . . . She pulled the wool over everybody's eyes." Reynolds concluded, "Better businessmen than I have handed over [to] her money with no security."[18]

Iri Reynolds conceded that he never pressed Mrs. Chadwick for an explanation of her relationship with Carnegie. "She gave me the impression Andrew Carnegie was back of everything," was all Reynolds would say. As recently as last summer, he testified, Cassie had shown him a $60,000 check with Carnegie's signature. Reynolds said that he had read the trust agreement, but it was only a skeleton copy—one lacking Carnegie's signature. Grossman doggedly pressed for details about the woman's finances, and Reynolds continued to repeat, "I will tell everything. I will keep nothing back." He explained how Wade Park had loaned Mrs. Chadwick $12,000 earlier in the year in return for a sealed package that she said contained a $250,000 certificate and $200,000 in US Steel bonds as collateral. The packages had been opened in November, and the contents were virtually worthless. Reynolds was emphatic that "I never loaned Mrs. Chadwick a cent with or without collateral without the consent of the [bank's] directors." Addressing accusations that he signed a receipt for specific stocks, bonds, or notes Mrs. Chadwick claimed she gave him, Reynolds replied, "I never signed such a receipt in my life." This was technically correct— Reynolds always provided only a dollar value for the purported securities, not a specific inventory.[19]

Reynolds testified that the last time he saw Mrs. Chadwick was on November 10, before her last New York trip, when she cashed a worthless check at Wade Park for expense money. Reynolds said Cassie left the impression she was seeing Carnegie to resolve her money problems. He would not discuss his personal losses to the woman, which reliable sources estimate at about $20,000, all the savings he had. Under the cover of social visits, Mrs. Chadwick would discover when Reynolds received some money, and she would later seek a personal loan on some pretense.[20]

Reynolds was adamant that he had not lodged at the Waldorf-Astoria during his last New York trip, press reports notwithstanding. He ruefully admitted, thanks to Cassie Chadwick, he did not have money enough "to stay there [at the Waldorf-Astoria] one hour." With a slight smile, Reynolds said that Mrs. Chadwick had written him recently to ask if he needed help since the Newton suit had caused a financial crisis at Wade Park.[21]

Grossman wanted Reynolds to estimate the value of the Chadwicks' personal property. According to Reynolds, who was neither an appraiser nor a jeweler, a "low estimate" would be $200,000. Last summer he had gone to New York on her behalf to retrieve $98,000 worth of jewels given as debt collateral. Reynolds did not know where the gemstones were presently. He did testify that Mrs. Chadwick's jewelry box was a foot and a half long and filled with diamonds and pearls. A ripple of laughter followed Reynolds's description of the jewels. "They were as nice and pretty a lot of pearls and diamonds as you ever saw." With that bit of humor, Reynolds concluded his exhausting two hours of questioning.[22]

The same day Reynolds was in Bankruptcy Court, a Cuyahoga County grand jury met to consider Mrs. Chadwick. Witnesses agreed that there were three Carnegie promissory notes: the $5 million one, one for $250,000—both currently in state prosecutors' hands—and one for $500,000, which was unaccounted for. A second $500,000 note was said to exist, but it had disappeared. C. K. Whitney, the Citizen's National bank director's son, was called to testify and, since he was believed to have one $500,000 note, produce it. The prosecutor asked Whitney how he came to have the note. He said Mrs. Chadwick had signed the note over to Beckwith and Spear and they had quarreled over who should hold the note, which was not due until January 7, 1905. As a compromise, the two bankers put it in an unmarked envelope, sealed it, and gave it to Whitney to hold as a "disinterested" party. The Whitneys were one of Citizen's National's largest depositors and hardly disinterested. Whitney put the sealed envelope said to contain the note and some other papers in a strongbox and left it in the bank vault. Whitney had brought the contents of the strongbox with him to the grand jury.[23]

Prosecutor Harvey Keeler asked if Whitney had the note, and Whitney theatrically responded by waving a bundle of papers to the jurymen. "I don't know, but it is supposed to be some place among these papers," he said. Whitney's search through the papers led through four envelopes as the suspense grew. At last, when the fifth envelope was opened, the $500,000 note with Carnegie's purported signature came to light. Surprise and murmurs of excitement came from the jurymen as they examined it. Finally, Whitney himself had a chance to scrutinize the piece of paper on which Beckwith and Spear had bet the future of Citizen's National Bank and no small part of Whitney's family's fortune. Whitney had kept this note a secret so absolutely that many people believed it was a myth.[24]

Whitney asked the prosecutor if he could hold the note until Mrs. Chadwick's trial. Astonishingly, Keeler agreed. Why Whitney was allowed to retain such a crucial piece of evidence was never explained. After the great reveal, Keeler read a telegram from Andrew Carnegie disavowing the notes. It says something of Carnegie's reputation in 1904 that he could disavow the note without ever seeing it and not be challenged. The grand jury indicted Mrs. Chadwick for forgery and passing the two bogus notes for $250,000 and $500,000. The maximum penalty was twenty years in prison. By 3:30 P.M. the paperwork was completed, and the all-male grand jury adjourned.[25]

Cuyahoga County prosecutor Harvey Keeler believed that Mrs. Chadwick could not have spent all the money she borrowed and had money or jewels hidden somewhere. The receiver for the defunct Citizen's National Bank, Robert Lyons, was of a like mind. "A woman as wise as Mrs. Chadwick," he guessed, "would be likely to put away a snug part of the money she obtained. She must have known that someday she would be caught." Keeler announced that Mrs. Chadwick was not the only person the grand jury was investigating. "If there are others, as I believe there were," Keeler said, "they shall be indicted." The prosecutor pointed his finger at "a certain attorney in New York City," whom he suggested was "next to Mrs. Chadwick, the arch-conspirator in all this deviltry." Keeler called the suspect "a mediator, an adjuster, a soft-spoken insidious worker, whose tracks almost baffle pursuit." This attorney always appeared after the mischief was done, according to the prosecutor. He cleaned up the loose ends and smoothed ruffled feathers. "The evidence against him is uncertain," Keeler admitted, and he did not know if there was enough solid evidence for an indictment. Keeler wisely never named the New York attorney, but most people believed it was Edmund Powers. Keeler's discretion was wise because this "mediator and adjuster" was never indicted by any grand jury and his identity remained a secret.[26]

CHAPTER SEVENTEEN

CHADWICKED

Dr. Chadwick was attempting to be invisible in Paris. On Sunday, December 11, he agreed to an interview with a correspondent from the *New York World*. The doctor insisted on a clandestine meeting in the billiard room of his hotel. He would seat himself just outside the door at the appointed time, and the two men would identify each other by carrying white handkerchiefs in their right hands. The doctor insisted on the cloak-and-dagger arrangements because American reporters in Paris were following him everywhere and he wanted to avoid their questions and insinuations. Additionally, Chadwick preferred not to talk to US Treasury agents investigating Cassie's diamond purchases in Brussels or to French creditors holding $30,000 in bad checks.[1]

When the two men met, a visibly nervous Chadwick insisted the reporter swear not to reveal his location. The newsman was impressed by the doctor's youthful appearance, guessing incorrectly that he was not over forty, shaving over a decade from his true age. The scribe's first question was part accusation: "Did you leave America because you knew the transactions charged against your wife were about to be ventilated?" Dr. Chadwick vigorously denied any knowledge beforehand. The reporter judged Chadwick sincere when he said he was "absolutely without an inkling" that his wife was doing the things of which she was accused. He insisted that his wife had never met Andrew Carnegie.[2]

Adopting a humble tone, Chadwick told the reporter he was "a practicing physician in Cleveland and making a good living," although he hadn't practiced for two years. The newsman asked Chadwick if his daughter had recently cabled Iri Reynolds for money. Chadwick bristled and replied, "That is something I will not deny or affirm." He continued, "A lot of big men are allowing a single weak woman [his wife] to bear the entire brunt of this affair." The doctor called Reynolds "an old and trusted friend" for whom he had "profoundest respect," but he denied that his wife ever told Reynolds in his presence that she was Carnegie's illegitimate daughter. Chadwick attempted to burnish his image by saying that he did not use tobacco or alcohol and that he and his daughter were definitely not going to the French Riviera as had been reported.[3]

The French press had taken to referring to Mrs. Chadwick as the "American Humbert" in reference to the imprisoned notorious French swindler Therese Humbert. Queried about this by the reporter, the doctor strenuously denounced the French papers for the comparison. Dr. Chadwick was emphatic: "That is impossible. The Humbert woman deliberately defrauded people." This ended the interview, and the reporter concluded that Dr. Leroy Chadwick was "a rather weak man, who could be easily controlled." The interview might have been over, but the comparisons between Mrs. Chadwick and Mme. Humbert had just begun.[4]

Mme. Therese Humbert, known in France as La Grande Therese, was one of Europe's greatest imposters. Therese rose from peasant roots to become one of Paris's wealthiest and most politically powerful women, a position she held for two decades. Mme. Humbert claimed to be the illegitimate daughter of an American millionaire, Robert Henry Crawford, who left her an inheritance of $20 million (100 million francs) in 1877. This fortune was purportedly in bearer bonds, which the Humbert family kept in a locked strongbox. French financiers and banks were eager to loan against this hoard even if almost no one outside Humbert's circle had seen the contents of the strongbox. A notarized inventory was available for the more skeptical creditors. The sheer size of the fortune added to its credibility. An anonymous friend of Therese explained that if she had laid claim to a few million francs, she could have borrowed only a few thousand francs against it. "But a hundred million!" the acquaintance exclaimed. "People took their hats off to a sum like that . . . their admiration prevented them from seeing straight."[5]

In 1896, a Paris bank failure was laid at Mme. Humbert's doorstep by a French prosecutor, who called the family's claims to wealth "the greatest swindle of the century." But the evidence was thin, and Therese succeeded in negotiating a settlement. By 1898, Therese had, by luck and guile, weathered the storm and regained much of her previous grandeur. It was but a brief respite. In 1902, a single, brave creditor sued over a paltry overdue loan of $26,000. On May 6, 1902, a judge signed an order for the infamous strongbox to be opened for an inventory. Therese and her entire clan vanished. The legendary strongbox contained only a red-leather jewel case containing a $2 broach, some shares in a defunct gold mine, and a few newspapers. The Humberts were charged with fraud.[6]

After a continent-wide manhunt, the family was arrested in Spain in December 1902. In August 1903, they went on trial in Paris. Some creditors talked of hypnosis and called Therese a sorcerer or an enchantress, but it was simpler than that. A prosecutor summed it up succinctly when he said that Therese had "raised burglary to the height of a work of genius." It was claimed that $140 million had passed through Therese's hands in the twenty years the fraud lasted and that she netted $10 million. Found guilty, Therese and her husband were sentenced to just five years' solitary confinement and hard labor, which was a light sentence considering the magnitude of the fraud. Therese was fifty-two. When she and her husband were released after five years, they disappeared completely. The Humbert swindle, its magnitude impossible to ignore, was widely reported throughout Europe and the United States. The similarities between the career of Therese Humbert and Cassie Chadwick were hard to miss. The American press began referring to Mrs. Chadwick as the "American Humbert," despite Dr. Chadwick's feeble protestations to the contrary.[7]

The next day, reporters found Dr. Chadwick in yet another Paris hotel. Cornered, he was asked if his wife was Toledo's notorious Madame Devere. The doctor indignantly responded, "How can people read such rot." However, he conceded, "There might have been much in her history with which I am unfamiliar." He went on to say that he only recently had heard the Devere name in connection with his wife, which was untrue. The doctor called the newspaper reports about his wife "an extreme shock" because she would never pass forged promissory notes. He denied that his wife had given him millions of dollars, and in fact he said he was forced to cable America for funds just yesterday. Reporters noted that Dr. Chadwick looked hunted as he weakly begged for people to leave him alone.[8]

Far from the lights of Paris, Charles Beckwith was having none of Leroy Chadwick's claims of innocence. Recalling those two worthless checks Dr. Chadwick had given him last August, a bitter Beckwith had this to say: "They ought to bring him back to this country and prosecute him to the full extent of the law. . . . He knew of the Carnegie notes as well as she did."[9]

Cassie Chadwick received unexpected support in New York from Hetty Green, the renowned nineteenth-century financial genius and notorious miser who was one of the wealthiest women in America. Although Mrs. Green had inherited a substantial sum herself, there were accusations that she forged an aunt's will to get even more. Hetty had made a fortune investing in Civil

War government bonds and railroad stocks, demonstrating a coolheaded, patient investment strategy that few men could match. Mrs. Green haughtily admitted she didn't know Mrs. Chadwick or her "kind," but she did have considerable experience with the male-dominated financial community. Mrs. Green felt that Mrs. Chadwick was only a tool of wealthy bankers and brokers. It was Hetty's opinion that "some of these big bankers and lawyers have been behind her, using her to get money." As for government prosecutors, a sore point with the seventy-year-old who had seen her share of legal trouble, Mrs. Green said, "You can't believe all the district attorneys about her either."[10]

On December 12, Cassie Chadwick, against the advice of her lawyers, voluntarily agreed to return to Cleveland. Her New York attorney, Phillip Carpenter, told reporters, "Mrs. Chadwick is not fearful of the result. She is entirely innocent of any crime." Her attorneys further indicated that she would not demand a change of venue because she thought Clevelanders would be sympathetic to her. Cassie failed to comprehend the effect the negative press coverage was having on the public's perception of her. Finding twelve souls in the potential Ohio jury pool who had no opinion on the case would be a challenge.[11]

Before leaving New York City, she agreed to meet—accompanied by her lawyer, Phillip Carpenter, and Marshal Henkel—with twenty of the city's reporters in the Tombs. The image she presented to the press was that of a cultured woman of wealth. Her clothes were fine: a broad-brimmed, fur-trimmed hat; a blue satin shirtwaist trimmed in lace; and a brown skirt. The reporters were less impressed by her rasping voice and disregard for grammar.[12]

Mrs. Chadwick declined to take questions, but instead she chose to embark on a rambling monologue. An attempt by an intrepid reporter to inject a question brought a sharp rebuke—"I can't be questioned"—backed up by a warning finger. She continued with a tirade aimed at the newspapers for printing falsehoods. She denied any rift between herself and Dr. Chadwick, and she declared that she had many offers of bail. She was returning to Cleveland to settle her affairs, Cassie emphasized, and face the charges against her. Carpenter confirmed the offers of bail but said those potential bondmen had demanded anonymity, which was impossible since bail was a matter of public record. Mrs. Chadwick reiterated her nervous state and delicate health. She mocked reporters by detailing her various secret comings and goings at Holland House, despite their watchfulness. She concluded by thanking Marshal Henkel publicly for his kindness.[13]

Cassie Chadwick had been good copy, and the New York press would miss her. East Coast bankers and financiers, however, breathed a sigh of relief. By the latest accounting, Cassie Chadwick had produced fraudulent documents totaling $17,296,000—over $400 million today. Before leaving New York, Mrs. Chadwick sent a note to Virgil Kline pledging she would be home soon and pay off all loans. One amazed creditor later responded, "You wouldn't think she'd get off a joke like this while she's locked up in jail." Attorney Carpenter summed up what many in New York financial circles thought when he asked reporters, "Does it not seem absurd that a woman saying she was the illegitimate daughter of Andrew Carnegie could go into a Cleveland bank and secure money on her mere assertion? If such is the practice in Cleveland, there ought to be a lunatic asylum founded for Cleveland bankers."[14]

Enterprising newspaper reporters in Cleveland had contacted every financial institution in the city to discover if Mrs. Chadwick was a customer. Only Wade Park Banking confirmed her as a client. Two banks that had once enjoyed her business were now defunct. No other banks admitted a relationship. Nervous Cleveland bankers felt these denials might not be sufficient to calm worried and distrustful depositors or prevent doubt from being cast on the entire region's financial system. Thus, the bankers collectively placed an announcement in the Cleveland papers informing the city that while a number of them had "intimate knowledge" of Mrs. Chadwick's financial transactions, only Wade Park held any Chadwick paper currently. This statement was signed by officers of thirty-eight Cleveland financial institutions.[15]

Andrew Carnegie's appearance as a witness would be necessary at any Chadwick trial. Carnegie preferred not to go to Cleveland. However, a mere affidavit, like the one he recently sent prosecutors in Cleveland disavowing the notes, would not suffice. To insure Carnegie's participation, the federal grand jury in Cleveland issued a subpoena for him to appear in Federal Court at 9:00 A.M. on Tuesday, December 13. Failure to appear was punishable by a fine of $250. A deputy marshal appeared at Carnegie's residence shortly after 10:00 A.M. on Saturday, December 10. After passing through the ironmaster's butler and secretary, the deputy was ushered into the library, where he found Carnegie reading a newspaper. The ironmaster read the summons, and then exclaimed, "Cleveland!" The deputy affirmed it. "Oh, Cleveland. Humph! Humph! I can't."[16]

The only way Carnegie could avoid a December trip to Cleveland was if he was ill and could present a doctor's certificate, much as Richard Brown had in 1890. This was not difficult for a man of Carnegie's wealth. Late Saturday afternoon, it was announced that Andrew Carnegie was suffering from an acute attack of his old nemesis, lumbago. Due to the winter weather, the doctor stated that it would be injudicious for his patient to travel to Cleveland.

To bolster his case, Carnegie canceled a trip to Washington, scheduled for Monday, December 12.[17]

The ironmaster did not wish to appear uncooperative, however. On Wednesday, December 14, he released a statement through his secretary reiterating that his only reason for not going to Cleveland now was the weather's effect on his health. He would be happy to give a deposition at his home, and later in the winter after returning from his winter home in Florida, he would go to Cleveland "whenever his testimony is needed." The government agreed. A lesser man might not have received such an accommodation from federal authorities, but Andrew Carnegie was no ordinary citizen.[18]

Cassie Chadwick, Freda, and five federal agents boarded New York Central's Buffalo Limited to Cleveland at 7:40 P.M. on December 12. Cassie was lodged in the train's buffet car, where she was guarded by two deputy US marshals and three secret service men. Her demand that her stateroom door only lock from the inside was ignored by the marshals, who wanted it kept ajar and, for good measure, wedged the windows shut. The women's luggage was searched, and a pair of scissors and two flasks of spirits were confiscated from Freda.

The overnight trip to northwest Pennsylvania was uneventful. From Erie westward, Mrs. Chadwick alternated between engaging in conversation and barely controlled weeping, accompanied by clenching her fist. "I'll fight this case," she could be heard to mutter. "It won't be long before the public knows the truth." Emil boarded the train at Ashtabula, Ohio, bearing a letter from Mary Chadwick in Paris. The November 30 letter was written just after Dr. Chadwick and his daughter had learned of Mrs. Chadwick's problems through a London newspaper. The affectionate and supportive letter was signed "your loving daughter, Mary," and it greatly cheered the recipient.[19]

If Cassie Chadwick had expected a warm welcome in Cleveland, she was seriously disappointed. Periodic reports reaching the train of a crowd at Union Station in Cleveland became increasing ominous. Fear of crowds caused Cassie to begin loudly wailing and demanding to detrain somewhere else. The Cleveland federal marshal had arranged to meet the train at Union Station, so no change in plans was possible. Learning this, the woman violently denounced everyone associated with her transportation.

As the train neared the station, she grew more concerned about how the crowd there would receive her. To counter any misconceptions Clevelanders might entertain, Cassie Chadwick embarked on a last-minute public relations blitz, issuing bulletins every quarter hour to the press corps on the train. She denied being Carnegie's daughter, calling the idea "ridiculous." She also denied that attorney Powers had represented himself as Carnegie's man. She said that if she had the millions the press claimed, she might have fled the country, an injudicious statement that hurt her chances of bail. Her tormentor Herbert Newton wasn't a banker at all, Cassie declared, but a mere machinist worth $200,000, at best. Her last issuance concluded, "I am coming back to fight for the $5,000,000 worth of securities and the trust certificate."[20]

A crowd estimated at ten thousand was on hand when Mrs. Chadwick's snow-covered train arrived at Union Station at 2:15 P.M. on Tuesday, December 13, three hours late. Waiting in the December cold for Mrs. Chadwick did nothing to improve the mood of the assembled ten thousand. The arrival of the train was greeted with hisses, jeers, hoots, and less kind epithets. When she saw the crowd, Mrs. Chadwick shrank from the Pullman's windows and sobbed, "I can't do it!" Once in the cavernous shed of Union Station, the prisoner demanded that the regular passengers detrain first to keep them from staring at her. The authorities refused. Freda wrapped Cassie securely in her brown full-length silk coat and placed a double-veiled empire hat on her head. Emil and a deputy marshal half carried her off the train. When Cassie stepped onto the platform from the Pullman, the crowd surged forward, trampling an iron fence and surging onto the tracks. Nearly two hundred surrounded the train, and it was all the fifty police detailed to crowd control could do to hold them at bay. Women threw away their hats for a clearer view, and old men fought for a better look. There were shouts of "There comes Cassie!" and "Where's the money?" followed by "Here's the notes!" and lastly, "How's father Andy?" Freda and a couple of enterprising newsmen led the way down the platform. Arms reached out for the chance to touch the infamous woman. Mrs. Chadwick recoiled and shuffled to a waiting carriage.[21]

Despite a crowded street and a dull, overcast day, which was terrible for taking pictures, photographers jostled for position as flashbulbs popped. Mrs. Chadwick was helped into a waiting carriage by Cleveland US marshal Frank Chandler. Her carriage was surrounded by vehicles carrying newsmen. Emil, holding a suitcase, and Freda, juggling several parcels, were left on the sidewalk as Mrs. Chadwick's carriage with two lawmen pulled away from the curb. One of the trailing carriages carried Associated Press reporters, who took pity on Emil and Freda and offered them a ride to the Federal Building. By the time Cassie arrived at the Federal Building twenty minutes later, she was almost prostrate. Marshal Chandler cleverly bypassed the Superior Street front entrance and headed for the west alley, where the wagon entrance for the post office was located. Unfortunately, the alley was full of coal and mail wagons. By the time these were cleared, the crowd had reassembled, filling the alley, the nearby roofs, and every window, including a sky bridge between buildings. Young boys made sport of throwing snow off the roof on those standing below.[22]

In the federal district attorney's office, Mrs. Chadwick was formally transferred from the custody of New York marshals to those in Cleveland. The office was closely guarded by police, Customs inspectors, and secret service men. On the advice of her attorneys, Mrs. Chadwick requested a preliminary hearing and was then hustled down a freight elevator to an alley, where her carriage waited. She covered her face with her hands and threw herself into the carriage. The crowd, tired of waiting and jostling for a look at the woman, was by now in a truly foul mood. They blocked the alley, forcing the carriage to run the gauntlet of spectators lining the street. At the jail, the entrance was blocked by another mob, so the police were ordered to use their clubs to clear a path. Several injuries left blood in the snow, but the crowd parted. Mrs. Chadwick entered the jail, a guest of Cuyahoga County sheriff Ed Barry, the man it was said, tongue-in-cheek, who entertained more than anyone else in Cleveland. This was not the kind of invitation Mrs. Chadwick would have sought. Asked her age, she told the turnkey she was thirty-eight; in New York, she had been fifty-one. She said she was born in the United States, but she gave no specific location.[23]

An hour and twenty minutes later, Mrs. Chadwick, now thoroughly broken, was lodged in cell 14 of the Cuyahoga County jail. The jail cells, nicknamed "pigeon holes" by the inhabitants, had stone floors and ceilings, three solid steel sides, and a grated front. A hinged shelf and a folding iron bed, supported by chains, completed the furnishings. This was not Holland House. During the day prisoners were permitted to mingle in a common room. Only two other female prisoners were present. Upon seeing her stark cell, Mrs. Chadwick fainted and was revived with water. Freda was permitted to go to the Euclid Avenue house to fetch some clothing and stay the night. She also made arrangements at the nearby Forest City Hotel for meals to spare Mrs. Chadwick unappetizing jail food, called slumgullion by the inmates. The jail remained besieged by the curious all evening, and police guarded every door in a rare instance of the jailers keeping people out of the lockup rather than in.[24]

One of Cassie's Cleveland attorneys, Sheldon Q. Kerruish, a partner in Virgil Kline's law firm, visited to discuss bail. A server from a local livery claiming an unpaid bill of $35 tried to serve a summons on her, but the sheriff dissuaded him. Mrs. Chadwick apparently rarely paid for transportation since another Cleveland livery company had also filed suit for $33.50 due for trips dating back to January 1. This failure to pay liverymen might haunt her since she had to provide her own transport to the courthouse or walk.[25]

On Wednesday, December 14, nineteen men were impaneled on a federal grand jury in Cleveland and rendered thirteen indictments in the Chadwick case, all in one day. The grand jury returned four indictments each against Beckwith and Spear, as well as five against Mrs. Chadwick. Legally, the charge was for "willfully misapplying funds of a national bank," and it stemmed from those checks certified with no funds in the bank. All nineteen members of the grand jury were rewarded for their fast work with a group picture, published in the *Cleveland Plain Dealer*, identifying them as the brave citizens who indicted Cassie Chadwick.[26]

By Thursday, December 15, Cassie was more relaxed and talking. While reclining on a couch in a corridor in the jail, she told an inquiring reporter that she was glad to be back among friends. The sheriff was "courtesy personified." Unlike her dark cell in the Tombs, the county jail environment was all "comfort and cheerfulness." She so liked the jail, she told the newsman, "I shall stay with Sheriff Barry at least until the bankruptcy case is settled." Did she think she had a choice? Why stay in jail, the reporters asked? It was not a matter of bail, she claimed, as she had received that very day an offer of bail from one of the wealthiest men in America. He was a friend since she was twelve and, publicity be damned, offered to publicly sign the bond. She declined, Mrs. Chadwick said, because of the protection the jail offered from the curious and hostile crowds she attracted. No one believed her.[27]

Mrs. Chadwick's intuition, she claimed, convinced her that her husband and stepdaughter had sailed from Liverpool, England, that very day. In reality, on December 15, Dr. Chadwick was still in Paris. The press reported that Mary and her father would go to England next week to await word of the doctor's possible indictment in Cleveland. This was pure speculation since Leroy Chadwick was refusing to answer any questions. As for rumors that her husband was penniless, Cassie scoffed, "He is plentifully supplied with money." In Paris at that very moment, the doctor was telling friends that he might resume his medical practice to earn his livelihood.[28]

Mrs. Chadwick asked a reporter how the people of Cleveland felt about her. They were divided, was the diplomatic reply, and many believed she was shielding an accomplice. Cassie promised to tell the truth eventually. She told the reporter, "You may assure my friends and those who believe in me that I

will not disappoint . . . I am an honest woman . . . I have never wrongfully obtained money from anyone . . . I will repay every dollar of my indebtedness."[29]

On the evening of December 15, two former jail matrons from the Ohio
Penitentiary arrived unannounced, and when she saw them, Mrs. Chadwick
covered her face and refused to address them. One of the visitors, Mrs. Flora
Kissinger, recalled that the Madame Devere of thirteen years ago seemed to
have some "pull" with the board of prison managers, gaining exceptional
privileges. The two Columbus women took a long look and left without public comment.[30]

Charles Beckwith was in Cleveland to testify before the Cuyahoga County
grand jury. He kept the jurymen's rapt attention through lunch and beyond
with the story of how he was "Chadwicked," a new slang term making the
rounds in financial circles. He reserved special vehemence for the New York
attorney who, according to Beckwith, presented himself as a Carnegie representative from Pittsburgh. Unfortunately for Beckwith, there were no independent witnesses willing to support this assertion.[31]

Released by the grand jury, Beckwith and his wife stopped by the county
jail to see Mrs. Chadwick. "You've ruined me, but I'm not sure you are a fraud,"
Beckwith told his former client. They shook hands. "It looks as if it's time for
you to tell all," Beckwith said, but Mrs. Chadwick made no reply. Beckwith
advised her to retain a good attorney and keep him. As he left, Beckwith's
voice broke as he told Mrs. Chadwick, "You know I've stood by you to my last
dollar." It was the last time the two would meet.[32]

New York attorney William Olcott admitted to the *New York Times,* "I was
a lamb, and I regret to say that for fifteen days I believed in Mrs. Chadwick
and was one of her many victims." Both former governor Frank Black and
Olcott had refused to represent her after repeated attempts by the woman.
Mrs. Chadwick begged to differ. She claimed that she had an appointment
with Black to discuss nonfinancial matters in New York in early December.
Only illness prevented her from keeping it. She further stated that Olcott had
sent her a nice letter in September, but she had misplaced it. Olcott's law firm
denied all of this and said that while she had recently tried to retain them to
defend her, they declined to take her call.[33]

The Chadwick money was making Cassie's jail stay far more pleasant than
that of most inmates. Sheriff Barry was offering her no special privileges, but
she was benefiting, according to the *Cleveland Plain Dealer,* from the rule that
"Money is almost as much good to a person in jail as it is to one outside." Her
meals were delivered by a nearby hotel kitchen, and the food was "just as sa-

vory," despite being served on the fifty-cent pine board in her cell. She had her favorite rocker from home and other trappings, including rugs, to make her cell more comfortable. Cassie Chadwick even received a delivery of flowers from Tom Porter, the former deputy hired to guard the Euclid Avenue home for the Elyria bank that held the mortgage. Porter said of the gesture, "Mrs. Chadwick always treated me fair and square." Porter's bank employer was said to be considering an offer to rent the house for public tours at fifty cents a head.[34]

As boredom set in, however, Mrs. Chadwick grew irascible and spiteful. She called for Sheriff Barry and spent an hour haranguing him about her treatment. The sheriff attempted to turn the episode into an interrogation, but the woman evaded his direct questions. He pointed out that if she could assist the poor depositors of Citizen's National, it would help her. "Oh, I am so sorry for the poor depositors . . . the Oberlin bank matter will be cleared up soon," she assured anyone listening. Barry pointed out that Iri Reynolds might be indicted, but Mrs. Chadwick insisted that he was a "dear friend," that no one would indict him. Sheriff Barry reminded her that newspapermen were waiting downstairs for her promised statement. Her response was, "Marshall [sic] Chandler told me this afternoon that I did not have to see anybody unless desired. I do not want to see the newspapermen, and that ends it."[35]

Mrs. Chadwick dispatched Emil and Freda to Marshal Chandler, with the complaint that Sheriff Barry was letting reporters harass her. This was patently untrue since no one was allowed to visit without Mrs. Chadwick's consent. Chandler contacted Cleveland federal district judge Francis Wing, on the circuit in Toledo, who issued a blanket order prohibiting visitors to *all* federal prisoners until he could sort the details. Chandler had to find the right balance in handling his celebrity prisoner. He was a Republican political appointee, and there were rumblings in Cleveland that one faction of the party wanted to replace him as part of a larger internal party power struggle that had nothing to do with Mrs. Chadwick. Mishandling the most infamous prisoner he would ever have in his custody could cost Chandler his job.[36]

Before enforcing the no-visitor order, Barry rounded up twenty or so reporters who had been hanging around the jail and marched on Mrs. Chadwick. Did she wish to make her long-promised statement? Angry, she refused to offer any comment. One out-of-town newspaperman managed to sneak a few private words to her. She told him, "Well, they haven't proved yet that I'm Madame Devere, anyhow," words she seemed to regret as soon as she uttered them.[37]

Playing the marshal and sheriff off against one another became a new diversion for Cassie. Sheriff Barry expanded the no-visitors order to bar Emil and

Freda. "If Mrs. Chadwick won't receive newspaper men and won't do this and that," Barry explained, "she won't have any visitors. She is scheduled for a quick disillusioning. [Marshal] Chandler asked that the maid and Emil be allowed to stay with her in jail, but they are going to clear out and stay out." Barry was going to enforce the new court directive to the letter. Visitation would henceforth be restricted to regular jail visitation, 1:00 to 3:00 P.M. weekdays. With no other female inmates, the scheming Cassie Chadwick found herself in virtual solitary confinement with only an occasional visit from a jail matron.[38]

Mrs. Chadwick appealed to Chandler, which only made Barry angrier. In reality, the federal authorities had no control over the jail. The county sheriff was legally responsible for all jail inmates, and his duty to a federal prisoner was to keep him or her safe and available when the marshal demanded it. Mrs. Chadwick sent Emil for her mail, and he delivered it directly to Barry, who had been opening and examining it over Cassie's objections. Now the sheriff refused to touch it without her written consent. She reluctantly gave it. Some legal minds believed that her recent actions, mood swings, and displays of temper were deliberate and a part of a strategy designed to reinforce an insanity defense.[39]

Insanity was a common defense for nonviolent crime. Iowan Mrs. Ellen S. Tupper was a nationally recognized honeybee expert in the 1870s and published a journal on beekeeping. To cover what were small debts, Mrs. Tupper began to forge notes and drafts bearing the signatures of prominent men in Iowa, including the governor. When discovered, she immediately confessed and made restitution of about $1,000. This crime was not publicized "to protect the good name" of the accused. Less than a month later, Mrs. Tupper was again caught negotiating forged paper, and it was reported that she had been so engaged for about two years. One wealthy citizen declined to file charges and was said to have "sustained in silence some loss." Her method seemed to be to pass one forged note to cover a previously forged note in an endless chain. Upon her arrest, Mrs. Tupper was quite ill, according to her physician, and had been "deranged" for two years. She was not indicted. Ellen was again arrested for forgery and in early March 1877 was tried in Davenport, Iowa, her forgeries amounting to at least $11,000. Her defense, according to one local newspaper, offered "the time worn and threadbare pleas of insanity." A jury quickly returned a not-guilty verdict on the grounds of insanity. One Iowa newspaper opined, "It is a libel upon the unfortunate insane and a farce upon justice to let pleas of insanity step between the criminal and deserved punishment." The episode had little effect upon Mrs. Tupper's reputation.

When she died in 1888, she was described in her obituary as a "remarkable woman" and a supporter of women's suffrage. No mention was made of her career as a forger and swindler.[40]

Mrs. Chadwick announced on Thursday, December 15, that J. P. Dawley, a prominent and combative defense attorney, had agreed to defend her. Dawley's clients ranged from murderers to crooked bankers. Dawley's hiring and Cassie's often-denied criminal past made an insanity defense less likely. The *Cleveland Plain Dealer* posed the obvious question of where the bankrupt woman found enough money to pay high-priced legal talent like Dawley, whose services "are not secured for a song." When Dawley made his initial call on his new client, he was accompanied by a wealthy Cleveland contractor whose presence left reporters speculating that perhaps a bail agreement was in the offing.[41]

On Saturday, December 17, Mrs. Chadwick, Beckwith, and Spear were arraigned in Federal Court on the grand jury indictments. The federal government would be the first to try the trio. All state evidence was surrendered to federal authorities. Federal district attorney John J. Sullivan had announced the arraignment for Monday but quietly changed the day to Saturday to deceive the expected Monday crowds. Not even the defendants and sheriff were forewarned. A doctor examined Mrs. Chadwick and suggested she take a carriage instead of walking to court. Sullivan's ruse worked as less than thirty people were present at the fifteen-minute proceeding.[42]

In court, the three defendants pled not guilty. The nearly deaf Mrs. Chadwick was puzzled. "Why was I brought here?" she queried of Dawley, who assured her it was just a formality that had no bearing on her trial. She was instantly relieved and more energetic. Dawley reserved the right to withdraw her plea in the future, leaving the door open to a plea deal or insanity plea. The bail for Beckwith and Spear was raised from $10,000 to $25,000 each, and the Oberlin men posted it within a couple of hours. Mrs. Chadwick's counsel didn't ask for bail, so she continued to reside in the best cell in the county jail, which, the *New York Times* pointed out, was still a cell in an Ohio county jail.[43]

Among those few observers in the courtroom was Irving Belford, Joe Lamb's defender back in 1890. Belford was seated not ten feet from Mrs. Chadwick, who sat resting her head in her hand. Belford's purpose seemed limited to a desire to unnerve the defendant. She never looked directly at Belford, stealing sidewise glances instead. "It was a mean trick," Belford admitted. He was certain Cassie Chadwick was Madame Devere.[44]

Cassie had to be helped into a carriage for her return trip to jail, and on the way she weakened perceptibly. Back in jail, she kept asking for medication given her in New York, which had been confiscated by her Cleveland jailers. The jail physician wisely refused, saying he was unfamiliar with the medication and feared its side effects. Many medications of the day were heavily laced with alcohol, narcotics, and even poisons, so this was a real concern. Nerve tonics were widely sold to women for the treatment of "fits, spasms, nervous head-ache, insomnia and nervous wakefulness." Some of these nostrums contained high levels of bromides, which were recognized to have depressing effects and, at high doses, could cause slurred speech, confusion, and psychotic behavior. Considering Cassie's hypochondria, she may have appreciated the patent med-icine that an enterprising Clevelander concocted. The untested nostrum car-ried the label proclaiming, "Cassie Chadwick's Nerve Tonic . . . for it was nerve which guided her life." Speculation about how much of Cassie's behavior could be blamed on medications she ingested was common among her keepers.[45]

Federal authorities were convinced Cassie's attorneys would offer an insan-ity defense, and the federal prosecutor, Sullivan, considered such a plea as her only solid chance to avoid prison. Sheriff Barry said he thought she was insane. Reportedly, federal prosecutors had already made preparations to have Mrs. Chadwick examined by psychologists or "alienists," as they were known. Some legal experts, perhaps in jest, suggested that the large bonuses and fees she paid for loans was proof of insanity. Lorain County, Ohio, prosecutor Lee Stroup estimated that as many as one hundred men from northern Ohio could have done business with Mrs. Chadwick and might be potential witnesses. "This is a remarkable affair," Stroup suggested. "There is no doubt but that hundreds of thousands have been borrowed in northern Ohio of which the public knows nothing. . . . The individuals who loaned her money are simply pocketing their losses and banks are maintaining strict secrecy in order to protect their credit."[46]

Ironically, one of Mrs. Chadwick's fellow inmates was a young woman charged with insanity, which Mrs. Chadwick called "a most terrible affliction." Victorian women were almost expected to develop mental disorders. Mentally and physically, women were believed to be infantile, developmentally arrested, and more primitive than men. Victorian women were expected to be nervous, cry, become hysterical, faint regularly, have poor judgment, and be easily in-fluenced. The most damning defect of all, according to prominent psychiatrist Prof. G. T. W. Patrick, writing in a widely read journal in 1895, was woman's "untruthfulness." According to the professor, "Deception and ruse in woman, far more than man, have become a habit of thought and speech." An 1890s book, titled *The Female Offender*, offered one of the first studies of female criminals. The authors concluded that female offenders were more primitive than other women, had masculine faces, and had oddly developed skulls. The book classi-fied swindling as a mental illness. With this backdrop of erroneous psychoanal-ysis, a female offender appearing to be insane and throwing herself on the mercy of the court was culturally acceptable, if not expected. In the late 1800s, insane asylums served as catchall facilities for violent and difficult women. Adding fuel to the fire for a possible insanity plea by Cassie, the superintendent of the Mas-sillon State Hospital for the Insane secretly examined her in late December.[47]

Marshal Chandler and Sheriff Barry were good friends, but that friend-ship was being put to the test by Mrs. Chadwick. Chandler had asked Barry to grant Emil and Freda open visitation. Barry had ended this privilege after learning through the Pittsburgh papers that the prisoner was telegraphing around the country through her son and nurse. Emil and Freda were also discovered smuggling luxury items into the jail. In retaliation against Bar-ry's order, Chandler said that Cassie's attorney, J. P. Dawley, would require a marshal's pass to see his client. "It's ridiculous," Barry scoffed of the pass. If a federal judge sided with Chandler and allowed Emil and Freda in outside of visitation hours, Barry said he would demand a release from federal author-ities for Mrs. Chadwick's security. Some authorities in the case suggested the sheriff-marshal feud might be resolved by sending the prisoner to Toledo, where federal authorities also used the county jail, the same lockup that had been Madame Devere's home for over a year.[48]

US Customs officials in Cleveland and New York had embarked on their own hunt for Chadwick treasure. There was much speculation that Mrs. Chadwick—nicknamed the "Duchess of Diamonds" by the press after hear-ing of her large, overflowing jewelry box—had squirreled away some of her gems to keep them out of the hands of creditors and receivers. Where were they, the Treasury agents wanted to know. They were especially interested in her repeated trips to Belgium, the diamond capital of Europe, suspecting she might have purchased gems there and failed to declare them when she returned to the United States, which was smuggling under the law.[49]

A trunk or satchel was believed to be missing from the Chadwick luggage seized in New York. Both Emil and Freda were severely questioned by Treasury agents about the missing luggage. Freda, claiming to be a mere employee, could shed no light on the matter. Emil, his mysterious Cleveland trip in early De-cember in question, was viewed as a coconspirator by some New York papers. He stated that the Holland House manager in New York—motivated by a de-sire to see the woman and the crowds she attracted depart—advised his mother to move her luggage to avoid attachment. Emil did not know where it went.[50]

On Sunday, December 18, Dr. Chadwick and Mary left Paris for London. By Tuesday, they were at sea. Some reporters claimed that the doctor exhibited a thick roll of cash whenever he paid a bill, tipped liberally, and carried a heavy suitcase, which never left his hand. The story was pure fabrication. Leroy Chadwick was reduced to booking cramped, second-class staterooms costing $57 each and paying for them with Mary's emergency funds.[51]

The Boston creditor, Herbert Newton, was in Southampton, England, to personally verify that Dr. Chadwick was on the Hamburg America steamer *Pretoria*, bound for the United States. Newton's lawyers confirmed that they intended to include the doctor in their civil suit for notes totaling $90,000, which Chadwick had personally signed.[52]

The Federal Bankruptcy Court wanted Cassie Chadwick to testify at the hearing currently in session. Attorney Dawley argued vigorously against it, citing self-incrimination, and maintained his client was too ill to appear. The Bankruptcy Court ordered her examined by two independent physicians before compelling her presence. Both Emil and Freda were ordered to answer the receiver's queries in his thus far fruitless attempt to locate hidden assets, primarily gemstones. Both were represented by Chadwick family attorney Sheldon Kerruish in the role of defender.[53]

Freda testified on December 19, stating that she was paid $45 a month to administer massage treatments, act as a maid, and answer the telephone because of Mrs. Chadwick's deafness. The court was very interested in the financial nature of those phone calls. However, Freda had been well coached by Kerruish, and she failed to remember any of the details. Attorney Grossman, in his role as inquisitor, questioned Freda at length about the missing luggage from Holland House, specifically a bag said to contain papers and a steamer truck of clothing. She denied any knowledge and said that Mrs. Chadwick's French maid, Adele Miny, was delegated to pack clothing and jewelry. Freda claimed that she saw only a little jewelry as Mrs. Chadwick rarely wore any. As Freda remembered it, only one trunk and two handbags went to New York, not the twenty-plus fantasy previously described in the New York papers. The steamer contained clothing, one handbag held articles for use on the train, and the other had important papers. Only Mrs. Chadwick handled the bag containing papers. Freda said that one handbag and the steamer trunk were removed from the hotel to avoid attachment by a New York merchant, but she didn't know where they were sent. Grossman accused Freda of playing a role in hiding the luggage, which she indignantly denied.[54]

Nineteen-year-old Emil Hoover was questioned sternly for half a day. Emil said he was in school on Long Island when the press broke the story and learned about the lawsuit when his mother telephoned to warn him about the publicity. He knew of the missing luggage—he testified they were a trunk and a handbag—but had made no effort to locate them. Of his mother's jewelry, he said that, like Freda, he had seen only a dozen rings, a sunburst brooch, and two watches, but never the large box Iri Reynolds had claimed existed. Emil explained that his quick trip to Cleveland had been to deliver two safety deposit box keys to his mother's brother-in-law, Daniel Pine, who was to retrieve some papers from the deposit box. Wishing to avoid the press, Emil took the keys to Chadwick family attorney Sheldon Kerruish, who took them to Pine. Within an hour, Pine and Kerruish had retrieved a package that had been sealed by Mrs. Chadwick. Emil said he presumed the package contained valuable papers. He told the Bankruptcy Court, "I never inquired what it contained." He took it to New York and placed it in his mother's hands. His mother, he said, was capable of taking care of her own business affairs and didn't take him into her confidence regarding financial matters. "I never bothered her about her affairs," Emil said. "She may explain them to me when she is prepared." Emil testified that "Dr. Chadwick cautioned me last summer to be careful as to how I spent my money." He conceded that he met with Freda on Saturday evening, December 17, to discuss their testimony. Of the missing satchel, Emil claimed not to know its contents. He said Freda thought it might contain his mother's jewelry.[55]

Mrs. Mary Londraville, a now former housekeeper for the Chadwicks, testified that she had taken two satchels to a meeting in Cleveland between Mrs. Chadwick's attorneys and Herbert Newton's. After the meeting, Mrs. Chadwick left for New York, according to Mary, and told her to take one large satchel to her brother-in-law, Daniel Pine. Mrs. Londraville believed the bag contained important papers. She said that Emil Hoover picked up the satchel from Pine, telling him that attorney Dawley wanted the bag. Emil told Mary that he didn't know what the satchel contained. While Emil convincingly claimed to know little of the satchel's contents, bankruptcy authorities believed Mrs. Chadwick was hiding something important in it. This courtroom testimony concerning the missing satchel had convinced Nathan Loeser, the bankruptcy receiver, that, according to the Cleveland Plain Dealer, "there is tangible property of Mrs. Chadwick's secreted at some place." Vigorous efforts to recover it would be pursued, Loeser said.[56]

A little over a week later, the two missing pieces of luggage—a satchel and a steamer trunk—were located in New York and forwarded to Cleveland for examination. They proved a dead end. When they were examined by authorities on January 5, they were found to contain only clothing with a retail value of $4,000 or $5,000. The clothing was expensive to be sure, but not the tens of thousands in missing jewelry the Bankruptcy Court was hoping to find.[57]

On Tuesday afternoon, December 20, Cassie Chadwick made her much anticipated appearance in Bankruptcy Court in Cleveland. To get into the courtroom, she was forced to run a gauntlet of curious spectators, who stubbornly refused to leave when asked by bailiffs and deputies to disperse. Trembling after her encounter with the crowd, Mrs. Chadwick sank into a chair and held her head in her hands. Much to the disappointment of everyone present, but on the advice of her attorney, she refused to give her name, be sworn in, or answer any questions, repeatedly citing the Fifth Amendment. Frustrated bankruptcy officials conceded the day to her and adjourned the session.[58]

CHAPTER EIGHTEEN

A NOBLE THING

Iri Reynolds appeared before the Cuyahoga County grand jury on December 20. He admitted that he had been shown the $5 million Carnegie note by Mrs. Chadwick back in March 1903, when she originally left it with him. According to Reynolds, the woman wrote on the back "Pay to the order of Iri Reynolds, trustee." Reynolds also told the grand jury that he had read a skeleton (unsigned) copy of the trust agreement, not the original. He denied any complicity in the Chadwick money schemes. While many of those who had lost money blamed Reynolds in part, he was generally seen as a sympathetic figure and a victim of Mrs. Chadwick's duplicity.[1]

The same county grand jury indicted Dr. Leroy Chadwick on December 22 for forgery. The indictment, based on Iri Reynolds's crucial testimony, alleged that Chadwick knew the $5 million Carnegie note was a forgery when his wife endorsed it over to Reynolds. When the doctor's ship docked in New York, he would be detained. County prosecutor Harvey Keeler was asked by newsmen if the grand jurors had discussed indicting others in the case. "Well, yes," said Keeler, "but there was not enough evidence to indict." Why not? "Why, the defendants could have sworn they trusted the woman's word," replied Keeler. Couldn't Dr. Chadwick use the same defense, the press wanted to know. "Yes," Keeler admitted, "but there are some things he must explain." The prosecutor's honesty reflected the difficulty both the state and federal government would face in convicting anybody with the primarily circumstantial evidence available. Ohio's case against Leroy Chadwick was a response to public demands for action. Neither Edmund Powers nor Iri Reynolds was indicted. Powers, the lawyer, had skated on the edge of criminality, while Reynolds left many people believing he had $5 million in securities instead of merely a promissory note.[2]

Dr. Chadwick had enjoyed an excellent reputation in Cleveland. His wife's attorney, Dawley, scoffed at the indictment, calling it "folly." Dawley defended Dr. Chadwick, saying, "He knew nothing of whatever his wife may have been engaged in and as far as that $5,000,000 note, upon which he was indicted, is concerned, he never even saw it." Dawley was taking Cassie's word on this. Friends of the doctor had warned him before their marriage that Cassie Hoover had a dark past, but Leroy wouldn't hear it. Supporters said he had been duped as completely as Cassie's many creditors. Prosecutors argued that the doctor's involvement in the quest for loans and his part in wining and dining potential creditors abetted her schemes. A family friend said that if Dr. Chadwick was a guilty accomplice, he should have "taken the first steamer for South Africa." But Chadwick hadn't. He could see what was coming for months, but his characteristic lack of initiative left him a spectator to his wife's downfall.[3]

The newspapers, in search of a new angle, published the rumor of a possible Chadwick divorce. Dawley denied all rumors of marital discord. "There is no possibility of a divorce suit." Virgil Kline, Dr. Chadwick's attorney in Cleveland, had no comment. In his written confession, Charles Beckwith, a sick man drifting away from reality, said that Mrs. Chadwick once showed him a divorce petition she had prepared and accompanying bruises on her body to support a claim of spousal abuse. Marshal Chandler scoffed at the suggestion of abuse and suggested that any injuries were props that Cassie employed in the effort to hoodwink the old banker.[4]

December 22, the same day Dr. Chadwick was indicted, Wade Park Banking Company announced it was being taken over by the Cleveland Trust Company. Iri Reynolds was one of the liquidating trustees in a sign of the banking community's confidence in him. In a public statement, Cleveland Trust officials said, "We believe the affairs of the Wade Park Banking Company have been conservatively and honestly administered." Those were reassuring words, but in truth, Wade Park had been weakened by the Chadwick scandal and was still under a sixty-day prohibition on withdrawals. When the prohibition expired in January, it would likely face a run by depositors. The bank had become another casualty of Cassie Chadwick.[5]

The only Christmas visitors to Mrs. Chadwick's dark and gloomy jail cell were Freda and J. P. Dawley. She declined the traditional jailhouse Christmas privilege granted inmates to roam the cell block freely. During the preceding week she had been subjected to the indignity of being examined by a state psychologist seeking to determine her mental state. Dr. C. J. Aldrich, another alienist, was sent by attorney Dawley to examine her, but he was blocked by the authorities. On New Year's Eve, she was measured by a secret service agent employing the Bertillon system for criminal identification. Contrary to protocol, Cassie was not photographed because the authorities decided there were enough photos of her in circulation.[6]

Just days after his grand jury appearance, Charles Beckwith suffered a serious heart attack at his home. The old banker's life hung by a thread, a result of the worries and troubles of the last few weeks, according to his doctor. Hardest for Beckwith was watching his reputation for honesty and integrity crumble. A recent announcement by federal bank examiners that Citizen's National's couple dozen or so stockholders faced tens of thousands in personal liability may have been the last straw for Beckwith. Should the old banker be incapacitated or die, the Chadwick prosecutors would lose their most important witness.[7]

Aboard ship in the middle of the Atlantic, Dr. Chadwick was unaware of his indictment in Cleveland. Detaining the doctor in New York was county sheriff Ed Barry's duty, and Mrs. Chadwick implored him to treat her husband kindly. Dr. Chadwick's impending arrest was, from Cassie's point of view, "the worst thing that has happened during all of the trouble." Barry said that special consideration would be given to Mary Chadwick to insure she would be lodged with friends when her father was detained. Overall, the sheriff, who knew the doctor personally, expressed the deepest sympathy for the man's situation. Barry would be leaving office in a few days; nevertheless, he was prepared to travel to New York to do his duty. Although Barry had been given extradition papers to force Chadwick to return to Ohio, county authorities believed that they would not be needed. Attorney Dawley observed, "Why you couldn't keep him [the doctor] away from Cleveland if you wanted to."[8]

Sheriff Barry traveled first to Albany to get the New York governor's stamp of approval on the extradition order. However, nitpicking bureaucrats in Albany placed a roadblock in Barry's path by refusing to approve the paperwork on the grounds that Ohio had not proved that Dr. Chadwick was in the state on March 5, 1903, when the alleged forgery was committed. Unfazed, Barry left the papers in Albany to be corrected and hurried to New York City. The sheriff's concern was not that Chadwick might flee but that someone in Herbert Newton's camp might persuade Massachusetts authorities to arrest Dr. Chadwick in New York and spirit him to Boston.[9]

The steamship *Pretoria*'s captain added confusion when he docked his ship in Hoboken, New Jersey, instead of New York on New Year's Eve. Dr. Chadwick had been silent and withdrawn on the voyage back to the States, spending most of his time on deck to avoid his jail cell–sized, five-by-six-foot second-class cabin. In his rare conversations with fellow passengers, most of whom were German and unaware of his notoriety, the doctor expressed his desire to return to Ohio and complained his wife had spent "several hundred thousand dollars" of his and his daughter's funds.[10]

When the *Pretoria* reached Hoboken, Sheriff Barry, worried about Newton's men, hitched a ride on the revenue cutter that met the ship in the harbor. On Barry's heels was a pack of braying lawyers, including that persistent creditor, Elyria's W. L. Fay. Barry was unable to prevent a Boston lawyer from serving Chadwick with papers that included him in the Newton lawsuit. After a long conference in Mary's cabin, Barry and Chadwick departed. They had agreed to take the Pennsylvania Railroad train to Cleveland that afternoon and, according to the sheriff, "We will travel as two gentlemen and old friends . . . the doctor will not be under arrest, and will not even be under detention." With no extradition papers for New Jersey, this was Barry's only recourse. The Chadwicks' luggage was not searched despite Customs authorities' frenzied search for valuable assets. New Jersey authorities, however, demanded that Barry and Chadwick explain why an Ohio sheriff was detaining a passenger in their port. Thus, Dr. Chadwick, Mary, and Sheriff Barry, accompanied by a half dozen local police detectives, went to the Hoboken police court, trailed by two or three hundred people. The horse pulling the carriage carrying the Chadwicks slipped on ice, and a freight wagon behind it appeared on a collision course. While Leroy Chadwick gawked at the unfolding calamity, Sheriff Barry leaped out and halted the freight horse single-handedly, saving the Chadwicks from injury. Once in police court, it was clear that the Hoboken police had mistakenly thought Dr. Chadwick was a fugitive, an impression created by Newton's lawyer. Sheriff Barry explained the situation and made an impassioned plea for Chadwick to be allowed to return to Cleveland. "He is my lifelong friend, and I ask that my friend be allowed to accompany me." The Hoboken judge agreed.[11]

Mary Chadwick, a pretty, diminutive eighteen-year-old, prepared to go to relatives in Florida. Mary had given over her inheritance, pegged at "several thousands," to Cassie to manage. Mrs. Chadwick had spent some of it to purchase an expensive wardrobe for Mary for the recent European trip. The rest of the money disappeared. Mary told eager reporters, "I have always been devoted to my stepmother. I willingly made her guardian of all my money. I hate to believe that mother wrongfully used my money, although apparently it is all gone. We have nothing." That Mary's mother left the money to her minor daughter and not in her father's care said volumes about the doctor's ability to manage money. Mary Chadwick would never see her stepmother again.[12]

Unlike his wife's arrival in Cleveland with its crowds and anticipation, Dr. Chadwick slipped into town at 7:30 A.M. Sunday, New Year's Day, virtually unobserved, except by a few newsmen. He immediately went to the courthouse, where Sheriff Barry registered him as a person of suspicion. Bond was already arranged ($10,000) and waiting when Dr. Chadwick arrived, guaranteed by attorneys Kline and Dawley personally. Dr. Chadwick was free to go.[13]

On the courthouse steps, Leroy Chadwick read a statement to the assembled reporters. "I am inexpressibly shocked at the recent turn of events. I am innocent of all charges against me. . . . I am entirely without information as to the case except what I read in the Paris papers." When informed that his wife had been measured using the standard Bertillon system, like all jail inmates, he exclaimed, "That is the last straw measuring her in that way." Told that Mrs. Chadwick and Madame Devere were suspected of being one and the same, he was stunned. "Oh, no! I do not believe such a thing can be possible. If she is, I have never suspected it." Then he admitted, "I did not know her history." He explained that when he met the former Mrs. Hoover, he was a widower with an invalid sister, bedridden mother, and eight-year-old daughter to care for. "Would I not be glad to know someone who would take an interest in my household and bring order out of chaos?" Addressing his financial situation, he said, "I am a penniless pauper. You know how I have lived. Now see me coming back in the second cabin. I am homeless and without a dollar." He said he used Mary's spending money for the return passage. Dr. Chadwick said he was contemplating writing a book for "educated" men to explain his wife's business affairs. Sales would have been brisk, and a bankrupt man like Dr. Chadwick certainly needed the money. However, the book never materialized.[14]

Dr. Chadwick went from the courthouse to the jail, where his reunion with his wife was described by the *Cleveland Plain Dealer* as "pathetic in the extreme." The couple broke down and wept, clinging to each other. Mrs. Chadwick made every effort to explain her actions to her husband and pled her innocence. "Trust me, trust me," she begged between bouts of weeping. "Don't think I would deceive you." But Dr. Chadwick appeared skeptical.[15]

The couple was joined by J. P. Dawley, and the three conversed for an hour. Mrs. Chadwick again wept when the men stood to leave. Her husband tried to reassure her, but his words did not offer unqualified support: "I do not say

I won't trust you; only give me time to collect my thoughts. I can only hope that everything will come out all right as you say."[16]

Dr. Chadwick's visit to his wife in jail deepened the rift between federal and state authorities. Marshal Chandler and prosecutor Sullivan were upset that Dr. Chadwick visited the prisoner without their permission since the doctor was a possible coconspirator. Chadwick's conference with his wife was in contradiction to a recent court order that required all visitors to apply to the marshal for a pass. Chandler and Sheriff Barry had a heated telephone conversation, and Barry was adamant that he was in charge of the lockup. Shortly thereafter, two burly deputy US marshals arrived at the jail and spent the day sitting in the turnkey's office, watching the women's ward lest any other unauthorized visitors appear.[17]

On Tuesday morning, January 3, 1905, Dr. Chadwick appeared in state court, where his bond was reviewed and reduced to $5,000. Chadwick was introduced to the county prosecutor, Harvey Keeler, an elected official, who remarked with a smile, "We are getting notoriety out of this thing." Chadwick replied, "Yes, but I would rather have your kind of notoriety than mine." The doctor preferred to avoid the press and was successful in keeping his picture out of the newspapers.[18]

That afternoon Marshal Chandler, flexing his federal muscle, refused to let a crestfallen Dr. Chadwick have a private conference with his wife. "I cannot differentiate between federal prisoners whether their names be Chadwick or Smith," said the unmoved marshal.[19]

Denied easy access to the Chadwicks, press attention shifted to the Chadwick home on the corner of Euclid and Genesee. The Elyria Loan and Trust Company held the actual mortgage and had assigned Tom Porter to guard it. This was as much to prevent Newton's men from occupying the place as to keep the simply curious at bay. Porter had moved into the servants' quarters. Fine weather on New Year's Day brought crowds of curious onlookers to point and gawk. A few intrepid souls marched up to the front door and rang the bell to ask for a tour of the house. Porter had "numerous" but "effective" ways of sending the curious on their way.[20]

The doctor spent New Year's night at Virgil Kline's home. The next night, January 2, Tom Porter let the homeless Leroy Chadwick spend the night in his Euclid Avenue home. Longtime Chadwick employees—three house servants and Freda—were owed almost $700 in back wages and sought reassurances from the head of household. Dr. Chadwick had little reassurance to offer. Late in the day, the doctor put aside the stack of mail he was reading and turned his attention to the magnificent pipe organ, letting its melancholy notes add to the old place's gloomy atmosphere.[21]

The New Year brought a new man to the county sheriff's office, George Mulhern. On January 5, US attorney Sullivan presented the neophyte sheriff with his written opinion stating that the marshal held sway over the federal prisoners. Two deputy marshals physically prevented attorney Dawley and Dr. Chadwick from seeing the prisoner that afternoon. Dawley became apoplectic. The feisty lawyer, 125 pounds, told the deputy twice his size that "You have the advantage in weight, else I would throw you through that window for your impertinence." Dawley continued his expletive-laden tirade when a second, even larger deputy marshal threatened him with arrest. That only further incited Dawley, who was escorted out by the deputy. When that lawman tried to return to the lockup, the jailer, a sheriff's man, refused him admittance, asking, "Have you got a permit from the sheriff?"[22]

For Dawley, his inability to see his client wasn't just an injustice, it was an insult. He was determined to instruct Chandler in the law, which, according to Dawley, permitted the prisoner reasonable access to her lawyer whenever she desired. Dawley called Chandler "nothing more or less than a constable who is attached to the federal court." In no time, the county prosecutor produced his own opinion, which agreed with Dawley, and gave Dr. Chadwick unlimited visitation privileges as long as he was accompanied by an attorney. A parlay was later held between the new sheriff, the marshal, Sullivan, and a county attorney. Nothing was resolved, except all agreed that Dawley could see his client whenever he pleased. This impasse would need to be settled by a federal judge.[23]

The newspapers suggested that the marshal's desire to regulate Mrs. Chadwick's visitors was instigated by Customs agents searching for smuggled gemstones. They didn't want Chadwick conspiring with his wife to conceal any valuable jewelry. Zealous Treasury officers went so far as to order J. P. Dawley to turn over any gemstones he might have received as a retainer. Dawley found this humorous. "I have not received so much as a pewter shoe buckle from either" was his reply. Also, "it is just as certain that I have no diamonds of my own."[24]

Customs agents grandly announced that they had traced in excess of $250,000 in gemstones and jewelry owned by Mrs. Chadwick, of which $60,000 were actually located in a New York bank. "It is scarcely an exaggeration to say that Mrs. Chadwick handled pearls, rubies, sapphires, garnets and emeralds almost by the peck," one Customs official said with a straight face. The federal

Customs agents and bankruptcy officials had questioned Mrs. Chadwick's employees to little avail. A few pieces were held by individual creditors as security. Citizen's National Bank had an emerald ring and a diamond sunburst brooch in its vaults. The brooch was said to be quite stunning, a single large diamond surrounded by thirty smaller ones set in two rows. W. L. Fay of Elyria was questioned about the alleged $20,000 in gems he held as collateral. The Bankruptcy Court suspected they were worth more than the debt Fay claimed. However, Fay, who had tried to serve Dr. Chadwick with a summons in New Jersey, was not intimidated by the government. He defiantly refused to surrender the gems unless an outstanding loan was repaid. Treasury officials were pressuring anyone with Chadwick gems to pay the 10 percent duty unless they could prove that Cassie had paid it. Despite the heavy-handed approach, Customs expected to receive only $8,000 to $10,000 in duty.[25]

The Federal Court in Cleveland settled the jail visitation issue by ruling that the county sheriff had ultimate control over operation of the jail, a well-established fact in Ohio. Rules governing the management of inmates were made by county Common Pleas Court judges and carried the weight of law, the Federal Court opined. The idea of moving Mrs. Chadwick to Toledo was resurrected. Sheriff Mulhern said he "would be tickled half to death" if she was relocated. In truth, despite all the arguing and legal maneuvering over visitation, few people were actually requesting to see the prisoner. Aside from reporters, only Freda, Emil, Dawley, and Dr. Chadwick had been denied.[26]

By the second week of January, Mrs. Chadwick's lawyers declared themselves ready for trial. Could an impartial jury be impaneled in Cleveland? Dawley told the press, "I doubt there is not a newspaper reader in Ohio who has not read something of the case." Asked if casting doubt on Mrs. Chadwick's chances of a fair trial was an attempt to garner sympathy for his client, Dawley replied, "Why of course I will work up public sentiment if I can." The extensive newspaper coverage of the access dispute had worked in his client's favor, in Dawley's opinion.[27]

Andrew Carnegie set the standard for philanthropy in twentieth-century America, and he proved to be Oberlin's savior after all. His secretary confirmed rumors flying about Oberlin since mid-December that Carnegie was offering to make good on the losses of those Citizen's National depositors who could not help themselves—the aged, the infirm, veterans, widows, the poor, and students. In addition, Carnegie agreed to assist the YMCA, which lost $2,700. The ironmaster reportedly did not wish to see innocent persons suffer because of the forgery of his name. It was reported that these losses would reach $200,000, but this was a gross exaggeration. The shrewd Carnegie knew his offer wouldn't cost him anywhere near six figures, but he let the higher figure stand unchallenged for its publicity value.

Carnegie's involvement was the work of Rev. W. R. Cadmus, an Elyria clergyman who was moved by the story of an Oberlin student who lost all in the bank failure. A relief committee was formed, and Cadmus wrote a short and moving letter to Carnegie, describing the suffering of the bank's small depositors. "A man who was charitably disposed might find a worthy field in Oberlin," Cadmus suggested to the ironmaster. Moved and sensing a public relations windfall, Carnegie promptly replied with an offer of aid. He asked Cadmus to oversee the project by providing a list of those most in need. Carnegie praised Reverend Cadmus: "I am glad to know of one man who is fit for both earth and heaven." However, the steel king did not believe in helping those who could help themselves, like governmental agencies, businessmen, and stockholders. Only a handful of depositors lost over $5,000—the village, the township, the school district, Oberlin Business College—not to be confused with Oberlin College—and L. T. Whitney and Company. Andrew Carnegie was the recipient of considerable goodwill in Oberlin, and student leaders at the college telegraphed their thanks.[28]

A relief committee, headed by Oberlin College president Churchill King, announced receipt of a Carnegie check for $15,000 in mid-January. Citizen's National had almost $450,000 in deposits when its doors closed, and half that amount was lost forever. Although it would not help him personally, Charles Beckwith said, "My heart was cheered to receive the news that the poor and needy who had their last dollar in the bank would be reimbursed." Federal district attorney John J. Sullivan observed, "It was a noble thing for Mr. Carnegie to do. He could not have done anything more appropriate." Iri Reynolds commented, "Mr. Carnegie is simply giving a practical illustration of his philanthropy," then added, "but I wish he would pay up the losses of all the depositors." Reynolds was voicing the collective wishful thinking of Cassie Chadwick's creditors, who saw hope fading that Andrew Carnegie would save them. While Mrs. Chadwick offered no comment on Carnegie's generosity, she did what Victorian women often did when given shocking news—she collapsed in a faint.[29]

Andrew Carnegie wasn't finished in Oberlin. President King, on a trip to the East Coast, met with Carnegie in New York to thank him for his generosity. King told Carnegie that Oberlin College needed a library, a project that had been pitched unsuccessfully to philanthropists, local donors, and alumni for two years. Carnegie reflected, and the canny Scotsman, who would eventually finance 2,800 libraries worldwide and donate $5.2 million to the New York Public Library alone, made an offer. He would put up $125,000 for the project if Oberlin College would raise $100,000 for their endowment. This was more than Carnegie, who never attended college, was in the habit of giving for college libraries. However, his sympathy for small colleges had intensified after an unfavorable reaction to his recent remarks given to a gathering of New York Ivy League alumni. After the ironmaster's speech, some of those Ivy Leaguers publicly mocked small colleges in general. This stung Carnegie, who truly supported small colleges because he believed they made college accessible to the masses. The endowment money was donated almost immediately by an anonymous Boston man. Oberlin's Carnegie library was completed in May 1907 at a cost of $155,600 of which $150,000 came from Andrew Carnegie.[30]

In Cleveland Federal Court on January 18, J. P. Dawley requested bail for his client. Presiding judge Francis Wing set bail at $20,000 on the federal charges. There was no joy in this for Cassie since the woman who once regularly borrowed tens of thousands could not find $5,000 now. Even if she did, the county prosecutor immediately indicated that he would arrest her on state charges, which would require even more bail. And if that were not enough, authorities in Massachusetts were considering pressing criminal charges. The Duchess of Diamonds would remain behind bars.[31]

Charles Beckwith's condition continued to deteriorate throughout January. The old man, going blind and facing prison, expressed a desire to die. By the end of the month, Beckwith's physician doubted the banker would last another week. He didn't. Beckwith died at home on the evening of February 5 after two days of unconsciousness. The *Cleveland Leader* ran the headline "Grief Kills Old Banker," which was largely true. The medical cause of death was given as paralytic dementia, a form of nervous breakdown, and heart failure initiated by the stress caused by the Chadwick losses. Despite Beckwith's role in the failure of Citizen's National, Oberlin residents, on the whole, had pity for the man victimized by Cassie Chadwick. Beckwith joined W. B. Bedortha as the second Citizen's National official whose death was partially attributed to Mrs. Chadwick.[32]

Beckwith's death was a severe blow to federal prosecutors as the man would have been the star prosecution witness in the upcoming Chadwick trial. The conspiracy charge would now be much more difficult to prove. Scrounging for an alternative, the government proposed introducing the sworn deposition Beckwith had previously given Marshal Chandler. However, such evi-

dence might be ruled out in the face of inevitable defense objections on the
grounds that the Constitution guaranteed defendants the right to confront
their accusers. This was not possible with a dead man. Beckwith's confession
had consumed over eight hours, and the transcribed copy was stored in a safe
in the US attorney's office. The confession had also figured in the state grand
jury probe that led to the indictment of both Chadwicks. With no eyewitness
equal to Beckwith, federal and state prosecutors were scrambling to find an
alternative.[33]

The financial manipulations of Cassie Chadwick had caught the attention
of both Congress and the Ohio legislature. The comptroller of the currency
wanted Congress to make the 10 percent loan limit for national banks a federal law with violations punishable by one to ten years in prison. Meanwhile
in Ohio, a bill introduced for better oversight of state chartered banks failed
to even get out of committee. The Republican-dominated state and national
legislatures recognized the public desire to do something to further protect
depositors, but they surrendered to their respective banking lobbies. No new
legislation was forthcoming.[34]

Cassie Chadwick's second appearance in Bankruptcy Court was scheduled
for February 17 and would be her opportunity to formally contest her creditors'
claims. While most present expected a repetition of December's recitation of
the Fifth Amendment, an entirely different woman took the stand. Mrs. Chadwick was uncharacteristically cool, alert, focused, and talkative. She contested
or denied claims totaling just $3,500 out of over $1 million, an amount inflated
by bonuses, commissions, fees, and creditors who padded their claims. Herbert Newton, for example, held Cassie's personal notes for a total of $190,800,
but she testified that she never received anything like that in actual cash from
him. In fact, by her accounting, she had received just $78,000, in the form of
$28,000 in cash and the rest in Newton's personal notes. Two $15,000 notes
were used to settle another of her debts, while two $10,000 notes were negoti-
ated, yielding her only $5,000 cash for the pair. Of the $10,000 notes, one was
currently in Oberlin and the other in Belgium. The two $15,000 notes were
with a banker she declined to name. In sum she told the court that Newton
expected to realize a fantastic $112,800 in commissions for these transactions.[35]

Newton's attorneys disagreed. They claimed Newton loaned her $90,800.
The two $15,000 notes were held by Elyria banker E. E. Williams. Of the
$10,000 notes, one was definitely in Oberlin; however, the other, Newton
claimed, was in New York, not Belgium. How much she got for them at discount was not of immediate concern to Newton as he was responsible for the

full face value of his promissory notes. This had been a private transaction, nothing was legally recorded, and what few records existed were written in pencil on cheap paper. Nevertheless, even by Newton's accounting, he had added $100,000 for which he could produce no legitimate claim.[36]

Of the small claims, Cassie's denials were often vindictive. Faithful Freda had asked for $300 in unpaid wages, of which her employer contested $32. Attorney Virgil Kline, who came to her aid when she was arrested in New York, was denied $125 in fees. An elderly caretaker of the Euclid Avenue home requested payment for several months' back wages at $20 a month, but Cassie said his wage was only $15 a month. She expressed her outrage at what she considered excessive claims but offered little in the way of proof. As her creditors' attorneys took turns questioning her, each wanted to know exactly what Cassie thought she owed when she disputed a claim. She, in turn, refused to answer. "I have no idea," she would say smiling, "I no longer have my receipts, and I couldn't carry it all in my head." Creditors in general took issue with Mrs. Chadwick's "capricious and unreasonable objections." Her attorneys responded by pointing out that the government had seized all of her papers. "You still have that satchel full," retorted attorney Grossman, representing the bankruptcy receiver, referring to a grip filled with her papers that Emil had spirited out of Cleveland in early December. Cassie's attorneys refused to surrender the papers for examination.[37]

The facts she provided were few, but Mrs. Chadwick received credit for enlivening the normally dull bureaucratic proceeding by approaching it with zest, uncommon interest, and even humor. Only once did Cassie become acrimonious when an attorney defended a bill for $25. "Let him have it, he needs it," she snorted, touching off a shouting match. In truth, experienced creditors had inflated their claims, realizing that they might receive only pennies on the dollar, and Mrs. Chadwick clearly enjoyed watching them squirm. Her performance concluded after about an hour.[38]

On February 22, the federal grand jury in Cleveland issued additional indictments against Chadwick and Spear in the Oberlin bank failure. District Attorney Sullivan had decided to try Mrs. Chadwick first on the conspiracy charge, followed immediately by Spear, making the woman available to testify against Spear, if needed. Two indictments with a total of sixteen counts each were handed down for conspiracy to defraud a national bank. Once again, those checks certified when no funds were credited to the woman proved to be the basis of the indictments. Spear's creative bookkeeping resulted in a fifty-page indictment for him. Cassie's defense objected to these new indictments—the publicity alone was damaging—but had no recourse. The government was throwing all it had at the two remaining defendants in the hope something would stick.[39]

A week later on February 24, Cassie Chadwick returned to the stand in Bankruptcy Court. Although everyone hoped for a performance similar to the last one, Mrs. Chadwick's attorneys convinced her to remain silent, fearing that she might say something that might jeopardize her criminal case. She eloquently told the court, "My financial affairs are so closely allied with the case in federal court that anything affecting the one must necessarily affect the other." Dawley accused prosecutors of wanting "to ascertain our defense" through the Bankruptcy Court proceedings. Dawley pointed out that papers she had previously voluntarily surrendered to the government had resulted in two or three additional indictments. Attorney Grossman, representing the Bankruptcy Court, retorted, "We are reliably informed . . . that there is a large amount of property including big sums of money that ought to be in the hands of the [bankruptcy] Trustee." Cassie seemed to enjoy the exchange.[40]

The court ordered her to testify. Once sworn, Mrs. Chadwick refused to give her name and invoked her Fifth Amendment privilege while pleasantly smiling throughout. The newspapers noted that she was once more the shrewd, adroit, strong-minded woman of affairs she was reputed to be. Cassie appeared amused as various lawyers fought over her refusal to answer any questions. Over a two-hour period, multiple attorneys failed to get her to answer a single question. Referee Remington, acting as judge, alternated between cajoling Cassie and threatening her. She ignored him, since additional jail time and fines meant little to someone already in jail, financially destitute, and facing multiple criminal charges. Remington took his frustration out on Dawley, and the two lawyers clashed with vigor as Mrs. Chadwick sat smiling throughout. At the end of the day, nothing positive had resulted, and both sides agreed not to bring Mrs. Chadwick back to Bankruptcy Court until after her criminal trial.[41]

Customs agents scoured New York, Cleveland, Pittsburgh, Elyria, and Oberlin for the Duchess of Diamonds's gemstones. Previous reports of pawned jewelry proved a dead end. Customs Inspector Charles Leech said, "Mrs. Chadwick was never reduced to an extremity where she would even have to think of dealing with a pawnbroker." Government agents traced almost every major purchase she made in the last three or four years. Most of the jewelry in question had been given away or was held as collateral, and Customs agents were squeezing the recipients for the import duty. A spokesman for the Treasury said

Customs expected to collect $125,000 in precious stones and jewelry, which would be sold to pay the duty and satisfy creditors. Attorneys at work on the issue said that the government would need very strong evidence to seize the jewelry if the holders refused to pay, as many were. Mrs. Chadwick vowed to fight for her assets. She sent three letters to the secretary of the Treasury, complaining about the Customs inspector, Leech. Regarding a possible indictment for smuggling, Leech wryly observed, "At present it would seem that there are enough indictments against Mrs. Chadwick."[42]

Leech had an opinion on where the Chadwick money had gone. "It is absolutely certain that Mrs. Chadwick did not spend all or nearly all the money that came into her possession. . . . Figuring on the amount of money she is known to have raised and on the amount she is known to have spent for valuables and running expenses, a large balance remains. Unless the woman literally gave money away there must be a considerable balance left." While the Treasury searched for hidden thousands, Cassie made application to the Bankruptcy Court to retain personal and household items to the maximum $3,000 allowed.[43]

At the end of February, Mrs. Chadwick sent a letter to the Customs inspector, Leech, offering to discuss the origin of her jewelry. She claimed that all but one piece was purchased in the United States, while Leech was insisting just the opposite. Leech was not enthusiastic about another meeting: "Mrs. Chadwick's information is cheerfully and willingly given, but it is information that does not inform." In short, Leech was calling her evasive at best, a liar at worst. For her part, Cassie insisted that she was unable to work from inventory lists and must see each piece to recall its origin.[44]

The drawn-out and tedious bankruptcy hearings continued in March without Mrs. Chadwick. On March 1, W. V. Coons was called to testify. Acting befuddled at first, he said he kept no records, only scribbled notes, because the woman demanded secrecy. As his memory improved, Coons admitted loaning Mrs. Chadwick $85,000, plus a commission of $12,500, which was collateralized by nothing more than a letter from Iri Reynolds. There were no further loans to Mrs. Chadwick, he explained, because when he asked Reynolds to see the securities, Reynolds declined, calling it "a matter of trust." Coons said, "She offered me almost anything, but I would loan her no more."[45]

Coons said that he and H. Clark Ford persuaded other men to loan a total of $258,000. Coons could not remember if he profited from the transactions. When his original $85,000 loan was not paid, Coons pursued it in the courts in his hometown of Findlay, where he admitted it would receive little Cleveland press coverage. Raising questions in Cleveland about Cassie's creditworthiness could have harmed both parties, he said. Coons admitted he received more than the legal 6 percent interest on the principal. When asked if his transaction with Cassie Chadwick was extraordinary, Coons said, "Well, it was in this, that Mrs. Chadwick wanted nothing known about it or her affairs." Coons testified that eventually he got his principal back, and a pearl necklace worth $25,000.[46]

Henry Wurst of Elyria briefly appeared and claimed that he held uncollected Chadwick notes for $40,500. He would not admit to receiving a bonus for these loans.[47]

H. Clark Ford took the stand. He initially claimed client privilege to avoid testifying, but the court ruled against him. After discussing the Coons loan, Ford declined to say if he knew anything about $258,000 in loans to Mrs. Chadwick. After some heated discussion, Ford admitted to knowing about loans to Oberlin College for which he received no compensation. Ford said he negotiated a $25,000 loan on a necklace and loaned Mrs. Chadwick $3,000 total out of his pocket during their relationship. The personal loans were repaid. Ford, attracted by the high fees and retainers, said he eventually developed doubts about Mrs. Chadwick's truthfulness and creditworthiness. The Ford-Chadwick relationship deteriorated quickly as she missed loan payments. On December 1, 1903, Ford received a string of pearls from Cassie as collateral for a debt to Coons in the sum of $25,275. The Cleveland lawyer testified that he severed his relationship with the Chadwicks at the end of 1903. On January 8, Ford gave the pearls to Coons for the unpaid debt. Ford admitted that on February 15, 1905, Cassie Chadwick sent a note to him demanding a full accounting of his legal fees or she threatened to file their management contract with the Bankruptcy Court, primarily to embarrass him. Ford never filed a bankruptcy claim, and Cassie never released the contract.[48]

Sixty-eight companies or individuals had filed claims with the Bankruptcy Court totaling in excess of $1.5 million. Over half of this total was estimated and likely inflated. Claims from jewelers totaled just $55,000. Three well-known creditors hadn't filed claims: J. W. Friend, Charles Beckwith's estate, and Iri Reynolds.[49]

CHAPTER NINETEEN

A Most Dangerous Criminal

Cassie Chadwick's escapades were the stuff of fiction, and a theatrical production appeared during the winter of 1905. *From Clue to Capture* made the rounds of small-town opera houses in northern Ohio, beginning in Mount Vernon. This hastily written stage play featured a villainous Mrs. Badwick, who robbed widows, orphans, and the wealthy while engaging in Wild West–style gunfights. In the climactic scene, Mrs. Badwick is discovered robbing John D. Rockefeller's safe and stuffing the goods in her bodice. This forgettable play did nothing to improve the already unfavorable view most people held of Mrs. Chadwick. The jury for her trial would be drawn from northern Ohio, and negative characterizations of Cassie dismayed her attorneys, who were trying to win in the court of public opinion by portraying their client as a helpless woman victimized by greedy moneymen.[1]

Trial dates were always tentative, but Clevelanders realized that Cassie Chadwick's time in the dock was at hand when Andrew Carnegie arrived in town. No one in America would dare keep the ironmaster waiting or inconvenience him. Having arrived in New York from his winter home in Florida, Carnegie boarded his private railroad car in New York on March 2, 1905, to travel to Cleveland. He would be staying at the Cleveland home of old friend Sylvester T. Everett, a financier, whose home on the corner of Euclid and Case Avenues was one of the largest in the city. On the evening of March 3, county prosecutor Harvey Keeler and Citizen's National receiver Robert Lyons arrived at the Everett mansion, bearing the original Chadwick documents. Carnegie had seen only photographs of the documents, and finally he would see the originals. The promissory notes were of a stock fill-in-the-blank variety that could be purchased at any stationery store. The all-important trust agreement was written on cheap paper, not parchment or even good-quality office paper. The pages were unnumbered, unlike most legal documents. According to a handwriting expert, the same individual was responsible for all the documents, and the writing was that of a woman. There were some differences in style, which may have been a clumsy attempt to deceive. Misspellings abounded. Expenses were spelled "expences," and property was "proprty." The phraseology was incorrect. "Known all men" instead of the correct "know all men." "Indorced" instead of the correct "endorsed." And there were numerous erasures. Even the forgery of Carnegie's name was not consistent among the documents. It was commonly agreed that the forger had carelessly copied the documents from a proper legal model.[2]

Investigators had determined from eyewitnesses that five documents bearing Carnegie's name had been circulated. Two were notes held by Citizen's National for $500,000 and $250,000. Prior to his death, Charles Beckwith had sworn that there was another $500,000 note in circulation. Iri Reynolds had surrendered two documents with Carnegie's signature: the $5 million note bearing a date in 1902 and the certificate of trusteeship for $7.5 million. In case there was any doubt, the forger completed two trusteeship documents, exactly alike, but bearing different dates. Neither one was marked as a duplicate or voided as even the greenest law clerk would have done.[3]

Upon reading the trust agreement, Carnegie enjoyed a hearty laugh. "If anybody had seen this paper and then really believed that I had drawn it up and signed it, I could have hardly been flattered," he said. He chuckled at the misspellings and faulty punctuation. Shown the "securities" Mrs. Chadwick held, the ironmaster enjoyed another laugh when he compared the signatures on the notes to his own. "I see little resemblance here," Carnegie remarked, a hint of relief in his voice. "Why I have never drawn up any document that even resembles this agreement in all my life, and I have not signed a note in the last thirty years." Carnegie gladly provided handwriting samples for the county prosecutor.[4]

Carnegie might have found the documents amusing, but his writing was hardly an example of perfection. He was a notoriously poor speller using a form of written language that one biographer labeled "telegraphese," a nineteenth-century phenomena into which former telegraphers like Carnegie frequently lapsed. He preferred shorthand replacements like "enuf," "delite," or "offerd" for the correct spellings and strung together incomplete sentences with numerous dashes. Samuel Clemens, better known as Mark Twain, a Carnegie friend, once joked that Carnegie's spelling was a danger to the entire human race. Were the ironmaster's notorious grammatical errors all that far removed from what appeared in the Chadwick documents?[5]

After Keeler and Lyons left Carnegie, US attorney John J. Sullivan held a long meeting with the Scotsman to go over the evidence. He was followed by marshal Frank Chandler, who visited Carnegie for an hour. "We just got acquainted. Mr. Carnegie is a pleasant man," was the marshal's only comment. Chandler would be in charge of courthouse security and Carnegie's safety.[6]

After examining the government's evidence and satisfying himself that he was in no jeopardy, Carnegie put to rest all doubts about his willingness to testify in the Chadwick case. He declared to newsmen, "It is the duty of every good citizen to serve his country, and in a matter of justice no citizen should fail to do his best." He refused to discuss the case with reporters, having been prohibited by the prosecution from doing so. "You see, I am the servant of the government just now," he said. Andrew Carnegie had come to Cleveland without legal counsel, a sure sign of man who had nothing to fear.[7]

Despite Carnegie's poor opinion of the forged documents—no one even considered they were genuine—Cassie Chadwick liked her chances in court. She issued this statement on the eve of her trial: "I have great hopes for the outcome. I will be nervous, but that is not owing to the trial itself, but on account of the large number of people who will be looking at me. That unstrings me. I can hardly stand it." Of Andrew Carnegie, Cassie said, "Mr. Carnegie's presence in the city is very good news to me." This was not an opinion shared by most people following the Chadwick saga. Some pundits joked that Carnegie could help her now only if he followed Charles Beckwith's lead and dropped dead. Would she testify in her own defense, a reporter asked. "The possibilities are that I will not go on the stand in my own defense tomorrow," Cassie replied. "I may, but that isn't certain . . . I'm not sure I could stand it." Mrs. Chadwick dreaded the crowds of strangers, which was not surprising for a woman who cherished secrecy. She had complained to federal authorities about a deputy marshal who kept bringing friends to the jail for a "look."[8]

Cassie Chadwick's trial for conspiracy to defraud the Citizen's National Bank began on Monday, March 6, 1905, Judge Robert W. Taylor presiding. Cassie continued to refuse to request a change of venue, and if there was any discussion of a plea bargain, it was never mentioned publicly. The courtroom in Cleveland's Federal Building was a magnificent marble-columned, wood-paneled temple of justice decorated with the usual symbols: the scales of justice, the palm of peace, and a painting titled *The Common Law*. In short, it was a splendid setting befitting the most powerful legal force in the land, the US government. Cassie Chadwick would agree that she deserved nothing less.[9]

Judge Robert Walker Taylor, fifty-two, had just been appointed to the bench by President Theodore Roosevelt in January 1905. A staunch Republican, Taylor, clean-shaven with thinning hair, had attended Western Reserve University, and he had been a lawyer since 1877 and an Ohio congressman from 1895 to 1903 before ascending to the federal bench. As a judge, Taylor was a neophyte about to preside over a high-profile trial.[10]

Judge Taylor had replaced Francis J. Wing, who had stepped down from the federal bench to pursue a more lucrative private practice. Wing had attended Harvard, served as a prosecutor and a county judge, and was a federal judge from 1901 to 1905. Now Wing was looking up at the bench as part of Mrs. Chadwick's defense team, his first opportunity to cash in on his judicial credentials. The former judge, fifty-three, was an acknowledged expert in banking and finance law. Wing would be assisting ace defense attorney J. P. Dawley, fifty-seven, a bantam rooster with a stylish goatee, known for his fiery eloquence. Bringing up the rear of the defense team was Chadwick family attorney Sheldon Q. Kerruish. Courtroom observers were asking where the bankrupt Cassie Chadwick got the money to retain such legal talent, but the publicity was priceless to all the lawyers. James Southard, the prosecutor of Madame Devere, parlayed his success in court into a seat in Congress.[11]

If the Chadwick defense was stacked with legal talent, the prosecution was practically a one-man show. US district attorney for northern Ohio John J. Sullivan, forty-four, would try the case himself. Sullivan, who was orphaned at nine, began practicing law in 1885, served in the Ohio Senate, and, as a favorite of Mark Hanna, was appointed to his post in 1899 by President McKinley. Sullivan, bald except for a fringe of hair, concurrently served as president of a savings bank and Cleveland's check-clearing house. Sullivan and Taylor were related by marriage and close friends. The prosecutor had minimal assistance from two novice associates, Thomas H. Garry and Benjamin Parmely Jr. Although there were debatable conflicts of interest among the lawyers—Wing's previous rulings in the case, Sullivan with close ties to the local banking community—no one considered stepping aside in a high-profile case like this.[12]

Although the trial was not scheduled to begin until 9:30 A.M., spectators began arriving at the courthouse at 7:00. The first to arrive was a delegation of women, and women continued to predominate in the crowd. For most Victorian women, Cassie Chadwick was so unlike themselves, an odd creature who had navigated the male-dominated world of finance, that she had become the subject of endless gossip and a bit of admiration. All potential spectators were held one floor below the fifth-floor courtroom. At 9:15, a first rush was admitted, and when all the seats were taken, the doors closed, sealing in about 150 spectators. Everyone was encouraged to check overcoats, overshoes, hats, and particularly cameras at a special coatroom hastily constructed for the trial. *Cassie L. Chadwick, alias C. L. Chadwick, alias Madame Devere vs. United States of America* was about to begin.[13]

Mrs. Chadwick left the jail and passed through a large but generally quiet crowd on the arm of a deputy marshal. She entered a carriage for the trip to the courthouse, arriving at 9:45. To insure she wore the correct attire for the occasion, Freda had brought several of Cassie's dresses from Euclid Avenue, but the defendant had some difficulty deciding on one. Referring to her incarceration, she quipped to a jail matron, "It's very hard to arrange one's clothes while handicapped as I am." She finally settled on a black velvet gown and a white shirtwaist, covered by a black velvet coat with black braid and white cuffs. Her hat was black with long, white-tipped feathers trailing off the left side. A heavy veil covered her face, except while in court. The newspapers recorded every detail of Cassie's attire. The *Cleveland Plain Dealer* described her appearance as "sumptuous." Keen observers noted that one key element was missing. The woman known for buying gemstones by the dozens wore no jewelry, save a single plain gold ring, a disappointment to many.[14]

Jury selection began immediately. J. P. Dawley, clad in a waistcoat, his goatee neatly trimmed and wire-rimmed glasses on his nose, inquired of the first potential juryman, "Would you give to all witnesses the same consideration you would to Andrew Carnegie, notwithstanding his wealth and influence?" That question had no sooner ceased to echo in the courtroom when, as if on cue at 9:50, Andrew Carnegie arrived. Carnegie was fashionably late for court but received no judicial rebuke. He was given a reserved seat near the front, and as he walked there, he brushed by Mrs. Chadwick. She deliberately failed to notice him, pretending to be otherwise preoccupied with jury selection. Carnegie sat at an angle that allowed him to examine the defendant straight on, and he did so with an amused twinkle in his deep-set, blue-gray eyes. For her part, Mrs. Chadwick confined herself to occasional discreet sidewise glances at the steel king.[15]

Dawley continued his tedious examination of the jury pool. All admitted they had followed the case in the newspapers but promised impartiality. To a man, they were resolute that they would not be swayed by the idea that the federal government was the prosecution in this case. To the surprise of legal experts, Dawley asked each potential juror, "Have you read that Mrs. Chadwick was once arrested and convicted some years ago?" The question went against the accepted legal wisdom of not reminding a jury of a defendant's criminal past, but Dawley wanted the issue known upfront. He theatrically consulted with his client about each juror, and she played her part well by sitting coolly and calmly, glasses perched on her nose, fully engaged as if this were a meeting of a board of directors. She sized up each juror. She felt jurors should be asked if they knew the Customs inspector or the federal marshal, and she was quick to give her opinion of each potential juror. The defendant hid her nervousness, if there was any, and gave every appearance of being in complete control of the proceedings. In all, a dozen potential jurors were dismissed before Dawley was satisfied.[16]

Andrew Carnegie was an attentive observer. He was seated next to C. M. Stone, county Common Pleas judge, that morning. When the court took a recess, Carnegie and Stone discussed whether Mrs. Chadwick would take the stand in her defense. "I don't think she will," Carnegie said with surprising certainty. "Silence is golden."[17]

Prosecutor Sullivan was more cavalier about jury selection. After a couple of replacements on the jury, Sullivan, his bald head glistening with sweat, was satisfied. Jury selection proved easier than might have been expected considering the publicity surrounding the case. After just two hours, at 12:35 P.M., twelve men were sworn in and warned by Judge Taylor not to discuss the case. The jury was comprised of nine farmers, a real estate man, and two teachers. Their ages ranged from forty to sixty-five. They came from all over northeast Ohio, but by design, none were from Cleveland proper. As was the custom in 1905, their names, addresses, occupations, and group picture were published in the newspapers. Court adjourned for lunch.[18]

That wealthy and parsimonious New York investor, Hetty Green, enjoyed litigation and was constantly in and out of court. She famously told reporters, "The men on juries that have tried my cases have always treated me so nicely." Would Cassie Chadwick agree when the trial in Cleveland concluded?[19]

Eclipsing even the defendant as the main attraction, Andrew Carnegie didn't disappoint. Looking well for a man of sixty-nine, he was immaculately groomed and wore a glossy silk top hat. During the lunch recess, the iron-master smiled at everyone and made small talk about the fine March weather in Cleveland. Carnegie and Chadwick's attorneys met in the corridor, where Carnegie, himself barely five feet tall, joked about Dawley's diminutive stature. "I'd heard so much about you that I had come think you must be at least six feet high," Carnegie laughed as he shook Dawley's hand. All agreed that any cross-examination of the government's star witness by the defense would not be taken personally, and Carnegie, a veteran of congressional hearings, didn't want to be lightly handled. Dawley readily agreed. Carnegie complimented the attorney on his hardheaded method of jury selection. "I like a hard fighter," the steel king told the beaming defense attorney.[20]

As he entered the crowded elevator to go to lunch, Carnegie responded to a reporter, "Oh, I like Cleveland all right. I always did like your city." Carnegie complimented the marshal on his handling of the crowd. The ironmaster had taken an interest in the proceedings that morning, but he was collectively judged to be too big a distraction in court. He was not required to return after lunch, instead agreeing to stay near a telephone at the Everett home.[21]

John Sullivan began the afternoon session by explaining the conspiracy charge to the jury. Eight checks were the source of the sixteen counts in the indictment, which was confusing even to the well-informed person. Seven checks had been certified by Spear and one by Beckwith. Three were written to third parties and the remaining five to Mrs. Chadwick herself. They bore dates between August 1903 and October 1904, and they varied in amounts from $2,400 to $15,600. Sullivan went on to say that he expected the testimony presented to show that "the total capital of the Oberlin bank was $60,000, and that $67,000 was drawn out by Mrs. Chadwick on checks certified by President Beckwith and Cashier Spear."[22]

When Dawley rose to speak for the defense of Mrs. Chadwick, he chose to attack the indictment. "There was no conspiracy," he flatly told the jury. "She was not with President Beckwith or Cashier Spear when they made entries upon the books of the Citizen's National Bank of Oberlin. . . . She knows nothing of what they did in the bank. Beckwith and Spear acted in good faith believing Mrs. Chadwick to be a wealthy woman. If they loaned her more money than they should, that was their business. Mrs. Chadwick had nothing to do with that. . . . Even if there was fraud upon her part, that is not conspiracy." The government, her defense attorneys asserted, had no case. Period. No defense was necessary. Dawley was technically correct. Would the jury hew to the defense's narrow line of reasoning or would it take into account the suffering Mrs. Chadwick caused in Oberlin?[23]

The first witnesses for the prosecution were the former directors of the now defunct Citizen's National Bank. These men were asked basically the same set of questions and gave consistent answers with no new revelations. Mrs. Chadwick withstood the court proceedings well until 3:45 P.M., when former Citizen's bank director E. H. Halter of Oberlin testified. When Sullivan asked about his business interests, he ruefully replied, "I have none now," having been financially destroyed by the bank's failure. Mrs. Chadwick paled, summoned the matron, and asked to be excused because of the heat—not to mention the smell—from all the bodies in the courtroom and the nervous strain. In a small private room off of the courtroom, she experienced a slight fainting spell. Marshal Chandler had two nurses from a nearby hospital summoned. Owing to the late hour, Judge Taylor adjourned court until the next day.[24]

Dr. Leroy Chadwick was conspicuous by his absence in court. Enterprising reporters found him at his old Euclid Avenue home with friends. Asked why he wasn't at the trial, Dr. Chadwick laconically replied, "Oh, no, I don't care to go," and refused further comment. His wife had a more favorable explanation for the *Cleveland Plain Dealer:* "Dr. Chadwick is doing exactly right. It is at my request that he is not attending the trial. I got into this thing alone, and I'm going to get out of it alone."[25]

Day two of the trial, March 7, was likewise well attended, and women continued to outnumber men. One clever lady brought opera glasses, much to the amusement of veteran court observers. But why not? This was, above all else, good theater. The spectators took no less interest in day two of the proceedings but were denied the presence of Andrew Carnegie, who would appear only if the defense introduced new evidence. The man who was so interested in Mrs. Chadwick's jewels, Charles F. Leech, Cleveland collector for the customhouse, was not in attendance either, although his office was only two floors down. Leech explained to a reporter from the *Cleveland Leader:* "I am too busy, and have no curiosity." Leech, a political appointee, may have been busy, but it may not have all been on government business. In October 1905, Leech was accused of politicizing his office by appointing political hacks to lucrative positions and requiring employees to campaign and solicit political donations for favored officeholders.[26]

Mrs. Chadwick herself was in good spirits and laughed freely. Her mood was buoyed by the smaller and quieter crowds that greeted her outside the courthouse. Once court was in session at 9:30, she was alert and engaged. Alexander B. Marshall, vice president of Cleveland's First National Bank, was summoned by the prosecution to describe the details of the single October 1904 check Charles Beckwith had certified. In response to a prosecution question, Marshall explained that a certified check indicated that the check's maker had funds on deposit the day of certification only. This was the main reason, he told the jury, why certified checks were generally cleared as quickly as possible. Upon cross-examination by the defense, Marshall was asked to define a "good check," and, to no one's surprise, he said that it was one in which there were "funds in the bank to meet it." Pressured by the defense, Marshall conceded that these funds didn't necessarily have to be cash, but they could be other collateral or even established credit. Asked if there was anything irregular in the manner Mrs. Chadwick obtained money on certified checks, Marshall replied, "No, but it was unusual." The overcertification of checks, meaning certification when funds were *not* immediately available but would be shortly, Marshall admitted, was common banking practice.[27]

Harry Avery, formerly assistant cashier of Citizen's National, was summoned to the stand. He said he had seen Mrs. Chadwick at the bank but never personally transacted business with her. Avery claimed that he examined the bank's ledgers and never discovered any credit in Mrs. Chadwick's favor. The defense challenged Avery's assertion by demonstrating that she deposited a certified check for $10,000 on November 3, 1903. Avery maintained that Mrs. Chadwick's credits were not recorded in the correct journal, and the prosecution effectively showed that the woman never had more than $10,000 cash, credit, or collateral in Citizen's National, yet each of her eight certified checks was covered by the bank. Before court adjourned for lunch, the prosecution established that of the eight personal promissory notes given to Citizen's as collateral for the checks by Cassie Chadwick, only two were correctly numbered and noted on the bank's books. The remaining six were not properly recorded. It seemed obvious that cashier Spear, a gifted and educated bookkeeper, had made false and misleading entries on Citizen's National's journals.[28]

After lunch, the official receiver of the Oberlin bank, Robert Lyons, was called. The clean-shaven Lyons, looking every bit an accountant in stiff collar and wire-rimmed glasses, was the expert on the books of the Oberlin bank. He testified that the bank's ledgers balanced, except for the accounts with Cleveland's First National, where Citizen's National was the bank equivalent of overdrawn by $37,000. Furthermore, Lyons revealed that Mrs. Chadwick had only savings accounts in Oberlin, never any accounts upon which she could draw checks. With those revelations and twilight approaching, court adjourned. All spectators were required to remain seated until the defendant was escorted from court.[29]

Lyons resumed his testimony Wednesday morning, and he was questioned almost until noon. The highly technical and boring questioning about which bank ledger recorded what transaction and its correctness was pursued by the prosecution to show Mrs. Chadwick's lack of funds in Citizen's National. This testimony was confusing and mind numbing for the jury. Sullivan summarized for the twelve laymen. "The meat of this is: did she have money on deposit, regularly entered up to her credit before the checks were certified?

We should know what we are trying here. Evidence of absence of money in the bank is what we are after."[30]

The defense, however, wanted to leave the impression that perhaps Mrs. Chadwick did have the funds, which were either not located or not properly recognized as credits. Lyons was cross-examined by former judge Francis Wing, who asked if the examiner had perused all the ledgers for entries to Mrs. Chadwick's credit. Lyons had not, except for certain dates. Wing declared, "There could have been millions of dollars for all you know on other dates to her credit." Lyons shot back, "I have never been able to find them." Wing waved the bank's general ledger at the witness and roared, "You have not examined this book except at certain dates . . . there may be entries of which you know nothing!" Lyons parried, "There may be, but individual accounts are not kept in the [general ledger]." Lyons held fast in his claim that he could not find where Mrs. Chadwick had any credit in the bank on the days the checks were certified. This was something the jurors understood.[31]

Sullivan and Dawley sparred over the admittance of testimony relating to journal entries not pertinent to the actual charges faced by the defendant. Suddenly Mrs. Chadwick, who like many in the courtroom had slipped into a stupor, spoke up. "That is what I would like, bring it all in." No one was quite sure what she meant. Lyons's testimony concluded when Wing asked if offering a promissory note as collateral for a bank loan was contrary to accepted procedure. "No," Lyons conceded, then hastened to add, "but it is not quite proper." Court adjourned for lunch.[32]

Sharp-eyed courtroom reporters were quick to note the departure of an unidentified man who had been seated in the reserved front row of spectators. He was quickly identified as Thomas Woodyatt, a police magistrate from Ontario, who was present to have a look at Mrs. Chadwick. He told reporters that he wanted to see if she was the same woman who had come to the attention of Canadian authorities while trying to borrow on questionable promissory notes in Brantford, Ontario, the previous summer. He left convinced Mrs. Chadwick was that woman.[33]

Mrs. Chadwick took lunch in a small anteroom off the judge's chamber with Emil. When court resumed, Emil took a seat directly behind her. The largest crowd of spectators since Monday had become loud and unruly during the break, and the threat of arrest was required to quiet them. When court resumed, the spectators' interest was aroused by the appearance of Iri Reynolds, who was thin, bony, and looked very Victorian in his stiff collar and full mustache. Reporters noted that he was visibly nervous and that his fingers twitched uncontrollably as he took the stand. Reynolds glanced only briefly at the defendant. For her part, Mrs. Chadwick was cool, and once she settled her eyes on the banker, she never changed her gaze. The man's time on the stand was brief. The prosecution asked him to identify the defendant's handwriting on a check, a note, and a letter, which he did somewhat timidly, and that was all. The defense had no questions, and Reynolds was dismissed, leaving the crowd of spectators, who hoped for something more scandalous, disappointed.[34]

Practically nothing of Mrs. Chadwick's correspondence survived because her penchant for secrecy had led to its destruction. Therefore, no small amount of legal sparing was inevitable when prosecutor Sullivan sought to read the two October 1903 letters Cassie sent to Beckwith and Spear. They revealed Mrs. Chadwick conspiring to deceive the Elyria men, Wurst and Fay, and showed her pressuring Spear to certify a check for $15,600 when she knew she had no funds on deposit to cover it. Judge Taylor ruled that the letters were admissible as evidence. Everyone in the courtroom strained to hear Sullivan read Cassie's words as she directed the actions of Beckwith and Spear. The letters were damaging to her defense—and the source of many objections—because they demonstrated that she knew she was asking the bankers to bend the rules. When Sullivan finished the letters, the prosecution rested at 3:00 P.M. on March 8.[35]

The defense chose for its first witness a Cleveland accountant, T. C. Doolittle, to refute Lyons's and Marshall's testimonies by proving that Mrs. Chadwick's transactions with the Oberlin bank were not irregular or unusual. Looking fashionable with a full handlebar mustache and hair parted in the middle, Doolittle lectured on the dry technical aspects of bank bookkeeping. Most of Doolittle's testimony was not memorable, except he did manage to say in plain English that discounting promissory notes amounted to giving credit secured by the notes, which could then appear on a bank's books. Such actions didn't constitute fraud or conspiracy, in Doolittle's opinion. Before court adjourned for the day, Doolittle was given permission to dive into the books of the Oberlin bank overnight to do a bit of forensic accounting.[36]

The next morning, day four of the trial, Cassie Chadwick arrived in court ten minutes early and in good spirits. Commenting on her chances for the *Cleveland Plain Dealer*, she said, "Well, I'm feeling hopeful. I've one regret though, and that is that we didn't go into the whole thing. Yes, I'm sorry Mr. Beckwith wasn't here to testify and tell the whole story." As usual, the defendant didn't elaborate on what "the whole thing" was.[37]

T. C. Doolittle returned to the stand, having spent the previous evening and much of the night with Citizen's National's ledgers and journals. His sharp-eyed perusal of the books had located a $40,000 discount or credit to Mrs. Chadwick. The credit was duly noted in only one journal but not in the individual ledger where personal accounts were maintained. The defense argued this proved two things. One, that their client had credit at the bank. Two, that the bank's bookkeeping was faulty because it utilized a loose-leaf journal instead of a bound one, which made it easy to remove pages, perhaps ones with Mrs. Chadwick's credits. On cross-examination, Sullivan got Doolittle to admit that the credit would not appear in the individual journal if it was withdrawn on the same day, which was exactly what previous testimony by the bank's bookkeeper had indicated. Sullivan pointed to a $40,000 deposit to Oberlin College's account the same day. The defense objected that there was no proof these transactions represented the same money. However, a quick-witted Judge Taylor had Doolittle calculate the interest on these deposits and compare it to the interest credits of Mrs. Chadwick. The credits matched, proving that it was almost certainly the same $40,000. If Cassie had money in Citizen's National, it never stayed there for more than a day.[38]

At 10:45 A.M. March 9, the defense rested. Mrs. Chadwick, like Madame Devere, would not testify on her own behalf. Despite her proven ability to withstand hard questions from hostile lawyers in Bankruptcy Court, Dawley and Wing chose not to place her on the stand. They concluded that the appearance of guilt she would create by taking the Fifth Amendment would be no worse than the insinuation of guilt produced by her failure to defend herself in open court. Mrs. Chadwick's defense attorneys, convinced the prosecution had no case, decided there was nothing for them to refute. Dawley and Wing were certain they could easily persuade the jury to see things their way.

The jury was discharged for the remainder of the day so that the judge, prosecution, and defense could argue the legality of the case—and whether the prosecution had presented sufficient evidence. Nearly all of the spectators remained to listen to the spirited legal debate. Wing opined, for two and a half hours, that what Cassie Chadwick had done was not conspiracy since she was not a bank officer. He concluded by asking for a directed verdict of acquittal because "Congress has not made it an offense to solicit an officer of a national bank to certify a check." Wing drove home the defense's central argument, that the government's case was one of aiding and abetting to certify a check, which was not a federal crime. Wing reminded the jury that certifying checks when no funds were available was a common banking practice. The government's case, Wing said, was to punish Mrs. Chadwick for a crime that only an officer of a national bank could commit. "That is a fair statement of the government's case," agreed Judge Taylor.[39]

The judge nonetheless dismissed the directed verdict motion in favor of letting the jury have the last say. Cassie Chadwick was visibly disappointed by this but had been warned to expect it. Judge Taylor did strike two indictments in favor of the defense, leaving fourteen intact. Those struck concerned a check in which the certification date was some weeks after it was written. Because of this, Taylor ruled that the check was not a check at all but a promissory note. It was a fine point that made little difference to the overall picture. The afternoon's legal jockeying proved of great interest to the spectators who, after a generally boring trial, gave the discussion their rapt attention.[40]

White-haired Mrs. Charles Beckwith was in court daily with her son, forced to watch her husband being vilified. She was never summoned as a prosecution witness. Her once-pretty face was creased with wrinkles and pain as she quietly listened each day. A meeting on the first day with Iri Reynolds after court adjourned left her sobbing. After Judge Taylor threw out the directed verdict and court ended for the day, Mrs. Chadwick rushed to Mrs. Beckwith. The two spoke quietly and earnestly for five minutes while bailiffs kept a gaggle of curious women at bay. As Mrs. Chadwick expressed her sympathy, Mrs. Beckwith wept but didn't offer any comment. Suddenly, in mid-sentence, Mrs. Chadwick saw one of her attorneys, leaped to her feet, and rushed to him without even a parting word or handshake for the banker's wife. Cassie left the white-haired widow sitting alone on the bench, drying her tears.[41]

His presence no longer required, Andrew Carnegie was free to take his private railcar back to New York. The Cleveland trip proved uneventful for Carnegie. He did manage a pleasant evening speaking to the ladies of the library school at Western Reserve University and a day basking in the glow of his philanthropy at Oberlin College. Carnegie left town without comment or fanfare, but he was $64.40 richer in witness fees, plus court-approved travel expenses. In a lighter moment, Carnegie was heard to say, "The woman has shown one thing. My credit must still be good." The Chadwick case was barely a footnote in Carnegie's life. His biographer, David Nasaw, labeled the Chadwick episode "significant" in the ironmaster's life, "not because there is a scintilla of evidence that Cassie Chadwick was Carnegie's illegitimate daughter—she most certainly was not—but because the construction of the story and the notice it was given in the daily press tell us a great deal about Carnegie's place in American culture and society at the turn of the century."[42]

Mrs. Chadwick entered court Friday morning, dejected and depressed after the failure of the previous day's defense motions. "I have given up all hopes of acquittal. I have no chance in this court," she told reporters. Then she told reporters she believed the case should have been tried elsewhere, which was a complete reversal for the woman who wanted to be tried in Cleveland. She claimed to be on the verge of physical collapse and admitted that her presence was purely the result of the administration of strong stimulants.[43]

Mrs. Chadwick's depression was worsened by Sullivan, who stated that regardless of the outcome of this trial, he would immediately try Mrs. Chadwick on one of the remaining seven indictments, and so on. Reporters calculated that conviction on the fourteen indictments in this trial alone could result in twenty-eight years in prison and $140,000 in fines. Lastly, if the federal government failed to convict her, the State of Ohio stood ready to try.[44]

Closing arguments began with assistant prosecutor Thomas H. Garry's summation of the government's case. After quoting the law for half an hour, Garry concluded by telling the jury, "We want the facts and that is all you want. Mrs. Chadwick is charged with conspiracy to defraud depositors of a national bank. . . . Whoever draws money from a national bank and has no money in that bank is guilty of an offense."[45]

At 11:00 A.M., Francis Wing took the floor to defend Mrs. Chadwick. He reminded the jury that indictment didn't guarantee guilt. Wing restated the central theme of the defense—that Cassie Chadwick could not certify checks and was therefore not even indictable under the conspiracy statute. Her transactions with Citizen's National were common occurrences in banking. "She asked to have a check certified," he told the jurymen. "To form a credit for this, she gave her note for the amount of the check. The check was certified. She drew the money . . . paid eight per cent interest upon the note, and in the end paid the notes." According to Wing, "The notes could not have been worthless paper because they were redeemed."[46]

Francis Wing continued his oratory until 3:30 P.M., when he stopped and court was adjourned. Mrs. Chadwick was pale and restless during the day, sinking into a deeper funk as the prosecution spoke and brightening a bit when the defense had the floor. Her deafness protected her from much of the most accusative oratory. Emil Hoover sat behind his mother in court and listened intently to the arguments, his face a solemn mask revealing no emotion.[47]

The trial resumed in a rare Saturday session on March 11, and J. P. Dawley had the floor. Dawley told the jury that "popular clamor has no place in the courtroom." He urged the jury to "Be governed by the evidence, and not by prejudice. Listen only to the unadorned truths, as they fell from the witness stand." He agreed that the case was intricate. "It is hard for us lawyers to understand. It must be puzzling to you [the jury]." There is "just one thing you are to consider. That is conspiracy to have a check certified. There is not even the slightest evidence of conspiracy." He reminded the jury of their responsibility. "It is for you to decide [Mrs. Chadwick's guilt] and you alone."[48]

Dawley took up the controversial topic of women's rights promoted by activists in every corner of the country in 1905. It was a subject, like so many others, on which Cassie left no recorded opinion. Dawley denounced the current state of affairs in which women were second-class citizens. "My client belongs to the class of people which, in the eyes of the law, is coupled with convicts and idiots," Dawley told the all-male jury. "She has nothing to say about the making of laws because she is a woman. She was not informed regarding the laws of banks, and she had a right to suppose that what the bank officers did they had a right to do." Dawley thus reminded the jury that Mrs. Chadwick was a woman in a society that saw her as someone incapable of handling her own affairs.[49]

Dawley praised young Emil Hoover, who had stood by his mother throughout her ordeal. Mrs. Chadwick, on cue, burst into tears, and Emil placed his arm around his mother. The scene was said to be most affecting to all present, and that was Dawley's goal—to garner some last-minute sympathy for his client. In conclusion, he asked Judge Taylor to "impress upon the jury that the court is not an arena for prejudice and the consideration of outside influence." Dawley's words echoed across the nation the next day when he was quoted in the *New York Times*. Dawley concluded at 11:25 that morning.[50]

Prosecutor Sullivan had the last word. He told the jurors that he believed they were intelligent men. "A bank has been wrecked," he pointed out. "Have you thought what that means? Have you thought of those poor depositors?" Sullivan reminded the jurors the bank's failure meant "the comforts of men and women and children all swept away." This was a real concern for everyday Americans who watched banks fail daily and depositors like themselves suffer. The jury could sympathize. Sullivan turned, pointed at the defendant, and pronounced, "Death, destruction, sickness in your path." He continued, "There is no evidence that she ever had any wealth except the wealth of power that she had over men."[51]

Those letters read in court were key evidence, Sullivan told the jury, other-wise the defense would not have spent four hours trying to undermine them. In the prosecution's view, "those letters show the stupendous criminality" of Chadwick, Beckwith, and Spear. "I hope you are beyond, the enchanting bower of this Duchess of Diamonds," Sullivan lectured the jurymen. "She knew how to gain the confidence of men. . . . If you see nothing in those letters of the 'managing directress' of that bank, you can see nothing. . . . With her hypnotism, her magnetism, or something else, she controlled every dollar in that bank by reason of her bewitchery. She bought them body and soul."[52]

Sullivan asked the jury to return a verdict of not guilty *unless* the govern-ment had made a case beyond reasonable doubt. "The government wants to play fair," he impressed upon the jury. At 2:35 P.M., Sullivan concluded his sum-mation. He told the jury, "You have the opportunity today to do right. Also the same opportunity to do wrong." Sullivan, whom Dawley called a "steam engine in britches" for his courtroom oratory, told his captivated audience, "You have before you the most dangerous criminal in the world today."[53]

Judge Taylor's charge to the jury was universally acknowledged to be bal-anced. He sought to make sense of the seemingly redundant charges in which the odd-numbered ones were for conspiracy to certify checks for which in-sufficient funds were on deposit, and the even ones were for the same checks, but for not having the funds *credited* to the check's maker on the bank's books. Even if a depositor had placed funds in a bank, Taylor said, they would not be available to the depositor *until* they were actually credited in the correct bank ledger. This was a bookkeeping technicality that looked like charging the defendant with the same crime twice to most reasonable people.

At 3:33, the jury was given the case. The closing oratory had been exceed-ingly eloquent and held the attention of the crowded courtroom. In essence, the defense argued that Mrs. Chadwick had not committed an indictable crime, and certainly conspiracy had not been proved. The prosecution sought common sense from the jury—a bank had been wrecked and Mrs. Chadwick was the reason. The defense had logic on its side, the prosecution, emotion. Which path the jury would follow was the source of much speculation. Many who had followed the trial believed that the jury would return in a matter of minutes with an acquittal. Judge Taylor was one of them. After the jury retired, Taylor remained motionless on the bench, keeping court in session. Following the judge's lead, no one else moved. Mrs. Chadwick remained at the defense table, anxiously watching the clock and nervously wiping beads of perspiration from her forehead with a handkerchief. Her attorneys passed the time by conferring with the court stenographers. As the clock crept toward 4:00 P.M., Mrs. Chadwick became increasingly nervous, shifting her head from one hand to another as a cramp stiffened her right arm. She spoke to Emil. The women in the court stared intently at the defendant, although for once she was oblivious to it. Finally, after half an hour and no word from the jury, Judge Taylor called a recess, sensing perhaps a lengthy deliberation.[54]

Mrs. Chadwick asked Marshal Chandler to be taken to his office out of sight of the prying eyes of the women in court, who had remained even after a recess was officially declared. She stood and turned to look at the spectators, defiance in her eyes. Then looking straight ahead and without uttering a word, she left the courtroom, Emil at her elbow. A cramp in her arm was massaged by the ever-present nurses. She ate supper in the marshal's office, conversing amiably with staff members and holding a whispered discussion with her son. Only a few newspapermen remained to keep the vigil.[55]

At 5:30, the jury sent word that a verdict had been reached, but they requested a recess from their labors for supper. Deputy marshals escorted the jurors, men who understood the value of a free meal, to Kennard House for supper at the government's expense. It was later revealed that it took the jury less than an hour to arrive at a consensus. At dinner, the jury foreman told Marshal Chandler he could call the judge at his leisure. Judge Taylor, at his hotel and in no hurry himself, reported he would arrive at 8:30 P.M.[56]

At the appointed hour, the defendant was returned to court. Mrs. Chadwick, her spirits again deflated, sat at the defense table, supporting her head with her right hand and staring at a book on the table as she waited, the severe cramp in her arm forgotten in the tense excitement. Her son and two nurses sat close by. The jury returned and sat silently. Mrs. Chadwick, who once searched men's faces for some sign of weakness, now searched the face of each juror for some hope, some sympathy. Those twelve men sat stone-faced, no juror meeting the defendant's gaze directly. In the dimly lit courtroom, perhaps thirty observers were present, mostly newsmen, bailiffs, and prosecution assistants. Francis Wing sat alone at the defense table, a worried frown on his face.[57]

At 8:34, Judge Taylor made his judicial entrance. When he asked the foreman, farmer L. E. Humphreys from Richfield, Ohio, if a verdict had been reached, the answer was yes. All jurors nodded in agreement. The foreman handed the verdict to the clerk, W. F. Carleton. Mrs. Chadwick, unable to hear the clerk's barely audible voice, resumed staring at the table. The verdict was not guilty on the even-numbered counts but guilty on the odd-numbered counts, a nod to the unfairness of the initial indictments, which seemed to all but the hardest observers as prosecutorial persecution. Guilty on seven counts was enough to send the defendant to prison for a minimum of seven years. Judge Taylor would announce his sentence in a week.[58]

The nearly deaf defendant had not heard the verdict, but the commotion around her got her attention. Her attorneys had deliberately lowered her expectations, and now Wing turned and said to his client, who was leaning on Emil's arm, "We have lost Mrs. Chadwick." She looked to Emil for confirmation, her face flushed. Emil placed his arms around her neck and whispered into her good ear. She sank into her chair and gasped, followed by sobs of anguish. "I'm not guilty," she kept repeating. "Take me away!" Emil, tears staining his cheeks, tried to comfort her, but she recoiled even from him before collapsing in his arms.[59]

Eventually Mrs. Chadwick composed herself and, with two deputy marshals, walked from the courtroom with an air of defiance. Waiting for the elevator, she grew weak, but then suddenly she became hysterical. She tried to break away from the lawmen, giving the two deputies all they could handle. "I am not guilty. I am not guilty! Let me go, let me go, let me go, I say!" The elevator arrived, Emil put her arm over his shoulder, and he carried her on board. Downstairs in the marshal's office, she once again became hysterical. After fifteen minutes, she quieted with the help of the nurses, who liberally applied what the newspapers called restoratives, likely a stiff drink. Cassie Chadwick was half led, half carried, while moaning loudly, to a waiting carriage and jail, where her spirits rose as Francis Wing explained the appeals process to her, vowing to "fight it to the finish."[60]

The verdict was not what most observers expected. Sullivan was almost apologetic when he told inquiring reporters, "She's a woman, and the prosecution came in my line of duty . . . but I believe that an honest verdict has been given." His tone hardened. "I thoroughly believe, however, that society has no place for a woman with the record of this woman." Asked about Mrs. Chadwick's remaining federal indictments, he was noncommittal. "It is the duty of this office to prosecute, not persecute. I am of the opinion that after Mrs. Chadwick has spent several years in the penitentiary, the government will be content."[61]

An enterprising reporter telephoned Dr. Chadwick at home and asked if he had heard the verdict. He had not. The reporter told him the result and asked for a comment. Leroy Chadwick hung up.[62]

J. P. Dawley had plenty to say about the verdict against his client. He blamed the jury, composed of men he called simple farmers, for failing to deliberate two hours when two days were required. Dawley accused the jury of failing to try to understand the case and choosing the expedient of conviction instead. Dawley also pointed the finger at newly minted federal judge Robert Taylor, whom he said was a "little puzzled," and expressed dissatisfaction with many of the judge's rulings. In fact, in Dawley's opinion, the judge should have taken the case from the jury entirely. Dawley was "confident that we can obtain a complete reversal of the verdict" on appeal.[63]

There was a different mood in US district attorney John J. Sullivan's office, where by Monday his desk was covered with congratulatory messages. One that stood out was from Andrew Carnegie, who telegraphed, "Congratulations. The victory is all your own." Publicly, Carnegie offered no comment.[64]

The trial had hinged on the technical aspects of federal banking laws. The jury of common-sense men from Ohio might not understand the arcane details of banking operations, but they could understand that having checks certified by a bank when you had no funds on deposit was wrong. Bank failures were common occurrences in 1905. A guilty verdict had as much to do with the facts as sending a message that Ohioans were fed up with the financial chicanery, which filled the newspapers on a daily basis. In retrospect, a guilty verdict could be seen as inevitable.

The *Cleveland Leader* labeled Cassie Chadwick's financial acrobatics "the Chadwick system of frenzied finance." The term *frenzied finance* was in vogue in 1905, and it was synonymous with the shameful and unlawful manipulation of securities for financial gain. In 1906 Thomas Lawson published a book of that title describing the rise and fall of Amalgamated Copper a half dozen years before, which involved the shameless manipulation of its stock. *Frenzied Finance* was also the title of a 1916 satirical silent film about capitalism, starring Oliver Hardy.[65]

On Sunday, March 12, the *Cleveland Leader* offered editorial comment on the Chadwick verdict. Acknowledging that many were of the opinion that Mrs. Chadwick would be found not guilty, or freed by mistrial due not to innocence but to the difficulty of gaining conspiracy verdicts in general, the paper defended the trial's result. "Mrs. Chadwick has not earned sympathy, was the cause of uncomputable sorrow and heavy loss to hundreds, and was dangerous to credit. To have freed her would have been to put a premium on sharp practice, to reward fraudulent assurance, to encourage confidence men and women the world over. Her conviction offers a sharp and a needed lesson to bankers and credulous capitalists." The paper was of the opinion that if Mrs. Chadwick managed to escape confinement in the future on a legal technicality, the other indictments should be pressed.[66]

Editorial comment appeared in newspapers across the country. The *Pittsburgh Gazette* said, "Sympathy should be directed to those innocent victims rather than to the money lenders." The *Pittsburgh Post* suggested, "The jury's prompt agreement shows that they had no trouble in making up the verdict, which will be generally approved." The *Philadelphia Record* wanted more trials: "Mrs. Chadwick was easily convicted. . . . But there remain several financial gentlemen who helped the adventuress to execute her preposterous schemes. . . . It is hoped that the officers of justice are not going to stop with the incarceration of the woman." The *New York World*, no stranger to reporting fraudulent financial manipulation, asked, "Her more important victims yielded to the line of the 'rake off.' . . . But is the bonus for bank loans peculiar to Mrs. Chadwick's borrowings?" The *Detroit Free Press* also advocated further charges: "Unfortunately the negligence, if not active participation, of others made them equally deserving of prosecution." The *Chicago Tribune* tried to put the Chadwick affair in perspective as seen from that city: "If Mrs. Chadwick keeps her lips sealed . . . and is sent to prison, she will drop out of mind as well as sight . . . she will be almost forgotten . . . and two years hence if her name should be mentioned, people will ask, 'Who is Mrs. Chadwick?' Cassie Chadwick might be easily forgotten in Chicago, but not in Cleveland."[67]

The Chadwick case made fooling banks look easy. "It is easy if you know how," Ohio native David Rothschild told a *Cleveland Plain Dealer* reporter from his jail cell in a New York prison. Rothschild was doing nine years for creating the Federal Bank of New York, which a New York court said "was established solely for the benefit of Rothschild and his accomplices." The bank was not a national bank, despite the name, and was designed to also evade New York state banking laws. Rothschild and his associates created a financial entity that had no assets, and they siphoned off deposits for the use of themselves and other bank officers. The bank's eventual collapse had become a major scandal in New York.[68]

Rothschild had this to say about Cassie's success at hoodwinking money lenders with forged promissory notes: "There are hundreds, yes, I'll wager, a thousand, cases like this Chadwick one right here in New York, only the newspapers didn't get hold of them. I know of more than a hundred myself." He explained that these cases were kept quiet "because when a banker gets fooled that way he never will prosecute unless he is forced to. They would rather settle for any old thing on the dollar than let the public know how foolish they have been." Rothschild regretted that he was jailed in New York when money was so "dead easy" to obtain in Cleveland.[69]

Sunday morning following her conviction, Mrs. Chadwick was still distraught, but medication given to her for hysteria had quieted her. She saw only two callers during the day. She spent time with her son Emil, making small talk, and Dawley, who expressed optimism regarding her appeal. Notably absent from her callers was Dr. Chadwick, who had not seen his wife since before the trial. At home on Euclid Avenue, he offered no comment to the reporters who knocked at his door, except to say, "What else can I say!"[70]

CHAPTER TWENTY

NO ARTISTIC TASTE
AND NO CULTURE

On Monday, March 13, Cleveland's attention shifted from the federal court-house to the Chadwicks' Euclid Avenue mansion and the much-anticipated auction of the couple's personal property. Beckwith, Reynolds, Newton, and countless potential lenders had visited and been impressed. Iri Reynolds had estimated the value of the Chadwick household goods at $200,000. An independent appraiser retained by some of Cassie's hopeful creditors dashed those hopes. "The woman certainly had no artistic taste and no culture," he told reporters, "if she is to be judged by the truck with which she filled her house. People are led to believe that the Chadwick home was a treasure house, while in reality it was a curiosity shop of hopelessly bad brick-a-brac." The famous collection of mechanical clocks the appraiser described as of "positively hideous design." A cut-glass chair he called "in execrable taste." He went on to say that there was not an original painting in the house, and the bronzes were best for the "smelter." Still, he didn't doubt Mrs. Chadwick paid dearly for them. Commenting on her taste for imported goods, he suggested that she had not cheated the Treasury when she paid duty on the European items but rather had overpaid it on the overpriced gaudy furnishings. The appraiser expressed the opinion that Mrs. Chadwick had been imposed upon by merchants eager to sell her low-quality goods at high prices. The appraiser could not resist saying, "The sort of things she selected would almost make one say she deserved to be imposed upon." Nevertheless, it was this snobbish expert's opinion that her creditors might do better than expected because "people may be willing to pay dearly for those things because of the notoriety."[1]

Bankruptcy trustee Nathan Loeser conducted his own appraisal. He placed a value of $2,000 on the once $8,000 pipe organ. The expensive laces seized by Customs agents for which Mrs. Chadwick paid $5,000 had an auction estimate of $1,981. Two elaborate revolving French urns were valued at $600. A dozen rare Coalport china plates were appraised at $300 and silk rugs at $3,000. Paintings and chinaware that had cost Mrs. Chadwick dearly were in fact worth considerably less. Loeser signed off on an appraisal of the personal property at $31,130 and the real estate at $41,190, well under $100,000. Federal and state officials were arguing over control of the Euclid Avenue property. The federal bankruptcy trustee wanted it, but state officials were backing a claim by mortgage holder Savings Deposit Bank and Trust of Elyria for $42,000. Everything would be auctioned. Cassie Chadwick was unhappy with the results of the appraisals and the tone of the appraisers. "There are many articles which I noticed today are appraised at scarcely half their real worth," she huffed.[2]

Loeser felt that Mrs. Chadwick wasn't disclosing all her assets. He told reporters, "Some time ago Mrs. Chadwick was reported to have said she would tell all she knew in bankruptcy court if she was declared guilty of the criminal charges against her. Whether she will keep this promise remains to be seen." She had no real incentive to be of assistance, and Loeser conceded that the remaining state and federal indictments might keep Mrs. Chadwick's lips sealed. Per bankruptcy law, she was permitted to return to the Euclid Avenue house under guard and, as it turned out, in Dr. Chadwick's absence, to select $3,000 in personal items she would be allowed to keep before the contents were sold. After what would be her last visit to her Euclid home, she admitted crying in her old bedroom. She had met Tom Porter there, a former employee now guarding the place. Once back in jail, Cassie was seized by the odd desire for lemon pie. She implored her jailers to ask Porter's wife to bake one. "I'm so hungry for a lemon pie," she explained.[3]

Dr. Chadwick, with two attorneys in tow, visited his wife in jail on March 16. During the half-hour visit, the couple limited their discussions to the bankruptcy proceedings. Afterward, Mrs. Chadwick reiterated her desire to "pay every honest obligation I owe." Of her husband she said, "The talk that Dr. Chadwick and myself are estranged is nonsense." She insisted his rare visits were due to lack of privacy at the jail. The doctor, as usual, had no comment.[4]

Friday, March 17, was preview day for the Chadwick bankruptcy auction. Crowds descended on the Euclid Avenue house. Bona fide potential buyers were permitted a walk-through; the merely curious were not. The contents would first be offered en masse, and the bidding was expected to be lively. Mrs. Chadwick was morose at the prospect of her thousands of personal items being sold to a commercial museum proprietor of the P. T. Barnum type or, worse, to ordinary curiosity seekers.[5]

There were sixteen registered bidders from Cleveland, Chicago, Cincinnati, Philadelphia, New York, and Atlantic City who had posted $1,000 bonds for the chance to bid at the Saturday morning auction. Once the auctioneer began his chant, sharp bidding ensued in rather small $50 to $100 increments until the gavel fell at $25,200 on goods appraised at $23,984, one-third their estimated cost. Approximately $4,000 worth could not be sold due to contested ownership. The winning bidder was the Knickerbocker Galleries of East 29th Street, New York, and they paid in cash by day's end. Experienced observers agreed it was a good sale because of the celebrity association.[6]

Knickerbocker Galleries, in a shrewd publicity move, announced that Leroy Chadwick had been retained to demonstrate the enormous pipe organ for $100 a week at public exhibitions, first in Cleveland and later in New York. Chadwick himself was reluctant to admit the arrangement and preferred to view it as demonstrating the organ's quality to prospective buyers. Why the doctor would humiliate himself by helping the new owners was not obvious to his friends. Or his wife, who uncharitably commented, "The whole thing is ridiculous. It's silly." The arrangement ultimately fell through.[7]

On Tuesday, attorneys Dawley and Wing discussed with reporters their appeal of Cassie's conviction. Ever the optimist, Dawley said he was "absolutely certain" that the Appeals Court would order a new trial. Reporters asked why Cassie's defense had been based solely on the premise that the government didn't have a case. "Because we had no idea that the government could possibly convince any jury that there was any conspiracy," Dawley explained.[8]

The prosecution wasn't worried because established case law was on its side. A similar case had withstood scrutiny by the Appeals Court. While the slow wheels of justice turned, Mrs. Chadwick would remain in the county jail, which was fine with her.

The Ohio Penitentiary occasionally housed federal prisoners at the expense of the federal government, and Cassie would be the first woman incarcerated there under the arrangement. Warden C. B. Gould painted a chilling picture for newsmen of what the woman faced in Columbus. There would be no special favors. She would be put to work, if physically able, at either cooking, laundry, or sewing prison garb. She would be responsible for cleaning her whitewashed, stone-floored cell with its iron cot, stool, and table. She would be wearing common prison clothing, a simple blue-and-white striped dress. The cells were locked at 5:30 P.M., and the workday began at 6:00 A.M. Her only possible respite from dull prison life would be the privilege of ordering her meals from an outside restaurant, if she had money enough. Warden Gould foresaw a benefit to having this infamous female inmate. "I look for a large increase in visitors' fees after her arrival. A prominent or notorious character draws visitors and incidentally increases our revenue materially." Ohio was not above exhibiting its inmates for profit.[9]

Cassie Chadwick was back in Bankruptcy Court on March 25. She was willing to talk, but she was still a frustrating witness. Bankruptcy trustee Loeser's attorney and partner, Louis Grossman, questioned Mrs. Chadwick and asserted that she had debts in excess of $2 million, and only $100,000 in assets had been located. The woman scoffed at the $2 million figure and told the court, perhaps truthfully for once, "I swear that $750,000 will cover every penny I owe." Of that, only $517,000 were actual loans. The remaining $200,000-plus were commissions and bonuses claimed by lenders and loan brokers. Grossman asked her to assist in locating undiscovered assets. Cassie offered no details but suggested the government look in Canton, Pittsburgh, and New York.[10]

Cassie testified that she owed $200,000 to Cleveland banks, none of which had filed claims with the Bankruptcy Court. She declined to name them, lest their soundness be questioned, but agreed to give the court their names privately. She did admit that $58,000 was due her from Clevelander Charles H. Stewart, secretary-treasurer of Euclid Avenue Savings and Banking Company and a onetime Chadwick creditor, and $150,000 was the value of jewelry held by a Belgium gem dealer. Mrs. Chadwick stated that the total she owed in Pittsburgh was $225,000. Of this, she obtained $150,000 with the assistance of James Friend, who himself loaned $75,000. He didn't get any commission or bonus but did get jewelry valued at $79,000 for collateral. She tantalizingly hinted that personal friends held other assets for her but declined to divulge their names.[11]

To keep it out of the public record, the court permitted her to whisper to trustee Loeser the name of a Clevelander whom she said owed her $100,000. Mrs. Chadwick was emphatic in disputing New York travel agents, who said they were due an incredible $282,000, of which only $35,000 had been paid. She said she owed Iri Reynolds, who had not filed a claim, a small undetermined amount, but he owed her nothing. She admitted she owed W. L. Fay of Elyria $4,000 for stock in his fire-ravaged factory. None of Dr. Chadwick's three living brothers had ever received a penny, she said. She neglected to mention the money owed the estate of James Chadwick.

Bankruptcy authorities had been eager to see the contents of the missing satchel Emil had given attorney Dawley in December. Originally it was believed to hold jewelry, but Grossman now thought that it might contain a paper trail. Mrs. Chadwick told the court that it contained "nothing but letters."

Dawley, observing the proceeding, indignantly told Grossman, "You can see all the stuff if you so desire." Nevertheless, the suspicion would forever persist that the Duchess of Diamonds had hidden away some of her fortune where creditors would not find it and that the poker-faced Emil Hoover was made of sterner stuff than his demeanor suggested.[12]

On Monday, March 27, 1905, at 5:00 P.M., Cassie Chadwick returned to Judge Taylor's court for sentencing. She stood alone, without her son or husband. Judge Taylor sentenced her to ten years in the Ohio Penitentiary. The judge tacked on a $70,000 fine that no one expected the bankrupt defendant to pay, but it could prove useful if undisclosed assets were located. Cassie, on tottering legs and with an anguish expression, asked, "What does the world want to know of me now?" She asked to speak privately with Judge Taylor as she had done in Bankruptcy Court. He rebuked her, saying, "Whatever you have to say will have to be said now and in open court." She declined, and with that she walked resolutely from the courtroom. Softening some, Judge Taylor said she could stay in the county jail pending the outcome of her appeal. The following day, March 28, was her birthday, and while she looked sixty, she was actually forty-eight.[13]

Avoiding a second imprisonment would be a miracle for Cassie Chadwick. Overturning her guilty verdict on appeal would be difficult. It would be 1910 before parole for federal prisoners was an option. A presidential pardon was even more unlikely. President Theodore Roosevelt, once New York police commissioner, famously said, "Nothing must clog the wheels of justice." According to the rules for presidential pardons, Judge Taylor had to initiate the process, which seemed improbable, and then it must pass Justice Department review before reaching Roosevelt's desk. Even if all the stars aligned for her at the federal level, state authorities were ready to pounce with more criminal charges.[14]

On Wednesday, April 5, Mrs. Chadwick's attorneys filed preliminary paperwork with the Federal Circuit Court of Appeals in Cincinnati. District attorney Sullivan believed that with her appearances in Bankruptcy Court concluded—she continued to bicker with the authorities over the value of certain claims—Mrs. Chadwick should be sent to Columbus. However, the Appeals Court on April 6 granted her a stay of execution of her prison sentence, meaning she could remain in the county jail. She was radiant when told. "Of course, it is encouraging, but it is not less than we expected," she crowed to reporters as she vowed to fight all the way to the US Supreme Court.[15]

On April 15, Mrs. Chadwick and Spear were arraigned in Federal Court on new indictments for perjury. Mrs. Chadwick, one reporter wrote, "never in all her appearances in federal court appeared to better advantage." She was attired in a suit of black silk with a flowering veil partly covering a new hat. Both defendants pled not guilty. Bail was set for Mrs. Chadwick at $5,000 on the new perjury charges. That translated into $27,000 for those charges she was convicted of and $25,000 for the indictments for forgery and perjury. In total, $52,000 would be needed to free her. Mrs. Chadwick predicted cash bail would be raised in a week. She was so certain of release that she told reporters she planned to stay in Cleveland until her appeals case was heard, unless her health dictated a change of scenery. Federal and state authorities took a dim view of the woman's chances to raise the money because individuals publicly willing to sign her bail bond were nonexistent. Mrs. Chadwick's attorneys were very exacting in their preparation of the appeal, and it wasn't filed in Cincinnati until July 22, 1905.[16]

If Mrs. Chadwick was successful in obtaining a new trial, it would be October at the earliest before the Appeals Court ruled. There was serious doubt that a second trial for conspiracy could be won by the federal government. The State was willing to try her for forgery. Cuyahoga County prosecutor Harvey Keeler told reporters, "The case of forgery, in my opinion, is very clear and Mrs. Chadwick can be convicted upon that charge if anything." However, until the federal appeal was resolved, the State of Ohio could do nothing.[17]

The receiver for Oberlin's Citizen's National Bank, Robert Lyons, filed suit against the bank's shareholders to recover the bank's losses. Each shareholder was required to pay $100 per share, and the first lawsuits to collect were directed at two New York women, Celeste Ives and Alice Adams, who held fifteen and one share, respectively.

The Knickerbocker Art Gallery in New York City was to be the scene of eleven scheduled auctions of the Chadwicks' possessions. Enterprising New Jersey millionaire Abraham G. Nelson was the man behind the winning bid in Cleveland on March 17, and he had shipped all 2,846 lots of "Chadwickiana" to New York for resale. A crowd of several hundred, mostly women, gathered for the first auction, which included a dozen sideboards. On April 23, the *New York Tribune* published a list of auction items for its curious readers: a mastodon tusk tankard, a $700 ten-piece set of Coalport china, a $750 cut-glass loving cup of which the king of England was said to have a duplicate, a $1,000 one-of-a-kind crystal chair, nine hundred pieces of silver tableware, thirty-two silk rugs, two hundred souvenir spoons, and on it went. Auctioneer C. E. Smith said that the home was packed to the garret with goods, some never unwrapped. One bedroom contained dozens of rare tiger and polar bear rugs, still rolled; rich silk draperies were found in coalbins; and there were barrels of bric-a-brac in the barn. Napoleonic furniture was located in a US Customs warehouse, never having been retrieved after Mrs. Chadwick paid the duty. The sterling silver was found boxed in a clothes closet. So extensive was the collection that even auctioneer Smith failed to see how it all fit into the Euclid Avenue home. In truth, it hadn't. Auction insiders claimed that not all the items for sale were Chadwick's. The auctioneers had bulked up the sale with outside goods in order to cash in on the Chadwick mania. Cassie, who often mortgaged the same furniture more than once, certainly could appreciate this bit of larceny.[18]

Nelson, expecting a healthy profit from his investment, produced a thick, glossy auction catalog that featured a full-length photograph of Mrs. Chadwick, pictures of the infamous Carnegie securities, and a two-page biography. The actual list of auction material seemed almost an afterthought. The auctioneers shamelessly flattered Mrs. Chadwick, commenting that she did "not show her age, [was] good looking and very charming of manner." They credited her with being an important collector of ivories and an expert judge of rare Middle Eastern rugs.[19]

The first auction session was set for Wednesday, April 26, 1905. Items sold included pieces of the famous art collection, in shiny gold frames, which brought from $7.50 to $18. One painting, *The Harlem Fruit Vendor*, was said to have cost thousands, but it sold for hundreds. One of Cassie Chadwick's oak rockers, in which she sat while negotiating with bankers, lawyers, and financiers, went for just $2.50, and a huge brass bed, rarely occupied by both Chadwicks simultaneously, was sold for $67.50. The ivory collection, a $5,000 loving cup, and Mrs. Chadwick's wardrobe would be auctioned in two weeks, and two automobiles, one an imported French Panhard touring car, were on the way to New York from Cleveland. The $8,000 365-pipe Votey pipe organ was yet to go under the hammer.[20]

Mrs. Chadwick's day in court had passed, but the epidemic of bank fraud, embezzlement, and financial manipulation continued unabated. On April 1, the Lorain Citizen's Savings Bank closed. Its cashier, assistant cashier, and a teller were charged with conspiracy to embezzle $10,000 to help cover the cashier's stock gambling debts. The cashier, E. F. Kaneen, attempted to borrow money from both Carnegie and Rockefeller to save the bank. After Citizen's National closed, many depositors from Oberlin had moved their deposits to the Lorain bank.[21]

April 1905 was banker's month in the Cleveland Federal Court as several indicted bank officers from across northern Ohio were scheduled to stand trial. In addition to Arthur Spear from Oberlin, the two bank officers, Lewis P. Ohliger and J. Robert Zimmerman, who ruined the Wooster National Bank were present, having been arrested in Victoria, British Columbia, in early January. Ohliger's indictment ran to seventy-five pages. Originally the Wooster bank failure was blamed on Mrs. Chadwick, especially when it became known that she knew Ohliger from his days as a Cleveland revenue collector and that he had loaned her money. As it turned out, Ohliger needed no help defrauding his bank. Two Conneaut bankers, C. M. Traver and O. C. Lillie, faced trial for making false bookkeeping entries, embezzlement, and misapplying funds. Both were officers in the failed First National Bank of Conneaut, which had originally been forced to close on the false rumor it held some of Cassie Chadwick's notes.[22]

From Milwaukee came word of the arrest of the former president of the American Bankers Association, Frank G. Bigelow, for defrauding his bank of $1.5 million. Bigelow, like Spear, had made false bookkeeping entries to hide money he borrowed to cover losses he suffered speculating in wheat and securities futures. Bigelow was unapologetic, declined defense council, pled guilty, and was sentenced to ten years' hard labor. Bigelow was a typical Victorian gentleman banker, not unlike Iri Reynolds or Charles Beckwith. Adhering to their unwritten code, most bank officials caught defrauding national banks pled guilty and took their medicine. When the judge asked Bigelow if he had anything further to say after his guilty plea, Bigelow straightened, looked the judge squarely in the eye, and replied, "Nothing."[23]

To former Citizen's National Bank cashier Arthur Spear, it was clear that the government, with its fifty-page conspiracy indictment, had the momentum in its case against him. He was charged with falsifying bank records, conspiracy to defraud, and certifying checks when no funds were on deposit, not to mention perjury. Unlike Cassie Chadwick, Spear had willingly assisted prosecutors in investigating the bank's collapse, which strengthened their case. The government repaid Spear with a plea deal, and on May 4, 1905, Spear pled guilty to just one of the twenty-one counts against him, successfully convincing prosecutors that Charles Beckwith, unable to defend himself from the grave, had directed him to certify those checks and alter the bank's books. That one count was for a bookkeeping irregularity on February 9, 1904, when Spear had creatively added $5,000 to Cleveland's Colonial National Bank's account to hide a Chadwick loan. Spear, who had already said good-bye to his family, was sentenced to seven years, when five was the minimum. Judge Taylor was sympathetic to the thirty-seven-year-old Spear's youth and Beckwith's influence on him. Taylor said he doubted Spear intended to "rob" his employer. Nevertheless, the judge felt an example needed to be set because "neither the defendant nor Beckwith had the courage to stop the dealings with Mrs. Chadwick." Spear wished to leave for the Ohio Penitentiary immediately after sentencing to avoid being held in the jail with Mrs. Chadwick. As Spear was exiting court, federal prosecutor John Sullivan quietly slipped him a letter for the prison warden, recommending the former cashier for a clerk's position instead of hard labor.[24]

Mrs. Chadwick was much affected by Spear's punishment. She said, "I am so sorry for Mr. Spear. He was a good man . . . we were always good friends, and I know he was absolutely innocent of any intentional wrong doing." However, she refused to comment on Spear's attorney's contention that his client was a scapegoat for Beckwith and Chadwick. Had Beckwith lived to face sentencing, it is likely that, at his age, any prison sentence would have been a life sentence.[25]

A legal notice in fine print in the classified section of Cleveland newspapers offered the Chadwick real estate assets for bid, one way to solve the dilemma of whether the mortgage holder or the Bankruptcy Court should liquidate them: the large home on Euclid Avenue, appraised at $39,140; a nearby lot on Lincoln Avenue, appraised at $1,875; and a lot in Newburgh township, appraised at $200. Boston financier Herbert Newton, who won his lawsuit against Mrs. Chadwick by default when she was in jail, had hoped to realize some of the proceeds. As it was, Newton would have to stand in line behind secured creditors. And indeed, the old Chadwick home was sold to the mortgage holder, Savings Deposit Bank and Trust of Elyria, for a high bid of $35,000. The Elyria bank was due a total of $43,000, principal and interest from the Chadwick mortgage.[26]

The evening of May 17, Mrs. Chadwick decided to tell her version of her frenzied finance to an Associated Press reporter of her choosing and approved by Judge Taylor and her attorneys. She would take no questions. Seated in a comfortable rocking chair in her Cleveland jail cell, she began her monologue by claiming that since January 1, 1901, a total of $3,210,000 had passed through her hands. Of that amount, only $900,000 was borrowed; the rest was from sales of assets and income from her trust fund. Cassie offered no proof or independent witnesses to support this assertion. At the time of her arrest, she boasted she had $250,000 with which she could have fled the country had she wished. Yet again, she promised full disclosure in a book she planned to write. Her trust fund, she told the AP man, still existed, but it was no longer in her name or to her benefit. In the interview's most sensational revelation, Mrs. Chadwick said that Emil Hoover was not her son—she was likely trying to protect him—but declined to name his real parents. This rambling interview, in which the newsman could not question her, concluded as it began with an unsubstantiated assertion that she once had $1.7 million free and clear. In the end, there would never be a book, unlike her contemporary swindler, New Yorker Sophie Lyons, who in 1913 penned her autobiography, *Why Crime Does Not Pay.* This interview, lacking in supporting evidence as it was, was nevertheless as close as Cassie Chadwick ever got to providing an explanation of her finances. From the reporter's point of view, it was delivered with sincerity and little else to give it credibility.[27]

On October 10, 1905, the *San Francisco Call* reviewed Cassie Chadwick's crimes in light of scandals swirling about the collapse of East Coast life insurance companies caused by their speculative investment practices. According to the paper, "She has moved for a new trial, and on many grounds she should have it." The newspaper suggested that it was unfair to jail Mrs. Chadwick when men remained free for equally dubious acts that were far more harmful to the public. "It is a mean thing to punish a woman," the *Call* opined, "while men who did as bad or worse are living in country seats and keep a butler and coachman." The *Call* suggested that "The time may come when Cleveland will hold her up as a conservative operator in her line, by way of contrast to the wild and runaway plungers of New York City."[28]

The Cleveland Customs House held an auction on October 20, 1905, of Mrs. Chadwick's jewelry, which had been seized. The estimated value was $17,000, but the pieces sold for a disappointing aggregate of $2,147. Some minor excitement was caused by an unidentified woman in black, who appeared to have some familiarity with the jewelry and was speculated to be Mrs. Chadwick's representative. The lady bid on almost every lot, but she purchased none. The item with the highest sales price was nicknamed "Cassie's Football," a huge solitaire diamond valued at $800 that sold for $665 to a Standard Oil Company executive. A brooch set with an amethyst, surrounded by sixteen pearls, sold for just $65. The sale's results indicated that jewelers regularly overcharged Mrs. Chadwick and that her purported expertise in gemstones was perhaps overrated.[29]

CHAPTER TWENTY-ONE

ENCHANTRESS IN
HER LAST HOME

Cassie Chadwick's conviction was upheld by the US Circuit Court of Appeals in Cincinnati on January 10, 1906. There was no appeal to the Supreme Court. She was ordered to begin her sentence in the Ohio Penitentiary. No one believed her claims that she was not Madame Devere, and, in prison parlance, she would be a "second termer," a title few would covet. The prison, surrounded by a twenty-foot brick wall and located on Spring Street on Columbus's west side, was built in 1834. A women's section was completed three years later. It was cold, damp, dreary, and disease ridden. The Ohio prison stood as a glowing example of the nineteenth-century philosophy of prison as punishment, not rehabilitation. The cells were so narrow that an inmate sitting on a bed could extend his legs and touch the opposite wall. All able prisoners were required to work.[1]

The prison's warden, C. B. Gould, told reporters, "Mrs. Cassie L. Chadwick will be treated just as any other female prisoner in this institution." He said she would be able to refresh her seamstress skills by "making shirts for male prisoners, sewing on buttons and darning socks," health permitting. As for her accommodations, Mrs. Chadwick was the fifty-eighth woman in the state prison, which had cells for only fifty. According to Gould, "She will . . . have to accept a cellmate, the rule being that only older and more deserving women" get a private cell.[2]

The day before her departure for Columbus, Cassie Chadwick refused to meet with most of her jailhouse visitors. She said she wished to be "alone in meditation," in order to prepare herself for the coming ordeal. Emil stayed with her until 2:00 A.M., and after he left, she slept under the watchful eye of another female inmate, such was the concern for her mental state. The day before her departure from the jail, the woman who once berated staff at the best hotels in

New York personally complimented the sheriff and each of her jailers for her treatment over the last year.[3]

Cassie was awakened at 5:00 A.M. January 12, 1906, for her last breakfast in Cleveland—rolls and coffee. She dressed for her journey in a brown traveling suit with plaid trim, furs, and her signature large hat with ostrich feathers. She left the jail at 7:00 A.M. for the 7:25 train to Columbus in the custody of Marshal Chandler. *Cleveland Plain Dealer* reporter Karl Kitchen was among the bevy of reporters who crowded aboard the same Columbus-bound train. Kitchen saw Mrs. Chadwick seated at the rear of the passenger car, her face covered with a heavy veil. Compared with past crowds, few people, aside from fellow travelers, saw her at the station. However, there were enough overeager photographers pressing cameras against the passenger car's windows to force Cassie and her accompanying physician, N. Stone Scott, to retreat into a Pullman stateroom. The closed door was guarded by the marshals.[4]

Ironically, the conductor was the same one who had presided over the train that brought her under arrest from New York to Cleveland in December 1904. And the porter, Sam Jones, had served in the private car Mrs. Chadwick had leased to take a group of Clevelanders to New York to see Wagner's opera *Parsifal* two years earlier. After that New York trip, she gave Jones a $25 tip, but today all she had to offer was a smile after he brought her a pillow. Mrs. Chadwick spent the first part of the trip reading a book, appropriately titled *Consequences*. The second half of the trip she spent lying down and napping due to motion sickness. Understandably depressed, she said, "I am not very well, and I don't believe I will ever recover my health."[5]

Columbus, Ohio, as the state capital, was accustomed to seeing the famous and the infamous. Its citizens considered it good sport to jeer at the arrival of high-profile prisoners destined for the gloomy prison on Spring Street. An above-average crowd of two thousand waited none too patiently at Columbus's Union Station for a glimpse of Cassie Chadwick. She arrived in Columbus at 11:00 A.M. A carriage was waiting for her at the basement entrance, and as it entered the street, a chorus of "There's Mrs. Chadwick, look out for your pocket book," greeted her. During the carriage ride, the weak and worried prisoner asked Dr. Scott to check her pulse. It was okay, he informed her. A crowd of similar size and temperament at the prison was fooled by the warden, who had placed extra guards at the main entrance, only to have the carriage veer off and whisk Cassie into the prison via a less used female entrance. Through sheer force of will, she arrived to begin her prison sentence in better than expected condition.[6]

Once inside the prison walls and hidden from public view, Mrs. Chadwick physically collapsed due, it was said, to nerves and motion sickness. Her face and her hair were both the color of snow. She recovered quickly, although her deafness made communication difficult. She was identified by old prison employees as Madame Devere, and her 1891 record resurrected. She was assigned number 36680. Upon examination, a burn scar was found on the right elbow, exactly like one found on Lydia Devere in 1891. Mrs. Chadwick was given a coarse, ill-fitting prison dress. Meals from a nearby restaurant had been arranged, but she refused to eat her dinner. A prison doctor examined her, and he admitted her to the prison hospital for a couple of days of rest. After viewing his new charge, Warden Gould decided that she would be put to work sewing as the laundry labor would be too strenuous. Sewing had been her former occupation in prison, and it was not light work. Cassie, being a federal prisoner, was provided with a private cell after all, and the warden softened enough to say she could furnish her cell with a rug and a few other possessions she had brought. The Duchess of Diamonds had arrived in Columbus with just $3 in her pocket.[7]

The *Cleveland Plain Dealer* prophetically summarized Cassie Chadwick's situation with the headline "Enchantress in Her Last Home." Newspaper reporters carefully calculated Mrs. Chadwick's prison time. She would be given credit for the time in jail in Cleveland beginning the day of her conviction, so her earliest release date, with good behavior, would be November 11, 1911. She would be fifty-four. Dr. Scott predicted she would never leave prison alive.[8]

Arthur Spear, already settled into prison life, consented to be interviewed. Spear was asked if he might see Mrs. Chadwick in the lockup. He doubted it. "I am trying to forget that I ever knew Mrs. Chadwick, and I think I will succeed," was his terse reply. Spear's feelings were no doubt those of her other victims.[9]

In the spring of 1907, Cassie Chadwick was bankrupt and incarcerated, yet she and James Friend were not done with each other. The widow of one of Friend and Frank Hoffstott's partners, W. C. Jutte, sued the pair for conspiring to defraud Jutte's estate of as much as $5 million in bonds. Jutte, a millionaire coal mine operator, had slowly slipped into a violent insanity before his Atlantic City suicide in the spring of 1905. The lawsuit alleged that Friend and Hoffstott had taken advantage of Jutte while he was impaired by persuading him to give his partners $1 million in bonds as collateral for a loan of $300,000. The collateral disappeared, and Mrs. Jutte sued.[10]

Mrs. Chadwick became involved in March 1904, when Friend demanded better collateral for his loans to her than Cassie's promissory notes. She signed over to Friend on April 12, 1904, the $5 million worth of securities—and the power to sell them—purportedly held by Iri Reynolds. In addition, the lawsuit alleged that Friend wanted Mrs. Chadwick to secretly dispose of the $1 million in bonds Friend had acquired from Jutte. Friend told Mrs. Chadwick that he possessed the bonds because "Poor old Jutte is not able to take care of his own affairs." Cassie was said to have received an $87,000 loan for this service, the money likely coming from Jutte's holdings.[11]

Jutte's widow lost her case in February 1907, possibly because the judge was pressured by Friend. Mrs. Jutte's lawyers proposed to depose Mrs. Chadwick as part of an appeal. Friend did not want this to occur and persuaded former judge Francis Wing, one of Cassie's defense team, to go to Columbus to try to dissuade her from being deposed. To accomplish this, Wing told his former client, who was in declining health, that Friend would use his influence to destroy her chances of a pardon and keep her in prison. Cassie later told a reporter of Friend's attempt: "When a man threatens me when I am in prison, that is the hardest thing he can do." Mrs. Chadwick gave the deposition. Since her departure from Cleveland, Cassie had kept a locked satchel of papers by her side, the same one that had so excited the Bankruptcy Court, never letting anyone touch it and never letting it leave her sight. From it she extracted a memo from James Friend, dated June 24, 1904, in which Friend listed Cassie's "entire indebtedness" to him. The memo listed six loans between April 1903 and March 1904, totaling $728,200, not including interest charges. Each of the loans was payable whenever Friend demanded it. Much of the money loaned Mrs. Chadwick was likely W. C. Jutte's, which may have been Friend's attempt to launder it. The deposition was sealed by the court when Friend's lawyers argued, among other things, that its contents might ignite a financial panic in western Pennsylvania. It was later made public. James W. Friend died in December 1909, purportedly because of the strain caused by the Chadwick swindle, the Jutte lawsuit, and a disastrous strike at his Pressed Steel Car Company. The lead for Friend's *New York Times* obituary listed not his business accomplishments but his role as a Chadwick dupe. Friend was a shrewd and ruthless businessman who was ultimately bested by a mere woman, Cassie Chadwick.[12]

Incarcerated, Cassie Chadwick's health continued to decline. Her attitude, described as peevish, grated on the prison staff. She preferred to be screened from the admission-paying public and even shunned her fellow prisoners. Her son was her only regular visitor; her sisters, only occasionally. Cassie complained of stomach problems and indigestion. When she arrived at prison, her meals were sent in by a fashionable restaurant nearby, but her continued complaints led prison officials to blame the rich diet and forbade it. Confined to prison fare—a repetitious diet of beans, cornbread, bacon, and coffee—she lost thirty pounds as her undiagnosed condition worsened.[13]

In mid-September 1907, during a visit with Emil, Mrs. Chadwick collapsed into unconsciousness. Initially, prison authorities thought this was another charade on her part to arouse sympathy for a pardon and chose to downplay the seriousness of her condition. However, days later when she failed to recover her strength, Cassie was placed in the hospital under the constant care of the prison doctor, A. G. Helmick. From then on, she alternated between intervals of rationality, unconsciousness, and delirium. She never spoke of her financial or personal affairs, although prison hospital personnel strained to hear some delirious revelation.[14]

On October 7, the prison issued a bulletin describing her condition as critical. Dr. Helmick said, "Mrs. Chadwick is not so well. Her pulse is 115 this morning and she appears to be gradually growing weaker." Imprisonment had broken her will. While confined in Columbus, Mrs. Chadwick never attended the prison's chapel because she feared attracting a crowd. However, on October 8, she surprised everyone by accepting Catholic baptism by the prison's priest, which was regarded as a sign she had accepted her fate. The *Cleveland Leader* described her as "a physical ghost of even the broken woman who was brought to the prison."[15]

By October 10, Cassie Chadwick was semicomatose, her heart beating feebly. Emil and two of her sisters were summoned. Only Emil, working in Cleveland, responded. Prison officials administered the only treatment available, small doses of strychnine used as a stimulant, three times daily to keep her alive.[16]

Cassie Chadwick drew her last breath at 10:15 P.M. on October 10, 1907. Emil arrived just minutes later. Jail matrons were her only company in the bare stone room when she died. The official cause was neurasthenia—nervous exhaustion brought on by chronic depression—although no autopsy was performed. The woman was dead, but her locked satchel was still of intense interest. According to the *Cleveland Leader,* "for a long time penitentiary officers have been curious as to the contents of the big valise in which her papers were contained." After his mother's death, Emil Hoover took the valise back to Cleveland with him.[17]

Mrs. Chadwick's body was delivered to a local funeral home in Columbus. Rumors circulated that when embalming was completed, the body would be exhibited for a fee, as were deceased gangsters and highwaymen. A crowd gathered in anticipation, but Emil refused permission for the circus to continue.

Finding the money for burial proved to be a problem. Prison workers believed that Cassie had told Emil where to find the money to pay for her burial. Another rumor identified a wealthy but anonymous acquaintance as a potential source of funeral expenses. An unmarked pauper's grave was an alternative. But in the end, arrangements were made by relatives for burial in Woodstock, Ontario.[18]

On October 16, 1907, Cassie Chadwick was laid to rest in the cemetery of St. Paul's Episcopal Church in Woodstock. The funeral proved to be the biggest event in the history of the small town of Woodstock. For many rural Canadians in attendance, it was their first look at newsreel cameras on hand to record the burial of the famous adventuress. Services were held in the home of her sister, Mrs. Campbell. Rev. F. W. Thompson, of the College Avenue Methodist Church, made it clear that only those who could show that they were friends of the family would be admitted to the 2:30 P.M. service. Some of the railroad men involved in shipping the casket started a rumor that the coffin was far too light to contain Cassie Chadwick's earthly remains. But they couldn't know that she had lost considerable weight during her illness. Fueled by the restricted viewing and closed casket, rumors began to fly that the real Cassie Chadwick might be still alive, having successfully executed one last con. Reverend Thompson was obliged to issue a statement attesting that he personally had seen and identified the body.[19]

Beautiful flowers and a picture of the deceased lay on the lid of the casket. Two sisters, a brother, and Emil were the only family present. Reverend Thompson read a psalm and made general remarks, but he did not mention Mrs. Chadwick's checkered past. Cassie's pallbearers, a testament to her notoriety, were a who's who of Woodstock's prominent men, including the mayor, his brother, an alderman, and two physicians. One pallbearer was a local man, A. L. Dent, an old acquaintance of Cassie's from Woodstock who appeared at her Toledo trial and whose name was occasionally mentioned in connection with her. At the graveside, a photographer asked the reverend to raise and lower the coffin again for a better camera angle. His patience exhausted, Thompson shoved the man, who subsequently lost his balance and fell into the grave.[20]

A large granite monument, which would have suited Cassie's tastes and would discourage grave robbers, was placed over the grave announcing, "Elizabeth Bigley, wife of L. S. Chadwick, M. D. 1859–1907." Thus, Cassie Chadwick, whose downfall began with a Baptist minister in Cleveland, died a Catholic in Columbus but was buried by a Methodist clergyman in an Episcopal cemetery in Canada. Perhaps she believed even God could be deceived.[21]

Cassie's obituary in the *Cleveland Plain Dealer,* which had chronicled her criminal career as completely as any newspaper, included some observations about the woman. The paper had once called Mrs. Chadwick the "Heroine of High Finance," and it suggested that had she been a corporation with proper management, her talents might have made many people rich. While that appraisal might contain a grain of truth, the *Plain Dealer* concluded that she was simply psychologically incapable of resisting a criminal path. The newspaper concluded that had she employed an insanity defense, she might have avoided the lonely prison death she suffered.[22]

Cassie Chadwick might be dead, but she still held the fascination of a curious public and stubborn government investigators. She left not one but three wills. The first, dated from 1902, assumed an estate of $1 million. The 1902 will left funds to three Cleveland hospitals, $50,000 to the local humane society, and $100,000 to Western Reserve University. The will stipulated that the recipient label the money as "Chadwick Memorial Funds" or "Chadwick Building Funds." This will was invalidated by subsequent ones.[23]

The second will Cassie dictated to her attorney, J. P. Dawley, on January 17, 1905, during one of her periods of illness. It was witnessed by county jail employees and appointed Dawley and family attorney Sheldon Kerruish as executors. In this version, she left just $2,500 to her husband, and everything else was to go to Emil Hoover. When she signed the final copy, Cassie struck the words "my son" from the text because, it was said, she wished to spare her devoted Emil the stain of his infamous mother's reputation. Attorney Dawley had this to say to those who questioned if Emil was her son. "There is no doubt on that point," the lawyer said. "He is now occupying a position with a large commercial concern in a large city and is well thought of." Dawley refused to discourage the notion that there might be real assets in Cassie's estate, which led to speculation that he was hiding something.[24]

The third will, which would take precedence, had been dictated to Columbus attorney Thomas E. Powell only a few weeks before Cassie's death. Powell, a latecomer to the woman's stable of attorneys, was nonetheless typical of her choice in a barrister—a well-connected, prominent local defense attorney and former candidate for governor. Like many, he was drawn to her by the opportunity to meet the infamous Cassie Chadwick. Powell's opinion carried the force of his reputation, and he believed his client was insane. "Mrs. Chadwick was the victim of a peculiar form of insanity, and she had no idea of the value of money," Powell said. The man was no physician, and a lack of appreciation for the value of money was hardly a guarantee of insanity. Nevertheless, Powell said of his client, "She was the shrewdest person I ever met. There is nothing in the claim that she died in possession of a fortune. She received a little money while in the pen, but lately the remittances were few and she realized that her friends deserted her." Powell estimated, based on his discussions with Cassie, that she must have spent $1.3 million over the last ten years, something akin to $32 million today. He said he would not file the Columbus will for probate. Emil Hoover agreed, saying, "it would open the entire estate to the attacks of creditors." Not filing it would insure that there would be no final examination of what remained undisclosed in Mrs. Chadwick's financial records. Emil's statement led many to believe there were hidden assets.[25]

US attorney John J. Sullivan, with the total support of bankruptcy receiver Nathan Loeser, threatened to force Powell to file the will, despite the fact that probate was a state issue. "I suspected a long time that just this sort of thing would be attempted when Mrs. Chadwick died," Sullivan said, clinging to the secret assets scenario. Sullivan insisted it was a state crime not to file the will, and the only possible explanation for not doing so was to keep the contents of her valise, a source of torment for government investigators, secret. Sullivan and others suspected that among Cassie's papers in that all-important valise, there might be promissory notes bearing genuine signatures. He acknowledged she was a forger, but it was possible she had a genuine note or two. The prosecutor said that his office had a $500 claim for court expenses, not to mention all those other creditors waiting in line. He, for one, doubted she had stashed away any jewelry, although the Customs investigation was still open. Sullivan emphatically denied persecuting the woman, pointing out that several indictments had not been pursued. Powell, the well-connected attorney, wasn't likely to be easily intimidated, even by a federal prosecutor like Sullivan. It is unclear whether the will was filed or not.[26]

Under pressure from prosecutors, Emil Hoover surrendered to the Bankruptcy Court some of the contents from his mother's valise, which touched off a new round of speculation and frenzy. Included were seven bank passbooks. One came from Pittsburgh, three from New York, and three from Cleveland. Most showed routine deposits and withdrawals. One was from the third largest trust company in New York, the Knickerbocker Trust Company, which was on the verge of collapse in the developing financial panic. The passbook of the New York Corn Exchange Bank had served as a notebook in which Cassie had written a new skin-care recipe: "sulphate quinine 5 grains; sweet almond oil, one ounce."[27]

However, the real excitement was reserved for the passbook of Pittsburgh's Second National Bank, which seemed to show deposits totaling $305,000 in 1902, and *no withdrawals!* Nathan Loeser, the bankruptcy trustee, made it clear that any actual funds did not belong to Emil or Dr. Chadwick, but rather the long-suffering creditors. "Whatever estate there is belongs to the creditors and not to the relatives," Loeser said. "That fact seems to have been overlooked by certain people." The government remained suspicious of young Emil Hoover.[28]

The euphoria was short-lived. Twenty-four hours later, the Second National Bank issued a denial: "If the receiver at Cleveland has any passbook with the name of the Second National Bank of Pittsburgh on it, and having an entry for $305,000 to the credit of Mrs. Cassie Chadwick, he will find it is a forgery." The phantom funds were attributed to someone simply adding zeros. Charles Stanek, a bank examiner who had investigated Mrs. Chadwick, confirmed that he knew of several phony passbook entries in Cleveland and New York. He said, "In some instances, all the entries in the passbook were forgeries, while in others the original entry would be changed." He recalled one New York passbook in which a $200 deposit became $200,000. Stanek said he knew of no Pittsburgh banks with any Chadwick money. The bank examiner tantalizingly confided to reporters that not one-tenth of the evidence he had against Cassie Chadwick would see the light of day, even after her death. Nevertheless, it is remotely possible that James Friend, a man capable of working both sides of the law and well connected in Pittsburgh banking circles, had managed to make the funds disappear.[29]

With Mrs. Chadwick dead, Dawley spoke to the *Cleveland Leader,* which had most recently called the woman the "witch of finance," about his most famous client. "I believe that Mrs. Chadwick was born with a mental disease which developed into a form of insanity, and that her mind was dominated by criminal impulses which she could not control," Dawley said. "She was possessed of great egotism and imagined herself a great financier. . . . She was possessed of considerable cunning and wonderful mental force which is not inconsistent with insanity." Mrs. Chadwick, Dawley said, took a childish delight in displaying her power and the trappings of wealth. This and more were signs that "she was mentally unbalanced."[30]

Cassie Chadwick died on the cusp of the great banker's Panic of 1907, which began with a failed attempt by unscrupulous investors to corner the copper market. As a result, several large New York financial concerns teetered on the brink of collapse by mid-October. Dawley saw little ethical difference between Mrs. Chadwick's conduct and the rich New York bankers about to lose all. Dawley told reporters, "I am unable to draw any distinction between that class of individuals who pre-empt our insurance funds, railroads and other public industries to their own private gains by modern methods," he said, "and those who borrow money by paying large bonuses for it and making extravagant statements as to their ability to repay the loan." Perhaps Mrs. Chadwick's escapades would awaken the public mind, Dawley hoped, to the corrupt methods employed by great financiers.[31]

Cassie Chadwick was Dawley's most famous client, and he lost the case. He was bitter and blamed the loss on the popular sentiment that concluded his client was guilty before she ever faced trial. "Emotional impulse was allowed to over-ride the law," he claimed. Dawley blamed the huge crowds and unsympathetic spectators in the courtroom to which the jurors, as well as the defendant, were equally subjected. Dawley, however, was a learned and experienced defense attorney who should have known how to cope with the publicity and hostile public sentiment.[32]

Dawley said he didn't believe his client was related to Andrew Carnegie. However, he admitted that his intuition, instead of solid evidence, led him to believe she knew him. Dr. Chadwick, in Dawley's opinion, was innocent. The man trusted his wife with his daughter and signed over his ancestral home to her, Dawley pointed out. The doctor was rewarded with the loss of everything he owned and liability for several promissory notes he signed. On the issue of Madame Devere, Dawley couldn't bring himself to admit the truth. "I never have seen any evidence on that point." Finally, he was asked if Cassie Chadwick truly believed she was innocent of her crimes. "I do not believe that Mrs. Chadwick from her standpoint thought she had committed any crime," Dawley said. "Her notion was that she was a great financier, and that what she did was legitimate borrowing of money," he said.[33]

Cassie's sister, Mrs. York, had a simpler view of her sister's life: "It seems to me that my sister had a mania for doing just such things as that which got her into trouble."[34]

Although Cassie Chadwick died in October 1907, her bankruptcy proceedings lived on until 1909. A single surviving check provided a glimpse of how her creditors fared. A Cleveland merchant, the Fetterman-Miller Company, submitted a claim for $29 and received a check four years later from the Bankruptcy Court for sixty-two cents. This check represented a payout on the order of two cents on the dollar.[35]

Arthur Spear was successful in getting his prison sentence commuted by fellow Ohioan, President William Howard Taft, on February 28, 1910, after serving just under five years. To have been the beneficiary of presidential action suggests sympathy for his situation and help from some important friends. After his release, Spear disappeared. A prison record from the Ohio Penitentiary bears the notation "died 1910," and a newspaper announced his death in Detroit in November 1910. Yet, the Ohio cemetery where Spear was purportedly buried has no record of anyone being interred in his grave. What really happened to Arthur Spear remains a mystery.[36]

Iri Reynolds was poorer monetarily, but his reputation was little tarnished by Cassie Chadwick. Still a trusted banker, Reynolds was working as a bank appraiser in 1910. He died in April 1928 at the age of eighty-three. Prosecutor John Sullivan, a Roosevelt Republican, parlayed his success into a state appellate judgeship and a prominent role in the antitrust action against the Standard Ohio Company. Sullivan died in August 1930.[37]

Dr. Leroy Chadwick escaped prosecution primarily because of a lack of evidence against him. He left Cleveland as soon as he was certain he wouldn't be tried. He never visited Cassie in prison and did not attend her funeral. In November 1906, he received an annulment of his Canadian marriage to the woman on the grounds that neither were legal Canadian residents. With the Pittsburgh ceremony of doubtful legality, it could be argued in retrospect that Leroy Chadwick never actually married Cassie Hoover. In 1905, Leroy and daughter Mary moved to Florida, where one of Chadwick's brothers was a successful businessman. In 1908, the doctor filed for personal bankruptcy. He claimed personal debts of $1,750 and jointly with his deceased wife of $650,000, which included James Friend, $500,000; Herbert Newton, $90,000; Charles Beckwith, $5,000; and attorney J. W. Albaugh, $5,000. Chadwick claimed assets of only $175. He asked the court to allow him to keep his medical instruments and books. Census records in 1910 indicate that Dr. Chadwick was selling real estate in Florida and living on a small farm with his daughter and her husband near Jacksonville. According to family oral history, the doctor never practiced medicine again, and he was none too successful selling real estate. His main interest was in playing the organ in church. He died on August 2, 1924, in Jacksonville, never having remarried. After Leroy's death, most of the papers the family had collected regarding the Cassie Chadwick years were destroyed to protect Mary's reputation.[38]

Was Leroy Chadwick a willing participant in his wife's financial manipulations or just another in a long line of gullible dupes? Ample evidence exists that he was present at many of her discussions with lenders, signed promissory notes, gave Cassie control of his property, entertained creditors, and even wrote bad checks to cover her loans. Chadwick was judged by his peers to be basically an honest man but weak and easily manipulated. His great-nephew, James Chadwick, suggested that Leroy "was low on fuel in his mental pilot light." In the later years of their marriage, the doctor must have had suspicions about his wife's deteriorating finances because in the summer of 1904, he warned Emil to watch his money. Even a weak man like Chadwick had his limits, and he finally realized that his good name had been abused by his wife, and his daughter's modest inheritance squandered. Like so many of Cassie Chadwick's victims, Dr. Leroy Chadwick appeared to have lost everything and only wanted to forget. Chadwick's personality and inertia seem at odds with any idea that he had squirreled away a nest egg for the future. The old family mansion on Euclid was, for a time, a tourist attraction. Ironically, it was razed in the 1920s to make way for a house of worship on what became the corner of Euclid and East 82nd. The Chadwicks, like many of the Avenue's once-famous residents, faded from memory.[39]

Emil Hoover remains a question mark. How did he fit into the grand schemes of Cassie Chadwick? Cassie likely appropriated the last name Hoover from her widowed landlady, Mrs. S. C. Hoover, with whom she boarded in Cleveland in the 1880s. Emil's father was never publicly identified, but apparently he was known to several people. The boy was born in Cleveland in 1885 or 1886 on Euclid Avenue in what was known locally as the Judge Griswold house. His father has been described as a wealthy but corrupt middle-aged Democrat ward heeler. Emil's father had died by the late 1890s.[40]

During the Devere years, Cassie shamelessly used the poor boy as a prop, at one point passing him off as the illegitimate son of Richard Brown as the boy alternated between Toledo, Cleveland, and Ontario. After his mother's conviction in Toledo in 1891, Emil went to Ontario with his grandmother, his support being provided by an unnamed Clevelander. On the official record of the Ohio Penitentiary, Emil was listed as her son. When Madame Devere was paroled in 1893, Emil was reunited with his mother in Cleveland. Reliable but anonymous informants told of blackmail threats by the now Mrs. Hoover directed at men who might have been Emil's father, using the boy once again. Those same sources reported that these cases were quietly settled out of court. After Mrs. Hoover married Leroy Chadwick, Emil became, in 1900, Emil H. Chadwick, born in 1888. The boy went to the best private schools in Cleveland, North Carolina, and Long Island. His summers and vacations included extensive travel. Of the Chadwick years, one of Leroy's nephews later observed with some envy that "Emil had everything that a boy could want."[41]

After his mother returned to prison in 1906, Emil Chadwick reverted to Emil Hoover and remained in Cleveland. Following her death and burial in 1907, the youth disappeared from the record, although one source placed him working for a large Cleveland firm. According to the Chadwick family, after Cassie's death, attempts to locate Emil and offer him a safe place in Florida met with failure. The family believed that he returned to Ontario to his mother's birthplace, where he spent much of his early life. Since the US government never really let the boy out of its sights, who could blame him if he chose to disappear, rich or poor?[42]

Was there a well-concealed horde of gemstones with Emil's name on it? Federal authorities were convinced that Cassie Chadwick had not spent every dollar of the vast sums she raised. When she was arrested, she had virtually no personal jewelry. Where was her vast collection? Even the Chadwick family thought there might be a secret hoard stashed away. With Emil's disappearance, there was the intriguing possibility that he fled with a satchel of jewelry or suitcase of cash to begin a new life under an assumed name and in a new place.[43]

Cassie Chadwick was one of the great swindlers of the Victorian era. Her obsession with secrecy and silence meant that most of the details of her thirty-five-year run as an adventuress remain lost to history. Her prosecutors readily admitted that they made public only a fraction of the evidence they uncovered to protect their sources, witnesses, innocent people, and, in some cases, financial institutions. When she was arrested, Cassie owed close to $1 million and had borrowed millions of dollars on worthless paper, supposedly backed by Andrew Carnegie. The men with whom she did business, and they were all men, tried to explain why they had loaned this woman so much money on such flimsy collateral. But none admitted to the root cause—greed. Greed was something Cassie Chadwick knew how to exploit.

Canadians had their own view of Mrs. Chadwick, who always returned to her country of birth despite her endless attempts to distance herself from her roots. In many ways Canadians took a perverse pride in Cassie's success at the expense of the often overbearing Americans. Canadian writer John Crosbie, who produced a primarily fictional account of Cassie's life, said of her, "I don't regard her as having a criminal mind. Remember too that she was apparently quite amoral. She could be a madame, she could be a clairvoyant, she could be anything she wanted . . . she may have also been a little crazy." In 1985, Mary Evans of the Oxford Historical Society in Woodstock said of Cassie, "It was her personality." According to Evans, she wasn't pretty but possessed an alluring figure. But it was her ability to "charm anybody . . . especially bank managers" that was the key to her success. Swindling, Evans believed, was what Cassie excelled at. "She is probably still the best swindler that's ever existed." Of Cassie's Woodstock roots, Evans had this to say: "She's our naughty girl. Oxford county people all knew about her." Evans felt that Cassie wasn't getting her due. Had she been an American, Evans believed, Cassie's exploits would have spawned movies and filled history books. Perhaps Mary Evans was right.[44]

Who was Cassie Chadwick? By the standards of 1905, she was a criminal. She was responsible for the destruction of a national bank, which caused considerable suffering in Oberlin. Bank closures were commonplace in the nineteenth and early twentieth century, when banks lacked the oversight, and depositors the protections, of the federal government. The losses incurred by depositors—working men and women—were real and could be devastating. Cassie's crimes were taken seriously, as they should have been.

Was the woman insane? Many educated men seemed to believe so. Perhaps by the standards of the time, she was. Cassie, by all appearances, suffered from depression, hysteria, agoraphobia, delusions of grandeur, egomania, and hypochondria. She was a career criminal. A hundred years on, these conditions would not necessarily suggest she was insane. Many women accused of a wide range of crimes were sent to asylums in the nineteenth century. It was one way to avoid prison. Cassie Chadwick chose not to pursue this option.

In the twenty-first century, Cassie might be viewed as a woman rebelling against the male-dominated society that was entrenched at the dawn of the twentieth century. It is true that she did not conform to the conventions and morality of the era. Cassie did achieve a measure of control over her destiny that a majority of women in Victorian America did not. It is possible, if not likely, that many of those women who endured rowdy crowds to catch a glimpse of her, rose early to attend her trials, and followed her saga in the newspapers saw some of the traits of a feminist or suffragette in the woman. Cassie herself left no comment or explanation. Her actions suggest she was a woman who did not feel bound by the stereotypical gender roles of her time.

Contemporary accounts indicate that Cassie Chadwick saw herself as a financier or businesswoman, behaving much as Victorian men did in pursuit of wealth. During the Gilded Age, many of Cassie's business practices were commonplace, even if unethical. Fees, commissions, kickbacks, bribes, secret deals, and all the other tricks of crony capitalism were routine. Andrew Carnegie was a successful practitioner. When the *Cleveland Plain Dealer* suggested that Cassie might have been a successful corporation making many rich had she only been a bit more conservative in her ways, the paper was not entirely mistaken. It had worked for Hetty Green. Cassie's defense attorneys tried to paint her as a legitimate businesswoman, and the defendant appeared to agree with this portrayal. Unfortunately for Cassie, an all-male jury of everyday Ohioans did not agree.

However one chooses to view Cassie Chadwick, 120 years later, there should be little doubt that the woman was persuasive, imaginative, secretive, audacious, and clever. It is true that "obstacles vanished with her woman's tongue" and that she possessed "a monumental nerve." The men who prosecuted her believed it impossible for a woman to do what she did without a male accomplice. The authorities searched high and low, but they never found anyone they could charge. In the final analysis, it appears that with minimal outside assistance, Cassie Chadwick succeeded in perpetrating one of the greatest frauds in American history.[45]

It was simply pure genius.

NOTES

ABBREVIATIONS

CL   *Cleveland Leader and Herald*
CPD   *Cleveland Plain Dealer*
CP   *Cleveland Press*
NYT   *New York Times*
OSJ   *Ohio State Journal*
TDB   *Toledo Daily Blade*
HCF   H. Clark Ford

INTRODUCTION

1. *CL*, Oct. 11, 1907; Borowitz, *Unhappy Endings*, 23–24; Loth, *Gold Brick Cassie*, 59–65; Crosbie, *The Incredible Mrs. Chadwick*, 186–88; MacNee, *Outlaws, Mobsters and Crooks*, 2:263–64; Wade, *Great Hoaxes and Famous Imposters*, 12–18; Connolly, "Marvelous Mrs. Chadwick," *McClure's Magazine*, 9.

2. *CPD*, Jan. 13, 1906.

3. MacNee, *New York Sunday Morning Star*, Dec. 17, 1911, 281–90; *New York Sun*, Aug. 10, 1890; *Anaconda (MT) Standard*, June 26, 1896; *Ottumwa (IA) Register*, Feb. 7, 1876; Byrnes, *1886 Professional Criminals of America*, 200–201, 218, 243, 316–21; Spurling, *La Grande Therese*, 116–26.

4. Reading, *The Mark Inside*; Crosbie, *The Incredible Mrs. Chadwick*, foreword, n.p.; Camilla Cornell, "Carnegie's 'Daughter,'" *London Magazine*, Sept. 1985, 25–30.

5. "The Truth about Liars: Great Canadian Liars," DocZone, Canadian Broadcasting Corporation, 2009.

6. *CP*, Nov. 26, 1904; *TDB*, Mar. 26, 1891; *CL*, Mar. 12, 1905; *CL*, Oct. 12, 15, 1907.

7. Jonathan Allen, "Fake Heiress Who Dazzled New York Elite Gets 4 to 12 for Fraud," May 9, 2019, www.reuters.com; "Anna Sorokin: Fake Apologizes as She Is Sentenced," May 9, 2019, www.bbc.com/news/world-us-canada-48219100; Jason Keyser, "Small Town Swindle," *Lexington Herald Leader*, Apr. 29, 2012; "All the Queen's Horses," PBS, *Chicago Tonight*, Nov. 13, 2017, www.pbs.org/video/All-Queens-horses-tells-Story-rita-crundwell-burrum; *New York Herald*, Oct. 4, 1875.

1. MISS BIGLEY, HEIRESS TO $15,000

1. *TDB*, Jan. 13, 1890.

2. *TDB*, Jan. 17, 1890; *CL*, Jan. 17, 1890.

3. *CP*, Nov. 16, 1904; *Youngstown Vindicator*, Jan. 30, 1890; Laning, *The History and Story of the Doings*, 1–3, 70; *CL*, Oct. 12, 1907.

4. Cassie Chadwick File, Oxford Historical Society, Woodstock, ON, Canada.

5. *Youngstown Vindicator*, Jan. 30, 1890; *TDB*, Jan. 17, 1890; *New York Sun*, July 19, 1879; Borowitz, *Unhappy Endings*, 26–27.

6. *TDB*, Jan. 17, 1890; *New York Sun*, Oct. 6, 1888.

7. *New York Sun*, July 19, 1879; Loth, *Gold Brick Cassie*, 20.

8. *CL*, Jan. 19, 1890.

9. Laning, *The History and Story of the Doings*, 1–2.

10. Laning, *The History and Story of the Doings*, 1–2; *CL*, Jan. 19, 1890.

11. *CL*, Jan. 17, 19, 1890.

12. *TDB*, Jan. 12, 13, 17, 1890; *CL*, Jan. 12. 1890.

13. *TBD*, Jan. 14, 16, 1890; Loth, *Gold Brick Cassie*, 32; *Cleveland City Directory*, 12:271; Borowitz, *Unhappy Endings*, 27.

14. Goldsmith, *Other Powers*, 28–37, 425–27.

15. Goldsmith, *Other Powers*, 7, 31, 49.

16. Crosbie, *The Incredible Mrs. Chadwick*, 7; Goldsmith, *Other Powers*, 21–22; Laning, *The History and Story of the Doings*, 81.

17. *TDB*, Jan. 15, 1890; Laning, *The History and Story of the Doings*, 2.

18. *TDB*, Jan. 17, 1890; *Stark County (OH) Democrat*, Jan. 19, 1888; *Akron (OH) Democrat*, Dec. 27, 1899; *Daily Ohio Standard*, Oct. 12, 1866.

19. *TDB*, Jan. 18, 19, 20, 1890.

20. *CPD* Dec. 11, 1904.

2. MADAME DEVERE, EUROPEAN CLAIRVOYANT

1. *TDB*, Jan. 16, 1890.

2. *TDB*, Jan. 15, Apr. 15, 1890, Laning, *The History and Story of the Doings*, 45.

3. *CL*, Jan. 17, 1890; *TDB*, Jan. 14, 1890.

4. *TDB*, Jan. 15, 17, 1890; *CL*, Jan. 19, 1890; Loth, *Gold Brick Cassie*, 20; Crosbie, *The Incredible Mrs. Chadwick*, 114; *New York Sun*, Apr. 22, 1894.

5. *TDB*, Jan. 15, 17, 1890; *CL*, Jan. 19, 1890; *CP*, Nov. 28, 1904; Laning, *The History and Story of the Doings*, 51–52; Crosbie, *The Incredible Mrs. Chadwick*, 114, 134.

6. *TDB*, Jan. 15, 1890; *CP*, Nov. 28, 1904; Laning, *The History and Story of the Doings*, 51.

7. *TDB*, Jan. 15, 16, 1890.

8. *TDB*, Jan. 15, 1890; *CP*, Nov. 29, 1904.

9. *TDB*, Apr. 15, 26, 1890; *CP*, Nov. 28, 1890; Laning, *The History and Story of the Doings*, 45–46.

10. *TDB*, Apr. 15, 1890; Laning, *The History and Story of the Doings*, 45; Crosbie, *The Incredible Mrs. Chadwick*, 116.

11. *TDB*, Apr. 15, 1890; Laning, *The History and Story of the Doings*, 45.

12. *TDB*, Mar. 31, Apr. 15, 16, 19, 1890; Laning, *The History and Story of the Doings*, 45–46.

13. *TDB*, Apr. 16, 1890.

14. *TDB*, Apr. 16, 1890; Laning, *The History and Story of the Doings*, 46; *Youngstown Vindicator*, Jan. 27, 1890.

15. *TDB*, Jan. 15, 16, 26, 1890.

16. *TDB*, Jan. 15, 16, 1890.

17. *TDB*, Jan. 16, 1890.

18. *TDB*, Apr. 18, 1890.

19. *TDB*, Apr. 18, 1890.

20. *TDB*, Apr. 16, 1890; Laning, *The History and Story of the Doings*, 46.

21. *TDB*, Jan. 15, 21, 1890.

22. *TDB*, Jan. 15, 16, 1890; *CL*, Jan. 16, 1890.

23. *TDB*, Apr. 15, 1890; Laning, *The History and Story of the Doings*, 46.

24. *TDB*, Apr. 19, 1890.

25. *TDB*, Apr. 18, 1890.

26. *TDB*, Jan. 13, 14, Apr. 16, 1890.

27. *TDB*, Jan. 13, 16, Mar. 25, 1890; Butler, *History of Youngstown and Mahoning Valley Ohio*, 3:79, 671, 307, 375, 816–17.

28. *TDB*, Jan. 24, Apr. 15, 18, 1890; Laning, *The History and Story of the Doings*, 47; *Youngstown Vindicator*, Jan. 19–21, 1890.

29. *CL*, Jan. 17, 1890; *TDB*, Jan. 17, 1890.

3. FAMILY TROUBLES

1. *TDB*, Apr. 18, 1890.

2. *TDB*, Jan. 24, 1890.

3. *TDB*, Jan. 13, 17, 24, Mar. 20, 1890.

4. *TDB*, Apr. 15, 1890; Laning, *The History and Story of the Doings*, 47.

5. *TDB*, Jan. 13, 17, Apr. 15, 1890; Laning, *The History and Story of the Doings*, 47.

6. *TDB*, Mar. 22, 23, 1890.

7. *TDB*, Jan. 13, 15, 1890.

8. *New York Herald*, Oct. 4, 1875; *TDB*, Apr. 15, 18, 1890.

9. *TDB*, Apr. 19, 1890.

10. *TDB*, Jan. 24, Mar. 20, Apr. 15, 18, 1890.

11. *TDB*, Mar. 21, Apr. 24, 1890; *Youngstown Vindicator*, Jan. 25, 1890.

12. *TDB*, Apr. 19, 1890.

13. *TDB*, Apr. 19, 1890.

14. *TDB*, Apr. 19, 1890.

4. A CLEAR FORGERY

1. *New York Sun*, Nov. 10, 1889; *TDB*, Jan. 13, 17, 1890.

2. *TDB*, Jan. 13, 16, 1890.

3. *TDB*, Jan. 13, 1890; *CL*, Jan. 13, 1890.

4. *TDB* Jan. 14, 1890.

5. *TDB*, Jan. 16, 25, Apr. 16, 1890.

6. *TDB*, Jan. 13, 14, 15, 1890.

7. *TDB*, Jan. 13, 1890.

8. *TDB*, Jan. 13, 1890.

9. *TDB*, Jan. 14, 1890.

10. *TDB,* Jan. 13, 14, 1890; *Democratic Northwest,* Nov. 14, 1889.

11. *TDB,* Jan. 14, 1890.

12. *TDB,* Jan. 14, 1890.

13. *TDB,* Jan. 14, 1890.

14. *Youngstown Vindicator,* Jan. 14, 1890; *TDB,* Jan. 14, Mar. 25, 1890.

15. *New York Sun,* June 26, 1878, July 19, 1879.

16. *CL,* Jan. 17, 1890; *TDB,* Jan. 17, 1890.

17. *TDB,* Jan. 14, 1890.

18. *TDB,* Jan. 14, 1890.

19. *Youngstown Vindicator,* Jan. 18, 1890; *TDB,* Jan. 14, 1890.

20. *TDB,* Jan. 16, 25, 1890.

21. *TDB,* Jan. 16, 1890.

22. *TDB,* Jan. 15, 1890.

23. *TDB,* Jan. 15, 16, 1890.

24. *TDB,* Jan. 14, 1890.

25. *TDB,* Jan. 15, 1890.

26. *TDB,* Jan. 14, 15, 1890.

27. *TDB,* Jan. 14, 15, Apr. 16, 1890.

28. *TDB,* Jan. 15, 18, 1890; *CL,* Jan. 19, 1890.

29. *TDB,* Jan. 16, 1890.

30. *TDB,* Jan. 16, 1890; *Youngstown Vindicator,* Jan. 15, 1890.

31. *TDB,* Jan. 16, 1890.

32. *TDB,* Jan. 25, 1890.

33. *TDB,* Jan. 16, Mar. 21, 1890; *CL,* Jan. 17, 19, 1890; *Youngstown Vindicator,* Jan. 15, 1890.

34. *TDB,* Jan. 13, 14, 15, 16, 1890.

35. *TDB,* Jan. 16, 24, 25, 26, 1890.

36. *TDB,* Jan. 24, 1890.

37. *TDB,* Jan. 16, 21, 24, 1890; *Youngstown Vindicator,* Jan. 15, 1890.

38. *TDB,* Jan. 24, 1890.

5. AN UNPRINCIPLED ADVENTURESS

1. *TDB,* Jan. 16, 1890.

2. *TDB,* Jan. 15, 1890.

3. *CP,* Nov. 28, 1904; Laning, *The History and Story of the Doings,* 47–48; Crosbie, *The Incredible Mrs. Chadwick,* 126, 132.

4. *TDB,* Jan. 16, 21, 24, 1890.

5. *TDB,* Jan. 16, Feb. 24, 1890; *CL,* Jan. 17, 1890; *CP,* Nov. 28, 1904; Laning, *The History and Story of the Doings,* 44.

6. *TDB,* Jan. 16, 17, 1890; *Youngstown Vindicator,* Jan. 17, 18, 1890.

7. *TDB,* Jan. 18, 1890; Loth, *Gold Brick Cassie,* 42.

8. *TDB,* Jan. 16, Apr. 15, 26, 1890.

9. *TDB,* Jan. 16, 1890.

10. *TDB,* Apr. 19, 1890.

11. *Perrysville (OH) Journal,* Jan. 18, 1890; Loth, *Gold Brick Cassie,* 45.

12. *TDB,* Jan. 18, 20, 22, 1890.

13. *Youngstown Vindicator,* Jan. 19, 20, 21, Mar. 25, 1890; *CL,* Jan. 19, 1890.

14. *TDB*, Jan. 21, 1890.
15. *TDB*, Jan. 21, 25, 1890.
16. *TDB*, Jan. 22, 23, 1890.
17. *TDB*, Jan. 24, 1890.
18. *TDB*, Jan. 23, 1890; *Youngstown Vindicator*, Jan. 22, 1890.
19. *TDB*, Jan. 24, 1890.
20. *TDB*, Jan. 20, 24, 1890.
21. *TDB*, Jan. 24, 1890.
22. *TDB*, Jan. 24, 1890.
23. *TDB*, Jan. 24, 1890.
24. *TDB*, Jan. 24, 1890.
25. *TDB*, Jan. 24, 1890.
26. *TDB*, Jan. 24, 1890.
27. *TDB*, Jan. 20, 24, 1890.
28. *TDB*, Jan. 20, 24, 1890.
29. *TDB*, Jan. 24, 1890.
30. *TDB*, Jan. 24, 1890.
31. *TDB*, Jan. 24, 1890.
32. *TDB*, Jan. 25, 1890.
33. *Youngstown Vindicator*, Jan. 27, 1890.
34. *TDB*, Jan. 25, 1890.
35. *TDB*, Jan. 24, 25, 1890.
36. *TDB*, Jan. 25, 27, 29, 1890.
37. *TDB*, Jan. 24, 30, 1890.
38. *TDB*, Feb. 18. 1890.

6. A MOST NOVEL AND UNIQUE DEFENSE

1. *TDB*, Feb. 19, 24, Mar. 11, 12, 1890.
2. *TDB*, Feb. 19, 24, Mar. 11, 12, 1890.
3. *TDB*, Mar. 14, 19, 1890.
4. *TDB*, Mar. 20, 1890.
5. *TDB*, Mar. 20, 1890.
6. *TDB*, Mar. 21, 1890; *CL*, Mar. 22, 1890.
7. *TDB*, Mar. 20, 1890.
8. *TDB*, Mar. 20, 1890.
9. *TDB*, Mar. 19, 21, 1890.
10. *TDB*, Jan. 15, 16, 1890; *CL*, Jan. 16, 1890.
11. *TDB*, Mar. 24, 25, 1890.
12. *TDB*, Mar. 23, 25, 1890.
13. *TDB*, Mar. 25, 1890.
14. *TDB*, Mar. 25, 26, 1890.
15. *TDB*, Mar. 28, 1890.
16. *TDB*, Mar. 28, 1890.
17. *TDB*, Apr. 15, 16, 1890.
18. *TDB*, Apr. 15, 16, 1890.
19. *TDB*, Apr. 16, 17, 1890.
20. *TDB*, Apr. 17, 1890; Crosbie, *The Incredible Mrs. Chadwick,* 136.
21. *TDB*, Apr. 17, 18, 19, 1890.

22. *TDB*, Apr. 19, 1890.

23. *TDB*, Apr. 19, 1890.

24. *TDB*, Apr. 18, 19, 1890.

25. Shorter, *A History of Psychiatry*, 84–86.

7. GUILTY AS CHARGED

1. *TDB*, Apr. 19, 24, 1890.

2. *TDB*, Apr. 25, 26, 1890.

3. *TDB*, Apr. 25, 1890.

4. *TDB*, Apr. 25, 1890.

5. *TDB*, Mar. 22, Apr. 25, 1890.

6. *TDB*, Apr. 26, 27, 28, 1890.

7. *TDB*, Apr. 27, 1890.

8. *TDB*, Apr. 28, 1890.

9. *TDB*, Mar. 24, Apr. 17, 28, 1890.

10. *TDB*, Apr. 29, 30, 1890.

11. *TDB*, Apr. 30, 1890.

12. *TDB*, May 1, 1890.

13. *TDB*, May 1, 1890.

14. *TDB*, May 1, 1890.

15. *TDB*, May 2, 1890.

16. *TDB*, May 3, 1890.

17. *TDB*, Jan. 25, 1890, Jan. 1, 1891.

18. *TDB*, Dec. 7, 1893; Ohio Penitentiary Register of Prisoners No. 16, Jan. 1891–92.

19. *Youngstown Vindicator*, Dec. 13, 1904; *CPD*, Dec. 26, 1954; *CP*, Nov. 29, 1904.

20. *TDB*, Dec. 7, 1893; *CL*, Oct. 11, 1907; Crosbie, *The Incredible Mrs. Chadwick*, 126.

21. *TDB*, Dec. 7, 1893; *CL*, Oct. 11, 1907; Crosbie, *The Incredible Mrs. Chadwick*, 126.

22. Nasaw, *Andrew Carnegie*, 477; *CL*, Jan. 17, 1890; *TDB*, Dec. 7, 1893.

8. A SORT OF A BUSINESS ARRANGEMENT

1. Segrave, *Women Swindlers in America, 1860–1920*, 166.

2. *CL*, Oct. 21, 1907.

3. Loth, *Gold Brick Cassie*, 45.

4. *Stark County (OH) Democrat*, Jan. 19, 1888; *Philadelphia Evening Telegraph*, Feb. 12, 1867; Loth, *Gold Brick Cassie*, 46; *Philadelphia Evening Telegraph*, Feb. 12. 1867.

5. Goldsmith, *Other Powers*, 159.

6. *CL*, Oct. 11, 1907.

7. Laning, *The History and Story of the Doings*, 49.

8. Laning, *The History and Story of the Doings*, 51.

9. *New York Sun*, July 19, 1897; MacNee, *Outlaws, Mobsters and Crooks*, 287–90.

10. Laning, *The History and Story of the Doings*, 69.

11. *Cleveland Morning Leader*, Dec. 31, 1864; Nasaw, *Andrew Carnegie*, 76–79.

12. Cigliano, *Showplace of America*, 309; Laning, *The History and Story of the Doings*, 28–29.

13. US Census, Venango County, PA, 1860, Cuyahoga County, OH, 1880, www.Ancestry.com/LibraryEdition; Laning, *The History and Story of the Doings*, 69.

14. *CPD*, Nov. 30, 1904; *OSJ*, Nov. 30, 1904.

15. *CL*, Oct. 21, 1907.

16. *CL*, Oct. 21, 1907.

17. *CL*, Oct. 21, 1907.

18. *CL*, Oct. 21, 1907.

19. *CL*, Oct. 21, 1907.

20. *OSJ*, Dec. 6, 1904; *CPD*, Dec. 2, 1904.

21. *OSJ*, Dec. 7, 1904; Laning, *The History and Story of the Doings*, 30; *CPD*, Dec. 2, 1904.

22. *CPD*, Dec. 13, 14, 1904.

23. Laning, *The History and Story of the Doings*, 119–21; *CPD*, Dec. 13, 1904.

24. Laning, *The History and Story of the Doings*, 119–21; *CPD*, Dec. 13, 1904; Nasaw, *Andrew Carnegie*, 57, 62.

25. *CPD*, Dec. 2, 1904.

26. *CP*, Nov. 26, 27, 28, 1904; James Chadwick, personal communication, July 20, 1987, Cassie Chadwick file; Connolly, "Marvelous Mrs. Chadwick," 9.

27. Wallach, *The Richest Woman in America*, 89, 119; Slack, *Hetty*, xii, 30–32.

28. *New York Sun*, Sept. 27, 1891; *Wilmington Evening Journal*, Aug. 24, 1895; Slack, *Hetty*, 111.

29. *CPD*, Dec. 4, 1904.

30. *CPD*, Dec. 16, 20, 1904.

31. Laning, *The History and Story of the Doings*, 14–17, 73–74.

32. 1900 US Census, Cuyahoga County, OH, AncestryLibrary.com.

33. *TDB*, Jan. 27, 1900.

9. THE GREATEST BULL MARKET IN HISTORY

1. Nasaw, *Andrew Carnegie*, 583.

2. Nasaw, *Andrew Carnegie*, 585.

3. Nasaw, *Andrew Carnegie*, 586–87.

4. *CPD*, Dec. 1, 1904.

5. *CPD*, Nov. 29, 1904.

6. *CPD*, Nov. 30, 1904; Laning, *The History and Story of the Doings*, 11–12; Hatcher, *The Western Reserve*, 208.

7. *CPD*, Nov. 30, 1904.

8. *New York Tribune*, May 10, 1901; *New York Sun*, May 11, 1901; *New York Evening World*, Apr. 30, 1901.

9. *CPD*, Dec. 04, 1904; Wallach, *The Richest Woman in America*, 118; Sparkes and Moore, *The Witch of Wall Street*, 229.

10. *New York Sun*, May 10, 1901; Sparkes and Moore, *The Witch of Wall Street*, 229.

11. *New York Sun*, May 2, 10, 11, 1901; *New York Tribune*, May 10, 1901; *Stark County (OH) Democrat*, May 3, 1901.

12. *New York World*, May 9, 1901; Laning, *The History and Story of the Doings*, 17.

13. *New York World*, May 9, 1901; Laning, *The History and Story of the Doings*, 17.

14. Laning, *The History and Story of the Doings*, 17.

15. *New York Sun*, May 10, 1901; *New York Tribune*, May 10, 1901; Nasaw, *Andrew Carnegie*, 684.

16. *New York Tribune*, May 10, 1901; *New York World*, May 9, 1901; *New York Sun*, May 10, 11, 1901.

17. *New York Tribune,* May 10, 1901; *New York World,* May 9, 1901; *New York Sun,* May 10, 11, 1901.

18. *CPD,* Nov. 30, 1904, May 18, 1905.

19. *CPD,* Nov. 30, 1904; *New York Sun,* May 11, 1901; *New York Tribune,* May 9, 1901.

20. *CPD,* Nov. 30, 1904; *New York Sun,* May 11, 1901; *New York Tribune,* May 9, 1901.

21. Wallach, *The Richest Woman in America,* 89, 247; Sparkes and Moore, *The Witch of Wall Street,* 210; Slack, *Hetty,* 167.

22. Laning, *The History and Story of the Doings,* 15.

23. *CPD,* May 18, 1905.

24. *CL,* Oct. 20, 1907.

25. *CL,* Oct. 20, 1907.

26. Laning, *The History and Story of the Doings,* 122.

10. SPLENDID BUSINESS

1. *Akron (OH) Daily Democrat,* Jan. 2, 3, July 7, 1902; *New York Tribune,* Jan. 2, 3, Feb. 13, 1902; *Los Angeles Herald,* Jan. 3, 1902.

2. *CPD,* Dec. 1, 1904.

3. *CPD,* Dec. 1, 12, 1904; Laning, *The History and Story of the Doings,* 77; James A. Chadwick, personal communication, June 20, 1987.

4. *CPD,* Dec. 1, 12, 1904; Laning, *The History and Story of the Doings,* 77; James A. Chadwick, personal communication, June 20, 1987.

5. *Commemorative Biographical Record of the Counties of Huron and Lorain, Ohio,* 872.

6. *NYT,* Dec. 6, 1904; *CPD,* Dec. 1, 1904, Mar. 2. 1905.

7. *CPD,* Mar. 25, 1905.

8. *CPD,* Dec. 6, 1904; *NYT,* Dec. 16, 1904; Mark Twain, www.azquotes.com.

9. Conant, *A History of Modern Banks of Issue,* 67, 87, 92–93, 95.

10. *CPD,* Nov. 29, 1904.

11. *CL,* Feb. 6, 1905.

12. *CL,* Feb. 6, 1905.

13. *CL,* Feb. 6, 1905; US Census, 1900, Lorain County, OH, www.Ancestry.com/Library Edition.

14. *CL,* Feb. 6, 1905.

15. US Census, 1900, Lorain County, OH, www.Ancestry.com/LibraryEdition; Ohio Penitentiary Register of Prisoners, 1902–7.

16. *CPD,* Dec. 2, 6, 1904; *NYT,* Dec. 6, 1904; Laning, *The History and Story of the Doings,* 24.

17. *CPD,* Dec. 2, 6, 1904; *NYT,* Dec. 6, 1904; Laning, *The History and Story of the Doings,* 24.

18. *CPD,* Dec. 12, 16, 1904.

19. *CPD,* Nov. 29, 1904.

20. Laning, *The History and Story of the Doings,* 24.

21. *CPD,* Dec. 10, 1904.

22. Laning, *The History and Story of the Doings,* 70; *CPD,* Nov. 30, Dec. 12, 1904; *Washington Post,* Dec. 25, 1904.

23. *CPD,* Dec. 2, 17, 1904.

24. *OSJ,* Dec. 18, 1904; *CPD,* Dec. 11, 1904, Mar. 25, 1905.

25. *CPD,* Dec. 2, 1904.

26. *CPD*, Dec. 12, 1904.

27. *NYT*, Dec. 12, 1904; *CPD*, Dec. 20, 1904; Nasaw, *Andrew Carnegie*, 76–77.

28. *CPD*, Nov. 30, Dec. 1, 13, 1904; *NYT*, Dec. 4, 10, 1904; Laning, *The History and Story of the Doings*, 120–21.

29. *CPD*, Nov. 30, 1904; *NYT*, Dec. 4, 1904.

30. *CPD*, Dec. 20, 1904; *NYT*, Dec. 20, 1904.

31. *CPD*, Dec. 1, 13, 1904; *NYT*, Dec. 10, 13, 1904; Laning, *The History and Story of the Doings*, 120–21.

32. *CPD*, Dec. 10, 1904; Laning, *The History and Story of the Doings*, 112–13; Loth, *Gold Brick Cassie*, 64.

33. Laning, *The History and Story of the Doings*, 70; *CPD*, Dec. 8, 1904; *OSJ*, Dec. 11, 1904.

34. *CPD*, Nov. 30, 1904; *NYT*, Dec. 4, 1904.

35. *CPD*, Nov. 30, 1904.

36. *CPD*, Nov. 30, 1904.

37. *CPD*, Nov. 30, 1904.

38. *CPD*, Nov. 30, Dec. 4, 1904; *NYT*, Dec. 11, 17, 28, 1904.

39. *CPD*, Nov. 30, Dec. 4, 1904; *NYT*, Dec. 11, 17, 28, 1904.

11. H. CLARK FORD AND THE OBERLIN COLLEGE LOANS

1. Coates, *A History of Cuyahoga County and the City of Cleveland*, 3:171.

2. *CPD*, Mar. 2, May 25, 1905.

3. Unsigned memo, May 29, 1903, Ford Family Papers.

4. *CPD*, Dec. 1, 1904.

5. HCF to L. H. Severance, Aug. 1, 1903; HCF legal contract with Cassie Chadwick, June 8, 1903, Ford Family Papers.

6. Cassie Chadwick to HCF, June 1903, Ford Family Papers.

7. *CPD*, Dec. 12, 1904.

8. *CPD*, Dec. 1, 1904.

9. Cassie Chadwick to HCF, July 24, 1903, Ford Family Papers.

10. HCF to L. H. Severance, Aug. 1, 1903, Ford Family Papers; L. H. Severance to HCF, Aug. 3, 1903, Ford Family Papers.

11. *CPD*, Dec. 12, 1903.

12. Cassie Chadwick to HCF, Aug. 5, 1903, Ford Family Papers.

13. Cassie Chadwick to HCF, Aug. 6, 1903; A. A. McCaslin to HCF, Aug. 6, 1903, Ford Family Papers.

14. Cassie Chadwick to HCF, Aug. 6, 1903; *CPD*, Dec. 10, 1904.

15. *CPD*, Dec. 10, 1904; Cassie Chadwick to HCF, Aug. 6, 1903, evening, Ford Family Papers.

16. Cassie Chadwick to HCF, Aug. 13, 1903, Ford Family Papers.

17. Cassie Chadwick to HCF, Aug. 16, 1903, Ford Family Papers.

18. HCF legal contract with Cassie Chadwick, Aug. 18, 1903, Ford Family Papers; *CPD*, Mar. 2. 1905.

19. Laning, *The History and Story of the Doings*, 42, 63.

20. HCF legal contract with Cassie Chadwick, Aug. 18, 1903, Ford Family Papers.

21. Cassie Chadwick to HCF, Aug. 25, 1903, Ford Family Papers.

22. *CPD*, Dec. 11, 1904.

23. United States Circuit Court of Appeals, Sixth Circuit, *Cassie L. Chadwick . . . vs. United States of America,* June 6, 1905, 93–96, 228, Western Reserve Historical Society, Cleveland; *NYT,* Dec. 8, 1904.

24. United States Circuit Court of Appeals, Sixth Circuit, *Cassie L. Chadwick . . . vs. United States of America,* June 6, 1905, 93–96, 228; *NYT,* Dec. 8, 1904.

25. Cassie Chadwick letters to HCF, Sept. 6, 18, 1903, Ford Family Papers.

26. Cassie Chadwick letters to HCF, Sept. 29, 1903, Ford Family Papers; *CPD,* Nov. 30, Dec. 2, 1904, Mar. 25, 1905.

27. Cassie Chadwick to HCF, Sept. 29, 1903, Ford Family Papers.

28. Cassie Chadwick to HCF, Oct. 1, 1903, Ford Family Papers.

29. Cassie Chadwick to HCF, Sept. 29, Oct. 2, 1903, Ford Family Papers.

30. United States Circuit Court of Appeals, Sixth Circuit, *Cassie L. Chadwick . . . vs. United States of America,* 228.

31. Cassie Chadwick to HCF, Oct. 2, 1903, Ford Family Papers; *CPD,* Nov. 30, 1904; *New York Times,* Nov. 30, 1904.

32. *CPD,* Dec. 1, 1904, Mar. 25, 1905.

33. *CL,* Mar. 9, 1905.

34. *CL,* Mar. 9, 1905.

35. United States Circuit Court of Appeals, Sixth Circuit, *Cassie L. Chadwick . . . vs. United States of America,* 58, 93–96, 228.

12. THE CARNEGIE NOTES

1. *NYT,* Dec. 12, 14, 1904; *CPD,* Mar. 2, 1905.

2. *NYT,* Dec. 12. 1904.

3. *NYT,* Dec. 20, 1904.

4. *NYT,* Dec. 6, 1904; Crosbie, *The Incredible Mrs. Chadwick,* 119.

5. *CPD,* Dec. 13, 1904.

6. *NYT,* Dec. 12, 14, 1904; *New York Journal,* Dec. 17, 19, 1896.

7. *NYT,* Dec. 12, 13, 14, 1904.

8. *NYT,* Dec. 12, 1904.

9. *NYT,* Dec. 12, 13, 14, 1904.

10. *NYT,* Dec. 13, 1904; Byrnes, *1886 Professional Criminals of America,* 201; Segrave, *Women Swindlers in America, 1860–1920,* 157–62.

11. *CPD,* Nov. 30, Dec. 1, 1904; United States Circuit Court of Appeals, Sixth Circuit, *Cassie L. Chadwick . . . vs. United States of America,* 228; Laning, *The History and Story of the Doings,* 7, 116; *NYT,* Dec. 6, 1904.

12. Laning, *The History and Story of the Doings,* 77–78.

13. *NYT,* Nov. 30, 1904; *CPD,* Dec. 1, 2, 1904; Laning, *The History and Story of the Doings,* 7, 34.

14. *NYT,* Dec. 13, 1904.

15. *CPD,* Dec. 2, 1904; Laning, *The History and Story of the Doings,* 66.

16. *CPD,* Nov. 30, Dec. 2, 1904.

17. *OSJ,* Dec. 9, 10, 1904; *NYT,* Dec. 9, 1904; Laning, *The History and Story of the Doings,* 63.

18. *OSJ,* Dec. 9, 10, 1904; *NYT,* Dec. 9, 1904; Laning, *The History and Story of the Doings,* 63.

19. *CPD*, Dec. 11, 1904.

20. *NYT*, Dec. 19, 1904; *OSJ*, Dec. 10, 1904; Laning, *The History and Story of the Doings*, 63.

21. *CPD*, Dec. 11, 1904; Laning, *The History and Story of the Doings*, 63, 81–84.

22. Laning, *The History and Story of the Doings*, 82; *CPD*, Dec. 11, 1904; *NYT*, Dec. 6, 1904.

23. *CPD*, Dec. 11, 1904; Laning, *The History and Story of the Doings*, 81–84.

24. *NYT*, Nov. 30, 1904; Laning, *The History and Story of the Doings*, 82.

13. FRENZIED FINANCE

1. *CPD*, Dec. 20, 1904; *New York Evening World*, Feb. 15, 1904; *Stark County (OH) Democrat*, Feb. 16, 1904, https://ohiohistorycentral.org.

2. *CPD*, Dec. 1, 1904; *NYT*, Mar. 25, 1905.

3. *CPD*, Nov. 30, Dec. 1, 1904.

4. Laning, *The History and Story of the Doings*, 31–32.

5. Laning, *The History and Story of the Doings*, 31–32.

6. Laning, *The History and Story of the Doings*, 7, 32–33, 65–66.

7. *CPD*, Dec. 13, 1904.

8. *CPD*, Dec. 2, 1904; *NYT*, Dec. 13, 1904.

9. *NYT*, Dec. 13, 1904.

10. *CPD*, Dec. 1, 1904, Feb. 4, 1905.

11. *NYT*, Dec. 13, 1904; *CPD*, Dec. 13, 1904; Laning, *The History and Story of the Doings*, 70.

12. *CPD*, Mar. 3, 1905.

13. *NYT*, Dec. 13, 1904; *CPD*, Dec. 13, 1904.

14. *CPD*, Nov. 23, 1904.

15. *CPD*, Nov. 30, 1904.

16. *CPD*, Feb. 22, 1905; *CL*, Mar. 9, 1905.

17. *CPD*, Feb. 22, 1905; *CL*, Mar. 9, 1905.

18. *CPD*, Dec. 14, 20, 1904, Feb. 6, 1905.

19. *CPD*, Dec. 14, 20, 1904, Feb. 6, 1905.

20. *CPD*, Nov. 30, Dec. 7, 8, 1904.

21. *CPD*, Dec. 4, 7, 10, 1904; *NYT*, Dec. 6, 1904.

22. *CPD*, Nov. 23, 1904; Loth, *Gold Brick Cassie*, 136, 138; United States Circuit Court of Appeals, Sixth Circuit, *Cassie L. Chadwick . . . vs. United States of America*, 93–100, 144; *CPD*, Mar. 8, 1905.

23. *CPD*, Dec. 8, 1904, Mar. 8, 1905; United States Circuit Court of Appeals, Sixth Circuit, *Cassie L. Chadwick . . . vs. United States of America*, 87–100.

24. *CPD*, Dec. 8, 1904; United States Circuit Court of Appeals, Sixth Circuit, *Cassie L. Chadwick . . . vs. United States of America*, 87–100; *CPD*, Mar. 8, 1905.

25. Laning, *The History and Story of the Doings*, 114–15; *CPD*, Nov. 30, Dec. 9, 1904.

26. *CPD*, Dec. 28, 1904.

27. *CPD*, Dec. 28, 1904.

28. *CPD*, Dec. 12, 1904.

29. *NYT*, Dec. 9, 1904; *CPD*, Dec. 11, 23, 1904; Laning, *The History and Story of the Doings*, 81–84.

30. Laning, *The History and Story of the Doings*, 81–84.

31. *CPD*, Nov. 23, 1904.

32. *CPD*, Nov. 23, 1904; Laning, *The History and Story of the Doings*, 63, 83.

33. Laning, *The History and Story of the Doings*, 115.

34. *CPD*, Dec. 10, 1904; Laning, *The History and Story of the Doings*, 19.

35. *CPD*, Dec. 6, 1904.

36. *NYT*, Nov. 30, 1904.

37. *NYT*, Dec. 30, 1904; Laning, *The History and Story of the Doings*, 81–84.

38. Laning, *The History and Story of the Doings*, 83; *NYT*, Nov. 30, 1904.

39. *NYT*, Nov. 30, 1904; *CP*, Nov. 28, 1904.

40. *CPD*, Nov. 23, 27, 1904.

41. *CPD*, Dec. 6, 10, 1904; Laning, *The History and Story of the Doings*, 19.

14. ABSURD!

1. *CPD*, Nov. 22, 1904; *Youngstown Vindicator*, Dec. 5, 1904.

2. *CPD*, Nov. 30, 1904.

3. *OSJ*, Nov. 27, 1904; *NYT*, Nov. 29, 1904.

4. *CP*, Nov. 26, 1904.

5. *NYT*, Nov. 30, 1904.

6. *NYT*, Dec. 13, 1904.

7. *NYT*, Nov. 30, 1904; *CPD*, Nov. 30, Dec. 3, 1904.

8. *NYT*, Nov. 29, 30, 1904; *CP*, Nov. 26, 28, 1904; *CL*, Feb. 6, 1905; *CPD*, Nov. 23, 30, Dec. 3, 1904.

9. *CP* Nov. 26, 1904; *NYT*, Dec. 13, 1904.

10. *NYT*, Nov. 29, 30, 1904; *CPD*, Nov. 23, 30, Dec. 3, 1904; *CL*, Feb. 6, 1905.

11. *CPD*, Dec. 4, 1904; Nasaw, *Andrew Carnegie*, 696; *CPD*, Nov. 29, 1904.

12. *CPD*, Nov. 29, 30, Dec. 4, 1904; *OSJ*, Dec, 1, 1904; *CP*, Nov. 28, 1904; *NYT*, Nov. 30. 1904; Laning, *The History and Story of the Doings*, 4, 20; *Ohio State News*, Dec. 1, 1904.

13. *OSJ*, Dec. 1, 1904; *NYT*, Nov. 19, 1904; *CPD*, Nov. 29, Dec. 8, 1904.

14. *CPD*, Nov. 29, 30, 1904; *NYT*, Nov. 29, 1904.

15. *CPD*, Nov. 29, 1904.

16. *CP*, Nov. 28, 1904; *CPD*, Nov. 30, 1904.

17. *CPD*, Nov. 29, 1904.

18. *CPD*, Nov. 29, 30, 1904; *NYT*, Nov. 30, 1904; *Ohio State News*, Dec. 1, 1904; Laning, *The History and Story of the Doings*, 4, 20.

19. *CPD*, Nov. 29, 1904.

20. *CPD*, Nov. 29, 1904.

21. *NYT*, Nov. 30, 1904; *OSJ*, Dec. 6, 1904.

22. *NYT*, Nov. 30, 1904; *CPD*, Dec. 2, 1904.

23. Laning, *The History and Story of the Doings*, 11.

24. *NYT*, Dec. 3, 1904; *CPD*, Nov. 29, Dec. 1, 1904.

25. *CPD*, Nov. 30, 1904.

26. *NYT*, Nov. 30, 1904; *CPD*, Nov. 29, 1904.

27. *OSJ*, Dec. 1, 1904; *NYT*, Dec. 1, 1904.

28. *CPD*, Dec. 1, 14, 17, 1904; Loth, *Gold Brick Cassie*, 70; *NYT*, Dec. 14, 16, 1904.

29. *NYT*, Dec. 16, 1904; *CPD*, Dec. 10, 12, 1904.

30. *CPD*, Nov. 27, Dec. 3, 1904.

31. *CPD*, Nov. 27, Dec. 3, 1904.

32. *CPD*, Dec. 2, 1904.

33. *NYT*, Dec. 4, 1904; *CPD*, Nov. 30, 1904.

34. *CPD*, Dec. 31, 1904; *NYT*, Feb. 7, 1904.

35. *OSJ*, Dec. 3, 1904; *NYT*, Dec. 3, 1904; *CPD*, Nov. 27, 1904, Dec. 3, 16, 1904.

36. *NYT*, Dec. 3, 1904; *CPD*, Dec. 13, 1904.

37. *NYT*, Dec. 4, 1904.

38. *CPD*, Dec. 4, 1904.

39. *CPD*, Dec. 4, 1904.

40. *CPD*, Dec. 3, 4, 1911; *New York Sun*, Aug. 8, 1911; *New York Tribune*, Aug. 8, 1911.

41. *NYT*, Dec. 11, 1904; *CPD*, Dec. 11, 1904.

15. A MOST UNPLEASANT DUTY

1. *CPD*, Dec. 5, 1904.

2. *CPD*, Dec. 5, 1904.

3. *CPD*, Dec. 5, 6, 1904; *OSJ*, Dec. 6, 1904.

4. *CPD*, Dec. 5, 6, 1904; *OSJ*, Dec. 6, 1904.

5. *OSJ*, Dec. 6, 1904; *NYT*, Dec. 6, 1904.

6. *CPD*, Dec. 7, 1904.

7. *CPD*, Dec. 8, 1904.

8. *CPD*, Dec. 13, 1904.

9. *NYT*, Dec. 5, 1891; *New York Tribune*, Dec. 5, 1891.

10. *NYT*, Dec. 2, 1904; *CPD*, Dec. 7, 1904.

11. *CP*, Nov. 26, 1904; *CPD*, Nov. 23, 1904.

12. *CPD*, Nov. 26, 27, 1904; *CP*, Nov. 26, 1904; *OSJ*, Nov. 27, 1904; *NYT*, Dec. 1, 1904.

13. *OSJ*, Dec. 6, 1904.

14. *CP*, Nov. 26, 1904.

15. *CP*, Nov. 28, 1904.

16. *CP*, Nov. 28, 1904; Laning, *The History and Story of the Doings*, 65, 78–81.

17. Laning, *The History and Story of the Doings*, 27.

18. *CPD*, Dec. 4, 1904; Laning, *The History and Story of the Doings*, 64.

19. *CPD*, Dec. 4, 9, 10, 1904; Laning, *The History and Story of the Doings*, 64.

20. *NYT*, Dec. 12, 1904.

21. *NYT*, Dec. 1, 1904; *CPD*, Nov. 30, Dec. 2, 7, 1904; *Youngstown Vindicator*, Dec. 1, 1904.

22. *CPD*, Dec. 3, 1904.

23. *CPD*, Dec. 3, 1904.

24. *CPD*, Dec. 3, 1904.

25. *NYT*, Dec. 5, 1904.

26. Laning, *The History and Story of the Doings*, 59–60; *CL*, Oct. 11, 1907; *NYT*, Dec. 1, 2, 3, 5, 1904; *OSJ*, Dec. 11, 1904.

27. *CPD*, Dec. 3, 1904.

28. *NYT*, Dec. 4, 5, 1904; *CPD*, Dec. 4, 5, 6, 1904.

29. *NYT*, Dec. 7, 1904.

30. *CPD*, Dec. 4, 1904; *NYT*, Dec. 5, 1904.

31. *CPD*, Dec. 2, 3, 4, 1904.

32. *NYT*, Dec. 5, 1904; *CPD*, Dec. 8, 1904.

33. *CPD*, Dec. 5, 1904.

34. *CPD*, Dec. 6, 7, 8, 1904.

35. *NYT*, Dec. 5, 1904.

36. *CPD*, Dec. 8, 1904; *NYT*, Dec. 2, 1904.

37. *NYT*, Dec. 8, 1904.

38. *NYT,* Dec. 8, 1904.

39. *NYT,* Dec. 8, 1904.

40. *NYT,* Dec. 8, 1904.

41. *NYT,* Dec. 8, 1904.

42. *NYT,* Dec. 8, 1904.

43. *CPD,* Dec. 8, 9, 1904; *NYT,* Dec. 8, 1904.

44. *CPD,* Dec. 7, 9, 1904; *NYT,* Dec. 9, 1904; US Census, Cuyahoga County, OH, 1880, www.Ancestry.com/LibraryEdition.com.

45. *NYT,* Dec. 8, 9, 1904; *CPD,* Dec. 9, 1904; *NYT,* Dec. 8, 1904.

46. *NYT,* Dec. 8, 1904.

47. *NYT,* Dec. 8, 1904.

48. *CPD,* Dec. 9, 1904.

49. *CPD,* Dec. 9, 1904.

50. *CPD,* Dec. 9, 1904; *NYT,* Dec. 9, 1904.

51. *CPD,* Dec. 9, 1904; *NYT,* Dec. 9, 1904.

52. *CPD,* Dec. 9, 1904; *NYT,* Dec. 9, 1904; Levy, *The Nan Paterson Case,* 89–97.

53. *Youngstown Vindicator,* Dec. 4, 1904; *CPD,* Dec. 11, 1904.

54. *NYT,* Dec. 9, 1904.

55. *NYT,* Dec. 7, 1904.

56. *CPD,* Dec. 9, 14, 1904.

57. *NYT,* Dec. 7, 1904; *CPD,* Dec. 6, 10, 13, 1904.

16. SIMPLY A SUCKER

1. *NYT,* Dec. 9, 1904.

2. *CPD,* Dec. 7, 1904.

3. *NYT,* Dec. 8, 1904; *OSJ,* Dec. 10, 1904; *Youngstown Vindicator,* Dec. 8, 9, 1904.

4. *NYT,* Dec. 3, 9, 11, 1904; *CPD,* Dec. 9, 1904.

5. *CPD,* Dec. 10, 1904; *NYT,* Dec. 10, 1904.

6. *NYT,* Dec. 10, 1904.

7. *NYT,* Nov. 30, 1904; *CPD,* Nov. 30, Dec. 1, 3, 1904; *OSJ,* Dec. 4, 1904; *Youngstown Vindicator,* Dec. 13, 1904.

8. *NYT,* Dec. 16, 1904; *CPD,* Dec. 10, 12, 1904.

9. *NYT,* Dec. 7, 1904; *CPD,* Dec. 6, 10, 13, 1904; Connolly, "Marvelous Mrs. Chadwick," 9.

10. *CPD,* Dec. 10, 11, 1904; *NYT,* Dec. 12, 1904; Nasaw, *Andrew Carnegie,* 76–77.

11. *CPD,* Dec. 13, 1904.

12. *CPD,* Dec. 10, 11, 12, 1904; *NYT,* Nov. 30, 1904; *OSJ,* Dec. 4, 1904.

13. *OSJ,* Dec. 12, 1904.

14. *CPD,* Jan. 1, 1950; Connolly, "Marvelous Mrs. Chadwick," 9.

15. *CPD,* Nov. 30, Dec. 8, 10, 12, 1904; *NYT,* Dec. 8, 1904.

16. *CPD,* Oct. 11, 1904.

17. *CPD,* Dec. 13, 1904; Laning, *The History and Story of the Doings,* 119–20.

18. *CPD,* Dec. 13, 1904; Laning, *The History and Story of the Doings,* 119–20.

19. *CPD,* Dec. 13, 1904; *NYT,* Dec. 13, 1904; Laning, *The History and Story of the Doings,* 121.

20. *CPD,* Dec. 14, 1904.

21. *NYT,* Dec. 13, 1904; *CPD,* Dec. 13, 1904.

22. *NYT,* Dec. 13, 1904; *CPD,* Dec. 13, 1904.

23. *CPD,* Dec. 13, 1904; Crosbie, *The Incredible Mrs. Chadwick,* 118–19.

24. *CPD*, Dec. 13, 1904.

25. *NYT*, Dec. 13, 14, 1904; *CPD*, Dec. 13, 1904.

26. *CPD*, Dec. 12, 1904; *NYT*, Dec. 13, 1904.

17. CHADWICKED

1. *CPD*, Dec. 12, 14, 1904.

2. *CPD*, Dec. 14, 1904.

3. *CPD*, Dec. 13, 1904.

4. *CPD*, Dec. 14, 1904; *CPD*, Dec. 14, 1904.

5. Spurling, *La Grande Therese*, 17, 35, 39, 63–65, 68–75; *CPD*, Dec. 16, 1904.

6. Spurling, *La Grande Therese*, 74–84, 96–98; *New York Tribune*, Aug. 9, 1903.

7. Spurling, *La Grande Therese*, 104–6, 116–24; *New York Tribune*, Aug. 9, 23, 1903.

8. *CPD*, Dec. 12, 13, 14, 1904.

9. *CPD*, Dec. 14, 1904.

10. Laning, *The History and Story of the Doings*, 76–78; *CPD*, Dec. 12, 1904; *NYT*, Dec. 12, 1904.

11. *NYT*, Dec. 14, 1904; *CPD*, Dec. 13, 1904.

12. *NYT*, Dec. 14, 1904.

13. *NYT*, Dec. 13, 14, 1904.

14. *NYT*, Dec. 13, 14, 1904.

15. *CPD*, Dec. 4, 1904.

16. Nasaw, *Andrew Carnegie*, 662–64; *NYT*, Dec. 12, 1904.

17. Nasaw, *Andrew Carnegie*, 662–64; *NYT*, Dec. 12, 1904.

18. *CPD*, Dec. 15, 1904.

19. Laning, *The History and Story of the Doings*, 89, 92.

20. Laning, *The History and Story of the Doings*, 93–94.

21. Laning, *The History and Story of the Doings*, 90–93; *NYT*, Dec. 15, 1904.

22. Laning, *The History and Story of the Doings*, 90.

23. Laning, *The History and Story of the Doings*, 91; *CPD*, Dec. 15, 1904.

24. *CPD*, Dec. 14, 15, 1904; *NYT*, Dec. 15, 1904.

25. *CPD*, Dec. 15, 16, 1904.

26. *CPD*, Dec. 15, 16, 1904; *NYT*, Jan. 8, 1905.

27. *NYT*, Dec. 15, 1904.

28. *CPD*, Dec. 15, 16, 17, 1904.

29. *NYT*, Dec. 15, 1904.

30. *CPD*, Dec. 16, 1904.

31. *CPD*, Dec. 16, 1904.

32. *NYT*, Dec. 16, 1904; *CPD*, Dec. 16, 1904.

33. *NYT*, Dec. 14, 15, 1904.

34. *NYT*, Dec. 15, 1904; *CPD*, Dec. 15, 16, 1904.

35. Laning, *The History and Story of the Doings*, 95; *CPD*, Dec. 14, 1904.

36. Laning, *The History and Story of the Doings*, 95; *CPD*, Dec. 14, 1904.

37. Laning, *The History and Story of the Doings*, 96.

38. *CPD*, Dec. 16, 17, 1904; Laning, *The History and Story of the Doings*, 96.

39. *CPD*, Dec. 16, 17, 1904; Laning, *The History and Story of the Doings*, 96.

40. Segrave, *Women Swindlers in America, 1860–1920*, 78–79; *Argus (SD) Leader*, Mar. 19, 1888; *Ottumwa (IA) Register*, Feb. 7, 1876; *Toledo (IA) Chronicle*, Mar. 1, 1877.

41. *CPD*, Dec. 17, 18, 1904; Laning, *The History and Story of the Doings*, 96.

42. *CPD*, Dec. 18, 1904; Laning, *The History and Story of the Doings*, 97.

43. Laning, *The History and Story of the Doings*, 31; *NYT*, Dec. 15, 1904; *CPD*, Dec. 15, 1904.

44. *NYT*, Dec. 18, 1904.

45. Laning, *The History and Story of the Doings*, 99; Cramp, *Nostrums and Quackery*, 2:160–61, 1:567, 627.

46. *CPD*, Dec. 11, 12, 18, 19, 1904.

47. Patrick, "The Psychology of Women," 209–25; *CPD*, Dec. 31, 1904.

48. *CPD*, Dec. 18, 20, 1904; *OSJ*, Dec. 18, 1904.

49. *NYT*, Dec. 20, 1904.

50. *CPD*, Dec. 18, 1904.

51. *CPD*, Dec. 19, 1904.

52. *CPD*, Dec. 20, 23, 1904.

53. *CPD*, Dec. 18, 19, 20, 1904.

54. *CPD*, Dec. 18, 19, 20, 1904.

55. *NYT*, Dec. 18, 1904; *CPD*, Dec. 12, 1904.

56. *NYT*, Dec. 18, 22, 1904; *CPD*, Dec. 12, 1904.

57. *OSJ*, Jan. 2, 1905; *NYT*, Dec. 28, 1904, Jan. 6, 1905.

58. *CPD*, Dec. 21, 1904.

18. A NOBLE THING

1. *CPD*, Dec. 20, 1904.

2. *CPD*, Dec. 23, 1904.

3. *CPD*, Dec. 23, 28, 1904.

4. *CPD*, Dec. 25, 1904.

5. *CPD*, Dec. 22, 1904.

6. *CPD*, Dec. 26, 31, 1904; *NYT*, Dec. 26, 1904.

7. *CPD*, Dec. 29, 31, 1904; *NYT*, Dec. 28, 1904.

8. *CPD*, Dec. 26, 27, 1904.

9. *NYT*, Dec. 27, 1904.

10. *NYT*, Jan. 1, 1905.

11. *CPD*, Dec. 27, 1904, Jan. 1, 1905.

12. *CL*, Oct. 11, 1907; *NYT*, Jan. 1, 1905.

13. *CPD*, Jan. 2, 1905.

14. *CPD*, Jan. 1, 1905; *NYT*, Jan. 1, 1905.

15. *CPD*, Jan. 2, 1905; *NYT*, Jan. 2, 1905.

16. *CPD*, Jan. 2, 1905; *NYT*, Jan. 2, 1905.

17. *CPD*, Jan. 2, 1905; *OSJ*, Jan. 2, 1905.

18. *CPD*, Jan. 4, 1905.

19. *CPD*, Jan. 4, 1905.

20. *CPD*, Jan. 2, 1905.

21. *CPD*, Jan. 3, 1905.

22. *OSJ*, Jan. 6, 1905.

23. *OSJ*, Jan. 6, 1905.

24. *CPD*, Jan. 6, 1905.

25. *CPD*, Jan. 9, 1905; *NYT*, Dec. 28, 1904; Laning, *The History and Story of the Doings*, 12.

26. *NYT*, Dec. 28, 1904.

27. *CPD*, Jan. 8, 1905; *NYT*, Jan. 6, 1905.

28. *CPD*, Jan. 18, 25, Feb. 18, 1905.

29. *CPD*, Dec. 29, 1904, Jan. 18, 1905; *NYT*, Jan. 18, 1905.

30. *CPD*, Jan. 25, 1905; Nasaw, *Andrew Carnegie*, 605–7; Isabelle Smith, "Strange Acquisitions: How We Got the Carnegie Building," *Oberlin Review*, Apr. 19, 2019.

31. *CPD*, Jan. 20, 1905.

32. *NYT*, Jan. 18, Feb. 6, 1905; *CPD*, Feb. 6, 1905; *CL*, Feb. 6, 1905.

33. *CPD*, Jan. 31, 1905; *NYT*, Feb. 6, 1905.

34. *CPD*, Dec. 12, 1904.

35. *CPD*, Feb. 18, 1905.

36. *CPD*, Feb. 18, 1905.

37. *CPD*, Feb. 18, 1905.

38. *CPD*, Feb. 18, 1905.

39. *CPD*, Feb. 22, 1905.

40. *CPD*, Feb. 25, 1905.

41. *CPD*, Feb. 25, 1905.

42. *CPD*, Feb. 25, Mar. 16, 1905.

43. *CPD*, Feb. 25, 1905.

44. *CPD*, Mar. 1, 1905.

45. *CPD*, Mar. 1, 1905.

46. *CPD*, Mar. 2, 1905.

47. *CPD*, Mar. 2, 1905.

48. *CPD*, Mar. 2, 1905; Cassie Chadwick to H. Clark Ford, Feb. 15, 1904; W. V. Coons to H. Clark Ford, Jan. 8, 1904; H. Clark Ford receipt, Dec. 12, 1904, Ford Family Papers; Krass, *Carnegie*, 260–61; Nasaw, *Andrew Carnegie*, 378.

49. *CL*, Feb. 6, 1905.

19. A MOST DANGEROUS CRIMINAL

1. Loth, *Gold Brick Cassie*, 77, 119; *CL*, Oct. 21, 1907, Feb. 6, 1905.

2. Laning, *The History and Story of the Doings*, 107–8; *CPD*, Dec. 14, 1904.

3. Laning, *The History and Story of the Doings*, 108; *CL*, Mar. 6, 1905; *NYT*, Mar. 5, 6, 1905.

4. Krass, *Carnegie*, 664.

5. Nasaw, *Andrew Carnegie*, 62.

6. *CL*, Mar. 6, 1905; *NYT*, Mar. 5, 6, 1905; Nasaw, *Andrew Carnegie*, 72–73.

7. *CPD*, Mar. 5, 6, 1905.

8. *CPD*, Mar. 8, 1905.

9. US Census, Portage County, Ohio, 1900, www.Ancestry.com/LibraryEdition.

10. *CPD*, Aug. 31, 1903; *CL*, Oct. 21, 1907; Loth, *Gold Brick Cassie*, 123.

11. United States Circuit Court of Appeals, Sixth Circuit, *Cassie L. Chadwick . . . vs. United States of America*, 2–34.

12. Nasaw, *Andrew Carnegie*, 195–96; *CPD*, Dec. 8, 1904.

13. *CPD*, Mar. 6, 7, 1905; *NYT*, Mar. 6, 7, 1905.

14. *CPD*, Mar. 6, 1905; *New York Sun*, Mar. 7, 1905.

15. *CPD*, Mar. 6, 7, 1905.

16. *CPD*, Mar. 6, 7, 1905.

17. *New York Sun*, Mar. 7, 1905.

18. *New York Sun,* Mar. 7, 1905.

19. *NYT,* May 24, 1910.

20. *CPD,* Mar. 6, 7, 1905.

21. *CPD,* Mar. 6, 7, 1905.

22. US Circuit Court of Appeals, Sixth Circuit, *Cassie L. Chadwick . . . vs. United States of America,* 80–87.

23. *New York Sun,* Mar. 7, 1905; *CPD,* Mar. 3, 7, 1905.

24. *CPD,* Mar. 7, 1905; *NYT,* Mar. 7, 1905.

25. US Circuit Court of Appeals, Sixth Circuit, *Cassie L. Chadwick . . . vs. United States of America,* 80–87.

26. *CPD,* Oct. 8, 1905.

27. Laning, *The History and Story of the Doings,* 103; *CPD,* Mar. 7, 1905.

28. *CPD,* Mar. 7, 8, 1905; *NYT,* Mar. 7, 8, 1905.

29. *CPD,* Mar. 7, 8, 1905; *NYT,* Mar. 7, 8, 1905.

30. *CPD,* Mar. 8, 1905; *NYT,* Mar. 8, 1905.

31. *CPD,* Mar. 8, 9, 1905; *NYT,* Mar. 8, 9, 1905.

32. *CPD,* Mar. 8, 9, 1905; *NYT,* Mar. 8, 9, 1905.

33. *CPD,* Mar. 8, 9, 1905; *NYT,* Mar. 8, 9, 1905.

34. US Circuit Court of Appeals, Sixth Circuit, *Cassie L. Chadwick . . . vs. United States of America,* 53–58.

35. *CPD,* Mar. 10, 12, 1905.

36. *CPD,* Mar. 9, 1905.

37. *CPD,* Mar. 9, 1905.

38. *NYT,* Mar. 9, 10, 1905; *CPD,* Mar. 9, 10, 1905.

39. *NYT,* Mar. 9, 10, 1905; *CPD,* Mar. 9, 10, 1905.

40. *NYT,* Mar. 9, 10, 1905; *CPD,* Mar. 9, 10, 1905.

41. *NYT,* Mar. 9, 10, 1905; *CPD,* Mar. 9, 10, 1905.

42. Krass, *Carnegie,* 444, 502; Nasaw, *Andrew Carnegie,* 662–64, 607, 798–801; *CPD,* Mar. 8, 1905.

43. *CPD,* Mar. 10, 1905.

44. *CPD,* Mar. 10, 1905.

45. *CPD,* Mar. 10, 1905.

46. *CPD,* Mar. 10, 11, 1905.

47. *CPD,* Mar. 10, 11, 1905.

48. *CPD,* Mar. 12, 1905.

49. *NYT,* Mar. 11, 1905; *CPD,* Mar. 11, 1905.

50. *NYT,* Mar. 11, 1905; *CPD,* Mar. 11, 1905.

51. *New York Sun,* Mar. 12, 1905; *NYT,* Mar. 11, 12, 1905; *CPD,* Mar. 11, 12, 1905.

52. *CPD,* Mar. 11, 12, 1905; *NYT,* Mar. 11, 12, 1905; US Circuit Court of Appeals, Sixth Circuit, *Cassie L. Chadwick . . . vs. United States of America,* 53–58.

53. *CPD,* Mar. 11, 12, 1905; *NYT,* Mar. 11, 12, 1905; US Circuit Court of Appeals, Sixth Circuit, *Cassie L. Chadwick . . . vs. United States of America,* 53–58.

54. *CPD,* Mar. 11, 12, 1905; *NYT,* Mar. 11, 12, 1905; US Circuit Court of Appeals, Sixth Circuit, *Cassie L. Chadwick . . . vs. United States of America,* 53–58.

55. *CPD,* Mar. 11, 12, 1905; *NYT,* Mar. 11, 12, 1905; US Circuit Court of Appeals, Sixth Circuit, *Cassie L. Chadwick . . . vs. United States of America,* 53–58.

56. *CPD,* Mar. 11, 12, 1905; *NYT,* Mar. 11, 12, 1905; US Circuit Court of Appeals, Sixth Circuit, *Cassie L. Chadwick . . . vs. United States of America,* 53–58.

57. *CPD*, Mar. 11, 12, 1905; *NYT*, Mar. 11, 12, 1905; US Circuit Court of Appeals, Sixth Circuit, *Cassie L. Chadwick . . . vs. United States of America*, 53–58.

58. *CPD*, Mar. 11, 12, 1905; *NYT*, Mar. 11, 12, 1905; US Circuit Court of Appeals, Sixth Circuit, *Cassie L. Chadwick . . . vs. United States of America*, 53–58.

59. *CPD*, Mar. 11, 12, 1905; *NYT*, Mar. 11, 12, 1905; US Circuit Court of Appeals, Sixth Circuit, *Cassie L. Chadwick . . . vs. United States of America*, 53–58.

60. *CPD*, Mar. 11, 12, 1905; *NYT*, Mar. 11, 12, 1905; US Circuit Court of Appeals, Sixth Circuit, *Cassie L. Chadwick . . . vs. United States of America*, 53–58.

61. *CPD*, Mar. 12, 13, 1905.

62. *CPD*, Mar. 12, 13, 1905.

63. *CPD*, Mar. 12, 13, 1905.

64. *CPD*, Mar. 12, 13, 1905.

65. *CL*, Mar. 14, 1905.

66. *CPD*, Mar. 15, 1905.

67. *CL*, Oct. 20, 1907.

68. *CPD*, Dec. 11, 1904.

69. *CPD*, Dec. 11, 1904.

70. *CPD*, Mar. 12, 13, 1905.

20. NO ARTISTIC TASTE AND NO CULTURE

1. *CL*, Mar. 14, 1905.

2. *NYT*, Mar. 5, 14, 1905.

3. *NYT*, Mar. 16, 1905; *CPD*, Mar. 14, 1905.

4. *NYT*, Mar. 16, 1905.

5. *CPD*, Mar. 18, 1905.

6. *CPD*, Mar. 18, 1905.

7. *CPD*, Mar. 23, 1905.

8. *CPD*, Mar. 14, 1905.

9. *CL*, Mar. 14, 1905.

10. *CPD*, Mar. 25, 1905.

11. Laning, *The History and Story of the Doings*, 17; *Cleveland Directory Company, 1899*, 1248.

12. *CPD*, Mar. 25, 1905.

13. *CPD*, Mar. 29, 1905.

14. *CPD*, Dec. 8, 1904.

15. *CPD*, Apr. 6, 1905.

16. *CPD*, Apr. 15, 1905.

17. *Mansfield (OH) News Journal*, Apr. 21, 1905.

18. *NYT*, Apr. 27, 1905; *CPD*, Apr. 11, 1905, Dec. 26, 1954; *Catalog of Very Artistic Furnishings Collected by Mrs. Cassie Chadwick*, 1–5.

19. *NYT*, Apr. 27, 1905; *CPD*, Apr. 11, 1905, Dec. 26, 1954; *Catalog of the Very Artistic Furnishings Collected by Mrs. Cassie Chadwick*, 1–5.

20. *NYT*, Apr. 27, 1905; *CPD*, Apr. 17, 1905.

21. *CPD*, Mar. 31, Apr. 1, 5, 1905.

22. *CPD*, Dec. 5, 1904, Feb. 22, 1905.

23. *CPD*, Apr. 21, 25, 1905.

24. *CPD*, Feb. 22, May 4, 1905.

25. *CPD*, May 4, 1905.

26. *CPD*, Nov. 30, 1904, May 17, 1905; *NYT*, May 19, 1905.

27. *CPD*, Nov. 30, 1904; MacNee, *Outlaws, Mobsters and Crooks*, 285–86.

28. *San Francisco Call*, Oct. 10, 1905.

29. *New York Tribune*, Oct. 20, 1905.

21. ENCHANTRESS IN HER LAST HOME

1. Loth, *Gold Brick Cassie*, 168; "Ohio Penitentiary," www.forgottenoh.com.

2. *CPD*, Jan. 12, 1906.

3. *CPD*, Jan. 12, 1906.

4. *CPD*, Jan. 13, 1906; *OSJ*, Jan. 13, 1906.

5. *CPD*, Jan. 13, 1906.

6. *CPD*, Jan. 13, 1906; *OSJ*, Jan. 13, 1906.

7. Ohio Penitentiary Register of Prisoners, no. 16, Jan. 1891–92; *CPD*, Jan. 13, 1906.

8. *CPD*, Jan. 13, 1906.

9. *CPD*, Jan. 13, 1906.

10. *Waterbury (CT) Evening Democrat*, Nov. 5, 1907.

11. *Waterbury (CT) Evening Democrat*, Nov. 5, 1907.

12. *CL*, Oct. 21, 22, 1907; *Forest City (AR) Times*, Nov. 8, 1907; *Los Angeles Herald*, Sept. 6, 1906; *CPD*, Dec. 13, 14, 1904; *NYT*, Dec. 28, 1909.

13. *CPD*, Nov. 11, 1907; *CL*, Oct. 10, 1907.

14. *CPD*, Oct. 11, 1907; *CL*, Oct. 10, 1907.

15. *CL*, Oct. 7, 8, 1907.

16. *CL*, Oct. 11, 1907; *CPD*, Oct. 11, 1907.

17. *CL*, Oct. 8, 15, 1907; *CPD*, Oct. 11, 1907; Thomas, *Taber's Cyclopedic Medical Dictionary*, 948.

18. *CL*, Oct. 12, 1907; Crosbie, *The Incredible Mrs. Chadwick*, 226–40.

19. Crosbie, *The Incredible Mrs. Chadwick*, 119, 226–40; *CL*, Oct. 17, 1907; *Daily Sentinel Review*, June 25, 1975.

20. Crosbie, *The Incredible Mrs. Chadwick*, 119, 226–40; *CL*, Oct. 17, 1907; *Daily Sentinel Review*, June 25, 1975.

21. Crosbie, *The Incredible Mrs. Chadwick*, 119, 226–40; *CL*, Oct. 17, 1907; *Daily Sentinel Review*, June 25, 1975.

22. *CPD*, Oct. 11, 1907.

23. *New York Evening World*, Oct. 17, 1907.

24. *CPD*, Oct. 12, 15, 1907; *CL*, Oct. 12, 1907.

25. *CPD*, Oct. 13, 1907; Lee, *History of the City of Columbus*, 820.

26. *CL*, Oct. 13, 15, 18, 1907; *CPD*, Aug. 31, 1930.

27. *CL*, Oct. 20, 1907.

28. *CL*, Oct. 20, 1907.

29. *CL*, Oct. 20, 23, 1907.

30. *CL*, Oct. 11, 12, 1907.

31. *CL*, Oct. 11, 12, 1907.

32. *CL*, Oct. 11, 12, 1907.

33. *CL*, Oct. 11, 12, 1907.

34. *CL*, Oct. 11, 1907.

35. Cleveland Public Library Photograph Collection, Cassie Chadwick File.

36. *Marion (OH) Daily Mirror,* Nov. 20, 1910; Arthur Spear, Bertillon Record, Ohio Penitentiary.

37. US Census, Cuyahoga County, Ohio, 1910, www.Ancestry.com/LibraryEdition; *Cleveland Necrology Index,* www.deathindexes.com/Ohio; *CPD,* Aug. 31, 1930.

38. Loth, *Gold Brick Cassie,* 168; US Census, Duval County, FL, 1910, www.Ancestry.com/LibraryEdition; *New York Tribune,* Aug. 28, 1908; James A. Chadwick, personal communication, Oxford (ON) Historical Society, July 20, 1987.

39. Loth, *Gold Brick Cassie,* 168; US Census, Duval County, FL, 1910, www.Ancestry.com/LibraryEdition; *New York Tribune,* Aug. 28, 1908; James A. Chadwick, personal communication, Oxford (ON) Historical Society, July 20, 1987.

40. Loth, *Gold Brick Cassie,* 33; *CL,* Oct. 11, 1907; *Cleveland City Directory,* 12:271, 13:298.

41. Loth, *Gold Brick Cassie,* 83; US Census, Cuyahoga County, OH, 1900, www.Ancestry.com/LibraryEdition; *CPD,* Oct. 11, 1907; James A. Chadwick, personal communication, July 20, 1987.

42. James A. Chadwick, personal communication, Oxford (ON) Historical Society, July 20, 1987.

43. Cornell, "Carnegie's Daughter," 25–30.

44. Cornell, "Carnegie's Daughter," 25–30.

45. Laning, *The History and Story of the Doings,* 72–73; *The Canon (CO) Record,* Oct. 17, 1907.

Bibliography

PRIMARY SOURCES

Byrne, Thomas. *1886 Professional Criminals of America*. New York: Chelsea House Publishing 1969.

Carnegie, Andrew. *Autobiography of Andrew Carnegie*. Boston: Northeastern Univ. Press, 1986.

Cassie Chadwick File. Oxford (ON) Historical Society.

Catalog of Very Artistic Furnishings Collected by Mrs. Cassie Chadwick. New York: Kinckerbocher Art Galleries, 1905. Western Reserve Historical Society Library, Cleveland.

Chadwick, James A. Personal communication. Oxford (ON) Historical Society, July 20, 1987.

Ford Family Papers. Western Reserve Historical Society Library, Cleveland.

Laning, Jay Ford. *The History and Story of the Doings of the Famous Mrs. Cassie L. Chadwick*. Cleveland: Laning Company, 1905.

Ohio Penitentiary Register of Prisoners. Ohio History Center Library and Archives, Columbus.

Spear, Arthur. Bertillon Record, Ohio Penitentiary, Box 2, Ohio History Center Library and Archives, Columbus.

United States Circuit Court of Appeals, Sixth Circuit. *Cassie L. Chadwick, alias C. L. Chadwick, alias Madame Devere vs. United States of America*. June 6, 1905. Western Reserve Historical Society Library and Archives, Cleveland.

SECONDARY SOURCES

Borowitz, Albert. *Unhappy Endings*. Cleveland: Rowfant Club, 2001.

Butler, Joseph. *History of Youngstown and the Mahoning Valley Ohio*. Vols. 2, 3. Chicago: American Historical Society, 1921.

Cigliano, Jan. *Showplace of America: Cleveland's Euclid Avenue, 1850–1910*. Kent, OH: Kent State Univ. Press, 1991.

The Cleveland City Directory. Vol. 12, *Year Ending July 1883*. Cleveland: Cleveland Directory Co., 1882.

The Cleveland City Directory. Vol. 13, *Year Ending July 1884*. Cleveland: Cleveland Directory Co., 1883.

The Cleveland Directory, Year Ending July 1899. Cleveland: Cleveland Directory Co., 1898.

The Cleveland Directory, Year Ending July 1905. Cleveland: Cleveland Directory Co., 1904.

Cleveland Necrology Index. www.deathindexes.com/Ohio/cuyahoga-cleveland.html.

Cleveland Public Library Photograph Collection. Cassie Chadwick File, Cleveland.

Coates, William R. *Commemorative Biographical Record of the Counties of Huron and Lorain, Ohio.* Chicago: J. H. Beers and Co., 1894.

———. *A History of Cuyahoga County and the City of Cleveland.* Vol. 3. Chicago: American Historical Society, 1924.

Commemorative Biographical Record of the Counties of Huron and Lorain, Ohio. Chicago: J. H. Beers and Co., 1894.

Conant, Charles A. *A History of Modern Banks of Issue.* 5th ed. New York: G. P. Putnam and Sons, 1915.

Connolly, C. D. "Marvelous Mrs. Chadwick." *McClure's Magazine,* Nov. 1916–Apr. 1917.

Cornell, Camilla. "Carnegie's Daughter." *London Magazine,* Sept. 1985.

Cramp, Arthur J. *Nostrums and Quackery.* 2 vols. Chicago: American Medical Association, 1912, 1921.

Crosbie, John S. *The Incredible Mrs. Chadwick.* Toronto: McGraw-Hill Ryerson, Ltd., 1975.

Evtimova, Milena. "Oberlin's Mysteries of History." *The Oberlin Review,* Nov. 10, 2006, 1–2.

Galbreath, Charles B. *History of Ohio.* Vol. 1. Chicago: American Historical Society, 1925.

Goldsmith, Barbara. *Other Powers.* New York: HarperPerennial, 1999.

Guillain, G. *J. M. Charcot (1825–1893): His Life, His Work.* New York: Paul B. Hoeber, 1959.

Hatcher, Harlan. *The Western Reserve.* New York: Bobbs-Merrill Co., 1949.

Knox, John Jay. *A History of Banking in the U.S.* New York: Bradford, Rhodes and Co., 1900.

Krass, Peter. *Carnegie.* Hoboken, NJ: John Wiley and Sons, Inc., 2002.

Lee, Alford Emory. *History of the City of Columbus: Capital of Ohio.* Columbus: W. W. Munsell and Co., 1892.

Loth, David. *Gold Brick Cassie.* New York: Fawcett Publications Inc., 1954.

MacNee, Marie J. *Outlaws, Mobsters and Crooks: From the Old West to the Internet.* Vol. 2. Detroit: UXL, 1998.

Mangus, Michael, ed. *Ohio Encyclopedia.* Vol. 1. Hamburg, MI: State History Publications, 2008.

Miller, Carol Poh. *Cleveland: A Concise History.* Bloomington: Indiana Univ. Press, 1990.

Nasaw, David. *Andrew Carnegie.* New York: Penguin Press, 2006.

Newman, Levy. *The Nan Patterson Case.* New York: Simon and Schuster, 1959.

"Ohio Penitentiary." www.forgottenoh.com.

Patrick, G. T. W. "The Psychology of Woman." *Popular Science Monthly,* June 1895, 209–25.

Reading, Amy. *The Mark Inside: A Perfect Swindle, A Cunning Revenge and a Small History of the Big Con.* New York: Vintage, 2013.

R. L. Polk and Company's Toledo City Directory for 1888–1889. Toledo: Blade Publishing Co., 1888.

Robertson, Ross M. *History of the American Economy.* 3rd ed. New York: Harcourt, Brace, Jovanovich, 1973.

Segrave, Kerry. *Women Swindlers in America, 1860–1920.* Jefferson, NC: McFarland and Company Inc., 2007.

Shorter, Edward. *A History of Psychiatry: From the Era of the Asylum to the Age of Prozac.* Garden City, NJ: John Wiley and Sons, 1997.

Skeel, David A., Jr. *Debt's Dominion: A History of Bankruptcy Law in America.* Princeton, NJ: Princeton Univ. Press, 2001.

Slack, Charles. *Hetty: The Genius and Madness of America's First Female Tycoon.* New York: HarperCollins Publishers, 2004.

Smith, Isabelle. "Strange Acquisitions: How We Got the Carnegie Building." *The Oberlin Review,* Apr. 19, 2019.

Sparkes, Boyden, Samuel Taylor Moore. *Hetty Green.* Garden City, NJ: Garden City Publishing Co., 1930.

Spurling, Hilary. *La Grande Therese: The Greatest Scandal of the Century.* New York: Harper Collins Publishers, 2000.

Thomas, Clayton L., ed. *Tabor's Cyclopedic Medical Dictionary.* 14th ed. Philadelphia: F. A. Davis, 1982.

US Census, Cuyahoga County, OH, 1880. www.Ancestry.com/LibraryEdition.

US Census, Cuyahoga County, OH, 1900. www.AncestryLibrary.com.

US Census, Cuyahoga County, OH, 1910. www.Ancestry.com/LibraryEdition.

US Census, Duvall County, FL, 1910. www.Ancestry.com/LibraryEdition.

Wade, Carlson. *Great Hoaxes and Famous Imposters.* Middle Village, NY: Jonathan David Publishers, 1976.

Wallach, Janet. *The Richest Woman in America: Hetty Green in the Gilded Age.* New York: Anchor Books, 2013.

"Who Was Hetty Green?" *T. Rowe Price Investor,* Dec. 2010, 26.

Youngstown City Directory. N. H. Burch and Co., 1886–87.

Youngstown City Directory. Cleveland: Guthman and Van Fleet, 1880.

NEWSPAPERS

Akron (OH) Democrat
Anaconda (MT) Standard
Cleveland Leader
Cleveland Leader and Herald
Cleveland Plain Dealer
Cleveland Press
Daily Ohio Standard
Daily Sentinel-Review (Woodstock, ON)
The Democrat Banner (Mount Vernon, OH)
Democratic Northwest (OH)
Greenville (PA) Evening Record
Los Angeles Herald
Marion (OH) Daily Mirror
New York Herald
New York Sun
New York Sunday Morning Star
New York Times
New York Tribune
New York World
Oberlin Review
Ohio State Journal
Ohio State News
Ottumwa (IA) Register
Perrysville (OH) Journal

Philadelphia Evening Telegraph
San Francisco Call
Stark County (OH) Democrat
Titusville (PA) Morning Herald
Toledo Blade
Toledo Daily Blade
Toledo (IA) Chronicle
Washington Post
Waterbury (CT) Evening Democrat
Youngstown Vindicator

Index